HEBREW SCHOLARSHIP AND THE MEDIEVAL WORLD

This book brings together specially commissioned contributions by leading scholars from around the world, who study the place of Hebrew scholarship in the Middle Ages. Hebrew language is at the heart of the volume, but beyond that there is a specific focus on scholarly investigation and writing, interpreted in the broad sense to include not only linguistic study pursued for its own sake but also as applied in other areas, such as biblical commentary or poetic creation. At the same time there is a stress on contemporary scholarship, and several of the contributions survey recent research in major areas.

The place of Hebrew scholarship within a wider medieval world is a subject that receives special attention in the book – particularly the interaction between Jewish scholars and their Christian and Muslim counterparts.

NICHOLAS DE LANGE is Reader in Hebrew and Jewish Studies at the University of Cambridge. He is a former President of the British Association of Jewish Studies, and is a Council Member of the Jewish Historical Society of England. He is the author of many books, including *An Introduction to Judaism* (Cambridge, 2000).

HEBREW SCHOLARSHIP AND THE MEDIEVAL WORLD

EDITED BY

NICHOLAS DE LANGE

University of Cambridge

CAMBRIDGE
UNIVERSITY PRESS

PUBLISHED BY THE PRESS SYNDICATE OF THE UNIVERSITY OF CAMBRIDGE
The Pitt Building, Trumpington Street, Cambridge, United Kingdom

CAMBRIDGE UNIVERSITY PRESS
The Edinburgh Building, Cambridge CB2 2RU, UK
40 West 20th Street, New York, NY 10011–4211, USA
10 Stamford Road, Oakleigh, VIC 3166, Australia
Ruiz de Alarcón 13, 28014 Madrid, Spain
Dock House, The Waterfront, Cape Town 8001, South Africa

http://www.cambridge.org

First published 2001

Printed in the United Kingdom at the University Press, Cambridge

Typeface Monotype Baskerville 11/12.5pt *System* QuarkXPress™ [SE]

A catalogue record for this book is available from the British Library

ISBN 0 521 78116 7 hardback

For Raphael Loewe

הספר הזה מקדש

לכבוד מורי

רפאל הלוי לועווע

עשה לך רב וקנה לך חבר

Contents

PART THREE PRAYER AND POETRY

PART FOUR THE WORLD OUTSIDE

The contributors

WOUT VAN BEKKUM is Professor of Modern History of Judaism at the University of Amsterdam and a Reader in Hebrew Language and Literature at the University of Groningen.

DANIEL FRANK, formerly a fellow of the Oxford Centre for Hebrew and Jewish Studies and Wolfson College Oxford, is Assistant Professor of Hebrew Language, Department of Near Eastern Languages and Cultures at the Ohio State University.

ALBERT VAN DER HEIDE is Professor of Jewish studies at the Vrije Universiteit of Amsterdam and Reader in Medieval Hebrew at Leiden University.

WILLIAM HORBURY is Professor of Jewish and Early Christian Studies in the University of Cambridge and a fellow of Corpus Christi College.

MASHA ITZHAKI is a professor of Hebrew Literature at INALCO, Paris.

GEOFFREY KHAN is Reader in Semitic Philology at the University of Cambridge.

NICHOLAS DE LANGE is Reader in Hebrew and Jewish Studies in the University of Cambridge and a fellow of Wolfson College.

JUDITH OLSZOWY-SCHLANGER is Researcher in the Hebrew Palaeography section of the Institut de Recherche et d'Histoire des Textes, CNRS, Paris.

STEFAN C. REIF of the University of Cambridge is Director of the Genizah Research Unit and Head of the Oriental Division at the University Library, Professor of Medieval Hebrew Studies in the Faculty of Oriental Studies, and a fellow of St John's College.

ANGEL SÁENZ-BADILLOS is Full Professor of Hebrew Language and Literature at the Universidad Complutense, Madrid.

COLETTE SIRAT has studied Medieval Jewish Philosophy and teaches Hebrew Palaeography at the Ecole Pratique des Hautes Etudes, IVth Section. She is the head of the Hebrew section of the Institut de Recherche et d'Histoire des Textes, CNRS, Paris.

ADENA TANENBAUM is an assistant professor in the Department of Near Eastern Languages and Cultures at the Ohio State University. She is also on the faculty of the Melton Center for Jewish Studies at Ohio State University.

MICHAEL WEITZMAN (d. 1998) was Reader in Hebrew and Jewish Studies at University College London.

JOSEPH YAHALOM is Professor of Medieval Hebrew Poetry at the Hebrew University of Jerusalem and a member of the Academy for the Hebrew Language, Jerusalem.

IRENE E. ZWIEP is Professor of Hebrew, Aramaic and Jewish Studies at the University of Amsterdam.

Preface

Raphael Loewe, the doyen of medieval Hebrew studies in Britain, celebrated his eightieth birthday in 1999. In anticipation of this happy event, three of his colleagues and former pupils, Ada Rapoport-Albert, Michael Weitzman and the undersigned, decided to mark the occasion with the publication of a volume of essays. Sadly, Michael Weitzman died on 21 March 1998, at the age of fifty-one, and it was subsequently agreed that I should take over sole responsibility for editing the volume. Since Raphael Loewe has a longstanding association with Cambridge University, I was delighted that Cambridge University Press undertook to publish it.

The purpose of the present volume is not only to celebrate Professor Loewe's long life in the service of Hebrew scholarship, but also to celebrate in an appropriately scholarly fashion the current vibrancy of Hebrew scholarship relating to the medieval period and to reflect on its achievements during the latter part of the twentieth century.

The establishment of major Jewish research and teaching institutes in the United States in the latter part of the nineteenth century and of the Hebrew University, followed by other universities and institutes, in Israel in the twentieth, has borne abundant fruit, which has helped to offset to some extent the irreparable loss of the great institutions of eastern Europe. Meanwhile in the countries of western Europe the universities and state-funded research centres have continued to produce work of the highest level. The study of manuscripts, which is the backbone of medieval research, has proceeded apace, fuelled by remarkable discoveries such as the Cairo Genizah, and, more recently, dismembered manuscripts re-used in bindings, as well as the opening up of the collections in Russia, and particularly the two very rich Firkovitch collections in St Petersburg, referred to in several of the chapters in this book. Techniques for the study of manuscripts have been greatly refined and developed in the same period, largely in the context of a farsighted

Franco-Israeli collaborative project. Changing approaches to the study of medieval history have also had an effect, and in particular there has been a greater appreciation of cultural exchanges and influences between the Jewish communities and their environment.

The fifteen scholars who have contributed to the volume are all working at the forefront of current research. Some are approaching retirement while others are at the beginning of their scholarly careers, but all have made a significant mark. Together they represent most of the countries where Hebrew studies are currently being most vigorously pursued, and the main branches of the subject. Given the flourishing state of medieval Hebrew studies at present, there are many other distinguished scholars who might have contributed, but the limited scope of the volume imposed a choice. My aim has been to give priority to surveys of research and *status quaestionum* written by leading specialists, and to expositions of subjects that deserve to be better known.

I am grateful to all the scholars who willingly agreed to write for this volume, and in some case put up patiently with editorial bullying. Raphael Loewe himself made a welcome contribution by selecting and compiling the bibliography of his own writings. My pupil Lawrence Lahey made the index, the cost being covered by a grant from Tyrwhitt's Hebrew Fund (University of Cambridge). I am also grateful to those in Cambridge University Press without whom this book could not have seen the light of day.

NICHOLAS DE LANGE
Cambridge

Abbreviations

AJS Review	*Association of Jewish Studies Review*
BEK	*Bulletin d'Etudes Karaïtes*
BHM	*Bulletin of the History of Medicine*
BIJS	*Bulletin of the Institute of Jewish Studies*
BJGS	*Bulletin of Judaeo-Greek Studies*
BJRL	*Bulletin of the John Rylands Library*
BMGS	*Byzantine and Modern Greek Studies*
BSOAS	*Bulletin of the School of Oriental and African Studies*
BZ	*Byzantinische Zeitschrift*
DNB	*Dictionary of National Biography*
EJ	*Encyclopaedia Judaica*
HTR	*Harvard Theological Review*
HUCA	*Hebrew Union College Annual*
IEJ	*Israel Exploration Journal*
IMHM	*Institute of Microfilmed Hebrew Manuscripts*
IOS	*Israel Oriental Studies*
JA	*Journal Asiatique*
JAOS	*Journal of the American Oriental Society*
JBL	*Journal of Biblical Literature*
JC	*Jewish Chronicle*
JJS	*Journal of Jewish Studies*
JMS	*Journal of Mediterranean Studies*
JPS	*Jewish Publication Society*
JQR	*Jewish Quarterly Review*
JSHL	*Jerusalem Studies in Hebrew Literature*
JSJ	*Journal for the Study of Judaism in the Persian, Hellenistic and Roman Periods*
JSOT	*Journal for the Study of the Old Testament*
JSQ	*Jewish Studies Quarterly*
JSS	*Journal of Semitic Studies*

JTS	*Journal of Theological Studies*
JWCI	*Journal of the Warburg and Courtauld Institutes*
KS	*Kiryat Sefer*
MEAH	*Miscelánea de Estudios Árabes y Hebráicos*
MGWJ	*Monatsschrift für Geschichte und Wissenschaft des Judentums*
MHR	*Mediterranean Historical Review*
MRS	*Mediaeval and Renaissance Studies*
PAAJR	*Proceedings of the American Academy for Jewish Research*
RB	*Revue biblique*
REJ	*Revue des études juives*
RH	*Revue historique*
RHPR	*Revue d'histoire et de philosophie religieuse*
SBB	*Studies in Bibliography and Booklore*
SCI	*Scripta Classica Israelica*
TAR	*Tel Aviv Review*
TJHSE	*Transactions of the Jewish Historical Society of England*
TZ	*Theologische Zeitschrift*
USQR	*Union Seminary Quarterly Review*
VT	*Vetus Testamentum*
ZAC	*Zeitschrift für Antikes Christentum*
ZAL	*Zeitschrift für arabische Linguistik*
ZAW	*Zeitschrift für die alttestamentliche Wissenschaft*
ZDMG	*Zeitschrift der deutschen morgenländischen Gesellschaft*
ZDPV	*Zeitschrift des Deutschen Palästina-Vereins*
ZPE	*Zeitschrift für Papyrologie und Epigrafik*

I

New lines of investigation

CHAPTER ONE

The study of medieval Karaism, 1989–1999

Daniel Frank

During the past decade the study of Karaism, its history and literature has begun to flourish. Over one hundred and fifty publications have appeared – a modest figure, perhaps, in comparison with scholarship on Maimonides, kabbalah, or medieval Hebrew poetry, but impressive in its own terms. And while a handful of eminences dominated Karaite studies in the previous decades, over sixty scholars contributed to the field during the 1990s.[1] This growth may be attributed to three main factors: the general expansion of Jewish studies; the development of Judaeo-Arabic research in particular; and the reopening of the great Russian manuscript collections.

New scholars seek new areas of research; Karaite literature has proved attractive, at least in part, because of its relative neglect. At the same time, as the field of Judaeo-Arabic has come of age, attention has focused quite naturally on the extensive *oeuvre* of Karaite authors in tenth- and eleventh-century Jerusalem which includes pioneering works of Hebrew lexicography and grammar, theology, law, biblical exegesis, and Bible translations. Due to their abstruseness, magnitude and language, the great majority of these compositions remain unpublished. While substantial numbers of Karaite codices are available in Europe and the United States, by far the greatest repository of all Judaeo-Arabic manuscripts – especially Karaitica – remains the vast collections assembled by Abraham Firkovitch during the last century and preserved in the Saltykov-Shchedrin public library, St Petersburg. Until the recent collapse of the Soviet Union, Western specialists in Hebrew and Judaeo-Arabic literature were apt to speak of 'the

For Raphael Loewe:
Faith! Thine is understanding wide / As Ocean, and thy learning's art / With answers leaves all satisfied / In mind, thy law makes wise their heart. (*Ibn Gabirol*, 57)

[1] During the 1960s and 1970s the field was dominated by by the late Professors Nemoy, Scheiber, Vajda, and Zucker, together with Professors Ankori and Wieder *yibbadelu le-ḥayyim arukkim*. For an overview, see Frank (1990a).

Leningrad Problem', i.e. the possibility (probability?) that other, probably better manuscripts of the texts they were studying existed, inaccessibly, in Russia.[2] By the early 1990s, research trips confirmed the richness of the Firkovitch hoards. Judaeo-Arabic literature would require a complete reassessment. Lost works and forgotten authors could now be recovered. Even favourite classics would have to be reconsidered.[3] But the appalling condition of many manuscripts, and – even more dauntingly – the lack of any catalogue or reliable handlist made serious work in Russia virtually impossible.[4] Fortunately, through the indefatigable efforts of several Israeli scholars and a munificent benefaction, a photographic team was dispatched to St Petersburg where the entire collection of perhaps seventeen thousand items was microfilmed. The films were deposited at the Institute of Microfilmed Hebrew Manuscripts (IMHM), at the Jewish National and University Library, Jerusalem, where they are currently being catalogued. Since the Firkovitch material may be studied there alongside films of manuscripts from virtually every other major collection, the IMHM remains the single most valuable resource for serious work on Hebrew manuscripts.[5]

And in the field of Karaitica there has been real progress. At least seven doctoral dissertations have been completed during the past decade, as well as several substantial master's theses.[6] There have been quite a few important publications, as we will see presently. And most significantly, several promising collaborative projects have been launched. In what follows, I have tried to survey comprehensively – if not exhaustively – recent scholarship on medieval and early modern Karaism. Representative publications dealing with the sect's history over the past two centuries have also been noted.[7]

[2] On these manuscripts, their provenance and significance see Beit-Arié (1991) and Ben-Sasson (1991).

[3] E.g. the *dīwān* of Judah Halevi; see Y. Yahalom, 'The Leningrad Treasures and the Study of the Poetry and Life of Yehuda Halevi' (Hebrew), *Pe'amim* 46–7 (1991): 55–74.

[4] Paul Fenton's handlist (1991) proved to be an important tool until it was largely superseded.

[5] The IMHM now holds as well microfilms of the Hebrew-character manuscripts in the Institute of Oriental Studies (St Petersburg). This collection contains most of the old Karaite National Library, formerly in the Crimea.

[6] Doctoral dissertations: Astren (University of California, Berkeley 1993), Frank (Harvard 1991), Freund (Stockholm 1991; published) Kollender (Bar-Ilan 1991), Olszowy-Schlanger (Cambridge 1995; published 1998), Polliack (Cambridge 1993; published 1997) and Tirosh-Becker (Hebrew University 1999); published MA thesis: Livne-Kafri (1993).

[7] For reasons of space, not every item in the bibliography has been mentioned in the body of the text.

SCHOLARSHIP BY AND ABOUT CONTEMPORARY KARAITES

Several Karaites have published recently on the sect's history and rituals; primarily intended for internal consumption, these works contain important information on current practices. They are also invaluable communal documents, reflecting contemporary concerns, hopes and self-perceptions. Ḥayyim Halevi, former chief rabbi of the community in Israel, published two volumes: a collection of texts and studies (1994), intended to introduce Israeli Karaites to their literary heritage; and a textbook of *halakhah* (1996) derived from Aaron b. Elijah's *Gan Eden* (1354) and Elijah Bashyachi's *Adderet Eliyahu* (fifteenth century). A useful discussion of the Egyptian Karaite celebration of the Festival of *Maṣṣot* can be found in Yosef Elgamil's monograph (1996). The late Simon Szyszman wrote a concise overview of Karaite life in Europe from a sectarian perspective (1989); there is now a booklet as well on the Lithuanian community by Halina Kobeckaite (1997). Mourad El-Kodsi's touching account (1993) documents the encounter between a delegation of Egyptian Karaites to the eastern European communities in the summer of 1991.[8]

As modern Karaite communities have contended with the acculturation of the younger generation and the rapid loss of their cultural heritage, academics have begun to document their languages, liturgies and practices. Emanuela Trevisan Semi (1991) and Tapani Harviainen (1997) have surveyed the European centres and their populations. Trevisan Semi (1997) has compared the respective celebrations of Passover by Egyptian Karaites in Israel and Lithuanian sectarians in Trakai. Geoffrey Khan (1997b) has described the Arabic dialect of Karaites from Iraq, while Harviainen (1992, 1998) has documented the pronunciation of Hebrew by the Lithuanian and Istanbuli communities. Jehoash Hirshberg (1989, 1994) and Rachel Kollender (1991, 1994) have analysed and discussed features of Egyptian Karaite liturgical music.

For the most part, however, scholarly interest has focused on medieval and early modern Karaism; it is to the question of Karaite origins that we now turn.

[8] Mention should be made as well of the communal newsletters that appear at irregular intervals: *Bitta'on Benei Miqra* (Ramleh, Israel) and the *KJA* [Karaite Jews of America] *Bulletin* (Daly City, California). There are also dedicated sites on the Internet.

ORIGINS

If historians now reject the standard Karaite foundation myths, they have yet to reach a consensus on the sect's origins and early years.[9] Two scholars, Haggai Ben-Shammai and Yoram Erder, have investigated the problem from different vantage points and with differing results.[10] Ben-Shammai (1992a, 1993b) has re-examined the relationship between Karaism and Anan ben David, its putative founder. Distinguishing between Anan's Aramaic *Book of Commandments* and statements attributed to him in later Arabic and Hebrew sources, he argues that Anan was no scripturalist, but rather the founder of a distinct sect with its own rival tradition. True Karaism only began with Daniel al-Qūmisī (late ninth century) who abandoned Ananism. During the tenth century, some of Anan's descendants joined the Karaites in Jerusalem, bringing with them both their Davidic lineage and their ancestor's fame. As these Ananite leaders assimilated to Karaism, they rose to high positions in the sect, becoming its 'Princes' (*neśi'im*). True scripturalism, 'total rejection of any tradition and individual exegesis became hallmarks of early Karaism'.[11] This short-lived phase was necessarily succeeded, however, by the admission of a Karaite tradition (Ar. *naql*, Heb. *ha'ataqah*) as a valid source of legal authority during the latter half of the tenth century.

Erder has focused on the connection between the terminology and doctrines of the Karaites and Qumran literature. The latter, he argues, exercised a 'powerful influence' on the medieval sectarians and constituted 'an inexhaustible source of inspiration for them'.[12] While he rejects any historical connection between the ancient and medieval sects, he emphasizes the degree to which Qumranian notions were appropriated by the Karaites. He maintains that not only did the latter take over Qumran epithets, but that they were also indebted to the Dead Sea group – whom they styled 'Sadducees' – for halakhic teachings (1992, 1994a, 1998); even the name 'Karaites', he argues, derives from the Qumran phrase *qeri'ei shem* (1994b) rather than the notion of Scripture (*miqra'*) or religious propagandist (*qarra'*).[13] If Ben-Shammai and Erder differ in their approach to Karaite origins, they agree that the sect crystallized in the time of Daniel al-Qūmisī (latter half of the ninth century) who settled with his followers in Jerusalem.

[9] For a convenient survey of the stories concerning Anan b. David and Karaite origins, see L. Nemoy, *Karaite Anthology* (New Haven and London: Yale University Press, 1952), 3–8.

[10] For an instructive exchange between them on matters of method, see *Cathedra* 42 (1987): 54–86.

[11] Ben-Shammai (1993a: 329).

[12] Erder (1994b: 205, 207).

[13] The classic treatment of epithets shared by the two sects remains N. Wieder, *The Judean Scrolls and Karaism* (London: East and West, 1962).

HISTORY: THE TENTH AND ELEVENTH CENTURIES IN THE ISLAMIC EAST

Most of the early Karaites seem to have originated in Iraq or even further east. Their relations with the Geonim, especially Saadya ben Joseph, have remained a starting point in Karaite studies at least since Poznanski's day.[14] Robert Brody's splendid introduction to Gaonic culture (1998) and David Sklare's impressive monograph on Samuel ben Ḥofni Gaon (1996) are indispensable for an understanding of the intellectual world in which Karaism emerged.

The leading figure among Iraqi Karaites during the first half of the tenth century seems to have been Ya'qūb al-Qirqisānī. Bruno Chiesa and Wilfred Lockwood (1992) have published a portion of the commentary on Genesis, part of an ongoing project to edit and translate what remains of *Kitāb al-Riyāḍ*. Fred Astren (1995) and Chiesa (1988) have considered *Kitāb al-Anwār*, particularly the heresiographic section, in the context of medieval historiography and dialectics. Other studies include Nemoy (1992) – issued over sixty years after his first publication on *Kitāb al-Anwār* – and Khan (1990b).

THE JERUSALEM COMMUNITY

Gil (1992) and Ben-Shammai (1996) – both revised translations of earlier studies – together provide a sound historical and bio-bibliographic orientation. On the basis of a responsum by Yūsuf al-Baṣīr, Ben-Shammai (1992b, 1994a) has located the medieval Karaite quarter south-east of the Temple Mount on the site of the Ofel within Eudocia's wall.

The Jerusalem community, self-styled 'Mourners for Zion' or 'Lilies' (*Shoshanim*), have been the subject of several thematic studies. Walfish (1991) has emphasized their settlement or 'Aliyah' ideology, while Erder (1997a, 1997b) has highlighted their absolute rejection of the Diaspora – theologically, physically, and halakhically. Noting lines of continuity with earlier sectarian movements, he points up differences of legal opinion between tenth-century Karaites in Jerusalem and Iraq. Frank (1995) discusses biblical exegesis and liturgy as expressions of communal identity. Drory (1992, 1994) assesses the special roles assigned Hebrew and Arabic in the literary systems of tenth-century Karaites.

[14] See S. Poznanski, *The Karaite Literary Opponents of Saadiah Gaon* (London: Luzac, 1908); repr. from *JQR* o.s. 18–20 (1905–8).

The Karaites of tenth and eleventh-century Jerusalem were remarkable for their scholarship. Prolific authors, they were among the first Jews to employ certain literary genres. Their interest was absorbed in the Bible, which they sought to transcribe meticulously, translate precisely, and explicate fully. A thousand years ago, a typical Karaite biblical codex was three-tiered: the Hebrew text of the Bible in Arabic characters; a running Arabic translation; and a detailed commentary. There were also independent Hebrew grammars and dictionaries. Recently, scholarship on these various fields has proliferated.

ARABIC BIBLE TRANSCRIPTIONS

The peculiar Karaite practice of presenting the biblical text in Arabic characters has been regarded as a sign of extraordinary acculturation: the community must have been more comfortable with Arabic script than Hebrew. Geoffrey Khan (1992a) has questioned this interpretation. He sees the transcriptions as an attempt by certain sectarians to record their reading tradition independent of the Masoretic text championed by the Rabbanites. The phenomenon would belong, then, to a broader polemical context in which the Karaites sought to differentiate themselves as much as possible from rabbinic tradition. Since both Hebrew- and Arabic-character manuscripts exist, however, the practice may have been largely a matter of personal preference (1993). Khan has also edited a collection of such biblical fragments from the Genizah (1990a). Needless to say, this material provides important data for the history of Hebrew phonology (Khan 1992b). Tapani Harviainen has published a series of linguistic studies, based upon Arabic Bible transcriptions in the Firkovitch collections (1993, 1994, 1995, 1996a).

ARABIC BIBLE TRANSLATIONS

While Saadya Gaon's *tafsīr* has received much attention over the years, Karaite renderings of the Bible into Arabic have been virtually ignored. Meira Polliack (1997) has put matters right in her seminal monograph (see also 1993–4, 1996). In comparing and analysing a half-dozen Karaite versions, she has discerned certain distinctive trends: a resistance to Targum on both ideological and philological grounds; a predilection for extreme literalism, even at the expense of good Arabic; an emphasis on individualism and freedom of opinion; and above all, a conception of translation as an interpretative genre.

ARABIC BIBLE COMMENTARIES

Ben-Shammai (1991b) re-edited and translated a fragment of Daniel al-Qūmisī's Hebrew commentary on Daniel containing some interesting historical data; Qūmisī's exegetical works were important forerunners of the great Judaeo-Arabic commentaries composed during the tenth century. The studies by Erder and Frank mentioned above ('The Jerusalem Community') draw heavily upon the Bible commentaries of Japheth ben Eli.[15] His writings and those of his predecessor Salmon ben Jeroham remain largely unpublished, because of their size, language and obscurity. By any standard, they are important texts which should interest biblicists, historians, and philologists alike. Publications include: (1) a partial edition and French translation of Salmon's commentary on Psalms (Alobaidi 1996);[16] (2) an edition of Japheth on Habakkuk (Livne-Kafri 1993); and, (3) most importantly, a *catalogue raisonné* of Firkovitch manuscripts of Japheth's commentary on Genesis (Ben-Shammai et al. 2000) which, at last, organizes some of the Russian materials and permits the contemplation of an edition. The catalogue also includes a sample edition and translation of the introduction and commentary on Genesis 1:1–5 (by Sagit Butbul and Sarah Stroumsa) as well as an essay by Haggai Ben-Shammai on the manuscript tradition of Japheth's translation. A forthcoming study (Frank 2001) uses Firkovitch material to recover another 'lost' work – Salmon's Judaeo-Arabic commentary on the Song of Songs, the oldest extant on the book by a Jewish author. In comparing Salmon and Japheth's interpretations of the Song, the author assesses the book's special importance for the *Shoshanim* as well as the evolution of the Bible commentary within the tenth-century community.

HEBREW GRAMMAR AND LEXICOGRAPHY

One of the most exciting developments has been the rediscovery of an extensive Karaite grammatical literature composed in Judaeo-Arabic. Two figures, the exegete and teacher Joseph ben Noah and the grammarian Abū'l-Faraj Hārūn, were primarily responsible for Karaite advances in Hebrew grammar during the late tenth and early eleventh centuries.[17] Khan (1997a) provides an entrée to their complex grammatical theories; see also Basal (1998), Becker (1991), Maman (1996, 1997)

[15] On Japheth's attitude towards Islam, see also Erder 1997c.
[16] On the Psalms commentaries of Salmon and Japheth see Simon 1991.
[17] See the chapter by Geoffrey Khan in the present volume (chapter 5).

and Zislin (1994). Eldar (1994) has written a monograph on the curious treatise *Hidāyat al-qāri* ('Guidance to the Reader') whose author he has demonstrated to have been Abū'l-Faraj Hārūn; on this text see also Morag (1997). For other treatments of Karaite (and Rabbanite) lexical and grammatical writings during this period, see Eldar (1992), Maman (1992, 1995), Olszowy-Schlanger (1997) and Zislin (1990). The peculiar Hebrew employed by eleventh-century Byzantine Karaites has been described by Maman (1989) and Hopkins (1992).

RABBINIC CITATIONS IN KARAITE WRITINGS

Two Israeli philologists have become particularly interested in the extensive citations of rabbinic texts embedded in Karaite works, especially the Bible commentaries of Yeshuah ben Judah. Often transcribed into Arabic characters, these passages offer early, oriental attestations of *midreshei halakhah*; see Maman (1990, 1991) and Tirosh-Becker (1991, 1993).

YŪSUF AL-BAṢĪR

The leading scholar in the Jerusalem community during the first decades of the eleventh century was Yūsuf al-Baṣīr, a Jewish Mutazilite theologian and jurist. Georges Vajda's edition of al-Baṣīr's *Kitāb al-Muḥtawī*, a *kalām* treatise, appeared posthumously;[18] subsequently, a missing chapter was discovered and published (Vajda and Fenton 1991). Al-Baṣīr's extensive legal writings had been virtually ignored until the appearance of David Sklare's masterly survey (1995). Together with Ben-Shammai, he has also produced a detailed catalogue of al-Baṣīr manuscripts in St Petersburg; the volume includes a text edition by Ben-Shammai of material missing from the Vajda *Muḥtawī* as well as a short piece by Sklare on unknown Karaite works preserved in the Firkovitch collection (Sklare and Ben-Shammai 1997). A responsum by al-Baṣīr – the first ever published – appears in Ben-Shammai 1994a.

YESHUAH BEN JUDAH (ABŪ 'L-FARAJ FURQĀN BEN AL-ASAD)

Al-Baṣīr's successor in the Karaite community of Jerusalem, Yeshuah ben Judah, left behind an extensive *oeuvre* much of which has been preserved in manuscript. It is also the subject of a cataloguing project at the Jewish National and University Library. While his most extensive works

[18] (Leiden: E. J. Brill, 1985); see Ben-Shammai (1988–9).

were exegetical, he also composed at least one lament (Ben-Shammai 1998). He also seems to have been responsible for the Karaite recension of a Rabbanite work, 'The Differences between the Babylonian and the Palestinian [Rites]' (Elkin 1996).

MARRIAGE CONTRACTS

So far as is known, there exists no trove of medieval Karaite documents comparable to the Cairo Genizah. Our knowledge of the sect's social and economic history during the tenth to twelfth centuries is distinctly limited. All the same, Judith Olszowy-Schlanger (1998) has identified fifty-seven Karaite marriage documents in various Genizah collections. Her monograph includes an edition and translation of these texts together with copious annotation and an extensive introduction dealing with Karaite history, marriage law, the use of Hebrew (rather than Aramaic) in these texts, and palaeography. There is also a companion piece on Karaite divorce (1996).

THE EGYPTIAN COMMUNITY, ELEVENTH TO FIFTEENTH CENTURIES

With the destruction of the Jerusalem community in 1099 by the crusaders, the eastern centre of Karaism moved decisively to Egypt. Shulamit Sela (1994, 1998) has published important texts on the 'Headship of the Jews'. Paul Fenton (1992) has discovered a document relating to the old Karaite synagogue. Donald Richards (1993) has edited and translated an important court document dealing with Karaite rights in fifteenth-century Egypt. Nemoy (1991) published and translated a manual for ritual slaughterers by Israel al-Maghribī (fourteenth century); for a remarkable Sabbath hymn by the same author see Weinberger (1990a). Preparatory to an edition, Weinberger (1994) has surveyed the poetic *oeuvre* of Moses Darʿī (thirteenth century).

KARAISM IN SPAIN

The precise nature of Karaism in the Iberian peninsula remains an open question. Muslim writers – notably Ibn Ḥazm (d. 1064) – refer to the 'Ananite' sect and describe a scripturalist Judaism, but it is impossible to state with certainty which texts they read (Adang 1994, 1996). Ben-Shammai (1993b) has suggested that Spain may really have been the last stronghold of true Ananism. Once they had studied abroad in the

Land of Israel, however, these sectarians returned to Spain as Karaites, bringing with them the works of the Jerusalem school. What little we know of Iberian Karaites and Karaism derives almost entirely from citations in twelfth-century Rabbanite compositions; this material has been synthesized by Lasker (1992a). Several studies examine the attitudes of twelfth-century Rabbanite religious philosophers toward Karaism as well as the impact of Karaite writings on their thought: Moses ibn Ezra (Fenton 1997), Judah Halevi (Lasker 1990a) and Maimonides (Lasker 1991) were each impressed by Karaite scholarship, even as they rejected the sect's scripturalism.

THE BYZANTINE PERIOD (TWELFTH TO FIFTEENTH CENTURIES)

By the end of the eleventh century, the Karaite community in Byzantium had become self-sufficient.[19] Apart from Judah Hadassi's encyclopaedic *Eshkol ha-Kofer* – on which see Barthélemy (1989) – virtually nothing is known of Byzantine Karaite scholarship for the period 1150–1300. In recent years, several major figures active during the fourteenth and fifteenth centuries have commanded attention. Frank (1990b, 1991) and Lasker (1990b, 1992b, 1998) have written on the intellectual world of Aaron ben Joseph 'the Elder' and Aaron ben Elijah 'the Younger', both of whom were heavily influenced by Abraham ibn Ezra and Maimonides. Jean-Christophe Attias (1991, 1992) has examined the Karaite–Rabbanite *rapprochement* in fifteenth-century Constantinople. Leon J. Weinberger (1990a, 1991a, 1992, 1998) has edited and analysed a substantial corpus of Karaite *piyyut* from this period.

HISTORY OF IDEAS, RELIGIOUS PHILOSOPHY AND THEMATIC STUDIES

Medieval Karaite literature offers fruitful ground for students of Jewish thought. The first Karaite authors were heavily influenced by the Islamic environment in which they worked; the later Byzantine sectarians received a rich intellectual heritage which they sought to harmonize with Maimonides' *Guide*, Ibn Ezra's commentaries and other rationalistic Rabbanite works. Karaite perspectives can illuminate problems in intellectual history (Ben-Shammai 1991a; Chiesa 1989; Erder 1994a; Stroumsa 1992). Because of the long chain of Karaite scholarship, a diachronic approach can also yield interesting results (Fenton 1993; Lasker 1998;

[19] See Z. Ankori, *Karaites in Byzantium* (New York: Columbia University Press, 1959).

Miller 1992, 1999). The history of Karaite views on curriculum has, in fact, been shown to mirror the group's changing sense of identity (Walfish 1992).

LATER KARAISM

Rich materials for the history of Karaism in the west (Turkey, the Crimea, Poland, Lithuania) are readily available but remain underexploited; comparatively little has appeared on the subject since Jacob Mann's *Texts and Studies*, volume II: *Karaitica*.[20] Nemoy (1989) devoted a study to Isaac ben Solomon of Kalé (d. 1826), the author of a work on the Karaite creed. Henryk Jankowski (1997) has studied the Tatar dialect into which the Crimean Karaites translated the Bible. Philip Miller (1993a) edited and translated the account of Simhah Babovich's mission to the tsar in 1827; this text forms the centrepiece of his insightful monograph on the Crimean Karaites and their efforts to achieve recognition as a separate, non-Jewish entity.[21] This process of 'de-judaisation' is also the subject of Roman Freund's dissertation (1991). Finally, the attitudes of mainstream Jews – one hesitates to use the word 'Rabbanites' here – towards Karaites in the nineteenth century have been examined by Bartal (1994) and Trevisan Semi (1994, 1998).

CURRENT PROJECTS

As mentioned above, several co-operative projects are now in progress; these should help pave the way for the next decade of Karaite studies. Under the general direction of its director, Haggai Ben-Shammai, the Ben-Zvi Institute in Jerusalem is co-ordinating three important initiatives specifically devoted to Karaitica: (1) the edition (in Hebrew) of Samuel Poznanski's unpublished bio-bibliographical dictionary of Karaite scholars, copyists, and personages;[22] (2) the cataloguing of the Firkovitch materials (for now, see Sklare and Ben-Shammai 1997 and Ben-Shammai et al. 2000); and (3) a comprehensive bibliography of scholarship by and about Karaites which is being edited by Barry D. Walfish (University of Toronto). As no reliable, up-to-date survey of Karaite history and literature exists, Meira Polliack is editing a volume of commissioned studies entitled *Karaite Judaism: An Introduction*.[23] Finally, Geoffrey Khan (Cambridge University) is heading a project on Karaite grammatical writings in Judaeo-Arabic.

[20] Philadelphia: Jewish Publication Society of America, 1935.

[21] Miller (1993, 1994) has also devoted special attention to Karaite elites and their internal politics in the nineteenth century.

[22] On this work see Schur (1995: 237–8).

[23] Leiden: E. J. Brill. For now, the two small volumes by Schur (1992, 1994) remain handy, if somewhat untrustworthy, companions.

'Of late there has been a distinct revival of interest in the Karaites among Orientalists', wrote Elkan N. Adler just one hundred years ago in the catalogue to his newly acquired manuscripts.[24] If that interest has flagged at times during the past century, there have always been a few scholars who have cherished Karaite literature and furthered its study. There is good reason to believe that the next decade will bring wider recognition of this ancient sect and its contributions to Jewish learning.[25]

LITERATURE

Adang, Camilla 1994. 'Eléments karaïtes dans la polémique anti-judaïque d'Ibn Ḥazm'. In *Diálogo filosófico-religioso entre cristianismo, judaísmo e islamismo durante la edad media en la Península Ibérica*, ed. H. Santiago-Otero, 419–41. Turnhout: Brepols

1996. *Muslim Writers on Judaism and the Hebrew Bible: From Ibn Rabban to Ibn Hazm*. Leiden: E. J. Brill

Alobaidi, Joseph 1996. *Le Commentaire des Psaumes par le qaraïte Salmon Ben Yeruham: Psaumes 1–10. Introduction, Edition, Traduction*. Frankfurt a/M: Peter Lang

Astren, Fred D. 1993. 'History, Historicization, and Historical Claims in Karaite Jewish Literature'. University of California, Berkeley, Ph.D. dissertation

1995. 'History or Philosophy? The Construction of the Past in Medieval Karaite Judaism'. *Medieval Encounters* 1: 114–43

Attias, Jean-Christophe 1991. *Le Commentaire biblique: Mordekhai Komtino ou l'herméneutique du dialogue*. Paris: Cerf

1992. 'Intellectual Leadership: Rabbanite–Karaite Relations in Constantinople as Seen Through the Works and Activity of Mordekhai Comtino in the Fifteenth Century'. In *Ottoman and Turkish Jewry: Community and Leadership*, ed. A. Rodrigue, 67–86. Bloomington: Indiana University Turkish Studies

Bartal, Jacob 1994. 'The East European Haskalah and the Karaites: Image and Reality' (Hebrew). In *Proceedings of the Eleventh World Congress of Jewish Studies, Division B*, vol. II, 15–22. Jerusalem: World Union of Jewish Studies

Barthélemy, Dominique 1989. 'La Tradition manuscrite d'Eshkol ha-Kofer'. *BEK* 2: 5–22

Basal, Nasir 1998. 'Part One of *al-Kitāb al-Mushtamil* by Abū al-Faraj Harūn and its Dependence on Ibn al-Sarrāj's *Kitāb al-'Uṣūl fī al-Naḥw*' (Hebrew). *Leshonenu* 61: 191–210

Becker, Dan 1991. 'The "Ways" of the Hebrew Verb according to the Karaite Grammarians Abu-Al-Faraj Harun and the Author of the Me'or Ha'ayin' (Hebrew). *Te'udah* 7: 249–79

Beit-Arié, Malachi 1991. 'Hebrew Manuscript Collections in Leningrad' (Hebrew). *Jewish Studies* 31: 33–46

[24] E. N. Adler, 'Karaitica'. *JQR* o.s. 12 (1900): 674–87, at 675. Adler's manuscripts are now part of the collection of the Jewish Theological Seminary of America in New York.

[25] As this chapter was going to press I received Professor Daniel J. Lasker's insightful Hebrew survey of Karaism in the context of Jewish studies (Lasker, 2000).

Ben-Sasson, Menahem 1991. 'Firkovitch's Second Collection: Remarks on Historical and Halakhic Materials' (Hebrew). *Jewish Studies* 31: 47–67

Ben-Shammai, Haggai 1988–9. 'Review of Vajda, *Kitāb al-Muḥtawī*' (Hebrew). *KS* 62: 407–26

1991a. 'Transmigration of Souls in Tenth-century Jewish Thought in the Orient' (Hebrew). *Sefunot* n.s. 5 [20]: 117–36

1991b. 'Fragments of Daniel al-Qumisi's Commentary on the Book of Daniel as a Historical Source'. *Henoch* 13: 259–82

1992a. 'The Karaite Controversy: Scripture and Tradition in Early Karaism'. In *Religionsgespräche im Mittelalter*, ed. B. Lewis and F. Niewöhner, 11–26. Wiesbaden: Otto Harrassowitz

1992b. 'New Data on the Location of the Karaite Quarter in Jerusalem during the Early Islamic Period'. *Shalem* 6: 305–13

1993a. 'Return to the Scriptures in Ancient and Medieval Jewish Sectarianism and in Early Islam'. In *Les Retours aux écritures: fondamentalismes présents et passés*, ed. E. Patlagean and A. Le Boulluec, 319–39. Louvain–Paris: Peeters

1993b. 'Between Ananites and Karaites: Observations on Early Medieval Jewish Sectarianism'. In *Studies in Muslim–Jewish Relations*, vol. I, ed. R. L. Nettler, 19–29. Chur: Harwood

1994a. 'The Location of the Karaite Quarter in Medieval Jerusalem' (Hebrew). *Cathedra* 70: 59–94

1994b. 'Poetic Works and Lamentations of Qaraite "Mourners of Zion" – Structure and Contents'. In *Knesset Ezra: Literature and Life in the Synagogue, Studies Presented to Ezra Fleischer* (Hebrew), ed. S. Elizur et al., 191–234. Jerusalem: Ben-Zvi Institute

1996. 'The Karaites'. In *The History of Jerusalem: The Early Muslim Period, 638–1099*, ed. J. Prawer and H. Ben-Shammai, 201–24. Jerusalem: Yad Izhak Ben-Zvi/New York: New York University Press

1998. 'A Unique Lamentation on Jerusalem by the Karaite Author Yeshu'a ben Judah'. In *Mas'at Moshe: Studies in Jewish and Islamic Culture Presented to Moshe Gil* (Hebrew), ed. E. Fleischer, M. A. Friedman and J. Kraemer, 93–102. Jerusalem: Bialik Institute

Ben-Shammai, Haggai *et al.* 2000. *Judaeo-Arabic Manuscripts in the Firkovitch Collections: Yefet ben 'Eli al-Baṣri, Commentary on Genesis. A Sample Catalogue. Texts and Studies* (Jerusalem: Center for the Study of Judaeo-Arabic Culture and Literature/Ben-Zvi Institute

Brinner, William M. 1989. 'Karaites of Christendom – Karaites of Islam'. In *Essays in Honor of Bernard Lewis*, ed. C. E. Bosworth et al., 55–73. Princeton: Darwin Press.

Brody, Robert 1998. 'The Struggle against Heresy'. In *The Geonim of Babylonia and the Shaping of Medieval Jewish Culture*. New Haven and London: Yale University Press.

Chiesa, Bruno 1988. 'A Note on Early Karaite Historiography'. In *Essays in Jewish Historiography* (*History and Theory*, Beiheft 27), ed. A. Rapoport-Albert, 56–65. Wesleyan, CT: Wesleyan University; repr. Atlanta: Scholars Press, 1991

1989. *Creazione e caduta dell'uomo nell'esegesi giudeo-araba medievale.* Brescia: Paideia Editrice

Chiesa, Bruno and Wilfred Lockwood 1992. 'Al-Qirqisānī's Newly-found Commentary on the Pentateuch: the Commentary on Gen. 12'. *Henoch* 14: 153–80

Corinaldi, Michael 1996. 'Karaite Halakhah'. In *An Introduction to the History and Sources of Jewish Law*, ed. N. S. Hecht et al., 251–69. Oxford: Clarendon Press

Drory, Rina 1992. '"Words Beautifully Put": Hebrew Versus Arabic in Tenth-century Jewish Literature'. In *Genizah Research after Ninety Years*, ed. J. Blau and S. C. Reif, 53–61. Cambridge: Cambridge University Press

1994. 'The Role of Karaite Literature in the History of Tenth-century Jewish Literature' (Hebrew). *Dappim la-Meḥqar ba-Sifrut* 9: 101–10

Eldar, Ilan 1992. 'The Beginnings of Hebrew Lexicography in the Orient' (Hebrew). *Language Studies* 5–6: 355–82

1994. *The Study of the Art of Correct Reading as Reflected in the Medieval Treatise Hidāyat al-Qāri (Guidance to the Reader)* (Hebrew). Jerusalem: Hebrew Language Academy

Elgamil, Yosef 1996. *Sefer Imrot Yosef: Dinei Ḥag ha-Maṣṣot.* Ramleh: n.p.

El-Hawary, Mohamed 1994. *The Differences between the Karaites and the Rabbanites in the Light of Genizah Mss. Ms. Heb. f. 18 (fols. 1-33a), Bodleian-Oxford* (Arabic). Cairo: Dar El-Zahraa

Elkin, Zeev 1996. 'The Karaite Version of "Sefer Ha-Ḥilluqim Bein Benei Ereẓ-Yisrael Le-Benei Bavel"' (Hebrew). *Tarbiz* 66: 101–11

El-Kodsi, Mourad 1993. *The Karaite Communities in Poland, Lithuania, Russia and Crimea.* Lyons, NY: Wilprint

Erder, Yoram 1990a. 'The Date of the Paschal Sacrifice in the Light of the "Hezekiah Paschal" in the Early Karaite Halakha' (Hebrew). *Tarbiz* 59: 443–56

1990b. 'Early Karaite Halacha and Rabbinic Halacha in Light of the Controversies over the Time of the Paschal Sacrifice' (Hebrew). In *Proceedings of the Tenth World Congress of Jewish Studies, Division C*, vol. I, 170–6. Jerusalem: World Union of Jewish Studies

1992. 'The First Date in *Megillat Ta'anit* in Light of the Karaite Commentary on the Tabernacle Dedication' (Hebrew). *JQR* 82: 263–83

1994a. 'Early Karaite Conceptions about Commandments Given before the Revelation of the Torah'. *PAAJR* 60: 101–40; 61 (1995): xvii–xviii (corrections)

1994b. 'The Karaites' Sadducee Dilemma'. *IOS* 14: 195–226

1994c. 'Daily Prayer Times in Karaite Halakha in Light of the Times of Islamic Prayers'. *REJ* 153: 5–27

1995. 'The Centrality of Eretz-Israel in Early Karaite Circles as Reflected in the Halakha of Mishawayah al-Ukbari' (Hebrew). *Zion* 60: 37–67

1997a. 'The Negation of the Exile in the Messianic Doctrine of the Karaite Mourners of Zion'. *HUCA* 68: 109–40

1997b. 'The Observance of the Commandments in the Diaspora on the Eve of the Redemption in the Doctrine of the Karaite Mourners of Zion'. *Henoch* 19: 193–220

1997c. 'The Attitude of the Karaite, Yefet ben Eli, to Islam in Light of his Interpretation of Psalms 14 and 53' (Hebrew), *Michael* 14: 29–49
1998. 'Remnants of Qumranic Lore in Two Laws of the Karaite Benjamin al-Nihāwandī concerning Desired Meat' (Hebrew). *Zion* 63: 5–38
Fenton, Paul B. 1991. *Handlist of Judaeo-Arabic Manuscripts in Leningrad: A Tentative Handlist of Judaeo-Arabic Manuscripts in the Firkovic Collections* (Hebrew). Jerusalem: Ben-Zvi Institute
1992. 'La Synagogue qaraïte du Caire d'après un fragment historique provenant de la Genizah'. *Henoch* 14: 145–51
1993. '"À l'image de Dieu": l'interpretation de Genèse I, 26 selon quelques exégètes qaraïtes du moyen āge'. *Henoch* 15: 271–90
1997. *Philosophie et exégèse dans 'Le Jardin de la métaphore' de Moïse Ibn 'Ezra, philosophe et poète andalou du xiie siècle*. Leiden: E. J. Brill
Frank, Daniel 1990a. 'The Study of Medieval Karaism 1959–1989'. *BJGS* 6: 15–23.
1990b. 'Abraham ibn Ezra and the Bible Commentaries of the Karaites Aaron ben Joseph and Aaron ben Elijah'. In *Abraham ibn Ezra and his Age: Proceedings of the International Symposium*, ed. F. Díaz Esteban, 99–107. Madrid: Asociación Española de Orientalistas
1991. 'The Religious Philosophy of the Karaite Aaron ben Elijah: The Problem of Divine Justice'. Harvard University, Ph.D. dissertation
1995. 'The *Shoshanim* of Tenth-century Jerusalem: Karaite Exegesis, Prayer, and Communal Identity'. In *The Jews of Medieval Islam: Community, Society, and Identity*, ed. D. Frank, 199–245. Leiden: E. J. Brill, 1995
2001. 'Karaite Commentaries on the Song of Songs from Tenth-century Jerusalem'. In *With Reverence for the Word: Medieval Scriptural Exegesis in Judaism, Christianity, and Islam*, ed. Jane Dammen McAuliffe et al. Oxford: Oxford University Press (in press)
Freund, Roman 1991. *Karaites and Dejudaization: A Historical Review of an Endogenous and Exogenous Paradigm*. Stockholm: Almqvist & Wiksell
Gil, Moshe 1992. *A History of Palestine, 634–1099*. Cambridge: Cambridge University Press
Halevi, Ḥayyim ben Yiṣḥaq 1994. *Sefer Toledot Ḥayyim*. Ashdod: n.p.
1996. *Sefer ha-Ḥinnukh Ma'ayan Ḥayyim*. 2nd edn Ashdod: n.p.
Harviainen, Tapani 1992. 'The Karaites of Lithuania at the Present Time and the Pronunciation Tradition of Hebrew among them: a Preliminary Survey'. *Proceedings of the Ninth International Congress of the International Organization for Masoretic Studies 1989* (=Masoretic Studies 7), ed. A. Dotan, 53–69. Atlanta: Scholars Press
1993. 'Karaite Arabic Transcriptions of Hebrew in the Saltykov-Schedrin Public Library in St. Petersburg'. In *Estudios Masoréticos (X Congreso de la IOMS)*, ed. E. Fernández Tejero and M. Teresa Ortega Monasterio, 63–72. Madrid: Instituto de Filología del CSIC
1994. 'A Karaite Bible Transcription with Indiscriminate Counterparts of Tiberian *qameṣ* and *ḥolam* (Ms. Fikovitsh II, Arab.-evr. 1)'. In *Proceedings of the Eleventh Congress of the International Organization for Masoretic Studies (IOMS)*, ed. A. Dotan, 33–40. Jerusalem: World Union of Jewish Studies

1995. 'A Karaite Letter-for-letter Transliteration of Biblical Hebrew – Ms Firkovitsh II, Arab.-evr. 355'. *Textus* 18: 169–77

1996a. 'MS. Arab.-evr. 2 of the Second Firkovitsh Collection, a Karaite Bible Transcription in Arabic Script'. In *Studies in Hebrew and Jewish Languages Presented to Shelomo Morag*, ed. Moshe Bar-Asher, *41–*59. Jerusalem: Hebrew University/Bialik Institute

1996b. 'The Cairo *Genizot* and Other Sources of the Second Firkovitch Collection in St. Petersburg'. In *Proceedings of the Twelfth Congress of the International Organization for Masoretic Studies 1995* (=Masoretic Studies 8), ed. E. J. Revell, 25–36. Atlanta: Scholars Press

1997. 'Signs of New Life in Karaim Communities'. In *Ethnic Encounter and Culture Change* (= Nordic Research on the Middle East 3), ed. M'hammed Sabour and Knut S. Vikør, 72–83. Bergen: Nordic Society for Middle Eastern Studies

1998. 'The Karaite Community in Istanbul and their Hebrew'. In *Jewish Studies in a New Europe: Proceedings of the Fifth Congress of Jewish Studies in Copenhagen 1994*, ed. Ulf Haxen et al., 349–56. Copenhagen: C. A. Reitzel A/S International Publishers Det Kongelige Bibliotek

Hirshberg, Jehoash 1989. 'The Role of Music in the Renewed Self-identity of Karaite Jewish Refugee Communities from Cairo'. *Yearbook for Traditional Music* 21: 36–56

1994. 'Preservation and Renewal in the Paraliturgical Musical Heritage of the Karaite Jews in Israel' (Hebrew). *Proceedings of the Eleventh World Congress of Jewish Studies, Division D*, vol. II 49–56. Jerusalem: Magnes Press

Hirshberg, Jehoash and Roni Granot 1998. 'Duration in the Responsive Singing of Karaite Jews: Custom or Nature?' (Hebrew). *Pe'amim* 77: 69–89 (with musical examples on accompanying CD)

Hopkins, Simon 1992. 'Arabic Elements in the Hebrew of the Byzantine Karaites'. In *Genizah Research after Ninety Years*, ed. J. Blau and S. C. Reif, 93–9. Cambridge: Cambridge University Press

Jankowski, Henryk 1997. 'A Bible Translation into the Northern Crimean Dialect of Karaim'. *Studia Orientalia* 82: 1–84

Khan, Geoffrey 1990a. *Karaite Bible Manuscripts from the Cairo Genizah*. Cambridge: Cambridge University Press

1990b. 'al-Qirqisānī's Opinions concerning the Text of the Bible and Parallel Muslim Attitudes towards the Text of the Qur'ān'. *JQR* 81: 59–73

1992a. 'The Medieval Karaite Transcriptions of Hebrew into Arabic Script'. *IOS* 12: 157–76

1992b. 'The Pronunciation of the Minor *Ga'ya* as Reflected in Karaite Bible Manuscripts in Arabic Transcription' (Hebrew), *Language Studies* 5–6: 465–80

1992c. 'The Importance of the Karaite Transcriptions of the Hebrew Bible for the Understanding of the Tiberian Masora' (Hebrew). *Proceedings of the Ninth International Congress of the International Organization for Masoretic Studies 1989* (=Masoretic Studies 7), ed. A. Dotan, *17–*22. Atlanta: Scholars Press

1993. 'On the Question of Script in Medieval Karaite Manuscripts: New Evidence from the Genizah'. *BJRL* 75: 132–41

1997a. "Abū al-Faraj Hārūn and the Early Karaite Grammatical Tradition'. *JJS* 48: 314–34

1997b. 'The Arabic Dialect of the Karaite Jews of Hīt'. *Zeitschrift für Arabische Linguistik* 34: 53–102

Kobeckaite, Halina 1997. *Lietuvos Karaimai.* Vilnius: Baltos Lankos.

Kollender, Rachel 1991. 'Meqomah shel ha-musiqah ba-liturgiyah shel 'adat ha-yehudim ha-qara'im be-yisra'el' [The place of music in the liturgy of the Karaite Jewish community in Israel]. Bar-Ilan University, Ph.D. dissertation

1994. 'The Liturgical Musical Heritage of the Karaite Jews in Israel' (Hebrew). *Proceedings of the Eleventh World Congress of Jewish Studies, Division D*, vol. II, 57–64. Jerusalem: Magnes Press

Lasker, Daniel J. 1989a. 'Islamic Influences on Karaite Origins'. In *Studies in Islamic and Judaic Traditions*, ed. W. M. Brinner and S. D. Ricks, vol. II, 23–47. Atlanta: Scholars Press

1989b. 'Karaites, Developments 1970–1988'. In *EJ Yearbook, 1988–89*, 366–7. Jerusalem

1990a. 'Judah Halevi and Karaism'. In *From Ancient Israel to Modern Judaism . . . Essays in Honor of Marvin Fox*, ed. Jacob Neusner, et al., vol. III, 111–26. Atlanta: Scholars Press

1990b. 'Maimonides' Influence on Karaite Theories of Prophecy and Law'. *Maimonidean Studies* 1: 99–115

1991. 'The Influence of Karaism on Maimonides' (Hebrew). In *Sefunot* n.s. 5 [20]: 145–61

1992a. 'Karaism in Twelfth-century Spain'. *Journal of Jewish Thought and Philosophy* 1: 179–95

1992b. 'Aaron ben Joseph and the Transformation of Karaite Thought'. In *Torah and Wisdom . . . Essays in Honor of Arthur Hyman*, ed. Ruth Link-Salinger, 121–8. New York: Shengold

1993. 'Karaism and the Jewish–Christian Debate'. In *The Frank Talmage Memorial Volume*, ed. B. Walfish, vol. I, 323–32. Haifa: Haifa University Press/Hanover, NH: University Press of New England

1998. 'The Prophecy of Abraham in Karaite Thought'. *Jerusalem Studies in Jewish Thought* 14 (Sermonetta Memorial Volume): 103–11

2000. *Karaism and Jewish Studies* (Hebrew) (Jewish Culture in Muslim Lands and Cairo Geniza Studies, no. 1). Tel Aviv: Tel Aviv University, 29 pp.

Levy, Yaffa 1993–4. 'Ezekiel's Plan in an Early Karaite Bible'. *Jewish Art* 19–20: 68–85

Livne-Kafri, Ofer 1993. 'The Commentary on Habakkuk (Chapters 1, 3) by the Karaite Yefeth ben 'Eli al-Basri' (Hebrew). *Sefunot* n.s. 6 [21]: 73–113

Maman, Aharon 1989. 'Ha-'ivrit shel ha-qara'im' [The Hebrew of the Karaites]. *Weekly Newsletter of the Academy of the Hebrew Language* 8 (December), 8 pp.

1990. 'Rabbinic Hebrew in Karaite Works' (Hebrew). In *Proceedings of the Tenth World Congress of Jewish Studies, Division D*, vol. I, 37–44. Jerusalem: World Union of Jewish Studies

1991. 'Karaites and Mishnaic Hebrew: Quotations and Usage' (Hebrew). *Leshonenu* 55: 221–68

1992. 'The Lexical Element in David Alfasi's Dictionary Definitions'. In *Genizah Research after Ninety Years*, ed. J. Blau and S. C. Reif, 119–25. Cambridge: Cambridge University Press

1995. 'Medieval Grammatical Thought: Karaites versus Rabbanites' (Hebrew). *Language Studies* 7: 79–96

1996. 'The Infinitive and the Verbal Noun According to Abū-l-Faraj Harūn' (Hebrew). In *Studies in Hebrew and Jewish Languages Presented to Shelomo Morag*, ed. Moshe Bar-Asher, 119–49. Jerusalem: Hebrew University/Bialik Institute.

1997. 'The *'Amal* Theory in the Grammatical Thought of Abū-l-Faraj Hārūn' (Hebrew). *Massorot* 9–11: 263–74

Miller, Philip E. 1989a. 'Report of the IREX Mission to Leningrad, December, 1986'. *SBB* 17: 19–25

1989b. 'Evidence of a Previously Undocumented Karaite Presence in Galicia'. *SBB* 17: 36–42

1992. 'Was There Karaite Aggadah?' In *'Open Thou Mine Eyes . . .': Essays . . . Presented to Rabbi William G. Braude*, ed. H. J. Blumberg et al., 209–18. Hoboken, NJ: KTAV

1993a. *Karaite Separatism in Nineteenth-century Russia: Joseph Solomon Lutski's Epistle of Israel's Deliverance*. Cincinnati: Hebrew Union College Press

1993b. 'Prayerbook Politics: An Attempt to Print the Karaite Siddur in 1866 That Was Cancelled'. *SBB* 18: 15–26

1994. 'Spiritual and Political Leadership among Nineteenth-century Crimean Karaites'. In *Proceedings of the Eleventh World Congress of Jewish Studies, Division B*, vol. III, 1–8. Jerusalem: World Union of Jewish Studies

1998. 'Agenda in Karaite Printing in the Crimea during the Middle Third of the Nineteenth Century'. *SBB* 20: 82–8

1999. 'Karaite Pespectives on *Yôm Tĕrû'â'*. In *Kī Baruch Hu . . . Studies in Honor of Baruch A. Levine*, ed. R. Chazan et al., 537–41. Winona Lake, IN: Eisenbrauns

Morag, Shelomo 1997. 'The Art of the Correct Reading of the Bible: A Chapter in the History of Medieval Hebrew Linguistics' (Hebrew). *Massorot* 9–11: 243–61

Nemoy, Leon 1989. 'Isaac ben Solomon on the Karaite Creed'. *JQR* 80: 49–85

1991. 'Israel al-Maghribī's Tract on Ritual Slaughtering'. *Henoch* 13: 195–218

1992. 'al-Qirqisānī's "Thou Shalt Not Seethe a Kid in its Mother's Milk"'. In *'Open Thou Mine Eyes . . .': Essays . . . Presented to Rabbi William G. Braude*, ed. H. J. Blumberg et al., 219–27. Hoboken, NJ: KTAV

Olszowy-Schlanger, Judith 1996. 'La Lettre de divorce caraïte et sa place dans les relations entre caraïtes et rabbanites au moyen âge'. *REJ* 155: 337–62

1997. 'Karaite Linguistics: The "Renaissance" of the Hebrew Language among Early Karaite Jews, and Contemporary Linguistic Theories'. *Beiträge zur Geschichte der Sprachwissenschaft* 7: 81–100

1998. *Karaite Marriage Documents from the Cairo Geniza: Legal Tradition and Community Life in Mediaeval Egypt and Palestine*. Leiden: E. J. Brill

Polliack, Meira 1993–4. 'Alternate Renderings and Additions in Yeshu'ah ben Yehudah's Arabic Translation of the Pentateuch'. *JQR* 84: 209–26

1996. 'Medieval Karaite Views on Translating the Hebrew Bible into Arabic'. *JJS* 47: 64–84

1997. *The Karaite Tradition of Arabic Bible Translation: A Linguistic and Exegetical Study of Karaite Translations of the Pentateuch from the Tenth to the Eleventh Centuries*. Leiden: E. J. Brill

Richards, Donald S. 1993. 'Dhimmi Problems in Fifteenth-century Cairo: Reconsideration of a Court Document'. In *Studies in Muslim–Jewish Relations*, vol. I, ed. R. L. Nettler, 127–63. Chur: Harwood

Schenker, Adrian 1989a. 'Auf dem Weg zu einer kritischen Ausgabe von Jafet ben Elis Kommentar zu den Psalmen'. *BEK* 2: 29–38

1989b. 'Die Geburtswehen der messianischen Zeit nach Japhet ben Eli'. *BEK* 2: 39–46

Schur, Nathan 1992. *History of the Karaites*. Frankfurt a/M: Peter Lang

1994. 'Sources from Accounts of Pilgrims and Travelers for the History of the Karaites in Jerusalem, 1250–1948' (Hebrew). In *Proceedings of the Eleventh World Congress of Jewish Studies, Division B*, vol. I, 141–6. Jerusalem: World Union of Jewish Studies

1995. *The Karaite Encyclopedia*. Frankfurt a/M: Peter Lang

Sela, Shulamit 1994. 'The Head of the Rabbanite, Karaite and Samaritan Jews: On the History of a Title'. *BSOAS* 57: 235–67

1998. 'The Headship of the Jews in the Fāṭimid Empire in Karaite Hands' (Hebrew). In *Mas'at Moshe: Studies in Jewish and Islamic Culture Presented to Moshe Gil* (Hebrew), ed. E. Fleischer, M. A. Friedman and J. Kraemer, 256–81. Jerusalem: Bialik Institute

Shtober, Shimon 1994. 'Geographic and Topographic Aspects in Japhet ben Ali's Translation and Commentary to the Bible'. In *Proceedings of the Eleventh World Congress of Jewish Studies, Division A*, 151–8. Jerusalem: World Union of Jewish Studies

Simon, Uriel 1991. 'The Karaite Approach: The Psalms as Mandatory Prophetic Prayers'. In *Four Approaches to the Book of Psalms: From Saadiah Gaon to Abraham Ibn Ezra*. Albany: State University of New York Press

Sklare, David E. 1995. 'Yūsuf al-Baṣīr: Theological Aspects of his Halakhic Works'. In *The Jews of Medieval Islam: Community, Society, and Identity*, ed. D. Frank, 249–70. Leiden: E. J. Brill

1996. *Samuel ben Hofni Gaon and his Cultural World. Texts and Studies*. Leiden: E.J. Brill

Sklare, David in cooperation with Haggai Ben-Shammai 1997. *Judaeo-Arabic Manuscripts in the Firkovitch Collections: The Works of Yusuf al-Basir. A Sample Catalogue. Texts and Studies* (Hebrew). Jerusalem: Center for the Study of Judaeo-Arabic Culture and Literature/Ben-Zvi Institute

Stroumsa, Sarah 1992. '"What is man?": Psalm 8:4–5 in Jewish, Christian and Muslim Exegesis in Arabic'. *Henoch* 14: 283–90

Szyszman, Simon 1989. *Les Karaïtes d'Europe*. Uppsala: Acta Universitatis Upsaliensis

Tirosh-Becker, Ofra 1991. 'Preliminary Studies in Rabbinic Quotations Embedded in the Pentateuch Commentaries of the Karaite Scholar Yeshu'a Ben-Yehuda' (Hebrew). *Massorot* 5–6: 313–40

1993. 'A Linguistic Study of Mishnaic Quotations Embedded in Yeshu'a ben Yehuda's Commentary on Leviticus' (Hebrew). *Massorot* 7: 145–86

Trevisan Semi, Emanuela 1991. 'A Brief Survey of Present-day Karaite Communities in Europe'. *The Jewish Journal of Sociology* 33 (1991): 97–106

1992. *Les Karaïtes: un autre Judaïsme*. Paris: Albion Michel

1994. 'The Crimean Karaites as Seen by the French Jewish Press in the Second Half of the Nineteenth Century'. In *Proceedings of the Eleventh World Congress of Jewish Studies, Division B*, vol. III, 9–16. Jerusalem: World Union of Jewish Studies

1997. 'Testo, rito, pasto nella Pasqua caraita: trasformazioni tra i caraiti d'oriente e d'occidente'. *'Ilu: revista de ciencias de las religiones* 2: 185–97

1998. 'Le *Sefer Massa Qrim* de Deinard: but parodique ou polémique?'. *REJ* 157: 57–67

Vajda, Georges and Paul B. Fenton 1991. 'The Definitions of the Technical Terms of the Mutakallimûn in the Writings of Yûsuf al-Baṣîr' (Hebrew). *Da'at* 26: 5–34

Walfish, Barry D. 1991. 'The Mourners of Zion (*'Avelei Siyyon*): A Karaite *Aliyah* Movement of the Early Arab Period'. In *Eretz Israel, Israel and the Jewish Diaspora: Mutual Relations*, ed. M. Mor, 42–52. Lanham, MD: University Press of America

1992. 'Karaite Education in the Middle Ages'. *Dor le-Dor* 5: 156–80

Weinberger, Leon J. 1990a. 'Israel Dayyan's *Zemer* for the Sabbath'. *JQR* 81: 119–25

1990b. 'A Karaite *Piyyut* in a Rabbanite Mahzor' (Hebrew). *Hadoar* 19 September, 23

1991a. *Rabbanite and Karaite Liturgical Poetry in South-eastern Europe*. Cincinnati: Hebrew Union College Press

1991b. 'A New Poem by Abraham Ibn Ezra from a Karaite Mahzor' (Hebrew). *Bitsaron* n.s. 10 45/48 (Nisan 5751): 154–5

1992. 'Karaite *Piyyut* in Southeastern Europe'. *JQR* 83: 145–65

1994. 'Moses Dar'ī, Karaite Poet and Physician'. *JQR* 84: 445–83

1998. 'Karaite Synagogue Poets'. In his *Jewish Hymnography: A Literary History*. London and Portland, OR: The Littman Library of Jewish Civilization

Wieder, Naphtali 1994. 'An Unknown Ancient Version of the Haftarah Benedictions – The Use of *'emet* to Affirm Important Religious Principles' (Hebrew). In *Knesset Ezra: Literature and Life in the Synagogue, Studies Presented to Ezra Fleischer* (Hebrew), ed. S. Elizur et al., 35–46. Jerusalem: Ben-Zvi Institute

Zislin, Meir I. 1990. *Me'ôr 'Aiin ('Svetoch Glaza')*. Moscow: Nauka

1994. 'Principles in the Morphology of Abu al-Faraj Harun of Jerusalem' (Hebrew). In *Proceedings of the Eleventh World Congress of Jewish Studies, Division D*, vol. I, 72–6. Jerusalem: World Union of Jewish Studies

CHAPTER TWO

Hebrew scholarship in Byzantium

Nicholas de Lange

A NEGLECTED SUBJECT

Modern study of Hebrew scholarship in Byzantium has a relatively short history. Despite the ground-breaking publications of Samuel Krauss, on the eve of the First World War, and of Joshua Starr, on the eve of the Second, scholars have been slow to take up the challenge of investigating Byzantine Hebrew culture or even, indeed, to recognize its existence.[1] Despite these slow beginnings, a good deal of progress has been made in the last decades of the twentieth century, and it is my purpose in this chapter to draw attention both to the achievements and to some of the main gaps that remain to be filled. Having recently surveyed elsewhere the history of the use of Hebrew in Byzantium,[2] I shall endeavour to avoid repeating myself here, and shall focus on the study of Hebrew, rather than its use for prayer or communication, hard though it is to draw a firm distinction.

The ignorance and even contempt with which Byzantine Jewish culture has too often been treated reflects attitudes to Byzantium in general which have regrettably been widely prevalent in Western scholarship. Krauss (following in the footsteps of Perles) was ahead of his time in his positive appreciation of it. The estimate of Starr ('The contribution of Byzantine Jewry to the culture of their people appears to have been on the whole rather mediocre', 1939: 50) represents a more usual trend, even though his judgement is contradicted by some of the primary and secondary sources that he himself quotes in his book. The well-known problem of scholarly prejudice is compounded by a serious shortage of hard evidence. Although the Cairo Genizah materials had begun to be studied in Starr's day, very little had been clearly identified as Byzantine, and relatively few Byzantine Hebrew texts had been

[1] See de Lange (1989a). Full particulars of titles abbreviated in the notes may be found in the bibliography at the end of the article.

[2] See de Lange (1999a).

published. Starr is too willing to assume that the little that was known to him represents the totality of Byzantine Jewish cultural activity, and he tends to regard the figures whose importance is widely recognized (men such as Shabbetai Donnolo, Tobias ben Eliezer or Hillel ben Eliaqim, not to mention Karaites such as Tobias ben Moses or Judah Hadassi) as constituting exceptions to the general rule. It is against this background that we must judge the achievement of Zvi Ankori, who in his monumental if cumbersomely 'overwritten'[3] book *Karaites in Byzantium* revealed clearly for the first time the richness of Byzantine Jewish culture, both Karaite and Rabbanite, in the early centuries of the second millennium. For H. J. Zimmels, writing in the 1960s, there is no doubting the quality and historical significance of Byzantine Jewish scholarship in the period 711–1096 (for most of which southern Italy was under Byzantine rule): 'The Byzantine Empire and Italy were not only the first countries in Europe to receive directly the legacy of Jewish scholarship from Babylonia and Palestine; they were also the gates through which this was transmitted to Central Europe' (1966: 175). Nevertheless, while he is willing to accord cardinal importance to Italy, he too cannot avoid importing a note of scepticism about the contribution of the more central parts of the empire:

> It would be natural to imagine that during this period Jewish intellectual life should have flourished in the central provinces of the Byzantine Empire, extending over the Balkans and Asia Minor. The area was in close geographical and economic contact with the great centers of Jewish population and intellectual life of the East. Its Jewish population, at least until the beginning of the religious persecution in the 9th century, was it seems dense. Byzantium itself had a strong Karaite community, whose mere presence should have stimulated intellectual life among the Rabbanites. Moreover, it is to this period that there probably belongs the development of the Byzantine rite of prayer, which should have been greatly enriched by local poets and hymnologists. Nevertheless, at the period we are discussing, there are no more than scanty records of Jewish literary productions in this area . . . It is difficult to give the reason for this. The subsequent dwindling of Jewish life undoubtedly led to a failure to copy and preserve the works produced locally at this time, while those that did not come to the attention of the great centers of Jewish life in Spain, France and Germany tended to be overlooked both then and later on, when the printing-press had so much influence on the preservation of the Jewish intellectual heritage and the selection of those works which came to be regarded as classics. Nevertheless, in spite of all this, it can hardly be doubted that had works of real importance been produced in

[3] R. J. Z. Werblowski in *JSS* 8 (1963): 268.

Greece at this time they would not have been forgotten by posterity; and consequently it is improbable that the Greek literary production was of real significance. (1966: 176 f.)

Despite perceiving good historical reasons in favour of taking Byzantium seriously as an area of Jewish cultural productivity, Zimmels thus ends up falling into the positivist trap which argues directly from the shortage of surviving or lost works clearly labelled as Byzantine to the conclusion that nothing of importance was produced here. If in the case of southern Italy a corresponding cultural productivity is impossible to deny, that is in large part due to the chance survival of the chronicle of Ahimaaz of Oria. Without the documentation supplied by that family history, and by some archaeological discoveries, we should be almost as ignorant of the cultural life of the Jews in Byzantine Italy as we are of Jewish culture in Constantinople and other centres. Moreover, as we shall see, Zimmels and others grossly underestimated the amount of Byzantine Jewish material surviving; had they been in a position to rely on a more realistic assessment of this they would have surely been less reluctant to take the Byzantine empire as a whole as seriously as their historical instincts in some cases inclined them to do. Yet at the same time other scholars were evincing a more open-minded attitude. Schirmann, for instance, comments specifically on the 'Ahimaaz problem', and these words of one of the foremost students of Hebrew poetry of his century are particularly significant in view of Zimmels's argument from the supposed lack of Byzantine hymnology:

As is well known, south Italy was for a long time under the dominion of the Byzantine emperors, and from a cultural point of view its earliest synagogue poets belong to the Greek sphere. Yet at the same period there was also a considerable Jewish population in Byzantium proper, i.e. in Greece, Asia Minor and the adjacent islands, and there is no doubt that here too there were scholars who made their contribution to the development of Hebrew religious poetry. But unfortunately for Byzantine Jewry no Hebrew sources survive that preserve the memory of their earliest poets (up to the eleventh century). We have no book from Byzantium to parallel the family chronicle of the Italian Ahimaaz ben Paltiel. We possess tens, if not hundreds, of religious poems composed in the Byzantine empire, and we even know the names of some poets who may have lived there, but so far these have remained 'disembodied souls', whose origin cannot be conclusively demonstrated. (5727 (1966/7): 421; my translation)

A few years earlier Baron had polemicized vigorously against those who refused to acknowledge the Byzantine origin of much of the mystical Hebrew literature:

Modern scholars have been reluctant to accept the Byzantine provenance of much of that literature, mainly because of the absence of any reliable documentary evidence for the intellectual creativity of the Jewries in the Byzantine sphere of influence during the eighth to the tenth centuries when most of these works were written, rewritten, or compiled. But, weak as are all such *argumenta a silentio*, they are doubly weak in this case, for many independent hypotheses and observations converge on the point of showing that, though little of their intellectual creativity long maintained in oral form has come down to us, the 'thousand' Jewish communities of the Byzantine Empire pursued a vigorous intellectual career of their own . . . Certainly, those great nineteenth-century scholars who looked for the origin of many homiletical collections in Italy intuitively felt that it was in that area that Jewish homiletical creativity was at its highest. They should, however, have limited this geographical designation primarily to those parts of the Apennine Peninsula and Sicily which were under Byzantine domination. Nor is there any valid reason for assuming that other provinces of the Byzantine Empire lagged so far behind. Even in the sphere of jurisprudence Byzantine contributions were not quite so arid as is generally assumed. In fact, we have quite a few indications of the composition of several important halakhic works of the late geonic period by one or other Byzantine Jew. (1958b: 30–1)

Baron's approach is, in my view, incontestably correct. There are too many indications of the importance and indeed centrality of Byzantium in the history of Jewish culture to allow us to attach too much weight to the shortage of material evidence. On the contrary, once we rid ourselves of the presupposition that Byzantium was not a productive area, we are able to attribute to it a good deal of otherwise unlocalized or badly identified material. To take a few specific examples out of many that might be cited, Schirmann (5727 (1966/7): 421–2) draws attention to the case of an early eleventh-century *payyetan* (hymnographer) named Benjamin bar Samuel of Kostani, whose home town Leopold Zunz in the nineteenth century had transcribed as Coutances (in Normandy). According to Schirmann 'it is possible in my view to say almost with certainty that he came from the Byzantine Empire'. Secondly, an origin in Qayrawan has been suggested for the legal code *Sefer Hefets*, but recently Neil Danzig (1991/2): 103–9) has argued that an origin in Byzantium, possibly in southern Italy, is more likely. A good example of the same prejudice, from a much later period, is the fifteenth-century *Sefer Haqaneh.* Israel Ta-Shma (5740 (1980)) has argued, against the established view of a Spanish origin for this work, that it originated in Byzantium. Finally, we may consider the case of the Rabbanite scholar Mordecai Khomatiano. According to Solomon Rosanes,[4] his surname

[4] *Divrei yemei yisrael betogarmah* (History of the Jews in Turkey), vol. I (Tel Aviv, 1930), 26.

is to be transcribed Comtino, indicating an origin in the Comtat Venaissin. In fact the name Khomatiano or Comatiano (in Italian sources) is well attested among both Jews and Christians in Greek-speaking lands, and Mordecai himself describes himself as *haqostandini hayevani*, 'the Greek of Constantinople'.[5]

In fact when we reach the last phase of Byzantine history, the Palaeologan period, there is still less reason to be chary of recognizing the importance of Byzantium than in the earlier period, with which the authors cited above are primarily concerned. Yet even for the period before the First Crusade, which is the most obscure and least well-documented period in the history of Byzantine Jewry, new information is constantly appearing which demonstrates the importance of the region both in its own right and as a conduit between Asia and Europe.[6] Those still inclined to scepticism about Byzantine Jewish cultural productivity should bear in mind the high proportion of anonymous or pseudonymous texts among Hebrew writings of this period, a tendency which is paralleled in the Byzantine Christian literature of the time. We should not necessarily expect works to be clearly labelled with the name of the author and the place of writing. Another significant factor is the presence in Byzantium of a strong oral tradition. Material of considerable antiquity sometimes surfaces within later writings without having left any appreciable trace in the intervening period, and we may reasonably suppose that a good deal of teaching was transmitted from generation to generation in purely oral form.

NEW SOURCES OF INFORMATION

Our knowledge of Hebrew-language culture in Byzantium has been augmented in a number of ways in the past decades. The most important sources of new knowledge come from the study of manuscripts.

As has already been mentioned, some use was made of the Cairo Genizah materials by Joshua Starr in the 1930s, and indeed Jacob Mann a little earlier had already studied some documents of Byzantine provenance.[7] The focus at that time was, however, principally on documents, and the Genizah has not supplied much documentary material of unquestionably Byzantine provenance. S. D. Goitein, discussing a letter

[5] See Attias (1991: 20–1); cf. Bowman (1985: 149, note 68).

[6] See de Lange (1999a: 154–5) for some suggestions about extant texts of the ninth or tenth centuries that may have come from Constantinople.

[7] J. Mann, *Texts and Studies in Jewish History and Literature*, 2 vols (Cincinnati 1931; Philadelphia 1935).

from Salonika, raises the question why, among such a wealth of documents concerned with trade, we do not have a single commercial letter from Salonika, or Constantinople, or indeed anywhere else in Byzantium, in the Genizah. The same question could be asked, he observes, about the Jewish merchants of southern France and Spain, who had close trading links with Egypt. 'The answer to this puzzling question', Goitein remarks,

> may be found not in any facts concerning those lands and cities but in the character of the Genizah itself, which served in the 11th century mainly as a depository for a group of Tunisian merchants who were residing or had settled in Egypt. In any case, caution is appropriate, and we may not infer from this that the links between the Jews of Egypt and Salonika were cultural and religious alone.[8]

Precisely in the area of culture and religion it was becoming apparent by the 1970s (when Goitein's article was published) that the Genizah contained a certain amount of material of Byzantine origin.[9] Palaeographical and other techniques are not yet refined enough to permit the identification of fragments as Byzantine where the content gives no indication, but it can be confidently expected that once such criteria are available a good deal more Byzantine material will come to light.

It is too early to comment from a Byzantinological perspective on the opening up of the Firkovitch collections in St Petersburg, but it seems likely that these, too, will prove to be a valuable resource for the study of Byzantine Hebrew texts, particularly those originating in a Karaite milieu.[10]

A major advance is represented by the recent progress in Hebrew codicology and palaeography, coupled with the recognition of Byzantium as a distinct and important area of Hebrew manuscript writing. The situation is succinctly summed up by Malachi Beit-Arié as follows:

> The third branch of Hebrew booklore, which seems to be represented by a single homogeneous scribal entity, is the Byzantine. In several ways, in its

[8] S. D. Goitein, 'Early Evidence from the Genizah about the Community of Salonika' (Hebrew), *Sefunot* 11 (AM 5731–8 (1970/1–77/8)) [11–33]: 15.

[9] For Byzantine materials in the Cambridge Genizah collections see de Lange (1989b, 1992). On Genizah fragments containing Greek words see N. R. M. de Lange, 'Two Genizah Fragments in Hebrew and Greek', in *Interpreting the Hebrew Bible. Essays in Honour of E. I. J. Rosenthal*, ed. J. A. Emerton and S. C. Reif, 61 ff. (Cambridge, 1982) and de Lange (1996a). See also the remarks of David Jacoby in *BZ* 91 (1998): 110–12.

[10] See the chapter by Daniel Frank in the present volume (chapter 1). On Firkovitch himself see V. L. Vikhnovich, *Karaim Avraam Firkovich* (Russian) (St Petersburg, 1997).

style of writing, various scribal practices and codicological techniques, this entity formed a bridge between East and West, bearing witness to the influence of both major branches of Hebrew booklore. The impact of Greek script and its offshoots, such as early Slavonic and Glagolitic, on styles of Hebrew writing in the territories of the late Byzantine Empire before its decline has not yet been studied. Here again, a distinctive style of script, which is known to us from letters and documents dating from the early eleventh century preserved in the Cairo Geniza, together with characteristic technical habits, persisted despite political changes and the shrinking of the Byzantine Empire. Thus, Hebrew manuscripts produced until the end of the Middle Ages in the areas of the Greek islands and the Balkan peninsula, Asia Minor, Crimea and the western Caucasus display a common type of scripts, book design, graphic and technical practices, and copying formulas.[11]

In another study, Beit-Arié remarks that 'the relative large number of Byzantine manuscripts (about 10 per cent), which is close to that of the Oriental, may attest to the intellectual level and perhaps the size of the Jewish population in an area where our knowledge of the Jewish communities is not sufficiently wide' (1991: 169),[12] an indication of how the open-minded scholar can use manuscripts as a valuable source of historical information where other sources are in short supply. The formal recognition of a 'Byzantine zone' with its own booklore and scribal practices opens the way, once Byzantine manuscripts have been identified,[13] for the proper study of Hebrew manuscripts copied in Byzantium. When this considerable task has been achieved, we shall be able to see clearly for the first time which works were copied and studied in Byzantium. The same approach applied to manuscripts from the other zones will reveal valuable information about the reception of Byzantine Hebrew literature outside the empire.

Another source of new knowledge is the study of inscriptions. Relatively little has been achieved in this area, but a certain number of Hebrew epitaphs have been published, including some from southern Italy that are in verse.[14]

11 Beit-Arié (1993b: 32). Cf. Beit-Arié (1977: 17).

12 Elsewhere he declares himself impressed by the large proportion of Byzantine copies among undated Hebrew manuscripts (1991: 179, note 16).

13 Beit-Arié, in his *Supplement to A. Neubauer's catalogue of the Hebrew Manuscripts in the Bodleian Library* (Oxford, 1994), identifies nearly 120 Bodleian manuscripts as definitely or possibly being of Byzantine origin. See the review in *BJGS* 17 (Winter 1995): 16–21. This is an important first step, which needs to be repeated for other collections.

14 See Simonsohn (1974: p. 853) and Colafemmina (1980).

THE HEBREW LANGUAGE IN BYZANTIUM

The inscriptions also shed an interesting light on the use of the Hebrew language in Byzantine south Italy, and thus indirectly on the vexed question of when and how Hebrew reached Europe. There is little or no sign of Hebrew in Europe before the beginning of the ninth century, when we have the first dated Hebrew inscriptions in Venosa, to be followed in the tenth by writings in Hebrew, such as the *Josephon* and the works of Shabbetai Donnolo.[15] However, there are some indications that Hebrew arrived in Europe earlier, perhaps via Constantinople and the other main centres in the Empire.[16] There is no cogent reason to suppose that it came first to south Italy. However, the process by which Hebrew replaced Greek and Latin as the written and liturgical language of the empire, a drastic cultural transformation with far-reaching consequences, remains completely unknown. It must be assumed that a profound educational reform was involved, but this too remains *terra incognita*. We can witness the results in terms of the high level of literacy and scholarly production from the eleventh century on, but how this was achieved is unknown.[17]

A topic on which little or no work has been done is the Hebrew of the Byzantine Jews. There are some indications of the influence of both Arabic and Greek on Hebrew texts written in Byzantium, and this is a subject that would benefit from further study.[18]

SURVEYS OF HEBREW SCHOLARSHIP IN BYZANTIUM

There is to date unfortunately no full-scale general survey of Hebrew scholarship in Byzantium. Starr has a chapter in his book (covering the period down to the Fourth Crusade) headed 'Intellectual interests and literary productions'. In keeping with his general approach, it is intended to serve primarily as a key to the documents he cites in translation, rather than a thorough and critical account of the subject. Important in its day as a guide through poorly charted waters, it is now out of date and inadequate. Zimmels addresses an even more limited period, ending at the time of the First Crusade, when Hebrew culture had barely established

[15] See de Lange (1996b) and the literature cited in de Lange (1999a: p. 153). On southern Italy generally see Bonfil (1983).

[16] On Novella 146 of Justinian see de Lange (1999a: p. 151) and the literature cited there.

[17] See de Lange (1994).

[18] See Hopkins (1992) and Maman (1979). Some examples of Arabic and Greek influence are indicated in de Lange (1990a and 1996a).

itself, and is devoted almost exclusively to Italy. The period after the Fourth Crusade is studied by Bowman (*The Jews of Byzantium*), in his chapter entitled 'Language and literature'. Bowman, like Starr, writes around a collection of documents in translation, but he adds some useful general observations. He draws attention, for example, to the continuing engagement with Palestinian Judaism (with its strong homiletical and mystical interests) even at this late date and despite the pervasive influence of the Babylonian Talmud, and he remarks also on a strong interest in astronomy and Hebrew grammar. Bowman also devotes particular attention to religious poetry and to Karaite scholarship. The most recent survey (de Lange, 1999a), is a chronologically ordered treatment paying special attention to the role of the Hebrew language.

SPECIFIC TOPICS

Biblical study

In the year 1207 a certain Judah ben Jacob, writing at a place named Gagra,[19] copied the text of a work in Hebrew compiled by someone named as Joseph the Constantinopolitan, 'who gathered and collected the opinions of the teachers and added even from the strength of his wisdom'.[20] The title of the work is *'Adat Devorim* ('Swarm of bees', Judges 14:8), and it deals with the text and grammar of the Bible. The following year the same Judah ben Jacob copied in the same town an anonymous grammatical work with the title *Meor 'Ayin* ('Light of the Eye', cf. Proverbs 15:30). Both manuscripts survive, in the Firkovitch collections in St Petersburg. These treatises are heavily dependent on works originally written in Arabic in the early eleventh century by the Jerusalem Karaite Abū al-Faraj Hārūn,[21] and this activity seems to point to what Ankori has called the 'literary translation project' of Byzantine Karaism, aimed at translating Karaite classics from Arabic into Hebrew or a mixture of Hebrew and Greek, and revising them for the benefit of Byzantine Jews. In themselves they do not mark any advance on the work of the Jerusalem grammarian, but later Byzantine Karaite authors, such as Judah Hadassi, reveal a knowledge of grammatical theories developed in Spain.

[19] Usually identified as Gagry on the eastern shore of the Black Sea, but Ankori (1959: 125–8), argues that it was actually Germanicopolis in Paphlagonia, near the south-western shore of the same sea.

[20] Translation of the colophon in Bowman (1985: 217–18).

[21] On Abū al-Faraj Hārūn see the chapter by Geoffrey Khan in the present volume (chapter 5). The text of *Meor 'Ayin* is published with a Commentary by Zislin. *'Adat Devorim* has not yet been published; see Eldar (1994: 19).

At the same time it would probably be a mistake to suppose that there was no native tradition of textual and grammatical study in Byzantine Jewry. Discussing some Genizah fragments of otherwise unknown Bible commentaries, Richard Steiner has observed that they combine sophistication in the area of text criticism with backwardness in the area of grammar.[22] The commentaries in question seem to derive from Rabbanite circles uninfluenced by Arabic language. Later Rabbanites, too, were greatly influenced by the Spanish tradition of grammar.

The Byzantine commentators on the Bible have been insufficiently studied. Steiner has argued that historians of exegesis should recognize a Byzantine school alongside better-known schools such as the Andalusian or North French ones, and that this Byzantine school may prove to be the 'missing link' between the earlier Palestinian tradition and the medieval exegesis of Ashkenaz and Italy.[23] Later, western commentaries such as those of Rashi circulated in Byzantium, by far the most influential commentator being Abraham ibn Ezra.[24]

Piyyut *and prayer*

Piyyut (synagogal poetry) is one of the richest veins in Byzantine Hebrew culture, and one that testifies to the high level of Hebrew education at least among the most favoured strata of society. We are fortunate to have editions of a large number of such compositions, thanks to the efforts of Leon J. Weinberger, who has published several volumes of *piyyutim* from Byzantium and neighbouring countries (in which the contribution of Karaite poets is not neglected). A large part of his book *Jewish Hymnography* is devoted to these regions, and his discussions of the various genres and individual poets are illustrated by translated excerpts, thus opening up this difficult but rewarding field to non-specialist scholars.

The Byzantine Hebrew prayer rite, as represented by the *Mahzor Romania*, has not been much studied since Goldschmidt's important article. While the later manuscripts convey the impression of a somewhat eclectic tradition, the roots of the ritual go back to the old Palestinian rite, and there is room for further study of its history, together with the relationship between the Hebrew prayers and the Greek synagogue liturgy which it replaced.

22 In a so far unpublished lecture entitled 'The Byzantine Commentary to Ezekiel and Minor Prophets and its Place in the History of Biblical Exegesis'. See Steiner (1998–9: 155).

23 Cf. the preceding note.

24 See Bowman (1985: 134), and de Lange (1990b) with supplementary material in *BJGS* 17 (Winter, 1995): 20.

Rabbinic study

Zimmels is at pains to emphasize the importance of rabbinic scholarship in Byzantine lands from an early date, and the pivotal role of Byzantium in spreading such studies northwards to Ashkenaz and south into the Mediterranean regions and perhaps even to Spain. Byzantium was an important meeting place of the Palestinian and Babylonian schools, represented by the two Talmuds. More recently I. Ta-Shma, in a series of articles, has drawn attention to a variety of aspects of the connections between Byzantium and Ashkenaz. There is room for a good deal more work on this particular subject, and indeed on rabbinic studies in Byzantium generally. One line of investigation passes through the study of the manuscript tradition of the Mishnah and Talmud (as well as their commentaries): it would be profitable to investigate the manuscripts copied in Byzantium, as well as those copied elsewhere which were used and in some cases annotated in Byzantium.

Although it is conventional to portray the Karaites as staunch opponents of the rabbinic tradition, several prominent Byzantine Karaites were keen students of rabbinics, and towards the end of the period some students frequented both Karaite and Rabbanite masters.[25]

Philosophy and science

From the very beginning of Hebrew writing in Byzantium science is represented in an important group of medical writings from Italy.[26] Little work has been done on the subsequent medical and scientific traditions, or on the history of philosophy in Byzantine Jewry. Again, one approach would be through the study of manuscripts, which preserve not only a number of unpublished writings, but also many indications of an interest in these subjects, particularly during the last century of Byzantine rule, when a large number of mathematical and astronomical manuscripts were copied.[27]

OTHER WRITINGS

Several writers have underscored the importance of Byzantium in the transmission of mystical writings from the Near East to Europe.[28] Such

25 See Bowman (1985: 139–46), and the chapter by Daniel Frank in the present volume (chapter 1).

26 See Lieber (1984 and 1991); Baron (1958b: 240–6); Sharf (1975) and his book *The Universe of Shabbetai Donnolo* (Warminster, 1976).

27 See also Lévy (1996: 94).

28 E.g. Baron (1958b: 30–1); Bowman (1985: 129).

concerns endured throughout the period of Byzantine rule, particularly in the form of kabbalah.[29]

Polemical writings against Christianity are discussed in Krauss and Horbury (1996), with bibliographies.[30]

Finally, the Cairo Genizah has given us several specimens of Hebrew letters.[31] While these are not primarily concerned with scholarly matters (they deal mainly with personal or commercial subjects) they do illustrate the way that Hebrew functions as a vehicle for communication.

CONCLUSIONS

I hope to have shown in these pages the richness of Byzantine Hebrew writing, and its importance both in its own right and in relation to other centres of Hebrew scholarship. Byzantium stands at the centre of the medieval Jewish world, like the hub of a wheel, whose spokes radiate out in every direction, to Syria and Palestine, Iraq, and further east to Iran and the silk route, to Egypt and North Africa, to Spain, France and Ashkenaz, and north to Khazaria and Rus.[32]

In surveying the achievements of scholars in this area I have tried to draw attention also to some of the significant gaps in our knowledge, in the hope of encouraging researchers to tackle these in the near future. The study of Byzantine Hebrew writings is really in its infancy, and it offers challenging and interesting opportunities.

LITERATURE

Ankori, Z. 1959. *Karaites in Byzantium: The Formative Years, 970-1100*, Columbia Studies in the Social Sciences 597, New York

Attias, J.-C. 1989. 'Un temps pour enseigner, un temps pour apprendre: Karaïtes et Rabbanites à Constantinople au XVe siècle'. In *Politique et religion dans le Judaïsme ancien et médiéval*, ed. D. Tollet, 187–98. Paris

1991. *Le Commentaire biblique: Mordekhai Komtino ou l'herméneutique du dialogue*. Paris

29 E.g. Bowman (1985: 137, 156–61); Ta-Shma (AM 5740).

30 See especially p. 67 and the references given there, together with the entries on Judah Hadassi (pp. 218–19) and *Nestor the Priest* (pp. 236–8). See also Horbury's contribution to the present volume (chapter 13).

31 See de Lange (1992 and 1996a), and Z. Ankori, 'The Correspondence of Tobias ben Moses the Karaite of Constantinople', in *Essays on Jewish Life and Thought Presented in Honor of S. W. Baron*, ed. J. L. Blau et al. (New York, 1959), 1–38.

32 See the trading routes shown on the maps in N. de Lange, *Atlas of the Jewish World* (Oxford and New York, 1984), 38, 40.

1993. 'Eliahu Mizrahi, sur-commentateur de Rashi (Constantinople xve–xvie s.)'. In *Rashi 1040–1990, hommage à Ephraïm E. Urbach*, ed. G. Sed-Rajna, 475–81. Paris

Baron, S. W. 1957. *A Social and Religious History of the Jews: High Middle Ages, 500–1200*, vol. VI: *Laws, Homilies and the Bible.* 2nd edn, New York

1958a. *A Social and Religious History of the Jews: High Middle Ages, 500–1200*, vol. VII: *Hebrew Language and Letters.* 2nd edn, New York

1958b. *A Social and Religious History of the Jews: High Middle Ages, 500–1200*, vol. VIII: *Philosophy and Science.* 2nd edn, New York

Beit-Arié, M. 1977. *Hebrew Codicology: Tentative Typology of Technical Practices Employed in Hebrew Dated Medieval Manuscripts.* Paris (Reprinted with addenda and corrigenda, Jerusalem, 1981)

1991. 'The Codicological Data-base of the Hebrew Palaeography Project: A Tool for Localising and Dating Hebrew Medieval Manuscripts'. In *Hebrew Studies*, ed. D. Rowland Smith and P. S. Salinger, 165–97. London (appeared also in his *The Makings of the Medieval Hebrew Book*, and in French in *Méthodologies informatiques et nouveaux horizons dans les recherches médiévales*, 1992)

1993a. *The Making of the Medieval Hebrew Book: Studies in Paleography and Codicology.* Jerusalem

1993b. *Hebrew Manuscripts of East and West: Towards a Comparative Codicology* (Panizzi lectures, 1992). London

Benin, S. D. 1985. 'The Scroll of Ahimaas and its Place in Byzantine Literature' (Hebrew). *Jerusalem Studies in Jewish Thought* : 237–50

Bernstein, S. 1963. 'Jewish Synagogal Poetry in the Byzantine Empire' (Hebrew). In *Festschrift I. Alfenbein*, 56–74. Jerusalem

Bonfil, R. 1983. 'Tra due mondi: Prospettive di ricerca sulla storia culturale degli Ebrei nell'Italia meridionale nell'Alto Medioevo', *Italia Judaica*, vol. I, 135–58. Rome

Bowman, S. B. 1982. 'Jewish Epitaphs in Thebes'. *REJ* 141: 317–30

1985. *The Jews of Byzantium, 1204–1453.* University of Alabama Press

Colafemmina, C. 1980. 'Insediamenti e condizione degli ebrei nell' Italia meridionale e insulare', in *Gli Ebrei nell' Alto Medioevo*, vol. I (Spoleto, 1980), 197–227

1984. 'Una nuova iscrizione ebraica a Venosa'. *Vetera Christianorum* 21: 197–202

Danzig, N. 1991–2. 'The First Discovered Leaves of *Sefer Hefes*'. *JQR* 82: 51–136

David, I. 1971. *The Poems of Zevadiah* (Hebrew). Jerusalem

1975. *The Poems of Amittai* (Hebrew). Jerusalem

1977. *The Poems of Elia bar Shemaya* (Hebrew). Jerusalem

Eldar, I. 1994. *The Study of the Art of Correct Reading as Reflected in the Medieval Treatise Hidayat al-Qari* (Hebrew). Jerusalem

Fleischer, E. 1990. 'On Early Hebrew Poetry in South-eastern Europe' (Hebrew). *JSHL* 12: 209–13

Goldschmidt, D. 1964. 'On the Mahzor Romania and its Ritual' (Hebrew). *Sefunot* 8: 207–36

Hopkins, S. 1992. 'Arabic Elements in the Hebrew of the Byzantine Karaites'.

In *Genizah Research after Ninety Years. The Case of Judaeo-Arabic*, ed. J. Blau and S. C. Reif, 93–9. Cambridge
Kahana, M. 1990. 'The Commentary of R Hillel on Sifre' (Hebrew). *KS* 63: 271–80
Klar, B. 1974. *The Chronicle of Ahimaaz* (Hebrew). 2nd edn Jerusalem
Krauss, S. 1914. *Studien zur byzantinisch-jüdischen Geschichte*. Vienna
Krauss, S. and W. Horbury 1996. *The Jewish-Christian Controversy from the Earliest Times to 1789*, vol. I: *History*. Tübingen
de Lange, N. 1986. 'Hebrew–Greek Genizah Fragments and their Bearing on the Culture of Byzantine Jewry'. *Proceedings of the Ninth World Congress of Jewish Studies*, B, vol. I, 39–46. Jerusalem
1989a. 'Qui a tué les Juifs de Byzance?'. In *Politique et religion dans le judaïsme ancien et médiéval*, ed. D. Tollet, 327–33. Paris
1989b. 'Greek and Byzantine Fragments in the Cairo Genizah'. *BJGS* 5 (Winter): 13–17
1990a. 'A Fragment of Byzantine Anti-Christian Polemic'. *JJS* 41: 92–100
1990b. 'Abraham ibn Ezra and Byzantium'. In *Abraham ibn Ezra y su Tiempo*, ed. F. Díaz Esteban, 181–92. Madrid
1992. 'Byzantium in the Cairo Genizah'. *BMGS* 16: 34–47
1994. 'Jewish Education in the Byzantine Empire in the Twelfth Century'. In *Jewish Education and Learning*, ed. G. Abramson and T. Parfitt, 115–128. Chur
1995. 'Hebrew/Greek Manuscripts: Some Notes'. *JJS* 46: 262–70
1996a. *Greek Jewish Texts from the Cairo Genizah*. Tübingen
1996b. 'The Hebrew Language in the European Diaspora'. In *Studies on the Jewish Diaspora in the Hellenistic and Roman Periods*, ed. B. Isaac and A. Oppenheimer (*Te'uda*, 12), 111–37. Tel Aviv
1999a. 'A Thousand Years of Hebrew in Byzantium'. In *Hebrew Study from Ezra to Ben-Yehuda*, ed. W. Horbury, 147–61. Edinburgh
1999b. 'Etudier et Prier à Byzance'. *REJ* 158: 51–9
Lévy, T. 1996. 'La littérature mathématique hébraique en Europe (du XIe au XVIe siècle)'. In *L'Europe mathématique – mythes, histoires, identités*, ed. C. Goldstein et al., 85–99. Paris
Lieber, E. 1984. 'Asaf's *Book of Medicines*: A Hebrew Encyclopedia of Greek and Jewish Medicine, Possibly Compiled in Byzantium on an Indian Model', *Dumbarton Oaks Papers* 38: 233–49
1991. 'An Ongoing Mystery: The So-called *Book of Medicines* Attributed to Asaf the Sage'. *BJGS* 8 (Summer): 18–25
Maman, A. 1979. 'The Hebrew of Tobias ben Moses the Karaite' (Hebrew). Hebrew University, MA dissertation
1989. 'The Hebrew of the Karaites' (Hebrew). *Weekly Newsletter of the Hebrew Language Academy* 8 (December)
AM 5751 (1990/1). 'Karaites and Mishnaic Hebrew: Quotations and Usage' (Hebrew). *Leshonenu* 55: 221–68
Netzer, N. 1979. 'Lexicographical Aspects of the *Eshkol Hakofer*' (Hebrew). Hebrew University, MA dissertation
Perles, J. 1893. 'Jüdisch–byzantinische Beziehungen', *BZ* 2: 569–84

Pines, S. and S. Shaked 1986. 'Fragment of a Jewish–Christian Composition from the Cairo Genizah'. In *Studies in Islamic History and Civilization in Honour of Professor David Ayalon*, ed. M. Sharon, 307–18. Leiden and Jerusalem
Schirmann, J. AM 5727 (1966/7). *New Hebrew Poems from the Genizah.* Jerusalem
Schlossberg, E. 1995–6. 'Lexicographico-exegetical Generalisations in the Biblical Commentaries of Meyuhas ben Elijah' (Hebrew). *Sinai* 116: 42–56
Sharf, A. 1971. *Byzantine Jewry from Justinian to the 4th Crusade.* London and New York
1975. 'Shabbetai Donnolo as a Byzantine Jewish Figure'. *BIJS* 3: 1–18
Simonsohn, S. 1974. 'The Hebrew Revival among Early Medieval European Jews'. In *S. W. Baron Jubilee Volume*, ed. Saul Lieberman, English Section, vol. II, 831–58. Jerusalem
Starr, J. 1939. *The Jews in the Byzantine Empire, 641–1204.* Athens
Steiner, R. C. AM 5756 (1995/6). 'Linguistic Features of the Commentary on Ezekiel and the Minor Prophets in the Hebrew Scrolls from Byzantium' (Hebrew). *Leshonenu* 59: 39–56
1998–9. 'Textual and Exegetical Notes to Nicholas de Lange, *Greek Jewish Texts from the Cairo Genizah*'. *JQR* 89: 155–69
Ta-Shma, I. AM 5740 (1980). 'Where were Sefer Haqaneh and Sefer Hapeliah written?' (Hebrew). In *Studies in the History of Jewish Society in the Middle Ages and in the Modern Period* (Jacob Katz jubilee volume), 56–63. Jerusalem
AM 5753 (1992/3). 'On Greek–Byzantine Rabbinic Literature of the Fourteenth Century' (Hebrew). *Tarbiz* 62: 101–14
Walfish, B. 1993. 'An Annotated Bibliography of Medieval Jewish Commentaries on the Book of Ruth in Print and in Manuscript'. In *The Frank Talmage Memorial Volume*, ed. B. Walfish, 251–71. Haifa
Weinberger, L. J. 1971. 'A Note on Jewish Scholars and Scholarship in Byzantium'. *JAOS* 91: 142–4
1975a. 'Greek, Anatolian and Balkan Synagogue Poets'. In *Texts and Responses*, ed. M. Fishbane and P. R. Flohr (Festschrift for N. N. Glatzer), 108–119. Leiden
1975b. *Anthology of Hebrew Poetry in Greece, Anatolia and the Balkans.* Cincinnati
1985. *Jewish Poets in Crete: A Literary History.* Cincinnati
1988a. *Early Synagogue Poets in the Balkans.* Cincinnati
1988b. 'Hebrew Poetry from the Byzantine Empire: A Survey of Recent and Current Research'. *BJGS* 3 (Winter): 18–20
1991. *Rabbanite and Karaite Liturgical Poetry in South-eastern Europe.* Cincinnati
1992. 'Karaite *Piyyut* in Southeastern Europe'. *JQR* 83: 145–65
1998. *Jewish Hymnography: A Literary History.* London
Zimmels, H. J. 1996. 'Scholars and Scholarship in Byzantium and Italy'. In *World History of the Jewish People*, vol. XI, ed. C. Roth, 175–88. New Brunswick
Zislin, M. I. 1990. *Me'or 'Aiin ("Svetoch Glaza"). Karaimskaia grammatika drevneevreiskogo yazyka po rukopisi 1208 g.* (Pamyatniki Pismennosti Vostoka, 96). Moscow

CHAPTER THREE

Hebrew philology in Sefarad: the state of the question

Angel Sáenz-Badillos

THE FIRST STEPS IN THE KNOWLEDGE OF MEDIEVAL HEBREW PHILOLOGY

The scientific study of Hebrew philology began in the nineteenth century with distinguished scholars such as Ewald and Dukes (1844), Munk (1850–1), Neubauer (1861–2) and Jastrow (1886–9). W. Bacher, with his many editions and about seven hundred and fifty articles on the origins of Hebrew grammar, is generally recognised as the most notable researcher in this area.[1]

However, new discoveries in the twentieth century have in many cases substantially changed the panorama of medieval Hebrew philology. Kokovzow (1916), Poznanski (1895–1926), Yellin (1945), Wilensky (1923–34), Morag (1970–93), Téné (1971–83), Abramson (1963–91), Eldar (1979–98), Maman (1984–92) etc.[2] have made important contributions in this field.

In the two last thirds of the twentieth century there has been a remarkable improvement in the knowledge of the texts of the main Andalusian grammarians, and of other Oriental and North African authors. Among the latter, the edition of al-Fāsī's dictionary by S. L. Skoss,[3] the *Diqduqe ha-ṭĕʿamin* of Aharon ben Mošeh ben Ašer by A. Dotan,[4] the *'Egron* of Sĕʿadyah by N. Allony,[5] the *Risāla* of Yĕhudah ibn

[1] His work was very positively evaluated a few years ago by Fellman (1974), and in a more critical way by Dotan (1977). Bacher's *Die hebräische Sprachwissenschaft* (1892) and 'Die Anfänge der hebräischen Grammatik' (1895) were excellent in their time, and are still very useful.

[2] Other interesting perspectives were published in the last years, such as Loewe (1994), Schippers (1997), etc. See a general conspectus in Sáenz-Badillos and Targarona (1988).

[3] *The Hebrew–Arabic Dictionary of the Bible Known as Kitâmi al- Alfâz (Agron) of David ben Abraham al-Fâsî the Karaite (Tenth Cent.)*, 2 vols. (New Haven, 1936–45).

[4] *The Diqduqe ha-ṭeamin of Aharon ben Mošeh ben Ašer with a Critical Edition of the Original Text from New Manuscripts* (Hebr.) (Jerusalem, 1967).

[5] *Ha'Egron. Kitâb usûl al-shir al-ʿbrânî by Rav Seʿadya Gaon. Critical Edition with Introduction and Commentary* (Hebrew) (Jerusalem, 1969). Review by E. Goldenberg, "Iyyunim ba-' Egron šel rab̲ Sĕʿadyah Ga'on', *Lĕšonenu* 37 (1972–3): 117–36, 275–90; 38 (1973/4): 78–90.

Qurayš by D. Becker,[6] and the recent publication of significant sections of the grammatical work of Sĕʿadyah by A. Dotan,[7] have opened a new perspective on the origins of Hebrew philology.

THE TEXT OF HEBREW-SPANISH PHILOLOGISTS: MANUSCRIPTS AND EDITIONS

The main Andalusian texts on Hebrew philology are known to us in editions of uneven quality, and a few of the less important works are still incomplete or in a fragmentary state. Some of these works have been preserved in unreliable manuscripts, and many editions that appeared during the nineteenth century, or even during a good part of the twentieth century, are not trustworthy, due to the small number of manuscripts employed and to the lack of criteria for reconstructing the text history.

New materials have improved our textual knowledge in the last years and notable progress is to be expected in the years ahead. The philological fragments of the Cairo Genizah in Cambridge, whose process of classification was started years ago by David Téné, or those of Manchester, far fewer in number, will not substantially change the picture, but can contribute to a better knowledge of some works, particularly in Judaeo-Arabic. The most promising results may come from the Russian libraries, in particular those of St Petersburg and Moscow, which preserve many philological manuscripts not yet studied by Western scholars.

Which is the best way of editing medieval Hebrew philological works? As is well known, there is a big difference between the critical editions of ancient Greek and Latin authors and most editions in the field of Judaic studies. Although the peculiar nature of biblical or rabbinical works could justify a different approach, medieval Hebrew works are not very dissimilar to other medieval books, and we should learn from the experience acquired by our colleagues in other areas. To publish the text of one manuscript, with all its mistakes, even if we correct it with subjective conjectures, is not the best way to get a text close to the original one. We ought to study the history of the transmission of the text of every book, and to apply the modern criteria of the science of textual criticism.[8]

[6] *The Risâla of Judah ben Quraysh. A Critical Edition* (Hebr.) (Tel Aviv, 1984).

[7] A. Dotan, *The Dawn of Hebrew Linguistics. The Book of Elegance of the Language of the Hebrews by Saadia Gaon* (Hebr.) Critical edition with introduction, 2 vols. (Jerusalem, 1997).

[8] See Sáenz-Badillos 1990a.

Some of these texts have a very particular history. A dictionary, for example, was not considered by the copyists as a real 'author's work' that had to be respected in its original form, but rather as a practical instrument for working on Hebrew texts, and consequently they could find it more convenient to correct it, adding new meanings, new quotations or sections, eliminating the mistakes and the observed inconsistencies, or, in other cases, shortening it, leaving out the excursuses or other 'unnecessary explanations'.[9]

Parts of the books may have been lost, as in the case of the *Tešuḇot* of Dunaš against Mĕnaḥem: twenty out of one hundred and eighty replies by Dunaš disappeared from the text so soon that not even Mĕnaḥem's disciples, who answered almost immediately, had them before their eyes. Filipowski's edition, the only one that existed for more than one hundred years, did not include this passage, which returned to its original place in my critical edition of the *Tešuḇot* (1980).[10]

Filipowski did not know the numerous manuscripts that we know today when he published the *Maḥberet* of Mĕnaḥem ben Saruq (1854, harshly criticized by D. Kaufmann in 1886).[11] But what is worse, he felt free to change the order of the roots found in the manuscripts in order to make searching easier, to add 'forgotten' quotations or new meanings, and to avoid some of the inconsistencies detected by Dunaš.[12] In my own edition (1986), I came back to the manuscripts, taking into consideration the history of the text. Having only one manuscript of the *Tešuḇot* of Mĕnaḥem's disciples, S. Benavente (1986) carefully revised the text of the book, clearly improving on the edition of S. G. Stern (1870).

The text of the *Tešuḇot* of Yĕhudi ben Šešat, Dunaš's disciple, and the *Tešuḇot 'al Sĕ'adyah*, attributed without conclusive arguments to the same Dunaš ben Labraṭ,[13] and also preserved in a single manuscript, still present textual problems that are difficult to solve.[14]

In respect of the main authors of the golden century of Hebrew philology, the end of the tenth and the first half of the eleventh century, the state of the text of the original works in Judaeo-Arabic and of the Hebrew translations is uneven. Ḥayyūŷ's two fundamental works on the weak and geminated verbs were first known in the West in one of their

9 I have found these and similar problems in preparing the critical edition of the *Maḥberet* of Mĕnaḥem. See my introduction to the edition, and Yahalom and Sáenz-Badillos (1985–6).

10 See Sáenz-Badillos (1981).

11 See the introduction to my 1986 edition of the *Maḥberet*, 47 ff.

12 See the introduction to my edition of the *Maḥberet*, 46 ff.; Yahalom and Sáenz-Badillos (1985–6).

13 See Sáenz-Badillos (1991).

14 In spite of the good reproduction of the text of the manuscript of the second work published by Schröter in 1866.

Hebrew versions, that of Abraham ibn Ezra, published in 1844 by L. Dukes, or that of Mošeh ibn Chiquitilla, edited by J. W. Nutt in 1870 with English translation, besides the anonymous version found by N. Porges in 1885. The original Judaeo-Arabic text of these two treatises was edited by M. Jastrow in 1897, while in 1870 J. W. Nutt published the original text of his book on vocalisation (*Kitāb al-tanqīṭ* o *al-nuqat*), together with the translation by Abraham ibn Ezra. Of his fourth, exegetical work, the *Kitāb al-natf*, only some fragments published by P. Kokovzow (1916), N. Allony (1963) and I. Eldar (1979, 1980) have been preserved. The new materials from the Russian libraries justify a new edition of the Arabic and Hebrew texts, announced some time ago by D. Sivan and N. Kinberg (Sivan 1989).

Yĕhudah ibn Tibbon's Hebrew translation of the most significant work of Yonah ibn Ŷanāḥ, the *Kitāb al-tanqiḥ*, and in particular of the grammatical section, *Kitāb al-luma'*, called *Sefer ha-riqmah*, is probably the best available text, published by M. Wilensky in 1921, and reprinted with important additions by D. Téné in 1964. The Arabic text was edited by J. Derenbourg in 1886, and needs a new, more modern elaboration. The dictionary, *Kitāb al-uṣul*, was published in its original Judaeo-Arabic form by Neubauer (1873–5), and the Hebrew translation is known to us thanks to W. Bacher (1896). Y. Ratzaby (1966) and J. Blau (1972–3) found two new Yemenite manuscripts of the Arabic text that will have to be included in a critical edition, which unfortunately is still a desideratum.

The Judaeo-Arabic text of Ibn Ŷanāḥ's *Opuscula* was published, with a French translation, by Joseph and Hartwig Derenbourg (1880), but new editions are a true necessity. In 1996 María Angeles Gallego prepared the critical edition of the Judaeo-Arabic text of the *Kitāb al-taswi'a* (her Ph.D. thesis in the Universidad Complutense, Madrid, in the process of publication). The rest of his short works are still awaiting similar initiatives.

The works of other eleventh-century grammarians have been lost, and it does not seem likely that these texts will ever reappear. Such is the case of the philological works of Yiṣḥaq ibn Mar Ša'ul, Šĕmu'el ha-Nagid, or Levi ibn al-Tabbān, known thanks to a few indirect quotations. Of Ibn Gabirol's Hebrew didactic poem, the *'Anaq*, only about a quarter has been preserved, quoted in Ibn Parḥon's dictionary.[15]

Some fragments of the work of Mošeh ibn Chiquitilla on the masculine and the feminine, *Kitāb fī al-tadkīr wa-al-tā'nīt* have been published by

[15] Although I identified a part of this poem within a *dīwān* among the fragments of the Genizah (Sáenz-Badillos 1980), the verses belong to the previously known part.

Kokovzow (1916), Allony (1949), and Eldar (1998a). At the same time Kokovzow edited a few framents of the three principal works of Yĕhudah ibn Bal'am on homonyms, particles and denominative verbs.[16] The latest contribution to the knowledge of the text of these works is due to S. Abramson (1963). We also know in an incomplete way the comparative work of Yiṣḥaq ibn Barūn, *Kitāb al-muwāzana bayn al-luġa al-'ibrāniyya wa-al-'arabiyya*, whose main manuscript is preserved in St Petersburg, and was published by P. Kokovzow in 1890, with the addition of some new fragments in 1916.

None of the editions of Abraham ibn Ezra's five grammatical works that appeared before 1980 was completely reliable, and new editions were urgently needed. Allony worked on the *Safer yĕsod diqduq*, called also *Śĕfat yeter*, and his excellent, posthumous edition appeared in 1984. The answers against the *Critique to Sĕ'adyah* attributed to Dunaš ben Labraṭ have been conveniently edited by I. Oshri in his MA thesis of Bar-Ilan University (1988). Two Ph.D. dissertations approved in the Universidad Complutense not long ago include the critical edition of the *Śafah bĕrurah* (by Enrique Ruiz González, 1994), and that of *Sefer Moznayim* (by Lorenzo Jiménez Patón, 1995); we hope to see both published soon. The important text of the *Sefer Ṣaḥot* deserves a new critical edition.

The dictionary of Šĕlomoh ibn Parḥon, *Maḥberet he-'aruk̲*, was published many years ago by S. G. Stern (1844). The old editions of the works of Yosef Qimḥi and of his son Mošeh are far from having the required quality (except perhaps the *Sefer zikkaron*, edited by W. Bacher in 1888). Likewise the works of David Qimḥi, who was very popular among Jewish and Christian scholars, and the *Ma'aśeh 'efod* of Profeit Duran (published by Friedlaender-Ha-Kohen in 1865), need new scientific editions.

The important dictionary of the last Andalusian philologist who taught in Granada in the second half of the fifteenth century, Sĕ'adyah ibn Danan, *Al-ḍarūrī fī al-luġa al-'ibrāniyya*, was edited in 1996, in the Ph.D. dissertation of Milagros Jiménez (University of Granada).

THE DEVELOPMENT OF HEBREW PHILOLOGY DURING THE TENTH CENTURY

The study of the origins of Hebrew grammar in al-Andalus has been enriched in our days thanks to three main factors:

[16] See further details in Sáenz-Badillos and Targarona (1988), 154 f.

(1) Comparison with Arabic grammar and Qur'ānic exegesis.
(2) The study of Karaite grammar and exegesis.
(3) Better knowledge of Sĕ'adyah and other authors from the East and North Africa.

Thanks to these new perspectives we can understand much better the great enthusiasm for philological studies among the Jews of Cordova in the second half of the tenth century, continuing and developing the efforts of their predecessors in the East and in the north of Africa. Philology, like poetry, exegesis, philosophy and sciences, had become by this time an indispensable and fundamental element of Andalusian Hebrew culture, a characteristic note of the educational training of the Sephardic Jews.

The parallel with the dawning of philological studies among the Arabs, and the original connection of grammar with the interpretation of the sacred texts in both religions, as well as the connection of Hebrew philological views with the main trends of the different schools of Arabic grammar, provide us with a framework for the correct understanding of the fascination that Andalusian Jews felt for the grammar and the vocabulary of the holy language.[17] One of the first motives for the rise of Arab grammar and lexicography was the urgency of establishing a definitive text of the Qur'ān and to understand its meaning.[18] The style and form of its language became the *šāhid*, 'testimony', and the *ḥuyya*, 'proof', on which grammar had to be founded, while its text constituted *al-'asās*, 'the base', of any philological discussion.[19] It is obvious that the Bible had for the Jews a role similar to that of the Qur'ān in the Muslim world,[20] and served also as a challenge and a basis for studying the Hebrew language and discussing all its smallest details.

The attitude to the nature of the language and its grammar adopted

[17] See Khan (1990); Zwiep (1997). Cf. also my paper for the symposium organized in 1997 by the Casa de Velázquez, 'El contacto intelectual de musulmanes y judíos en el campo del estudio de la gramática y los comentarios a textos sagrados' (in press).

[18] Cf. M. G. Carter, 'Arabic Grammar', in *The Cambridge History of Arabic Literature. Religion, Learning and Science in the Abbasid Period*, ed. M. J. L. Young, J. D. Latham and R. B. Serjeant, (Cambridge, 1990), [118–38] 119. See the view of Ibn Khaldūn, in A. M. Turki, *Théologiens et juristes de l'Espagne musulmane. Aspects polémiques* (Paris, 1982), 349 f. See also G. Bohas, J. P. Guillaume and D. E. Kouloughli, *The Arabic Linguistic Tradition* (London and New York, 1990); C. H. M. Versteegh, *Arabic Grammar and Qur'ānic Exegesis in Early Islam* (Leiden and New York, 1993), 96 ff.

[19] See R. Talmon, 'Who was the First Arab Grammarian? A New Approach to an Old Problem' *ZAL* 15 (1985): 128–45.

[20] Hebrew grammarians speak frequently of *'ed*, 'testimony' (see, for example, Dunaš ben Labraṭ, *Tĕšuḇot*, ed. A. Sáenz-Badillos (Granada, 1980), 47*, etc.) and *rĕ'ayah*, 'proof' (see Mĕnaḥem ben Saruq, *Maḥberet*, ed. A. Sáenz-Badillos (Granada, 1986), 62*, etc., as well as Ibn Ŷanāḥ, *Sefer ha-riqmah*) to refer to concrete forms that appear in the Bible.

by Andalusian philologists can only be understood in its true dimension in the light of the different trends that existed in Arabic grammar. Some years ago this topic was presented in the form of a linguistic debate between the members of two antagonist 'schools', Bosra and Kūfa.[21] Today, many scholars see these names as embodying different attitudes to the language: the grammarians of Bosra, like Sībawayhi, tried to reduce the tongue to a small number of rules, in parallel to nature, logic or society; they sought for the basic form (*aṣl*), explaining through analogy and uniformity the derived forms and even the anomalies. The linguists of Kūfa, like al-Kisā'ī or al-Farrā', were prepared to admit the anomalies in their system, since they saw the expressions that in fact existed in the language and the literature as well founded and with normative force; the plural tradition (*naql*) was for them the first and more important source. Both trends were known and shared by Andalusian Hebrew philologists.

A better knowledge of the first Karaite exegetes and grammarians also illuminates the first steps of Andalusian Hebrew philology. The study of the Karaite manuscripts gathered by Firkovitch and preserved today in St Petersburg promises spectacular advances in this area. Even if the eighth century continues to be rather obscure, during the second half of the ninth century the active presence in Jerusalem of outstanding Karaites dedicated to the study of the Bible, such as Daniel al-Qūmisī, is well documented. The translations of the Bible into Arabic were accompanied by an interest in the grammar and vocabulary of the scripture reflected in many notes (Polliack 1997: xiv, 31 ff., etc.). There existed Karaite lists of grammatical terms, like the one published by Allony (1964), and lexica, antedating the work of Sĕ'adyah; remains of them have been found among the fragments of the Genizah (Polliack 1997: 35). The first large work on Hebrew grammar of Karaite origin seems to be *al-Diqduq* of Abū Yaqūb Yūsuf ibn Nuḥ, written at the end of the tenth century, although the grammatical tradition that he reflects may have its origin in the previous century (Khan 1999). The possible philo-Karaite tendencies of Mĕnaḥem ben Saruq constitute a well-known topic (Allony 1962 and 1965).

Among the Rabbanites, few authors have had so outstanding and innovative a role in the history of medieval Hebrew grammar as Sĕ'adyah Gaon. The small sections of the first normative and systematic grammar of biblical and rabbinical Hebrew discovered by Harkavy and Skoss have been completed with the publication by Dotan in 1997 of at least two-thirds of his work in Judaeo-Arabic, *The Book of Elegance*

[21] See the classic exposition of G. Weil, *Abu l-Bakarāt ibn al-Anbārī. Die grammatischen Streitfragen der Basrer und Kufer* (Leiden, 1913).

of the Language of the Hebrews. Allony had already published the *'Egron*, Sĕʿadyah's lexicographical work (1969), and his short treatise on the *hapax legomena* (1958), two books that had also a notable echo in al-Andalus. Other writings of philologists from the East (like Aharon ben Ašer) or North Africa (such as Ibn Qurayš or al-Fāsī), already mentioned, have illuminated in a decisive way the transition from Masora to Hebrew grammar, the origins of Semitic comparative linguistic study and the first steps of Hebrew lexicography.

Hebrew philology started in Cordova a few years after Sĕʿadyah's death, but developed very fast, with passionate debates accompanying it from the very beginning. As this was the first time that such subjects were dealt with in Hebrew, Mĕnaḥem had first of all to create an adequate terminology in this language.[22] His introduction to the *Maḥberet* starts by recalling that God has given to man the special gift of the faculty of speech so that he may express himself in an adequate, correct way: *lada ʿat nĕḵonah lĕ-dabber ṣaḥot* (1*). This Hebrew term, *ṣaḥot*, that we usually translate as 'correctness', is in some way the linguist's ideal, the use of the pure language of the scripture, in which there are no mistakes, in parallel to the Arabic concept employed by Sĕʿadyah.[23]

One of the main concerns of all Andalusian philologists was the search for a set of primitive, basic elements that permit all the forms that appear in the linguistic corpus to be explained. These elements can be seen as a static, unchanging structure from a synchronic perspective, or as a dynamic, ever-changing one from a diachronic point of view. Such are the two models chosen by Mĕnaḥem and Ḥayyūŷ respectively, both having precedents in Arabic grammar and lexicography.

For Mĕnaḥem the base of the language is constituted by a certain number of firm consonants[24] that subsist by themselves or, when they are less than three, with the help of other, 'servile', consonants.[25] Accepting the existence in Hebrew of basic units from one to five consonants (like other philologists of the time, such as al-Fāsī) he has serious problems in explaining the so-called 'weak' verbs, grouping together (with a synchronic criterion) forms that have completely different morphological and lexical origins.[26] However, the *Maḥberet* has an internal

[22] Cf. Sáenz-Badillos (1976); del Valle (1982).
[23] Morag (1970–1); Eldar (1989: 24), with bibliography on the issue.
[24] To this structural kernel he gives the name of *yĕsod*, 'base,' or synonyms such as *šoreš*, 'root', or *ʿiqar*, 'essence'. See, for example, *Maḥberet*, 73*, 11. 20 ff.
[25] *Maḥberet*, 2*. See Goldenberg (1979–80).
[26] In doing so, Mĕnaḥem is far removed from the philologists of Bosra, and also from Sĕʿadyah. See Khan (1999); Eldar (1989: 30).

logic. Měnaḥem did not seek with a diachronic perspective what we call today the 'verbal root', i.e. the form that historically underlies all possible variations that result from the inflection. He wrote a dictionary of 'bases', not of 'roots', a substantial difference in relation to other medieval lexica, like those of Ibn Ŷanāḥ or David Qimḥi, which are dictionaries of 'roots'. As a lexicographer, Měnaḥem is concerned to group together all the biblical forms sharing common consonants, classifying them according to the difference of meaning. No material change in the concept of 'base' was introduced by Dunaš ben Labrat in his *Tĕšuḇot ʿal Mĕnaḥem*. Only the *Tĕšuḇot ʿal Sĕʿadyah* marked a notable progress in the recognition of the triliteral root, but the problems concerning the authorship of this work and the difficulty in dating it before or after Ḥayyūŷ's work should make us very cautious.

Some specific aspects of the tenth-century grammarians have attracted the attention of scholars in the last decades, for instance, the topic of the holiness of the language, with the question of the legitimacy of the use of the language of the rabbinic writings,[27] the compatibility of the Hebrew consonants,[28] the different attitudes to comparative study,[29] the connection with the exegesis of the Bible[30] and the *hapax legomena*.[31]

In two suggestive studies, Richard Steiner (1992, 1998) has evaluated very thoroughly the lexicological work of Měnaḥem and Dunaš in comparison with that of Sĕʿadyah and Rashi. He discusses their attitude to the meaning of some particles, and to maximalism or minimalism in the number of meanings. John Elwolde has analysed the lexicographical theory on which the *Maḥberet* is founded (1995), underlining the fact that Měnaḥem decided to write in Hebrew since 'a language should be explicable from within itself' (463) and qualifying Měnaḥem's method as a 'distributional/taxonomic/inductive approach to semantic description' (464).

HEBREW PHILOLOGY IN AL-ANDALUS DURING THE ELEVENTH CENTURY

The last years of the tenth and the first half of the eleventh century marked a qualitative change in the perspective of Andalusian Hebrew philology, initiating the scientific study of the Hebrew language. It was

27 Allony (1962); Netzer (1983).
28 See the introduction to my edition of the *Maḥberet*, 25 ff.
29 See Téné (1980, 1983); Maman (1984).
30 See Sáenz-Badillos and Targarona (1998).
31 See Sáenz-Badillos (1986).

the fruit of deep reflection on the Hebrew language with the help of the grammatical works of the Arabs and on the basis of their fundamental principles.

This is particularly clear in the case of Ḥayyūŷ. He probably did not know directly *al-Kitāb* of Sībawayhi (d. 792), nor the dictionary attributed to al-Khalīl (d. *c.* 791), *Kitāb al-ʻayn*, although he may have read in depth writings of more recent representatives of the school of Bosra, such as the dictionary of Ibn Durayd (d. 934), *Kitāb al-yamhara fī-la-luġa*. However, it seems very likely that he became familiar with authors established in Cordova, like the Armenian al-Qālī (or al-Bagdādī) (d. 967), a disciple of Ibn Durayd, or his disciple al-Zubaydī from Seville (d. 989), whose abridged version of al-Khalīl's dictionary, and other short works on grammar, had considerable diffusion.[32]

Ḥayyūŷ substantially modified the concept of 'basis' of the first Hebrew philologists of the tenth century. He turned to the concept of *aṣl*, 'root' (which could be understood in different ways),[33] like most Arabic grammarians of Bosra. As Eldar (1998a: 50) has pointed out, for Sĕʻadyah the 'root' was the 'basic word-form (a 'leading form'), actually occurring, in which the word is cited (in a dictionary), and from which the rest of the paradigm is derived,' while Ḥayyūŷ understood it in a more abstract way, as 'an underlying base-form with which a corresponding given form is interrelated, and from which it is said to be derived or modified'. Like most Arabic grammarians, he adopted a 'triliteral' approach, considering that the basic pattern of any verbal root in Hebrew has three radicals.

One of the most important terms that Ḥayyūŷ learned from Arabic grammarians was the so-called *al-sākin al-layyin*; it refers to the consonants alef, waw, yod (and sometimes he'), and is usually translated as 'weak quiescent': when one of these Hebrew letters is not vocalized it can on occasion stay hidden, serving as a prolongation of the previous consonant and its vowel.[34] This principle enabled him to avoid the confusion and mistakes of the previous grammarians in respect of the weak verbs.[35] Even if the term had been already used by Dunaš ibn Tamim, Ḥayyūŷ drew all its consequences. Mošeh ibn Chiquitilla translated it as *'otiyot ha-seter*

[32] Cf. J. A. Haywood, *Arabic Lexicography* (Leiden 1965), 44 ff., 56 ff., 61 f.; A. G. Chejne, *The Arabic Language: Its Role in History* (Minneapolis, 1969), 46 f.

[33] See H. Blanc, 'Diachronic and Synchronic Ordering in Medieval Arab Grammatical Theory', in *Studia Orientalia Memoriae D. H. Baneth Dedicata*, ed. J. Blau et al. (Jerusalem, 1979), 158; Goldenberg (1979–80: 283 f.).

[34] See Haywood, *Arabic Lexicography*, 51; Goldenberg (1979–80: 286).

[35] See Goldenberg (1979–80); Eldar (1984).

(*wĕ-ha-mešek*), 'hidden [and prolongating] letters', while Abraham ibn Ezra preferred the expression *naḥ ne 'ĕlam*, 'a quiescent letter that can be concealed'.[36]

For Ḥayyūŷ, who saw the language from a diachronic perspective, there is no Hebrew verb with fewer than three letters,[37] and one of the main activities of the linguist has to be to recognize the cases in which the first, second or third consonant of the root is one of those weak 'hidden' letters, discovering the basic form that is at the root of all the other forms. This apparently simple principle was the basis of the substantial progress of Andalusian Hebrew philology in the eleventh century. After finding the basic form, by applying the method of *qiyās* or analogy it was possible to explain the derivation of all the actual forms that are found in the Bible.

Other aspects of Ḥayyūŷ's work have been objects of research in recent years, such, as the pronunciation of the *šĕwa'*, characterized as 'Sephardic',[38] his Sephardic pronunciation of the *qameṣ*,[39] etc.

Among the outstanding advances of recent years in respect of Yonah ibn Ŷanāḥ we should mention the studies of D. Becker on his Arabic sources (1992, 1995, 1996 and especially 1998). Examining the works of Arabic grammarians who preceded to him, Becker found a considerable amount of material that Ibn Ŷanāḥ took almost verbatim from the *Kitāb al-Muqtaḍab* of al-Mubarrad (second half of the ninth century), as well as from the works of other grammarians.

The best study of Ibn Ŷanāḥ's contribution to Hebrew grammar (he was the first Andalusian scholar who offered a systematic treatment of phonetic and morphosyntactic topics of Hebrew language and even an analysis of some aspects of the rhetoric of the Bible) is included in the additions to Wilensky's edition of *Sefer ha-riqmah* (1964), by D. Téné;[40] E. A. Coffin wrote a Ph.D. dissertation (1983) on his grammatical theories, while S. Abramson (1988: 195 ff.) studied his rabbinic and Gaonic sources. A. Maman has studied in detail Ibn Ŷanāḥ's use of linguistic comparative study on a triliteral basis (1984: 188 ff.).[41] M. Perez, in his Ph.D. dissertation (1978: 327 ff.) studied the different attitudes of the Hebrew linguists to the interchange and metathesis of

[36] See Sivan (1989); Targarona (1990: 5 f.).

[37] *Sefer Ḥayyūŷ*, repr. 1968 (*Šĕlošah sifre diqduq*), 12.

[38] *Sefer Ḥayyūŷ*, 4 f.; Ben-Hayyim (1956); S. Morag, *The Hebrew Language Tradition of the Yeminite Jews* (Jerusalem, 1963), 160 ff.

[39] Sivan (1988–9). Abramson (1988: 25 ff.) has studied the *Kitāb al-natf*.

[40] See *Sefer ha-riqmah*, vol. II, 706 f., with thirty-two novelties of phonetic and morphologic character.

[41] Maman has collected 342 original lexical comparisons in his works.

consonants, including Ibn Ŷanāḥ among the most decided defenders of the procedure. The lexicographical section of Ibn Ŷanāḥ's work, the peak of medieval Hebrew lexicography, deserves still deeper analysis.

Little new work has been done on the remaining Andalusian philologists of the eleventh century during the last decades. In 1895 Poznanski published fragments of the writings of Mošeh ibn Chiquitilla preserved as quotations in the works of Abraham ibn Ezra and other authors. Some fragments from the Russian libraries have begun to be published (Eldar 1998a), thanks to which we today know better his *Kitāb al-taḏkīr wa-l-tānīṯ*, a collection of biblical names grouped in different categories, with special attention to their gender.

Perez, in his Ph.D. dissertation (1978), dealt with the characteristics of Ibn Bal'am's philological exegesis, without forgetting his grammatical system. D. Pagis (1963) gathered the passages that allude to Ibn al-Tabbān as grammarian in medieval or later works.

Yiṣḥaq ibn Barūn, a disciple of Ibn al-Tabbān, has been studied by P. Wechter (1941, 1964) and A. Maman (1984) as a grammarian and lexicographer who applied the linguistic comparative method.

The *Sefer ha-ṣĕrufim* of Yiṣḥaq ibn Yašuš from Toledo, probably written in Arabic, is known exclusively thanks to the quotations of Abraham ibn Ezra. The same is true for *Sefer ha-mĕlaḵim*, written by David ha-Dayan ibn ha-Ger, from Granada (Eldar 1998b: 115f.).

The grammatical work of the Karaite philologists of the end of the tenth and of the eleventh century (especially Yūsuf ibn Nūḥ and Abū al-Faraŷ Hārūn), whose influence reached al-Andalus, is being currently studied by Khan, Eldar and others, and promises spectacular results.

HEBREW LINGUISTICS FROM THE TWELFTH CENTURY UNTIL THE EXPULSION

The twelfth century still witnessed original philological contributions in al-Andalus, even if after the arrival of the Almohads Jewish life quickly declined, and many Jews moved to the Christian kingdoms of the north. There, under new social and historical circumstances, a new, more traditional system of values arose, in which Andalusian culture (including philology) became less and less highly regarded, and was directly attacked by anti-rationalist groups. No wonder that Andalusian interest in the revival of the holy language and the study of its grammar and vocabulary was not matched in the Christian north of the peninsula.[42]

Abraham ibn Ezra, a true linguist who not only transmitted the philological knowledge of the eleventh century to European Jews but created his own grammatical system, has been particularly studied in the last decades. L. Prijs (1950) published a terminological study that, in spite of some limitations, is still valuable.[43] The volume of the Proceedings of the Congress on Abraham ibn Ezra, held in 1989 on the occasion of the 900th anniversary of his birth, edited by F. Díaz Esteban, includes some significant papers on different aspects of the contribution of Ibn Ezra to Hebrew grammar by Díaz Esteban, Glinert, Shai, Targarona and Sáenz-Badillos. Interest in Ibn Ezra as a grammarian seems to have grown in the recent years: at Bar-Ilan University L. Charlap (1995) dealt in her Ph.D. dissertation with the innovative and traditional elements in his linguistic system,[44] and Y. Oshri in his MA dissertation (1988) edited the text of Ibn Ezra's work against the *Critiques to Sĕʿadyah*. Furthermore, as previously said, two recent Ph.D. dissertations of the Universidad Complutense have been devoted to new critical, fully reliable editions of the *Śafah bĕrurah* (E. Ruiz González, 1994) and the *Moznayim* (L. Jiménez Patón, 1995), with serious studies of the author's own original philological contribution in both books.

It has been emphasized that Abraham ibn Ezra, a translator of Ḥayyūŷ and a follower of his main philological principles, did not accept the universal triliterism established by the great philologist, since he developed the concept of *naḥ neʿĕlam* in his own way, creating a new coherent system.[45]

[42] In the heat of the dispute against Maimonides and his followers, Mĕšullam de Piera, close to the kabbalist circle of Girona and an adversary of Maimonidean philosophy, laughed at the grammarians and asked 'Have you seen a grammarian who is Rav or Judge, a *naqdan* who is a leader of the community?' (H. Brody, 'Šire Mĕšullam de Piera' (Hebr.), *Studies of the Research Institute for Hebrew Poetry* 4 (1938): 41, n. 16, 40). A similar atmosphere can also be found among some groups in al-Andalus. Ibn Ŷanāḥ laments that linguists meet with contempt, incomprehension and suspicion from those dedicated to the traditional sciences of Judaism:

> Those who disdain this science and despise its problematic are the persons dedicated in any way to the science of the Talmud, due to their pride, because they do not understand very much of it. Somebody told me that one of their celebrities was saying that the science of the language was nonsense and that it was not worth occupying himself with it, that their masters are fatigued to no avail and those who study it are tired without having any fruit . . . The knowledge of the flexion and the language is for them a kind of enchantment, and they almost see it as an heresy. (*Sefer ha-riqmah*, 11 f.)

[43] See the review by Ben Ḥayyim (1951).

[44] The basis of her recent book on the subject (1999).

[45] See Sáenz-Badillos (1996).

On the grammatical work of the Qimḥis, on Šĕlomoh ibn Parḥon or on Profeit Duran, who are among the outstanding philologists of the last centuries before the expulsion, it is difficult to mention any new studies in the last decades,[46] in spite of the fact that their works have so many interesting aspects.

A few studies on the philological views of Sĕʿadyah ibn Danan, underlining his significance,[47] appeared a short time before the publication of the excellent edition of the original Judaeo-Arabic text of the lexicon by M. Jiménez (1996), thanks to which we are now able to follow the last steps of Hebrew lexicography until 1492.

EDITIONS OF THE WORKS OF HEBREW PHILOLOGISTS FROM SEFARAD

Abraham ibn ʿEzra'. *Mozne Lĕšon ha-Qodeš*, ed. W. Heidenheim (Offenbach, 1791)

ʿEl Sefer Moznayim de Abraham ibn ʿEzra', ed. L. Jiménez Patón, Ph.D. thesis, Universidad Complutense (Madrid, 1995)

Śĕfat Yeter, ed. M. Bisliches, Pressburg 1838; ed. G. H. Lippmann (Frankfurt a/M, 1843)

ʿ*Sefer ha-haganah ʿal Rav Sĕʿadyah Ga'on (ha-mĕḵunneh "Śĕfat yeter")*', Y. Oshri, MA, Bar-Ilan University (Ramat-Gan, 1988)

Yesod diqduq hu' Śĕfat Yeter. Critical ed., intro. and notes N. Allony (Jerusalem, 1984)

Sefer Ṣaḥot, ed. G. H. Lippmann (Fürth, 1827)

Sefer Ṣaḥot de Abraham Ibn ʿEzra. Edición crítica y versión castellana de C. del Valle Rodríguez (Salamanca, 1977)

Sefer ha-šem, ed. G. H. Lippman (Fürth, 1834)

Sapha Berura oder die gelauterte Sprache von R. Abraham Ebn Esra. Kritisch bearbeitet und mit einem Commentar nebst Einleitung versehen von G. H. Lippmann (Fürth, 1839; repr. Jerusalem, 1967)

'Safah Berurah de Ibn Ezra', ed. E. Ruiz González, Ph.D. thesis, Universidad Complutense (Madrid, 1994)

David Qimḥi. *Sefer ha-šorašim*, ed. J. H. R. Biesenthal and F. Lebrecht (Berlin, 1847; repr. Jerusalem, 1967)

Sefer miḵlol, ed. I. ben Aharon Rittenberg (Lyck, 1862; repr. Jerusalem, 1966)

ʿ*Et Sofer*, ed. B. Goldberg (Lyck, 1864; repr. Jerusalem, 1970)

Dunaš ben Labraṭ. *Sefer Tĕšuḇot Dunaš ben Labraṭ ʿim Haḵra'ot Rabbenu Ya'aqoḇ Tam*, ed. H. Filipowski (London and Edinburgh, 1855)

Tĕšuḇot de Dunaš ben Labraṭ. Ed. crítica y traducción española de A. Sáenz-Badillos (Granada, 1980)

[46] With the exception of Zwiep 1997. W. Chomsky's study of the *Miḵlol* appeared between 1933 and 1952.

[47] See Targarona (1994); Sáenz-Badillos (1991b, 1994).

? *Sefer Tĕšubot Dunaš ha-Levi ben Labraṭ ʿal Rabbi Sĕʿadyah Gaʾon.* Kritik des Dunašch ben Labrat über einzelne Stellen aus Saadia's arabischer Übersetzung des A. T. und aus dessen grammatischen Schriften, ed. R. Schröter (Breslau, 1866; repr. Israel 1971)

Mĕnaḥem ben Saruq. *Maḥberet Mĕnaḥem*, ed. H. Filipowski (London and Leipzig, 1854)

Mĕnaḥem ben Saruq, Maḥberet. Edición crítica e introducción de A. Sáenz-Badillos (Granada, 1986)

Mĕnaḥem's Disciples. *Sefer tĕšuḇot talmide Mĕnaḥem b. Yaʿăqoḇ b. Saruq*, ed. S. G. Stern (Vienna, 1870)

Tĕšuḇot de los discípulos de Mĕnaḥem contra Dunaš ben Labraṭ. Edición del texto y traducción castellana por S. Benavente Robles (Granada, 1986)

Mošeh Qimḥi. *Sefer mahălaḵ šĕḇile ha-daʿat, ʿim beʾur Elias Levita*, ed. Z. Pozner (Hamburg, 1785)

Sefer Sekhel tov, ed. A. Refael (Frankfurt, 1934)

Profiat Duran. *Maʿaśe ʾEfod.* Einleitung in das Studium und Grammatik der Hebräischen Sprache von Profiat Duran, nebst einer Einleitung, erlauternden und Kritischen Noten von den Herausgebern, und hebräischen Beilagen von dem Verfasser sowie von S. D. Luzzatto, zum ersten Male herausgegeben von J. Friedlander and J. Kohn (Vienna, 1865)

Sĕʿadyah ibn Danan. *Sefer ha-šorašim*, ed. M. Jiménez Sánchez (Granada, 1996)

Šĕlomoh ibn Gabirol. *Ibn Gabirols ʿAnak.* Neu herausgegeben mit einer Einleitung und Uebersetzung versehen von E. Neumark (Leipzig, 1936)

'El ʿAnaq, poema lingüístico de Šĕlomoh ibn Gabirol'. Critical edn and Spanish version A. Sáenz-Badillos. *MEAH* 29, 2 (1980): 5–29

Šĕlomoh ibn Parḥon. *Maḥberet he-ʿAruḵ lĕ-R.Šĕlomoh Parḥon*, ed. S. G. Stern (Pressburg, 1844; repr. Jerusalem, 1970)

Yaʿăqoḇ ben ʿElʿazar. *Kitāb al-Kāmil*, ed. N. Allony, Jerusalem 1977

Yĕhudah ibn Balʿam. *Šĕlošah Sĕfarim šel Rab Yĕhudah Ibn Balʿam*, ed. S. Abramson (Jerusalem, 1975)

Yĕhudah ibn Daud Ḥayyūŷ. *Grammatische Werke des R. Jehuda Chajjug. Sifre Diqduq meroš hamĕdaqdeqim R.Yehuda Hayyug*, ed. L. Dukes (Stuttgart, 1844)

The Weak and Geminative Verbs in Hebrew by Abū Zakariyyā Yahyā Ibn Dāwud of Fez, Known as Ḥayyūŷ. The Arabic Text now published for the First Time by M. Jastrow (Leiden, 1897)

Two Treatises on Verbs Containing Feeble and Double Letters by R. Jehuda Ḥayuŷ of Fez. Translated in Hebrew from the Original Arabic by R. Moses Gikatilia of Cordova; to which is added the Treatise on Punctuation by the Same Author translated by Aben Ezra, ed. from Bodleian MSS with an English translation by J. W. Nutt (London and Berlin, 1870; Hebrew text repr. Jerusalem, 1968: *Šĕlošah Sifre Diqduq*)

Yĕhudi ibn Šešet. *Tĕšubot Yĕhudi Ibn Šešet ʿal Tĕšuḇot talmide Mĕnaḥem*, ed. S. G. Stern (Vienna, 1870)

Tĕšubot de Yĕhudi Ben Šešet. Ed., traducción castellana y comentario E. Varela (Granada, 1981)

Yiṣḥaq ibn Barūn. *Kitāb al-muwāzana bayn al-luġa al ʿibrāniyya wa-l-ʿarabiyya*, ed. P. Kokowzow, St Petersburg 1890. New fragments in *Novye materialy dlia kharakteristiki Iekhudy Khaiudzha Samuila Nagida i nekotorykh drugikh predstavitelei evreiskoi filologicheskoi nauki v X, XI i XII veke* . . . (St Petersburg, 1916), 155–72

Yonah ibn Yanaḥ. *Le livre des parterres fleuries. Grammaire hebr. en arabe d'Abou'l-Walid*, ed. J. Derenbourg (Paris, 1889)

Sefer Harikma. Grammaire hébraïque de Jona ben Gannach, traduite de l'arabe en hébreu par Yehuda Ibn Tibbon, ed. B. Goldberg and R. Kirchheim (Frankfurt, 1856)

Sefer ha-Riqmah lĕ-R. Yonah Ibn Ganaḥ, bĕ-targumo ha-ʿib̲ri šel R. Yĕhudah Ibn Tibbon, ed. M. Wilensky (Berlin, 1929; repr. with additions by D. Téné, Jerusalem, 1964)

Le Livre des Parterres Fleuris d'Abou 'l-Walid Merwan Ibn Djanah, de Cordoue. Traduit en français sur les MSS arabes par le Rabbin M. Metzger (Paris, 1889)

The Book of Hebrew Roots by Abu'l Walīd Marwān Ibn Ganah otherwise called Rabbi Jonah. Now first edited, with an Appendix containing extracts from other Hebrew Arabic Dictionaries by A. Neubauer (Oxford, 1873–5; repr. Amsterdam, 1968)

Sepher Haschoraschim: Wurzelwörterbuch der Hebräischen Sprache von Abulwalid Merwan Ibn Ganah (R. Jona). Aus dem Arabischen in's Hebräische übersetzt von J. Ibn Tibbon, und mit Registern und einem Anhänge, Textberichtigungen zum Sepher Harikma, versehen von W. Bacher (Berlin, 1896; repr. Jerusalem, 1966)

Opuscules et traites d'Abou'l Walīd Merwān Ibn Djanāh de Cordoue. Texte arabe publié avec une traduction française par J. Derenbourg, H. Derenbourg (Paris, 1880; repr. Amsterdam 1969)

Yosef Qimḥi. *Sepher Sikkaron.* Grammatik der Hebräischen Sprache von R. Joseph Kimchi, zum ersten Male herausgegeben von W. Bacher (Berlin, 1888; repr. Jerusalem, 1968)

Sepher ha-Galuj von R. Joseph Kimchi. Zum ersten Male herausgegeben von H. J. Mathews (Berlin, 1887; repr. Jerusalem, 1967)

SELECT BIBLIOGRAPHY

Abramson, S. 1963. 'Sefer ha-taŷnis (ha-ṣimmud) lĕ-rab̲ Yĕhudah ben Bal'am'. *Sefer Ḥanok̲ Yalon. Qob̲eṣ ma'ămarim*, ed. S. Liberman et al., 51–149. Jerusalem

1979. 'Pĕraqim še-nogĕʿim lĕ-Rab̲ Yĕhudah Ḥayyūŷ u-lĕ-Rab̲ Yonah b. Ŷanāḥ'. *Lĕšonenu* 43: 260–9

1988. *Mi-pi baʿăle lĕšonot.* Jerusalem

1991. 'Lo' Rab̲ Šĕmu'el ha-Nagid wĕ-lo' Rab̲ Yonah ben Ŷanāḥ'. *Sinai* 108: 1–6

Allony, N. 1944–5. 'Mĕqorot lĕ-tolĕdot ha-diqduq ha-ʿib̲ri bi-yme ha-benayyim'. *Lĕšonenu* 13: 211–22

1949. 'Šĕride Sefer ʿal lašon zakar wĕ-lašon nĕqeb̲ah, Kitāb al-tadkir wa-l-tanit̲ me'et R. Mošeh ha-Kohen ibn Chiquitilla'. *Sinai* 24: 34–67

1951. 'An Unpublished Grammar of Abraham ibn 'Ezra'. *Sefarad* 11: 91–9
1958. '*Kitāb 'al-sib'īn lafẓa lĕ-Rav Sĕ'adyah ga'on*'. In *Sefer zikkaron li-k̲b̲od Y. Y. Goldziher*, ed. S. Löwinger et al., vol. II, 1–48. Jerusalem
1962. 'Hasqafot qaraiyyot bĕ-Maḥberet Mĕnaḥem wĕ-ha-millim ha-bodĕdot bĕ-'erek 'glb''. *'Oṣar Yĕhude Sĕfarad* 5: 21–54
1963. 'Qeṭa' ḥadaš mi'Sefer ha-Qorḥa' lĕ-Rab̲ Yĕhudah Ḥayyūŷ'. *Beth Mikra* 16: 90–105
1964a. 'Rĕšimat munaḥim qara'it me-ha-me'ah ha-šĕminit'. In *Sefer ha-zikkaron le-B. Korngrin*, ed. A. Vayzer et al., 324–63. Tel Aviv
1964b. 'Šĕlošah qĕṭa'im ḥadăšim me-ḥibbure ibn Bal'am'. *Beth Mikra* 20/21: 87–122
1965. 'Haqdamat Dunaš li-Tšub̲otaw lĕ-'Maḥberet' Mĕnaḥem'. *Beth Mikra* 22: 45–63
1983. 'Geniza Fragments of Hebrew Philology.' In *Festschrift Papyrus Erzherzog Rainer*, 229–37. Vienna
Bacher, W. 1881. *Abraham ibn Esra als Grammatiker. Ein Beitrag zur Geschichte der hebräischen Sprachwissenschaft*. Budapest
1882. *Die Grammatische Terminologie des Jehuda b. Dawid (Abu Zakarja Jahja ibn Daud) Hayyug*. Vienna
1884. 'Die hebräisch–arabische Sprachvergleichung des Abulwalid Merwan Ibn Ganāḥ'. In *Sitzungsberichte der kaiserlichen Akademie der Wissenschaft*, Philosophisch-Historischen Classe 106: 96–119
1885a. 'Etymologisirende Wörterklärung bei Abulwalid Merwan ibn Ganah'. *ZAW* 5: 138–51
1885b. *Leben und Werke des Abulwalīd Merwān ibn Ganāḥ (R. Jona) und die Quellen seiner Schrifterklärung*. Budapest and Leipzig
1885c. 'Die hebräisch–neuhebräische und hebräisch–aramäische Sprachvergleichung des Abulwalid Merwan Ibn Ganāḥ'. *Sitzungsberichte der kaiserlichen Akademie der Wissenschaft*, Philosophisch-Historischen Classe: 110 ff.
1892. *Die hebräische Sprachwissenschaft vom 10. bis zum 16. Jahrhundert* (=J. Winter and A. Wünsche, *Die jüdische Literatur*, vol. II, 133–235, Trier)
1894a. 'Die hebräischarabische Sprachvergleichung des Abu Ibrahim ibn Barun'. *ZAW* 14: 223–49
1894b. 'Remarques sur le Petah Debarai, grammaire hébraïque anonyme, et sur le Sekhel Tob de Moise Kimhi'. *REJ* 29: 292–7
1895. 'Die Anfänge der hebräischen Grammatik'. *ZDMG* 49: 162, 335–92
1900. 'Fragment du lexique de Saadia ibn Danan'. *REJ* 41: 268–72
1902. 'Die Echtheit der Dunasch zugeschriebenen Kritik gegen Saadja'. *MGWJ* 46: 478–80
1911. 'Die "Wortvertauschungen" im Kitab al-Luma' des Abulwalid'. *MGWJ* 55: 233–40
1974. *Die Anfänge der hebräischen Grammatik and die hebräische Sprachwissenschaft vom 10. bis zum 16. Jahrhundert*, comp. L. Blau with suppl. by D. Friedman and intro. by L. Fellman. Amsterdam

Becker, D. 1980. 'Hašlamot lĕ-Kitāb al-Muwāzanah (*Sefer ha-Hašwa'ah*) lĕ-Iṣḥaq ben Barūn'. *Lĕšonenu* 44: 293–8
1992. 'The Dependence of R Yona b. Ganāḥ on Arab Grammarians' (Hebrew). *Lĕšonenu* 57: 137–45
1995. 'Concerning the Arabic Sources of R Jonah ibn Janāḥ' (Hebrew). In *Te'udah*, vol. IX: *Studies in Hebrew Language in Memory of Eliezer Rubinstein* (Hebrew), ed. A. Dotan and A. Tal, 143–68. Tel Aviv
1996. 'Linguistic Rules and Definitions in Ibn Janāḥ's *Kitāb al-Luma'* (*Sefer ha-Riqma*) Copied from the Arab Grammarians'. *JQR* 86: 275–98
1998. *Arabic Sources of R Jonah ibn Janāḥ's Grammar* (Hebrew). Tel Aviv: The Jacob and Shoshana Schreiber Chair for the History of the Hebrew Language
Ben-Ḥayyim, Z. 1951. 'He'arot lĕ-munḥe ha-diqduq šel RAbA'. *Lĕšonenu* 17: 241–7
1956. 'Lĕ-'inyan kĕlale ha-šĕwa' šel R. Yĕhudah Ḥayyūŷ'. *Lĕšonenu* 20: 135–8
Ben-Menahem, N. 1940–1: 'Śafah Bĕrurah šel R.' Abraham ibn 'Ezra'. *Sinai* 8: 43–53
Blau, J. 1972–3: 'A Note on the Manuscripts of ibn Janah's Dictionary' (Hebrew). *Lĕšonenu* 37: 232–3
Charlap, L. 1995. 'Innovation and Tradition in Rabbi Abraham Ibn Ezra's Grammar according to his Grammatical Writings and to his Bible Exegesis.' Bar Ilan University, Ph.D. dissertation
1999. *Rabbi Abraham Ibn-Ezra's Linguistic System. Tradition and Innovation* (Hebrew). Beer-Sheva
Chomsky, W. 1952. *David Ḳimḥi's Hebrew Grammar (Mikhlol)*. New York (first part, Philadelphia 1933)
Coffin, E. A. 1983. 'Ibn Janah's *Kitab al-Luma'*: A critique of medieval grammatical tradition'. Ph.D. thesis, University of Michigan (University Microfilms International, Ann Arbor)
Díaz Esteban, F. 1990. 'Abraham ibn Ezra y el 'Sefer 'Oklah wĕ-'Oklah'.' In *Abraham ibn Ezra y su tiempo. Actas del Simposio Internacional. Madrid, Tudela, Toledo. 1–8 febrero 1989*, ed. F. Díaz Esteban, 79–88 Madrid
Dotan, A. 1977: 'Wilhelm Bacher's Place in the History of Hebrew Linguistics'. *Historiographia Linguistica* 4, 2: 135–57
1987. 'From the Beginning of Medieval Hebrew–Arabic Lexicography'. *Proceedings of the Third International Conference on the History of Language Sciences, Princeton, 19–23 August 1984*, ed. H. Aarsleff and L. G. Kelly, 77–84. Papers in the History of Linguistics. Amsterdam
1990. 'De la Massora à la grammaire: Les débuts de la pensée grammaticale dans l'hébreu'. *JA* 278: 13–30
1995. 'Balšanut u-ḇalšanut mašwah bi-yme ha-benayim. 'Iyyun bĕ-sugiyah mi-mišnato šel Yĕhudah Ḥayuŷ'. In *Tĕ'udah*, vol. IX: *Studies in Hebrew Language in Memory of Eliezer Rubinstein*, ed. A. Dotan and A. Tal, 117–30. Tel Aviv
Eldar, I. 1979: 'Qeṭa' min "Kitāb al-Natf" lĕ-Rab Yĕhudah Ḥayyūŷ li-Trey 'aśar'. *Lĕšonenu* 43: 254–9

1980. 'Tiqqunim lĕ-qeta' min 'Kitab al-Natf' li-Trey 'aśar'. *Lĕšonenu* 44: 240
1984. 'Gilgulo šel muṣag 'al-sākin al-lyn' (ha-naḥ ha-rafeh) mi-Sĕfarad lĕ-'ereṣ Yiśra'el'. *MEAH* 33, 2: 1–9
1985. 'E' davvero Yehudah ibn Bal'am l'autore della Hidāyat al-qāri?' *Henoch* 7: 301–24
1989. ''Askolat ha-diqduq ha-'andalusit: tĕqufat ha-rešit'. *Pĕ'amim* 38: 21–33
1990. 'The Grammatical Theory of Ḥayyuj' (Hebrew). *Lĕšonenu* 54: 169–81
1994. *Torat ha-qĕriah ba-Miqra'. Sefer Horayat ha-qore' u-mišnato ha-lĕšonit.* Jerusalem
1998a. 'Hebrew Philology between the East and Spain. The Concept of Derivation as a Case Study'. *JSS* 43: 49–61
1998b. 'Šarid nosaf min 'Kitāb al-taḏkir wa-l-tānīṯ' lĕ-Mošeh ha-Kohen ibn Chiquitilla'. *Ben 'Eḇer la-'Araḇ*: 113–28
Elwolde, J. F. 1995. '*The Maḥberet* of Mĕnaḥem – Proposals for a Lexicographic Theory, with Sample Translation and Notes.' In *Words Remembered, Texts Renewed. Essays in Honour of John F. A. Sawyer*, ed. J. Davies, G. Harvey and W. G. E. Watson, 462–79. Sheffield
Ewald, H. and L. Dukes 1844. *Beiträge zur Geschichte der ältesten Auslegung und Spracherklärung des A.T.*, 3 vols. in 1. Stuttgart
Fellman, J. 1974. 'Wilhem Bacher, Pioneer in the History of Hebrew Linguistics.' In *Die Anfänge der hebräischen Grammatik and Die hebräische Sprachwissenschaft vom 10. bis zum 16. Jahrhundert*, ed. W. Bacher; repr. Amsterdam
Glinert, L. 1990. 'The Unknown Grammar of Abraham Ibn Ezra: Syntactic features of 'Yĕsod Diqdud'.' In Díaz Esteban 1990: 129–36
Goldenberg, G. 1979–80. ''Al ha-šoḵen he-ḥalaq wĕ-ha-šoreš ha- 'iḇri'. *Lĕšonenu* 44: 281–92
Jastrow, M. 1886–9. 'Jewish Grammarians of the Middle Ages'. *Hebraica* 3 (1886): 103–6, 171–4; 4 (1887/8): 26–33, 118–22; 5 (1888/9): 115–20
Kaufmann, D. 1886. 'Das Wörterbuch Menahem ibn Saruk's nach Codex Bern 200.' *ZDMG* 40: 367–409
Khan, G. 1990. 'al-Qirqisānī's Opinions concerning the Text of the Bible and Parallel Muslim Attitudes toward the Text of the Qur'an'. *JQR*, 81: 59–73
1998. 'The Book of Hebrew Grammar by the Karaite Joseph ben Noaḥ'. *JSS* 43: 265–86
1999. 'The Early Karaite Grammatical Tradition'. In *Jewish Studies at the Turn of the Twentieth Century: Proceeding of the Sixth EAJS Conference, Toledo 1998*, ed. J. Targarona and A. Sáenz-Badillos, vol. I, 72–80. Leiden
Kinberg, N. 1987. 'Some Syntactic Notions of Judah Ḥayyuj' (Hebrew). *Lĕšonenu* 52: 144–56
Kokovzow, P. 1916. *Mi-sifre ha-balšanut ha-'ibrit biyme ha-benayyim.* St Petersburg; repr. Jerusalem 1970
Loewe, R. 1994. 'Hebrew Linguistics'. In *History of Linguistics*, vol. I: *The Eastern Traditions of Linguistics*, ed. G. Lepschy, 97–163. London and New York
Maman, A. 1984. 'The Comparison of the Hebrew Lexicon with Arabic and Aramaic in the Linguistic Literature of the Jews from Rav Saadia Gaon

(10th Cent.) to Ibn Barun (12th Cent.)' (Hebrew). Hebrew University, Ph.D. dissertation

1992. 'The Lexical Element in David Alfasi's Dictionary Definitions.' In *Genizah Research after Ninety Years. The Case of Judaeo-Arabic*, ed. J. Blau and S. C. Reif, 119–125. Cambridge

Morag, Š. 1970–1. 'Re'šit ha-millona'ut ha-'ibrit wĕ-ha-'ărabit'. *Molad* 3 (26): 575–82

1993. 'Maḥăloqet Mĕnaḥem wĕ-Dunaš wĕ-tahălik ha-tĕḥiyyah ha-'ibrit bi-Sfarad'. *Pĕ'amim* 56: 4–19

Munk, S. 1850–1. 'Notice sur Abou'l Walid Merwan ibn Djana'h et sur quelques autres grammairiens hébreux du Xè et du XIè siècles, suivie de l'introduction du Kitab al-Luma' d'ibn Djana'h en arabe avec une traduction française'. *JA* (1850) 1: 297–337; (1850) 2: 550, 201–47, 353–427; (1851) 1: 85–93

Netzer, N. 1983. *Mishnaic Hebrew in the Work of Medieval Hebrew Grammarians (During the Period of Original Creativity: Saadia Gaon–Ibn Bal'am)* (Hebrew). Hebrew University, Ph.D. dissertation

Neubauer, A. 1861–2. 'Notice sur la lexicographie hébraïque, avec des remarques sur quelques grammairiens postérieurs a Ibn-Djanā'h'. *JA* (1861) 2: 44–176; (1862) 1: 47–81; 127–55, 359–416; (1862) 2: 201–67

Pagis, D. 1963. 'Mĕqorot li-f'ulato šel Levi ibn al-Tabbān bĕ-meḥqar ha-lašon'. *Lĕšonenu* 27: 49–57

Perez, M. 1978. *Paršanuto ha-pilologit šel R. Yĕhudah ibn Bal'am.* University of Bar-Ilan, Ph.D. dissertation

1981. 'R Jehuda ibn Bal'am's Methods in Explaining Hapax Legomena' (Hebrew). *Lĕšonenu* 45: 213–32

Polliack, M. 1997. *The Karaite Tradition of Arabic Bible Translation. A Linguistic and Exegetical Study of Karaite Translations of the Pentateuch from the Tenth and Eleventh Centuries* CE. Leiden, New York and Cologne.

Porges, N. 1885. 'Bruchstucke einer hebräischen Übersetzung des Buches über die Schwachlautigen Verba von Chajudsch'. *MGWJ* 34: 321–31

Poznanski, S. 1895a. 'Die Zusätze in der Nutt'schen Ausgabe der Schriften Hajjug's'. *ZAW* 15: 133–7

1895b. *Mose B. Samuel Hakkohen ibn Chiquitilla, nebst den Fragmenten seiner Schriften.* Leipzig

1898. 'Un fragment de l'original arabe du traité sur les verbes dénominatifs de Juda ibn Bal'am'. *REJ* 36: 298–301

1906. 'L'original arabe du traité des verbes dénominatifs de Juda ibn Bal'am'. *REJ* 51: 152–3

1909a. 'Les Ouvrages lingüistiques de Samuel Hannaguid'. *REJ* 57: 253–67

1909b. 'Encore les ouvrages lingüistiques de Samuel Hannaguid'. *REJ* 58: 183–8.

1916. 'Hebräisch–arabische Sprachvergleichung bei Jehuda ibn Bal'am'. *ZDMG* 70: 449–76

1925–6. 'New Material on the History of Hebrew and Hebrew–Arabic Philology during the X–XII Centuries'. *JQR* n.s. 16: 237–66

Prijs, L. 1950. *Die Grammatikalische Terminologie des Abraham ibn Esra.* Basle

Ratzaby, Y. 1966. ' "Kitāb al-uṣul" lĕ-r. Yonah ben Ŷanāḥ (Milu'im wĕ-tiqqunim mi-tok̲ kĕtab̲-yad temani bilti noda')'. *Lĕšonenu* 30: 273–95

Sáenz-Badillos, A. 1976. 'En torno al Mahberet de Menahem ben Saruq'. *MEAH* 25, 2: 11–50

1980. 'El 'Anaq, poema lingüístico de Šĕlomoh ibn Gabirol'. *MEAH* 29, 2: 5–29

1981. 'Les Tesubot de Dunaš ben Labraṭ contre le Mahberet de Menahem. Matériaux nouveaux'. In *Mélanges D. Barthélemy*, ed. P. Casetti, O. Keel and A. Schenker, 347–71. Fribourg and Göttingen

1986: 'Los 'hapax legomena' bíblicos en Mĕnaḥem ben Saruq'. In *Salvación en la Palabra, Homenaje al Prof. A. Díez Macho*, ed. D. Muñoz León, 783–809. Madrid

1990a. 'La obra de Abraham ibn 'Ezra' sobre las "Críticas contra Sĕ'adyah".' In Díaz Esteban 1990: 287–94

1990b. "Eqronot lĕ-hahdarat ḥibburim balšaniim mi-yme ha-benayim'. *Lĕšonenu* 54: 1990: 217–30

1991a. 'Sobre el autor de las 'Tĕšub̲ot 'al Sĕ'adyah'.' In *Exilio y Diáspora. Estudios sobre la historia del pueblo judío en homenaje al Profesor Haim Beinart*, ed. A. Mirsky et al., 26–43. Jerusalem

1991b. 'Ha-mab̲o' ha-diqduqi bĕ-'ib̲rit lĕ-millono šel Sĕ'adyah ibn Danan'. *Kenes Barṣelona. The 8th Hebrew Scientific European Congress*, 33–8. Jerusalem

1994. 'La teoría de las vocales de Sĕ'adyah ibn Danan'. In *History and Creativity in the Sepahardi and Oriental Jewish Communities*, ed. T. Alexander et al., [3]–[13] Jerusalem

1996. 'Some Basic Concepts in the Linguistic System of Abraham Ibn 'Ezra'.' In *Studies in Hebrew and Jewish Languages Presented to Shelomoh Morag*, ed. M. Bar-Asher, *125–*149. Jerusalem

Sáenz-Badillos, A. and J. Targarona 1988. *Gramáticos hebreos de al-Andalus (siglos X–XIII). Filología y Biblia.* Córdoba

Schippers, A. 1997. 'The Hebrew Grammatical Tradition.' In *The Semitic Languages*, ed. R. Hetzron, 59–65. London

Shai, H. 1990. 'Abraham Ibn Ezra's Hebrew Commentary to the Bible and Mediaeval Judaeo-Arabic Commentaries and Grammaries'. In Díaz Esteban 1990: 309–16

Sivan, D. 1988–9. 'Ḥayyūŷ hayah hogeh qameṣ sĕfaradi'. *Lĕšonenu* 53: 90–92

1989. 'Biblical Hebrew Roots and Quiescents According to Judah Ḥayyuj's Grammatical Works'. *HUCA* 60: 115–27

Steiner, R. 1992. 'Meaninglessness, Meaningfulness, and Super-meaningfulness in Scripture: An Analysis of the Controversy surrounding Dan. 2: 12 in the Middle Ages'. *JQR* 82: 431–49

1998. 'Saadia vs Rashi: on the Shift from Meaning-Maximalism to Meaning-Minimalism in Medieval Biblical Lexicology'. *JQR* 88: 213–58

Targarona, J. 1990. 'Conceptos gramaticales en el Sefer Moznayim de Abraham ibn 'Ezra''. In Díaz Esteban 1990: 345–52

1994. 'La clasificación de las consonantes hebreas en Sĕ'adyah ibn Danan'. In *History and Creativity in the Sepahardi and Oriental Jewish Communities*, ed. T. Alexander et al., 15–26. Jerusalem

Téné, D. 1971–2. 'Linguistic Literature, Hebrew' (part I). In *Encyclopaedia Judaica* XVI: 1352–90. Jerusalem

1980. 'The Earliest Comparisons of Hebrew with Aramaic and Arabic'. In *Progress in Linguistic Historiography*, ed. K. Koerner, 355–77. Amsterdam

1983. 'Hašwa'at ha-lĕšonot wi-ydi'at ha-lašon.' In *Hebrew Language Studies Presented to Professor Zeev Ben-Ḥayyim* (Hebrew) ed. M. Bar-Asher et al., 237–87. Jerusalem

Valle, C. del 1976. 'Gramáticos hebreos españoles. Notas bibliográficas'. *Repertorio de Historia de la Ciencias Eclesiásticas en España* (Salamanca) 5: 243–98

1977. *La obra gramatical de Abraham ibn 'Ezra*. Madrid

1981a. *La escuela hebrea de Córdoba*. Madrid

1981b. 'Die Anfänge der hebräischen Grammatik in Spanien'. In *The History of Linguistics in the Near East*, ed. C. H. M. Versteegh et al., 153–65. Amsterdam

1982. *Die Grammatikalische Terminologie der fruehen Hebraeischen Grammatikern*. Madrid

Wechter, P. 1941. 'Ibn Barun's Contribution to Comparative Hebrew Philology'. *JAOS* 61: 172–87

1964. *Ibn Barun's Arabic Works on Hebrew Grammar and Lexicography*. Philadelphia

Wilensky, M. 1923. 'Sefer Śafah Bĕrurah'. *Dĕḇir* 2: 274–302

1926. 'Al Dĕḇar Sefer ha-Yĕsod wĕ-Sefer Śefat Yeter lĕ-Rabbi Abraham ibn 'Ezra'. *Kirjath Sepher* 3: 73–9

1934. 'Who was the Author of the Criticism against Saadia (Tesubot)?' *JQR* 24: 209–16

Yahalom, Y. and A. Sáenz-Badillos 1985–6. ''Ariḵah wĕ-nusaḥ bĕ-kitbe ha-yad šel Maḥberet Mĕnaḥem'. *Lĕšonenu* 48/9: 253–68

Yellin, D. 1945. *Tolĕdot hitpattĕḥut ha-diqduq ha-'iḇri, 'im mišqale ha-šemot ba-lašon ha-'iḇrit*. Jerusalem

Zwiep, I. 1997. *The Mother of Reason and Revelation: A Short History of Medieval Jewish Linguistic Thought*. Amsterdam

CHAPTER FOUR

Some recent developments in the study of medieval Hebrew liturgy

Stefan C. Reif

In order to establish a starting point for this survey of recent developments, it will perhaps be helpful to summarize what was covered in the volume that I published some seven years ago and that was based on research done until the early 1990s.[1] In that attempt to provide a fresh scientific overview of Jewish liturgical history, three chapters were devoted to what may with some degree of justification be called the Jewish medieval period in that it comes between the Talmudic age and the past three centuries of modernity. In covering the millennium that ranged from the seventh to the seventeenth century, the volume dealt with a number of central topics. Firstly, it traced the process by which there emerged a formal, authoritative liturgy that was committed to writing and attempted to explain such a development by reference to the influences of political centralization, the challenges of other religious groups, and the standardization of Jewish religious law. It was argued that the emergence of the synagogue at the centre of Jewish religious life and the adoption of the codex for transmitting rabbinic traditions played central roles in the developments of the Geonic age.[2] The next chapter moved on to what are often referred to as the 'high middle ages' and traced the manner in which the Babylonian rite had a major influence on the prayer-books of later communities while that of the Palestinian homeland left only remnants of its traditions. As the newer centres became stronger and more independent, they opted for their own liturgical expression and there emerged a host of textual variations between and within the oriental and occidental communities. Leading scholars and major works focused on the text, obligation and meaning of prayer and the bound prayer-book greatly extended its content from simple text to compendious, synagogal and communal

[1] Stefan C. Reif, *Judaism and Hebrew Prayer: New Perspectives on Jewish Liturgical History* (Cambridge, 1993). The present survey is offered as a humble tribute to a scholar whose personal friendship and scholarly co-operation I have enjoyed for over thirty years. [2] Reif, *Hebrew Prayer*, pp. 122–52.

coverage.[3] In the remainder of the study it emerged that the major themes of the immediate pre-modern centuries were demographical change, the revolution of printing and the growth of mysticism. The self-assured and cultured Jews of Spain came to dominate the forms of worship in the synagogues of their new homelands and the wide availability of printed editions had a democratizing effect on the evolution of texts. The mystical trends of Egypt, Franco-Germany and Spain reached their peak in Safed and no longer had to enter the prayer-book by the back door. Introductory and concluding sets of prayers increased in number while internal and external censorship forced textual amendments. As more systematic thought was given to the ramifications of communal prayer, so the claims of theology, grammar, women, non-Jews and departed relatives competed for liturgical attention, thus laying the foundations of more revolutionary developments in the subsequent period of political emancipation.[4]

In many ways, the most important publication of the past decade in the field of Jewish liturgy is a collection of studies that were originally written in the course of the previous half-century. Naphtali Wieder's researches into the text of the prayer-book began during the Second World War when he was one of the remarkable band of scholarly refugees from central Europe who took up residence in Oxford and brought a refreshing input into academic Jewish studies in the United Kingdom. Wieder, a brilliant lecturer, an outstanding researcher and an inspired compiler of scholarly data, who taught at Jews' College and University College in London, and then at Bar-Ilan University in Israel, deciphered and closely analysed hundreds of Hebrew codices and Genizah fragments from many collections around the world and published numerous articles in periodicals and *Festschriften*, mostly in Hebrew.[5] An astonishing characteristic of his work is how often he was a trail-blazer in a field of Jewish studies whose insights and interpretations were neither widely noted nor adequately appreciated until many years later. He was the scholar who first drew detailed attention, in 1947, to the liturgical innovations proposed by R. Abraham Maimuni in thirteenth-century Cairo and pointed to the characteristics they had in common with the contemporaneous Sufi attitudes to worship. His *Judean Scrolls and Karaism*, which appeared in 1962, was the first balanced, historical and non-

[3] Reif, *Hebrew Prayer*, pp. 153–206.
[4] Reif, *Hebrew Prayer*, pp. 207–55.
[5] Naphtali Wieder, *The Formation of Jewish Liturgy in the East and the West* (Hebrew) (2 vols., Jerusalem, 1998).

polemical attempt to trace the detailed parallels between these two Jewish sects, and for many years his liturgical studies quietly but convincingly set the tone for critical examination of Jewish prayer-texts from talmudic to modern times. He consistently overwhelmed the reader with extensive and intricate data, only moving slightly towards the presentation of a broader, historical overview in his later work. Either because of his reticence in addressing his scholarly publications to any more than a few leading specialists or because what he was attempting to say was not yet fashionable, it took many years for the remainder of the academic world to catch up with him.[6]

The appearance of two volumes of his collected articles has now rectified the situation and will undoubtedly make a major impact on the field. Although the texts of the previously published items have unfortunately been reproduced photographically rather than reset, the author has added new material and made fresh comments to many of these, as well as contributing five fresh studies. English articles have been translated into Hebrew and important indexes have been prepared by P. Zackbach but, sadly, there are no English summaries for the student less familiar with contemporary Hebrew. What immediately strikes the reader is the author's range of competence. Thoroughly convinced as he always has been that proponents of *Wissenschaft des Judentums* cannot be one-subject scholars but must range widely across Hebrew and Jewish literature, he clearly demonstrates his own practical adherence to this philosophy by explaining Talmudic, halakhic and mystical passages, annotating midrashic and poetic sources, commenting on Aramaic and Judaeo-Arabic texts, and subjecting liturgical formulations to linguistic as well as historical analysis. It will be no surprise even for those less acquainted with his work to come across articles that reconstruct the history of prayers, readings and expressions such as *yismaḥ mosheh*, *kol nidrey*, the morning benedictions, *ba-meh madliqin*, *qeṣ*, *barukh hu u-varukh shemo*, and the widely forgotten blessings for virginity and wine.[7] What may attract greater attention, and perhaps a degree of

[6] See his volumes *Der Midrasch Echa Zuta: Übersetzung, Kommentierung und Vergleich mit Echa Rabbati* (Berlin, 1936); *Islamic Influences on the Jewish Worship* (Hebrew) (Oxford, 1947; reproduced from what had originally appeared in the Manchester periodical *Melila* 2 in 1946); and *The Judean Scrolls and Karaism* (London, 1962). Wieder's life, from his birth in Sziget, Hungary, in 1905 to his current retirement in Jerusalem, is a remarkable scholarly tale but not one that he has ever wished to see detailed or discussed. By his choice, the only data provided about him in his collected essays is the list of sources where the articles originally appeared.

[7] Wieder, *Formation of Jewish Liturgy*, pp. 295–322, 368–90, 199–218, 323–51, 492–501, 259–80, 619–21 and 234–41. Most of my review in *JJS* 51 (2000) is incorporated here by kind permission of the editors.

astonishment, is the extent to which such a variety of factors led to adjustments in the wording of some daily prayers. Some Jews found that the numerical value of two uncomplimentary words in the *'alenu* prayer (*lhvl wlryq*) was equivalent to that of the names of Jesus and Muhammad and this inevitably led many others to do their utmost to alter these, and also some other words in that prayer. An archaic formula used to draw the congregation's special attention to the next part of the service was the dramatic use of the word *ha-qol* in the sense of 'hearken!' but once the original meaning and context became unclear it was amended to *ha-kol* and differently understood. The problematic and unattested expression *benei maron* in the Mishnah *Rosh Ha-Shanah* 1.2 and in the *musaf 'amidah* repetition on New Year is simply a corruption of the single Greek word *noumeron* (Latin *numerus*), in the sense of 'a column of soldiers'. There are a number of early liturgical manuscripts that testify to the old pronunciation preserved in the word that appears as *rabbouni* in Mark 10:51 and John 20:16.[8] If the word *ḥaver* was widely perceived to refer to a distinguished scholarly leader, the phrase *ḥaverim kol yisra'el* became problematic since it was manifestly untrue, and alternative phraseology had to be substituted. The European Jews were familiar with so many languages in which an expression very similar to the Hebrew *fi* was crude and offensive that they felt obliged to eliminate it from the prayers, and indeed from Masoretic texts, and replace it with the forms *feh* and *piy*, even if the context made such forms grammatically inappropriate. The enigmatic liturgical use of the word *hw'* may still convey a meaning that it already had in the Qumran scrolls, namely, that of a divine epithet.[9]

Also important for the development of Jewish liturgical study are the general trends that Wieder has convincingly identified throughout his liturgical researches. Versions that are widely characterized as Palestinian may sometimes appear in what are undoubtedly Babylonian texts and historical developments should therefore not be oversimplified. The logic, order and clarity of the prayers came to have major significance and any item that did not meet what were regarded as the required standards was subject to adjustment or replacement. When a rabbinic reticence to use biblical verses was overcome and they were used in the liturgy, the sense presupposed is not uncommonly to be found in the interpretations given to them in the standard Talmudic–midrashic sources. While Sa'adya Gaon constructed his

[8] Wieder, *Formation of Jewish Liturgy*, pp. 453–68, 181–4, 440–7 and 502–6.
[9] Wieder, *Formation of Jewish Liturgy*, pp. 141–54, 469–91 and 395–439.

prayer-book on the basis of contextual and philosophical considerations, the amendments made to it by his successors were often motivated by a desire to make it more user-friendly and liturgically convenient. The rabbinic use of Psalms selections is at times parallel to Karaite and Christian custom and changes attributed to the kabbalists of Safed may be identified in earlier literature, albeit with different rationalization.[10] Early texts such as those from the Genizah should not be lightly dismissed as erroneous but may provide the only remaining testimony to a long-forgotten liturgical practice. Wieder also contributes in the region of a hundred additional texts to the reconstruction of Sa'adya's *siddur* and its transmission and carefully points out those instances in which he calls into question liturgical theories proposed by A. Mirski, A. M. Habermann, E. Fleischer, I. Ta-Shma and M. Bar-Ilan.[11] In sum, what Wieder has convincingly demonstrated is that there is hardly a word, a phrase or a paragraph in the medieval Hebrew prayer-book for which the assiduous researcher cannot uncover a dynamic and controversial history.

In a recent conference devoted to Jewish and Islamic liturgy, Shalom Goldman devoted his presentation to Wieder's Hebrew monograph on *Islamic Influences on the Jewish Worship.* He argued that the work displayed remarkable erudition, was rich in primary rabbinic sources, and contained copious and provocative notes. He regretted that Wieder's description and analysis of R Abraham Maimuni's liturgical innovations and the relevant Judaeo-Arabic texts had not received the attention they deserved.[12] In fact, Wieder's monograph has now reappeared in the new volume of his collected essays and Mordechai Friedman has made considerable progress in preparing a study of the liturgical controversies between the son of Maimonides and his contemporaries. That study has to date taken the form of various scholarly articles which deserve summary and assessment in the present context.

Friedman has expanded the earlier Genizah researches of such scholars as Jacob Mann and Ezra Fleischer and impressively clarified the history of the liturgical controversies between the Palestinian and

[10] Wieder, *Formation of Jewish Liturgy*, pp. 561–621 and 352–57.

[11] Wieder, *Formation of Jewish Liturgy*, pp. 561–658; 52 and 361; 393–4, 441 and 521; 179, 274, 287, 289 and 646–67; 613; and 764–6.

[12] S. Goldman, 'An Appraisal of Naphtali Wieder's *Islamic Influences on Jewish Worship* on the Fiftieth Anniversary of its Publication', *Medieval Encounters* 5/1 (1999): 11–16. That issue of *Medieval Encounters* consists of nine of the papers delivered at a conference devoted to '*Avoda* and *'Ibāda*: Ritual and Liturgy in Islamic and Judaic Traditions' arranged by Seth Ward at the University of Denver, Colorado, in March 1998.

Babylonian communities.[13] There were undoubtedly Palestinian liturgical practices, still in existence in the Middle Ages and relating for example to the synagogal lectionaries, that had had their origins in the age of the *tanna'im*. As the authority of the Babylonian Talmud grew during the Amoraic and Gaonic periods and the associated application of its religious law and ritual took increasingly greater hold on the wider communities of the Near East and the Mediterranean area, attempts were made to force these practices followed in the homeland to come into line with the views of the Diaspora majority. One of the most famous and powerful examples of attacks on the Palestinian rites was that of the Babylonian scholar Pirqoi ben Baboi of the eighth to ninth centuries. He not only objected to the alternative cycles of pentateuchal and prophetic lectionaries and the inclusion of benedictions, petitions, mystical texts and poetry but also noted how the Babylonians had had to convince the Palestinians to recite a daily *qedushah*, and expressed his opposition to their reading the Torah at the afternoon service of a festival, as well as of the regular Sabbath. The synagogue of the Palestinian Jews in Fustat, which, according to Friedman, may well have been built as early as the beginning of the seventh century, before the rise of Islam, was one of the havens of the 'western' customs and it is possible that early in its existence it had developed a compromise custom whereby its congregants read from their texts according to the Babylonian cycle but listened to a communal reading from a scroll that adhered to their own ancient practice. By the beginning of the thirteenth century, most of the Palestinian communities and their customs had disappeared and the emigrés in the Ben Ezra synagogue in Fustat were left alone to carry the banner of their traditions and to defend them against growing opposition. Conscious as they were of the responsibility, they drew up a kind of 'trust deed' in 1211 which summarized their liturgical formulations and synagogal customs, including the special roles of the Torah scroll and the reading of the Song of the Sea (Exodus 15) and the Ten Commandments (Exodus 20), as well as the more extensive use of liturgical poems and biblical verses, and confirmed their adherence to these. No sooner had they done so than one of their number addressed an

[13] Mann touched on the subject in his volumes *The Jews in Egypt and in Palestine under the Fatimid Caliphs* (reprinted edn with preface and reader's guide by S. D. Goitein; 2 vols. in 1, New York, 1970), and *Texts and Studies in Jewish History and Literature,* 2 vols. (Cincinnati and Philadelphia, 1931–5); and the reprint of Philadelphia and New York, 1991, with Gershon Cohen's important essay on 'The Reconstruction of Gaonic History'), while Fleischer dealt with it in some detail in his *Eretz-Israel Prayer and Prayer Rituals as Portrayed in the Geniza Documents* (Hebrew) (Jerusalem, 1988); see Friedman (n. 17 below) for further details.

enquiry to one of the leading halakhic authorities (*rosh ha-seder*) in Egypt who had emigrated there from Iraq, R Joseph ben Jacob, arguing the importance of adhering to their traditional ways in the face of pressure to change, claiming earlier acceptance of these by non-Palestinian rabbinic luminaries, and questioning the standing of any other rabbinic court to dictate otherwise. There is little doubt that he hoped for a formal ratification of his community's intention of continuing what many had come to regard as its heterodoxical ways and equally little doubt that Joseph's responsum was designed to disappoint such an expectation and to demonstrate a total unwillingness to brook any departure from the established Babylonian, now virtually universal, practice. While Maimonides had defined the Palestinian customs as erroneous, he had recognized the strength of their communal adherence to these. He had unsuccessfully attempted to put a stop to the triennial cycle of lectionaries and had reluctantly declined to stir up further controversy by ruling further against the rites of the Jews from the Holy Land. Joseph ben Jacob was considerably less tolerant of deviations from what he regarded as the norm and, adopting or perhaps continuing the maximalist position of Pirqoi, he defined such deviation as nothing less than heresy. This approach was virtually identical to that of his contemporary, R Abraham ben Moses, the only son of Maimonides himself.[14]

Friedman has also added to the research of Wieder, Goitein and Fenton in the matter of the role of R Abraham ben Moses as leader of the Cairo community on the one hand and of the Jewish Sufi-like mystics on the other.[15] R Abraham's ambition, like that of both R Joseph ben Jacob and R Yeḥiel ben Eliaqim, was to eliminate the Palestinian liturgical customs from the Cairene community but part of his agenda was also to force the adoption of pietistic customs in the synagogue not as an option but as a religious requirement. He saw the standardization of prayer-texts, lectionaries and synagogal customs as well as the wider use of ritual ablution, of kneeling and of prostration, as vital to the improvement of the spiritual experience during prayer and as practices

[14] M. A. Friedman, 'Opposition to Palestinian Prayer and Prayer Rituals as Portrayed in Responsa Found in the Genizah (from the Responsa of R Joseph Rosh Ha-Seder)', in *Knesset Ezra. Literature and Life in the Synagogue: Studies Presented to Ezra Fleischer*, ed. S. Elizur, M. D. Herr, G. Shaked and A. Shinan. (Hebrew) (Jerusalem, 1994), 69–102.

[15] Wieder, *Islamic Influences*; S. D. Goitein, 'Abraham Maimonides and his Pietist Circle', in *Jewish Medieval and Renaissance Studies*, ed. A. Altmann (Cambridge, MA., 1967), 145–64 and his earlier Hebrew version of the paper in *Tarbiz* 33 (1963): 181–97; P. B. Fenton, 'A Mystical Treatise on Prayer and the Spiritual Quest from the Pietist Circle', *Jerusalem Studies in Arabic and Islam* 16 (1993): 137–75.

that should be adopted by all congregants because they had originally been part of standard Jewish observance, subsequently preserved only by the Muslims. He himself was convinced that he had won a major victory against the 'Jerusalemites' by unifying the customs of the Babylonian and Palestinian Jews in the early period of his authority and took pride in the fact that he had achieved more in this respect than his great father, who had been unable to overcome the powerful opposition of R Sar-Shalom (Zuṭa) ha-Levi ben Moses, the Palestinian leader. Various Genizah documents do, however, reveal that the war of words between him and his opponents continued from the time of his father's demise in 1204 virtually until his own death in 1237. Initially, the practice of referring to the leader of the Jewish community in parts of the synagogal liturgy (*reshut*), as well as in official documents, as an expression of allegiance, had to be abandoned by the leadership because of objections to R Abraham's authority and ideology and it took almost a decade before he was able to reassert this right for himself. Only by taking such action could the leadership forestall the creation of additional synagogues that would regard themselves as independent of the communal leadership. His opponents saw R Abraham's pietistic campaign not as a defence of tradition but as a radically novel religiosity bent on mimicking Sufi practice and his rejection of Palestinian practice as an attempt to destroy well-established and authentic rituals. So incensed and desperate were they that on more than one occasion they appealed to the Muslim authorities to rule that his modes of worship were unconscionably innovative. He, for his part, was so convinced of the rectitude of his arguments that he found support for them in Tannaitic sources. According to his interpretation of a passage in the Tosefta,[16] there was already then an established custom uniformly to kneel in rows facing the ark where the scrolls were kept and to conduct all the prayers in the direction of Jerusalem.[17]

Recent Genizah research has demonstrated that a Hebrew responsum written by R Yeḥiel ben Eliaqim, and previously discussed by Abrahams and by Mann, was penned in 1211 and related to the controversy between R Abraham and his opponents about the use of the *reshut* as an acknowledgement of the authority of Maimonides' son.[18] It turns

[16] Tosefta, *Megillah* 3(4).21 (ed. S. Lieberman, p. 360, ll. 77 ff).

[17] M. A. Friedman, '"A Controversy for the Sake of Heaven": Studies in the Liturgical Polemics of Abraham Maimonides and his Contemporaries', *Te'uda* 10, ed. M. A. Friedman (Tel Aviv, 1996), 245–98.

[18] I. Abrahams, 'A Formula and a Responsum', in *Jews' College Jubilee Volume*, ed. I. Harris (London, 1908), 101–8; Mann, *The Jews*, vol. I, 237–41 and 267, and vol. II, 301–5.

out that R Yeḥiel was not from Aleppo but from Byzantium or Christian Europe and that he was active in Fustat from 1211 until at least 1238. His responsum was composed in reply to a request for guidance from the supporters of R Abraham who thought that the newly arrived scholar might be willing to speak out against the earlier removal of the *reshut*. The favourable and unequivocal response that they received was inspired by the developments of the previous six years and reflected the increased success and growing power of R Abraham. It contributed to the reintroduction of the *reshut* and the consequent recognition of R Abraham's authority in acts of communal worship, as well as in formal documentation.[19]

During the thirty-year period in which R Abraham held the leadership of the Cairo community, those loyal to the Palestinian traditions in the Ben Ezra synagogue fought hard against his attempts to change communal worship by eliminating their customs and introducing pietistic rituals. It would appear that a Genizah letter addressed to the court physician, Samuel ben Solomon ha-Levi, entreating him to intervene with the sultan in defence of these traditions, was drafted in response to the pro-R Abraham offensives of 1211, including the attack of R Joseph ben Jacob on the extensive use of liturgical poetry by the Palestinians. The subject of the letter and the type of request make this identification a plausible one and it fits neatly with other developments known from the Genizah. While Maimonides had been prepared to tolerate liturgical poems for the sake of avoiding communal controversy, he recited his prayers in his own study-centre where they could be avoided. His son and his supporters took a firmer line and demonstrated in their rulings a determination to rid the synagogue of liturgy that they regarded as a departure from the halakhically authorized formulations and a distraction from the required concentration. Those anxious to enlist the support of the Muslim court against such an approach claimed that those promoting it lacked integrity and probity and were set on depriving them of a synagogal activity that was of major cultural and aesthetic importance and constituted one of the few spiritual pleasures left to them.[20]

It should also be noted that Gerald Blidstein's examination of the

[19] M. A. Friedman, 'R. Yehiel b. Elyakim's Responsum Permitting the *reshut*', in *Mas'at Moshe: Studies in Jewish and Islamic Culture Presented to Moshe Gil*, ed. E. Fleischer, M. A. Friedman and J. A. Kraemer (Hebrew) (Jerusalem and Tel Aviv, 1998), 328–67.

[20] M. A. Friedman, 'A Bitter Protest about Elimination of *piyyuṭim* from the Service: A Request to Appeal to the Sultan', *Pe'amim* 78 (1999): 128–47.

halakhic work of R Abraham has revealed the degree to which he was conscious of the competing claims on him as an individual pietist on the one hand and as a communal leader on the other. Attempting a balance of the theological and the practical sides of his commitments, and seeing this as a continuation of his father's similar efforts, he argued for a reciprocal relationship between the individual and the community. He claimed that his quarrel with those who were opposed to his elitist spiritualism was not with the broader community but with some of its specific leaders.[21]

Some comments on research developments in another area of ritual devotion are now in order. While it had already been appreciated that saints, tombs and holy places had played an important liturgical role in Judaism, Christianity and Islam, particularly in the area of pilgrimage and more popular religion, there was some suspicion that references to the dead in acts of worship had their origins in Christian circles.[22] The recent researches of Josef Meri have, however, demonstrated more clearly the extent to which veneration of relics, of the dead and of holy books was also a major element in Muslim and Jewish spirituality. The object was to achieve blessing and intercession for the worshipper and the ritual included the recitation of verses and prayers, circumambulation of the site, and the use of water and earth from the sacred source. Some activities at the Ka'ba were already characteristic of pilgrimage to Mecca at least from, if not earlier than, the time of Muhammad. Unsurprisingly, the theologians were not always enamoured of this form of religiosity and there are known objections on the Muslim side from Ibn Taymīya in the thirteenth century, on the Karaite side from Sahl ben Masliah in the tenth century, and on the rabbinic side from the *ge'onim* Nissim, Sherira and Hai.[23] It therefore emerges that the concern with the dead in Ashkenazi liturgical practice from about the eleventh century may have had earlier oriental precedents, even if some of the more immediate inspiration was derived from local Christian custom. As far as liturgical rituals at holy sites are concerned, current studies of medieval Rabbanite and Karaite custom vis-à-vis pilgrimage to Jerusalem attest to an additional manifestation of the role of the holy place in popular worship.

Two of these studies, by Ezra Fleischer and Haggai Ben-Shammai, deserve closer attention. That the Genizah texts reveal the special

[21] G. (Y.) Blidstein, 'The Congregation and Public Prayer in the Writings of Rabbi Abraham, the Son of Maimonides', *Pe'amim* 78 (1999): 148–63. [22] Reif, *Hebrew Prayer*, 218–20.

[23] Josef W. Meri, 'Aspects of *baraka* (Blessings) and Ritual Devotion among Medieval Muslims and Jews', *Medieval Encounters* 5/1 (1999): 46–69 (see note 12 above).

prayers and biblical verses recited by pilgrims on their visits to Jerusalem was already noted by Jacob Mann and more recent research has been done on the subject by Mordecai Margaliot, Elhanan Reiner and Moshe Gil.[24] Ezra Fleischer has now closely examined some ten Genizah fragments, eight of them from Cambridge, and added substantial detail to our knowledge of the ceremony and the recitations that accompanied each part of the approach to the Holy City, the circumambulation of its walls, and the final arrival at the Temple Mount.[25] It is not yet clear where each of the gates mentioned in the Genizah texts was actually located but it can be postulated with some confidence that the custom of adding to the spiritual dimension of a visit to Jerusalem by such liturgical activities, formally entitled in Judaeo-Arabic *ṣlw't 'l'bw'b 'lqwds* (= 'Prayers at the Gates of Jerusalem'), was already well established by the time of the crusader invasion at the end of the eleventh century. Although there are some minor inconsistencies in the data provided in each of the fragments, an overall picture emerges and permits a number of important conclusions. The twenty names actually refer to the ten gates of the city (rather than the Temple Mount) and the Jewish quarter was at that time to the south of the Temple Mount, between the Temple wall and the southern city wall. The ritual may be traced in both Rabbanite and Karaite circles, and it would appear that it was the 'Mourners of Zion' who instituted the practice. The biblical verses recited at each gate were chosen to match its name and the special prayers and supplications were added to these verses only at the first and last 'stations'. Some of these were known from other liturgical contexts and took the form of benedictions, and poetic items were also used, in one case borrowed from the mystical *hekhalot* texts.[26]

Ben-Shammai's study is concerned with a Karaite manifestation of such a ritual. He deals with a manuscript that has preserved a large fragment of the *Book of Concealment* (*Kitāb al-tawriya*) by the Karaite author Yeshu'ah ben Judah (hitherto not attested in specific text) dealing with the interpretation of difficult pentateuchal expressions.[27] The colophon

[24] Mann, *Texts*, vol. I, 459; M. Margaliot, *Hilkhot 'Eres Yisra'el Min Ha-Genizah*, ed. I. Ta-Shma (Jerusalem, 1973), 138–41; E. Reiner, 'Concerning the Priest Gate and its Location', *Tarbiz* 56 (1987): 279–90; and M. Gil, *Palestine during the First Muslim Period (634–1099)* (Hebrew), 3 vols. (Tel Aviv, 1983), vol. I, 519–33.

[25] The Genizah fragments are T-S K27.2, NS 265.13, H10.278, H11.72, NS 315.276–77, NS 154.46, NS 195.23, NS 208.73 at Cambridge University Library; Adler 2893, f. 2b at the Jewish Theological Seminary of America in New York; and 100.f.35–36 at the Bodleian Library in Oxford.

[26] E. Fleischer, 'Pilgrims' Prayer and the Gates of Jerusalem', in Fleischer et al. (eds.), *Mas'at Moshe*, 298–327.

[27] The manuscript is Firkovitch II Evr.-Ar. I 4816 in the Russian National Library in St Petersburg.

is dated 1046 and is followed by a lamentation on the destruction of Jerusalem and the Temple which is remarkable not only for its language and content but also for what it reveals more generally about the period and the ambience in which it was composed. Its few lines have much to tell us about the ceremonies of the 'Mourners of Zion' in Jerusalem during the eleventh century. Locals and pilgrims participated in ceremonies in the course of which they recited the book of Lamentations and other poems that bemoaned the loss of Jerusalem and the Temple and expressed sorrow about their current state. They walked around the walls of the city reciting biblical passages and prayers at particular sites and such leaders and scholars as Yeshu'ah ben Judah, who apparently composed this lamentation, were among the participants in this moving mourning ritual.[28]

Although the close study of medieval halakhic and liturgical texts currently being done by scholars in North America does not generally match its equivalent in Israel, a recent volume is an exception to this rule and undoubtedly constitutes a helpful contribution to our understanding of the development of the Hebrew prayer-book in the Middle Ages. Although based on her doctoral dissertation, which was begun with the late and lamented Jacob Petuchowski, Ruth Langer's study is of a higher standard than many such efforts produced for the purpose.[29] In addition to defining how the talmudic authorities justified their replacement of the Temple worship with the adoption of regular prayers for daily, Sabbath and festival use, and tracing some of the ramifications of Jewish liturgical controversy in the modern world, the body of her work is concerned with the tensions created in the Gaonic and medieval periods between those who wished to follow a narrow interpretation of Talmudic principles in the area of prayer texts with those who accorded at least equal authority to established custom and practice. She exemplifies these tensions by dealing with the three major issues of (a) the halakhic status of non-Talmudic benedictions such as those for the tokens of virginity and for the priest to recite at the redemption of the first-born child; (b) the acceptability of the insertion of *piyyuṭim* (liturgical poems) into the body of the standard prayers as well as around them; and (c) the individual recitation of the *qedushah*, in the three contexts of

[28] H. Ben-Shammai, 'A Unique Lamentation on Jerusalem by the Karaite Author Yeshu'a ben Judah', in Fleischer et al., *Mas'at Moshe*, 93–102.

[29] R. Langer, *To Worship God Properly: Tensions between Liturgical Custom and Halakhah in Judaism* (Cincinnati, 1998). She has also written an important critique of the views of E. Fleischer in *Prooftexts* 19 (1999): 179–204 but that is concerned with the earlier rabbinic liturgy rather than with its medieval development.

the pre-*shema*' benedictions, the *'amidah*, and the *qedushah desidra* after the *'amidah*. A great wealth of texts, from Genizah fragments, codices and printed editions, are cited, translated and annotated and although the general treatment is thematic, there is also an accompanying analysis that pays close attention to the historical development.

I have certain critical comments to make in connection with some definitions, presuppositions, translations and omissions in Langer's treatment but these may be left for a different context.[30] For our purposes here, we may summarize some of her important conclusions that appear to me to be perfectly acceptable interpretations of the evidence. There is throughout the medieval period a tension between the acceptance of established custom and the desire to standardize halakhic theory and practice. This is also manifest when rabbinic authorities who are used to prayers as they are recited in one centre being confronted with alternative and, to their mind, questionable formulations preferred in another. Decisions are made that are undoubtedly seen as halakhic but they are reached under the influence of historical, geographical and cultural considerations as well as what might be described as more clinically legal ones. In Langer's words: 'Liturgical halakhah thus was shaped not only by the historical circumstances of its great codifiers, but also by changes in the cultural status of minhagim. These changes altered the balance between the authority of the particular minhag and the authority of the relevant halakhah.'[31] Substitute 'textual variants' for 'minhagim' and the broader point is made. Tendencies in one centre did not match those of another and even within major rites one has to be aware of internal divergences. Responses to such difficulties varied from the total acceptance or rejection of a tradition to various degrees of compromise being made with it, sometimes in the form of amended or conflated texts, at other times in the form of an ideological, historical or exegetical re-assessment. While the mystics left their mark on the prayers at a number of junctures in liturgical history, there was always some ambivalence about whether the prayer of the ordinary individual should be on a par with that of the ascetic and what the textual ramifications would be of either decision.

While it was common twenty years ago to bemoan the limited extent of scholarly work on the medieval history of the Hebrew prayers, it must today be acknowledged that the range of recent research has been such

30 My review is scheduled to appear in *JSS* 45 (2000) or 46 (2001) and I am grateful to the editors and to the publisher, Oxford University Press, for permission to incorporate into this chapter some of the comments I make in that review.

31 Langer, *Worship*, 251.

that it is impossible to do it justice in the space allocated to a chapter such as this. All that may be done in these concluding remarks is to note the existence of other important work and leave closer assessment of it to another context. Editions of the work of Shabbethai Sofer and Solomon ben Nathan of Sijilmasa,[32] as well as an English translation of Elbogen's classic, have appeared.[33] Collections of useful essays have been published by the late J. J. Petuchowski, by Israel Ta-Shma, by Joseph Tabory and by Lawrence Hoffman,[34] and a linguistic study of the Yemenite rite has been completed by Isaac Gluska.[35] My own contribution has been by way of a number of essays in Hebrew and English publications.[36]

What Wieder points out in the cases of *kol nidrey* and *'alenu* could justifiably be applied to many others in the medieval history of the Hebrew prayer-book. In the first instance, he writes: 'The Babylonian *ge'onim* rejected it completely; the Karaites criticized it strongly; the halakhists of every generation persistently drew attention to the halakhic and ethical problems bound up in its recitation.'[37] In connection with the latter prayer, his comments include the following: 'One generation of substitute expressions gave way to another or both came to be used in conflated versions. New textual formulations were created as a result of the struggle and against a background of constant deletions and erasures.'[38] This assessment of the internal dynamic of medieval Hebrew prayer-texts is one that has undoubtedly been fortified by the scholarly researches of the past decade.

[32] *Sefer ha-Medaqdeq ha-Gadol . . . Shabbetai Sofer*, ed. I. Satz and D. Yitschaki (Hebrew) (2 vols., Baltimore, 1987 and 1994); *Siddur R. Shelomo b. R. Natan*, ed. and trans. S. Hagi (Jerusalem, 1995).

[33] *Jewish Liturgy: A Comprehensive History by Ismar Elbogen*, ed. Raymond Scheindlin (Philadelphia, Jerusalem and New York, 1993).

[34] J. J. Petuchowski, *Studies in Modern Theology and Prayer*, ed. E. R. and A. M. Petuchowski (Philadelphia and Jerusalem, 1998); I. M. Ta-Shma, *Early Franco-German Ritual and Custom* (Hebrew) (Jerusalem, 1992); J. Tabory, *From Qumran to Cairo: Studies in the History of Prayer* (Hebrew and English) (Jerusalem, 1999) and see also his *Pesah Dorot: Peraqim Be-Toledot Lel Ha-Seder* (Tel Aviv, 1996). P. F. Bradshaw and L. A. Hoffman have edited six volumes in the series 'Two Liturgical Traditions' published by the University of Notre Dame Press from 1991 until 1999.

[35] Isaac Gluska, *The Yemenite Weekday Prayer: Text and Language* (Hebrew) (Jerusalem, 1995).

[36] 'Written Prayers from the Genizah: Their Physical Aspect and its Relationship to their Content' (Hebrew) in *From Qumran to Cairo: Studies in the History of Prayer*, ed. J. Tabory, 121–30 (Jerusalem, 1999); 'The Early Liturgy of the Synagogue' in *The Cambridge History of Judaism*, vol. III, 326–57 (Cambridge, 1999); 'The Genizah and Jewish Liturgy', *Medieval Encounters* 5.1 (1999): 29–45; 'Jewish Prayers and their Cultural Contexts in the Roman and Byzantine Periods' (a Hebrew essay accepted for publication in a forthcoming volume on the Byzantine period being edited by Lee Levine).

[37] Wieder, *Formation of Jewish Liturgy*, p. 368.

[38] Wieder, *Formation of Jewish Liturgy*, p. 466.

II

The Hebrew language

CHAPTER FIVE

The early eastern traditions of Hebrew grammar

Geoffrey Khan

Many of the grammatical concepts that are found in our modern textbooks of Hebrew have come down to us from the medieval grammatical tradition. These include central aspects of derivational morphology, such as the triliteral root and the derived verbal stems (*binyanim*), with which all students are familiar. The origin of these concepts is to be found in the writings of the Hebrew grammarians of Spain from the eleventh and twelfth centuries CE. The key figure in this school of grammarians was Judah ben David Ḥayyūj, who, at the beginning of eleventh century, published treatises on verbs that laid the foundations of the Hebrew grammatical tradition that is still with us today.

In the Middle Ages, there were traditions of Hebrew grammatical thought also in the east, i.e. in Iraq and Palestine. These traditions were mostly older than the grammatical tradition of the Jews of Spain. It was indeed in the east that Hebrew grammatical thought first arose. Until recently, relatively little was known about the activities of the early eastern Hebrew grammarians. Descriptions of the development of Hebrew grammatical thought have largely concentrated on the well-known works belonging to the western tradition of the grammarians in Spain.

Over the last decade numerous manuscripts have become available to scholars that contain unedited and sometimes hitherto unknown texts of the eastern Hebrew grammarians. The majority of these are in the Firkovitch collections of manuscripts belonging to the National Library of Russia in St Petersburg or in collections of manuscript fragments from the Cairo Genizah. These manuscripts have brought to light Hebrew grammatical texts from the tenth and eleventh centuries CE. It is now clear that there were numerous streams of Hebrew grammatical

It is a pleasure to dedicate this article to Professor Raphael Loewe as a token of thanks and admiration. He enlightened my first steps in Hebrew grammar and medieval Hebrew texts. His teaching was an inspiration to me as a student and its formative influence will always remain with me.

thought in the east. These traditions differ in many respects from the familiar western tradition of the grammarians of Spain.

The eastern texts may be classified broadly into Masoretic treatises, the works of Karaite grammarians and the works of Saadya Gaon. Fragments of Masoretic treatises and also of Saadya Gaon's grammatical writings have been known for some time. There has been little awareness among scholars, however, of the scope and importance of the works of the Karaite grammarians. It used to be assumed that Saadya Gaon was a pioneer in the field of Hebrew grammatical thought and that his grammatical works arose in virtual isolation. The newly discovered Karaite texts, however, provide evidence that circles of Karaite grammarians were in existence during the lifetime of Saadya Gaon in the first half of the tenth century. There are a few parallels between the grammatical concepts and terminology of Saadya and those of the Karaites, which suggests that there was some contact between the traditions. The Karaite traditions, however, did not develop directly from the grammatical thought of Saadya but had independent and possibly earlier roots. In the present state of research it seems that the Karaite grammatical tradition grew out of the Masoretic tradition rather than the teachings of Saadya. In this chapter I shall present a brief survey of the works of the Hebrew grammarians of the east that are now known to scholarship. The Masoretic texts will be discussed first, on account of their chronological precedence. This is followed by a description of the works of the Karaite grammarians, since the Karaite grammatical tradition, at least in its early stages, was closely allied to the Masoretic tradition. The works of Saadya are considered after those of the Karaites, although his writings predate the extant Karaite texts. This is because Saadya's works are considered to stand alone and are not as closely associated with the Masoretic tradition as the early Karaite grammatical texts. Grammatical texts written after the eleventh century in the east are not included in the survey.

MASORETIC TEXTS

Some of the earliest known texts that contain elements of Hebrew grammatical thought are anonymous treatises that are associated with the activities of the Masoretes. These are generally short texts that have been preserved at the end of medieval Bible manuscripts. Some are found in independent manuscripts. These treatises developed from the Masoretic notes that were written in the margin of Bible manuscripts.

In the vast majority of cases the Masoretic notes are descriptive statements that draw attention to details of orthography, vocalization and accent signs in order to ensure the correct transmission of the biblical text. Many of the treatises systematize the statements that are made in the Masoretic notes by collating material that belongs together and seeking general principles. A few of the treatises go beyond descriptive statements concerning the distribution of orthographical features, vocalization and accents in the biblical corpus and discuss principles of the language using theoretical concepts of grammar. These are mainly concerned with aspects of phonology, which relate directly to the recitation of the text, though some other features of grammar are also touched upon.

The masoretic notes in the margin of Bible codices were written in Aramaic, the vernacular language of the Masoretes in the pre-Islamic period. Much of this material had been transmitted orally for some time before being committed to writing around the seventh or eighth centuries CE. Already in the Aramaic Masoretic notes one finds occasional references to grammatical categories such as gender and number. Some of the notes concerning pronunciation, moreover, attest to a form of phonetic theory. It can be said, therefore, that grammatical elements are found in the early Masoretic tradition, which may go back as far as the Talmudic period.[1] It is important to note, however, that the existence of these elements of grammatical thought should not lead us to define the general activity of the Masoretes of this period as 'grammar'. The main purpose of their work was still to preserve the *text* of scripture rather than investigate the rules of the *language* of scripture. The use of grammatical categories was ancillary to this purpose.

The majority of the attested Masoretic treatises are written in Hebrew or Arabic rather than Aramaic. The choice of Hebrew or Arabic reflects the period in which the text was written. The Hebrew treatises appear to have been composed some time between the seventh and ninth centuries. In the tenth century Masoretic literature began to be written in Arabic. Some of these Arabic texts contain Hebrew terminology and even whole passages in Hebrew, many of them quotations from earlier Masoretic texts. Other texts are almost exclusively Arabic. It appears that there is a chronological difference between these two types of text. The texts with the Hebraic elements are datable to the tenth century, whereas those that lack them are from the eleventh.

[1] See A. Dotan, 'De la Massora à la grammaire. Les débuts de la pensée grammaticale dans l'Hébreu'. *JA* 278 (1990): 13–30.

Grammatical concepts are found in some of the Hebrew treatises, which appear to predate the tenth century. Most of the known Masoretic treatises that are written in Hebrew can be found in the corpus of Hebrew texts published by S. Baer and H. L. Strack.[2] These were culled mainly from medieval Bible manuscripts. The texts that contain grammatical material include numbers 36 and 71 of the corpus, which deal with both phonology and morphology.

Another Hebrew text that emanated from Masoretic circles is a list of Hebrew technical terms that are referred to as *diqduqe ha-miqra*, 'The principles for elucidating the fine points of Scripture'.[3] As is the case with other Masoretic texts written in Hebrew, this text is datable to before the tenth century. The text opens with a short introduction that refers to the transmission of the biblical text and its interpretation by hermeneutical methods. This is followed by the list of terms. The terms refer to concepts that can be classified as Masoretic, grammatical and rhetorical–exegetical. Many of the rhetorical–exegetical terms relate to the relation between the cantillation and the meaning of the text. This demonstrates that within Masoretic circles at this period there was a concern to establish general principles not only with regard to the correct textual transmission and recitation of scripture but also the analysis of its grammar and certain aspects of the meaning of verses. One should recall that already in Talmudic times the 'reading' of the Bible did not involve simply pronouncing the letters of the texts, but also having awareness of the sense units that were expressed by the accents in the cantillation.[4]

A number of Arabic Masoretic texts are extant that concern the biblical reading tradition and its phonological principles. Many of these are datable to the tenth century. As remarked above, a feature of the Arabic texts from the tenth century is that some of the terminology and even sections of the text itself are in Hebrew. These Hebrew elements may be regarded as vestiges from the earlier Hebrew tradition of Masoretic

[2] *Die Dikduke ha-Teamim des Ahron ben Moscheh ben Ascher und andere alte grammatisch-massorethische Lehrstücke* (Leipzig, 1879).

[3] The various versions of this text were published in N. Allony, רשימת מונחים קראית מהמאה השמינית, in כתבי החברה לחקר המקרא בישראל לזכר ד"ר י. פ. קורנגרין ז"ל, ed. A. Wieser and B. Z. Luria (Tel Aviv, 1964), 324–63. Some of the versions appeared in earlier publications. These include C. Ginsburg, *The Massorah*, (London, 1905), vol. IV, 36, col. 2 and J. Mann, 'On the Terminology of the Early Massorites and Grammarians', in *Oriental Studies Published in Commemoration of the Fortieth Anniversary (1883–1923) of Paul Haupt as Director of the Oriental Seminary of the Johns Hopkins University*, ed. C. Adler and A. Ember (Baltimore and Leipzig, 1926), 437–45.

[4] This is shown, for example, by Babylonian Talmud, *Nedarim* 37b, where the phrase ויבינו במקרא (Neh. 8:8) is interpreted as 'the division [of the verses] by accents' (זה פיסוק טעמים).

treatises. Some of the texts datable to the tenth century include treatises on vowels,[5] treatises on the *shewa*,[6] and a treatise on the consonants.[7] These are anonymous works, whose authorship cannot be established with certainty.[8]

THE KARAITES

The two most important Karaite grammarians in the Middle Ages were 'Abū Ya'qūb Yūsuf ibn Nūḥ (second half of the tenth century) and 'Abū al-Faraj Hārūn (first half of the eleventh century). Numerous manuscripts of the works of these scholars have been preserved, mainly in the Firkovitch collections of the National Library of Russia. A number of grammatical works of other Karaite scholars that are datable to the tenth and eleventh centuries are also extant. There are references in the medieval texts also to Karaite grammarians whose works have not directly survived. Yūsuf ibn Nūḥ, who was writing in the second half of the tenth century, on numerous occasions cites the opinions of earlier Karaite grammarians.

The Diqduq of Yūsuf ibn Nūḥ

During most of his adult life Yūsuf ibn Nūḥ resided in Palestine. According to the chronicle of Ibn al-Hītī, he had a college (*dār li-l-'ilm*) in Jerusalem consisting of seventy Karaite scholars, which appears to have been established around the end of the tenth century.[9] He was one of the foremost Karaite scholars of his age. One source includes Ibn Nūḥ in a list of scholars whom it describes as the 'teachers of Jerusalem'.[10]

One Hebrew grammatical text that is attributed to Yūsuf ibn Nūḥ is

[5] E.g. *Kitāb al-muṣawwitāt* 'The Book of Vowels' (ed. N. Allony, ספר הקולות – כתאב אלמצותאת למשה בן אשר, *Lĕšonénu* 29 (1964–5): 9–23, 136–59) and *Seder ha-simanim* 'The Order of Signs' (ed. N. Allony, סדר הסימנים, *HUCA* 35 (1964): א–מ).

[6] E.g. the texts published by K. Levy (*Zur masoretischen Grammatik* (Stuttgart, 1936)) and N. Allony (מדקדוק המסורה, *Lĕšonénu* 12 (1943–4): 145–55).

[7] Ed. N. Allony, 'עלי בן יהודה הנזיר וחיבור 'יסודות הלשון העברית, *Lĕšonénu* 34 (1973–4): 75–105, 187–205.

[8] N. Allony, who edited many of them, attributed them to various medieval scholars who are known from other sources, such as Moshe ben Asher and 'Eli ben Yehudah ha-Nazir. In most cases there is no decisive evidence for these attributions and they should be treated with caution.

[9] G. Margoliouth, 'Ibn al-Hītī's Arabic Chronicle of Karaite Doctors'. *JQR* o.s. 9 (1896–7): 433, 438–9. Ibn al-Hītī was writing in the fifteenth century. See J. Mann, *Texts and Studies in Jewish History and Literature* (Philadelphia, 1935), vol. II, 33–4.

[10] Mann, *Texts and Studies*, II, 31. The other scholars in the list are his contemporaries Yefet ben 'Eli and 'Abū al-Surri ibn Zuṭa.

extant. This work is written in Arabic and is referred to in the colophons simply as *al-Diqduq*.[11]

The *Diqduq* of Ibn Nūḥ is not a systematically arranged description of the Hebrew language with the various aspects of grammar presented in separate chapters but rather a series of grammatical notes on the Bible, together with sporadic exegetical comments.[12] The work covers the entire Bible, selecting words and phrases that are deemed to require elucidation and analysis. The work was intended to be used as an aid to the reading of the Bible. It does not offer instruction on the rudiments of Hebrew grammar but rather concentrates on points that Ibn Nūḥ believed may be problematic for the reader or concerning which there was controversy.

The main concern of the *Diqduq* is the analysis and explanation of word structure. On various occasions aspects of phonology and also the syntactic and rhetorical structure of a verse are taken into account, but this is generally done as a means of elucidating the form of a word. The *Diqduq* is not a comprehensive grammar of Hebrew, either in its arrangement or in its content. It concentrates on what are regarded as problematic grammatical issues.

In his analysis of word structure Ibn Nūḥ attempted to find consistent rules governing the formation of words. The ultimate purpose of his grammatical activity, however, was not the analysis of the Hebrew language *per se* but rather the application of grammatical analysis in order to elucidate the precise meaning of the biblical text.

A guiding principle of his approach was that one category of linguistic form consistently has one type of meaning. In order to establish the precise meaning of the biblical text, therefore, it was thought to be essential to analyse the form of words.

In the system of derivation morphology that is presented by Ibn Nūḥ, most inflected verbal forms are derived from an imperative base form. According to a statement by 'Abū al-Faraj Hārūn, this practice was also followed by the Kūfan school of Arabic grammar. The Kūfan school represented an early tradition of Arabic grammatical thought, which was current before the tenth century, which may point to the early roots of the Karaite tradition.[13] The base of inflected nouns is generally stated to be the singular form of the noun in the absolute state.

[11] For further details concerning Ibn Nūḥ see G. Khan, *The Early Karaite Tradition of Hebrew Grammatical Thought: Including a Critical Edition, Translation and Analysis of the Diqduq of 'Abū Ya'qūb Yūsuf ibn Nūḥ on the Hagiographa* (Leiden, 2000).

[12] An edition of the *Diqduq* to the Hagiographa has been prepared by G. Khan (*The Early Karaite Tradition of Hebrew Grammatical Thought*).

[13] See G. Khan, ''Abū al-Faraj Hārūn and the early Karaite Grammatical Tradition'. *JJS* 48 (1997): 318–25.

Ibn Nūḥ also refers to abstract roots that underlie the linguistic forms. These consist of letters alone without vowels. It should be noted, however, that he considers the medial vowel letters *waw* or *yod* in forms such as קוּם and שִׂים to be letters belonging to the abstract root, though did not regard final *he* to be a radical.

Although the *Diqduq* is written in Arabic, much of its grammatical terminology is Hebrew. These appear to be vestiges from an earlier period, when Hebrew was generally used by Karaite scholars in their writings. We see this, for example, in the Hebrew works of the Karaites Benjamin al-Nahawendi and Daniel al-Qūmisi from the ninth century.

The *Diqduq* of Ibn Nūḥ is closely allied in many ways to the work of the Masoretes and some of the Hebrew terms of the *Diqduq* can be found also in the Hebrew Masoretic literature dating from before the tenth century. The fact that there is very little treatment of pronunciation in the *Diqduq* is likely to reflect the intention of Ibn Nūḥ that his work would complement Masoretic treatises on the reading tradition.

On many occasions in Ibn Nūḥ's *Diqduq*, a variety of different opinions are cited. The proponents of these are always left anonymous. Very frequently he presents these divergent opinions without asserting any preference of his own. The issue as to why a word has one form rather than another is sometimes referred to by the term *mas'ala* ('question', pl. *masā'il*). This is generally used when there is an apparent inconsistency with other related forms or with some general rule. These questions often formed issues of debate among the grammarians, and Ibn Nūḥ frequently cites the opinions of others as to their solution. His method was to attempt to reach the truth by exploring many possible paths. The practice of presenting various views on an issue appears also to have had a pedagogical purpose. It encouraged enquiry and engagement rather than passive acceptance of authority.[14]

The *Diqduq* of Ibn Nūḥ is the earliest extant text that can be identified with certainty as a Karaite grammatical work. Ibn Nūḥ, however, was certainly not the earliest Karaite grammarian. Other Karaite scholars of his generation wrote grammatical works. Judah Hadassi, for instance, refers to a grammar book of Sahl ben Maṣliaḥ.[15] A number of grammatical concepts are found in the lexicographical work of the Karaite David ben Abraham al-Fāsī[16] and in the Bible commentaries of Yefet

[14] The presentation of alternative interpretations that often complement each other and have a didactic purpose is found also in Karaite Bible translations and exegetical texts: see M. Polliack, *The Karaite Tradition of Arabic Bible translation* (Leiden, 1997), 26–31, 181–99, 263–8.

[15] Judah Hadassi, *Eshkol ha-Kofer* (Gozlow, 1836), 167, letter ט, 173, letter צ.

[16] *The Hebrew–Arabic Dictionary of the Bible Known as Kitāb Jāmiʿ al-'Alfāẓ (Agrōn) of David ben Abraham al-Fāsī the Karaite*, ed. S. Skoss, 2 vols. (New Haven, 1936–45).

ben 'Eli. All of these scholars belonged to the generation of Ibn Nūḥ. As we have seen, Ibn Nūḥ himself refers to other anonymous scholars ('*ulamā*') of grammar. Some of these may have been his contemporaries, yet some are referred to as deceased.[17] 'Abū al-Faraj Hārūn attributes some grammatical concepts to the teachings of earlier Karaite grammarians in Irāq.[18] The traditions of this earlier Iraqi school described by 'Abū al-Faraj correspond closely to what we find in Ibn Nūḥ's *Diqduq*. Ibn Nūḥ was an immigrant to Palestine from Iraq, where he was, it seems, a pupil of the Iraqi circle of Karaite grammarians.

According to a passage in one anonymous medieval Karaite source, the discipline of grammar began in Isfahan.[19] The Karaite al-Qirqisānī, writing in the first half of the tenth century, refers to Hebrew grammarians from Isfahan, Tustar and Basra.[20] Some Karaite grammatical fragments in Judaeo-Persian have, indeed, been preserved in the Cairo Genizah. These are likely to reflect the grammatical tradition of the early Iranian schools. One fragment[21] is from a treatise on grammatical *masā'il*, i.e. problematic issues. A number of fragments of Karaite Bible commentaries written in Judaeo-Persian that are largely grammatical in character are also extant.[22]

A number of fragments of minor grammatical works are extant that are closely associated with the *Diqduq* of Ibn Nūḥ. These include a treatise on Hebrew verbs that is attributed in the text to a certain Sa'īd. The clear parallels that this work exhibits with the *Diqduq* show that the author belonged to the circle of Ibn Nūḥ and may possibly be identified with a Karaite grammarian known as Sa'īd Shīrān.[23] The treatise contains numerous paradigms that illustrate the inflections of verbs. Another text that should be mentioned in this context is an anonymous treatise on grammar that appears to be a short digest of the main grammatical issues that are included in Ibn Nūḥ's *Diqduq*. This is extant in a few Genizah fragments.[24]

17 E.g. II Firkovitch Ev. Arab. I 4323, f. 9a, הדה הו מדהב בעץ̇ אלעלמא רחמה אללה, 'This is the opinion of one of the sages, God have mercy upon him', where the blessing *raḥimahu allāh* suggests that the man in question is deceased.

18 E.g. *al-Kitāb al-kāfī*, MS II Firk. Ev. Ar. I 2437, f. 37b: אלדי דהב אלי דלך מן אלדקדוקיין קום מן אלעראקיין . . ., 'Those who have held this opinion from among the Hebrew grammarians are a group of the Iraqis.'

19 Mann, *Texts and Studies*, vol. II, 104–5.

20 *Kitāb al-'anwār wa-l-marāqib*, L. Nemoy (ed.), vol. I (New York, 1939), chapter 17, 140.

21 T-S Ar. 31.238.

22 See S. Shaked, 'Two Judaeo-Iranian Contributions'. In *Irano-Judaica*, ed. S. Shaked, 304–12 (Jerusalem, 1982).

23 Short extracts of this text were originally published by A. Harkavy (1891), who erroneously identified its author with Saadya Gaon. The full surviving text has now been edited by G. Khan, *Early Karaite Grammatical Texts* (Atlanta, 2000).

24 The fragments are published in Khan, *Early Karaite Grammatical Texts*.

The works of 'Abū al-Faraj Hārūn

'Abū al-Faraj Hārūn ibn Faraj lived in Jerusalem in the first half of the eleventh century AD. According to the chronicler Ibn al-Hītī he was attached to the Karaite college that had been established by Yūsuf ibn Nūḥ. After the death of Yūsuf ibn Nūḥ, 'Abū al-Faraj took over the leadership of the college.[25]

'Abū al-Faraj Hārūn wrote several Arabic works on the Hebrew language. The largest of these is a comprehensive work on Hebrew morphology and syntax consisting of eight parts entitled *al-Kitāb al-muštamil ʿalā al-'uṣūl wa-l-fuṣūl fī al-lugha al-ʿibrāniyya* ('The comprehensive book of general principles and particular rules of the Hebrew language'), which was completed in 1026 AD.[26] He composed a shorter version of the work called *al-Kitāb al-kāfī* ('The sufficient book').[27] We have a few fragments of two additional works that appear to be epitomes of *al-Kitāb al-kāfī*. One of these is referred to by 'Abū al-Faraj simply as *al-Mukṯaṣar* ('The short version') and the other was entitled *Kitāb al-ʿuqūd fī taṣārīf al-lugha al-ʿibrāniyya* ('Book of the pearl-strings on the grammatical inflections of the Hebrew language').[28] In the introduction to *Kitāb al-ʿuqūd* it is stated

[25] Ibn al-Hītī, ed. Margoliouth, 433.

[26] For a summary of the contents of the *al-Kitāb al-muštamil* see W. Bacher, 'Le grammairien anonyme de Jérusalem et son livre', *REJ* 30 (1895): 232–56, who publishes a few short extracts. Recent studies of aspects of grammar in *al-Kitāb al-muštamil* have been published by A. Maman (המחשבה הדקדוקית בימי הביניים: בין הקראים לרבנים. *Language Studies* 7 (1996): 79–96; המקור ושם הפעולה בתפיסת אבו אלפרג הרון, in *Studies in Hebrew and Jewish Languages Presented to Shelomo Morag*, ed. M. Bar-Asher, 119–49 (Jerusalem, 1996)) and N. Basal ('Part One of *al-Kitāb al-Muštamil* by 'Abū al-Faraj Hārūn and its Dependence on Ibn al-Sarrāj's *Kitāb al-'Uṣūl fī al-Naḥw*'. *Lĕšonénu* 61 (1998): 191–209). An edition of *al-Kitāb al-muštamil* is being prepared by A. Maman.

[27] See S. Skoss, *The Arabic Commentary of ʿAli ben Suleimān* (Philadelphia, 1928), introduction, 11–27; M. Gil, *Palestine during the First Muslim Period (634–1099)* (Tel Aviv, 1983), vol. I, section 938, and the references cited there. Extracts from *al-Kitāb al-kāfī* have been published by S. Poznański ('Abou l-Faradj Haroun ben al-Faradj le grammairien de Jérusalem et son *Mouschtamil*', *REJ 30* (1896): 197–213), M. N. Zislin ('Glava iz grammatičeskovo sočineniya al-Kafi Abu-l-Faradža Xaruna ibn al-Faradž'. *Palestinskiy Sbornik* 7 (1962): 178–84; 'Abu-l-Faradž Xarun o spryaženii Ebreyskovo glagola'. *Kratkie Soobščeniya Instituta Narodoe Azii* 86 (1965): 164–77), N. Allony (קטעי גניזה בספריה הלאומית בוינה, in *Festschrift zum 100-jährigen Bestehen der Papyrussamlung der Österreichischen Nationbibliothek: Papyrus Erzherzog Rainer (P. Rainer Cent.)* (Vienna, 1983), 229–47, and D. Becker, ("לפי המדקדקים הקראים אבו אלפרג' הארון ובצל 'מאור העין' שיטת הסימנים של 'דרכי הפועל העברי", in *Studies in Judaica*, ed. M. A. Friedman (Tel-Aviv, 1991), 249–75. A full edition and English translation of *al-Kitāb al-kāfī* is currently being prepared by G. Khan, J. Olszowy-Schlanger and M. Angeles Gallego.

[28] Fragments of *Kitāb al-ʿuqūd* were published by H. Hirschfeld ('An Unknown Grammatical Work by Abul-Faraj Harun', *JQR*, n.s. 13 (1922–3): 1–7). N. Basal has published some leaves that he identifies as coming from *al-Mukṯaṣar* of 'Abū al-Faraj ('Excerpts from the Abridgment (*al-Muḫtaṣar*) of *al-Kitāb al-Kāfī* by Abū al-Farağ Hārūn in Arabic Script', *IOS* 17 (1997): 197–225).

that this work is more concise than *al-Muḵtaṣar*.[29] Also extant are a few leaves of a grammatical commentary on the Bible which appears to have been the work of 'Abū al-Faraj.[30] He treated the pronunciation and accents of biblical Hebrew in the separate work *Hidāyat al-qāri* ('The guide for the reader'), which he produced in both a long and a short version.[31]

Most of the grammatical works of 'Abū al-Faraj are systematically arranged studies of the Hebrew language as an independent discipline. He, indeed, sometimes goes beyond a description of specifically Hebrew grammar and discusses general principles of language. The perspective of these works, therefore, differs from that of Ibn Nūḥ's *Diqduq*, the primary purpose of which was the investigation of scripture by grammatical analysis rather than the study of the language *per se*. They are closer in spirit to the grammatical treatise of Saadya (see below). Another similarity to the approach of Saadya and divergence from that of Ibn Nūḥ is the categorical approach of 'Abū al-Faraj. He rarely presents alternative opinions.

'Abū al-Faraj refers to the grammarians of earlier generations such as Ibn Nūḥ as *al-diqdūqiyyūna*. He did not use the term *diqdūqiyyūna* to designate all people engaged in the study of grammar. He makes an explicit terminological distinction between the Arabic grammarians (*al-nuḥā*) and the early Karaite Hebrew grammarians (*al-diqdūqiyyūna*).[32] Moreover, the way he uses the term *diqdūqiyyūna* in his writings implies that they were a set of scholars distinct from himself and that he did not regard himself as one of their number. He considered, it seems, that the nature of his own grammatical investigation was different. Whereas his primary purpose was the systematic investigation of the language, the primary purpose of the earlier Karaite grammarians was to investigate the fine points of scripture. The term *diqduq* in this context, therefore, designated this 'detailed investigation of scripture through grammatical

[29] קד כנת אכ̇תצרת אלכאפי פי אללגה . . . וסאל סאיל אן אכ̇תצר מכ̇תצר אכ̇ר אוג̇ז מן אלמכ̇תצר אלמד̇כור 'I summarized the book *Kāfī fī al-lugha* . . . and somebody asked me to make another short version that is more concise than the aforementioned short version' (Hirschfeld, 'An Unknown Grammatical Work', 5).

[30] British Library Or. 2499 ff. 1–21 (G. Margoliouth, *Catalogue of the Hebrew and Samaritan Manuscripts in the British Museum*, (London, 1899), vol. I, no. 276). The leaves contain grammatical notes to the Pentateuch, and the books of Joshua and Judges. There is no colophon, but the text refers the reader to *al-Kitāb al-muštamil* and *al-Kitāb al-kāfī* for further details on some point of grammar, which suggests that the author was 'Abū al-Faraj.

[31] The attribution of this work to 'Abū al-Faraj Hārūn has only recently been established: see I. Eldar, *The Art of Correct Reading of the Bible* (Hebrew) (Jerusalem, 1994), 40–3.

[32] This is seen, for example, in the passage from *al-Kitāb al-kāfī* that is published in G. Khan, ''Abū al-Faraj Hārūn and the Early Karaite Grammatical Tradition', *JJS* 48 (1997): 318.

analysis' and did not have the simple sense of 'grammar' as an independent discipline, which it subsequently acquired.

'Abū al-Faraj incorporated a number of elements from the earlier Karaite grammatical tradition, though he diverges from the approach of his Karaite predecessors in many aspects. He follows closely the approach to grammar that had been adopted by most Arabic grammarians of his time. He maintains, for example, that the infinitive is the source of derivation of all inflected forms of a verb. This is the view of the so-called Basran school of Arabic grammarians, which had become the mainstream tradition by the tenth century. In this respect, therefore, he broke away from the earlier Karaite tradition, according to which the imperative form was the base of derivation. 'Abū al-Faraj, moreover, uses in most cases the Arabic grammatical terminology that was current in the Basran tradition rather than the Hebrew terminology of the earlier Karaite tradition.

The work of 'Abū al-Faraj known as *Hidāyat al-qāri* ('The guide for the reader') could be classified as a treatise on orthoepy rather than on grammar. It describes in detail the phonetics of the Tiberian reading tradition of the Bible and gives instructions for correct pronunciation. It should be taken into account, however, that his grammatical work *al-Kitāb al-muštamil*, although systematic in its treatment of morphology and syntax, devotes very little attention to pronunciation. It appears that *Hidāyat al-qāri* was intended to complement *al-Kitāb al-muštamil* by supplying a systematic treatment of the phonetics of Hebrew. In this respect, therefore, the attitude of 'Abū al-Faraj parallels that of Ibn Nūḥ, who also refrained from dealing with Hebrew pronunciation in his grammatical work, on the grounds, it seems, that this was dealt with in the Masoretic treatises.

Some minor Karaite grammatical works are extant that are largely dependent on the writing of 'Abū al-Faraj Hārūn and were written in the eleventh century. One such work is the grammatical treatise in Hebrew known as *Me'or 'ayin*, which has been published on the basis of a single surviving manuscript.[33] The text was written by an anonymous author in Byzantium some time during the second half of the eleventh century. The work is largely derivative from the works of 'Abū al-Faraj Hārūn, especially, it seems, *al-Kitāb al-kāfī*, the epitome of *al-Kitāb al-muštamil*. Some elements, however, appear to be drawn directly from the early Karaite grammatical tradition represented by Ibn Nūḥ.

[33] M. N. Zislin (ed.), *Me'or 'ayin* (Moscow, 1990). The manuscript is II Firk. Ev. IIA 132[1]. An important contribution to the assessment of this text is made by A. Maman in his review of the edition by Zislin in *Lĕšonénu* 58 (1994): 153–65.

One of the immediate sources of *Me'or 'ayin* appears to be an anonymous Arabic grammatical work that is extant in a number of manuscripts.[34] This text is referred to in the colophon simply as *al-Mukṭaṣar* ('The digest'). It is largely devoted to verbal inflections, but also contains chapters on other grammatical topics. The author was an anonymous scholar who mentions 'Abū al-Faraj Hārūn as his contemporary and so the work should be distinguished from the short version of *al-Kitāb al-kāfī* referred to in one source as *al-Mukṭaṣar* that was written by 'Abū al-Faraj himself. It is clear that the work is dependent on 'Abū al-Faraj to a large extent, though the author had access also to earlier Karaite sources.

SAADYA GAON

Among the manifold literary works that have come down to us from the pen of Saadya Gaon, we have a book on Hebrew grammar known as *Kitāb faṣīḥ lughat al-'ibrāniyyīna* ('The book of elegance of the language of the Hebrews'). This work originally consisted of twelve sections. Large fragments of some of these have survived in various manuscripts, a definitive edition of which has recently been made by A. Dotan.[35]

Saadya was born in Fayyum district of Egypt in 882 CE. He left Egypt when he was a young adult and resided for a few years in Tiberias, which was an important centre for Masoretic studies and also for Hebrew liturgical poetry (*piyyut*). We learn from the Muslim author al-Mas'ūdī[36] that, while in Tiberias, Saadya was the pupil of a certain 'Abū Kaṯir Yaḥyā ibn Zakaryā, who is described as *al-kātib al-ṭabarānī*, 'the Tiberian scribe', and belonged, it seems, to the circle of Tiberian Masoretes. Saadya subsequently settled in Iraq, where he spent the remainder of his life. In the year 928 he was appointed as head of the academy of Sura.

In the opinion of Dotan, the *Kitāb faṣīḥ lughat al-'ibrāniyyīna* was written by Saadya when he was in Tiberias. It should be noted, however, that while he was still in Egypt he had already devoted his attention to grammar. When he was twenty years old he produced the first edition of a Hebrew lexicon known as *ha-Egron* ('The collection'),[37] which reflected

34 The text, which was first discovered by M. Zislin, is preserved in the manuscript Ev. Arab. I 2591 in the Firkovitch collection in St Petersburg. A number of fragments of the work can be found in the Cairo Genizah.

35 A. Dotan, *The Dawn of Hebrew Linguistics* (Jerusalem, 1997). An earlier edition, with an English translation, was made by S. Skoss (*JQR* n.s. 33 (1942): 171–212; n.s. 42 (1952): 283–317).

36 'Abū al-Ḥasan 'Alī ibn al-Ḥusayn al-Mas'ūdī, *Kitāb al-tanbīh wa-l-'išrāf*, ed. M. J. de Goeje (Leiden, 1894; Bibliotheca Geographorum Arabicorum 8), 113.

37 *Ha'Egron. Critical Edition with Introduction and Commentary*, ed. N. Allony (Jerusalem, 1969).

a number of grammatical concepts that were subsequently elaborated in his grammar book. This lexicon was originally written in Hebrew and at some later stage reworked in an Arabic edition. Other lexicographical works by Saadya include a treatise on *hapax legomena* in the Bible known as *Kitāb al-sab'īna lafẓa al-mufrada* ('Book of the seventy unique words')[38] and a short work on difficult words from the Mishnah entitled *'Alfāẓ al-Mišna* ('The words of the Mishnah').[39] The work on *hapax legomena* had an anti-Karaite polemical aim, in that it was written to demonstrate that the oral law was indispensable for understanding these words. We should mention here also Saadya's commentary on the mystical text *Sefer Yeṣira*, which he wrote in 931 in Iraq.[40] The *Sefer Yeṣira* is largely concerned with the mystical qualities of the letters of the Hebrew alphabet and Saadya's commentary expatiates on various aspects of the pronunciation of the Hebrew letters. Finally, we have a few fragments of a grammar book known as *Kitāb naḥw al-'ibrānī* ('The book of Hebrew grammar') which appears to be a shortened version of Saadya's *Kitāb faṣīḥ lughat al-ibrāniyyīna*.[41]

Although Saadya's grammar book *Kitāb faṣīḥ lughat al-'ibrāniyyīna* appears to have been written in Tiberias and incorporates some details of the Tiberian Masoretic tradition, it is clearly independent of this tradition. Unlike the *Diqduq* of Yūsuf ibn Nūḥ, which was intended primarily as an investigation of the biblical text and as a complement to the Masoretic texts on the Tiberian reading tradition, the grammar book of Saadya treated the Hebrew language as an independent discipline. As far as we know, Saadya's grammar book was the first work on Hebrew grammar that had this independent perspective. It should be noted, however, that elements of Hebrew grammatical thought are found in Masoretic texts that predate Saadya. As we have seen, there are also references to Karaite Hebrew grammarians at the beginning of the tenth century, who appear to have been contemporaries of Saadya.

The surviving fragments of the grammar book of Saadya contain detailed discussions of phonology and morphology. The inclusion of sections on phonology may be taken as evidence that Saadya regarded his work as independent of the Masoretic texts on the Tiberian reading

38 Ed. N. Allony, ספר הזכרון לכבוד יצחק גולדציהר, I, (1957–8), 1–48.

39 Ed. N. Allony, *Lĕšonénu* 18 (1951–3): 167–78.

40 *Commentaire sur le Séfer Yesira ou Livre de création par le Gaon Saadya de Fayyoum*, ed. and trans. Mayer Lambert (Paris, 1891).

41 The fragments were edited by I. Eldar (*Lĕšonénu* 45 (1980–1). 105–32) and N. Allony (*Sinai* 90 (1981–2): 101–27).

tradition. As we have seen, neither Ibn Nūḥ nor 'Abū al-Faraj Hārūn devoted attention to phonology in their grammatical works.

In various places in his grammar, Saadya discusses general principles that are common to all languages that were known to him and also general linguistic issues such as the origin of human language. In this respect Saadya's grammar is close in spirit to the works of 'Abū al-Faraj Hārūn, which also touches upon general principles of human language.

Saadya differs from the Karaites in that he extends his treatment of Hebrew grammar to include not only the language of the Bible but also material from Rabbinic and even payṭanic Hebrew. Not only was Saadya concerned with the language of a wider range of Hebrew literature than the Karaite grammarians, but he also intended his work to go beyond an analysis of the language of a closed corpus and to discuss principles of the creative use of language. This involved the establishing of principles for the analogical formation of new words, mainly for the use of poets.

The central concept in Saadya's treatment of Hebrew morphology is that all words are derived from a nominal base. Verbs were derived from infinitive forms or from other types of verbal nouns. In some contexts Saadya also refers to the letters that formed the abstract root of words. These did not include the vowel letters aleph, waw and yod, but did include final he. Another fundamental aspect of his treatment of morphology is his division of the letters of the Hebrew alphabet into eleven base letters, which occur only as root letters, and eleven servile letters, i.e. letters that, in the formation of words, are attached to the fundamental root letters.

Finally, it should be noted that Saadya's presentation is largely categorical and there is very little discussion of differences in opinion and alternative views. This should be contrasted to the style of Yūsuf ibn Nūḥ and his circle, who explore various opinions concerning most issues. In this respect also, the approach of 'Abū al-Faraj is closer to that of Saadya.

THE INFLUENCE OF SAADYA ON THE KARAITES

In various places in the foregoing discussion, we have indicated parallels and differences between Saadya and the Karaite grammarians. The key Karaite grammatical texts, the *Diqduq* of Yūsuf ibn Nūḥ and the works of 'Abū al-Faraj Hārūn, were written later than the *Kitāb faṣīḥ luġat al-ʿibrāniyyīna* of Saadya. As has been shown, the Karaite grammatical tradition by no means derives wholly from the work of Saadya, but rather has its roots elsewhere. Some parallels between the Karaites and Saadya may have arisen by the common environment in which the texts were written rather than by direct influence. The adherence of both Saadya and 'Abū al-Faraj to the notion that verbs are derived from a nominal base, for example, may in each case be the result of the influence of the contemporary teachings of the Baṣran school of Arabic grammarians. There are, nevertheless, some parallels between the Karaite texts and Saadya's grammatical work which are more easily accepted as the result of influence of Saadya on the Karaites. These include, for example, the concept of verbal paradigms, which is found in the Karaite treatise on Hebrew verbs attributed to a Karaite known as Saʿīd, and the division of the letters of the Hebrew alphabet into servile and base letters, which is found in the grammatical works of 'Abū al-Faraj. Some phonetic concepts used by 'Abū al-Faraj in his *Hidāyat al-Qāri* also seem to be derived from Saadya.[42]

IMPORTANCE OF THE DISCOVERY OF THE EASTERN GRAMMATICAL SOURCES

The recent advances in our knowledge of the eastern traditions of Hebrew grammatical thought are of importance for the history of the development of the discipline in the Middle Ages. The discovery of the Karaite grammatical texts now makes it clear that Hebrew grammatical thought was far more widespread and developed in the east than scholars had previously thought.

The study of the eastern texts, in fact, have more than antiquarian interest. As was remarked at the beginning of this chapter, many of the basic concepts of Hebrew grammar that are still with us today are a heritage from the Spanish school of grammarians. Knowledge of the eastern sources may in some respects, therefore, give us new insights into the Hebrew language and its analysis. This certainly applies to the pronunciation of Hebrew. Many of the eastern sources describe the original Tiberian pronunciation tradition of Hebrew, which was only imperfectly known to the grammarians of Spain.

[42] Eldar, *The Art of Correct Reading*, 14.

CHAPTER SIX

Banner, miracle, trial? Medieval Hebrew lexicography between facts and faith

Albert van der Heide

INTRODUCTION

The story of the discovery of the grammatical structure of Hebrew has often been told and is, by and large, well known to all Hebraists.[1] It is an established fact that it was the study of Arabic by Muslim scholars that served Jewish scholars as an example in their effort to determine the meaning of the words of Hebrew and to reduce the grammatical forms to their roots. Like the Qur'ān for the Muslims, the Hebrew Bible was the chief object of this enterprise. The study of the language in fact became part and parcel of the study of the Bible.

After the pioneering efforts of Saadya Gaon in the first half of the tenth century, Hebrew studies culminated in the application of the principle of triliterality to Hebrew by Judah Ḥayyuj around 1000 CE. The extensive elaboration of this principle in a grammar and a lexicon by Jonah ibn Janaḥ around 1040 resulted in the first complete description of biblical Hebrew (*Kitāb al-Tanqīḥ*). During this first pioneering century of scholarship, Hebrew grammars and dictionaries, with a few notable exceptions, were written in Arabic. Later, grammatical works came to be written in Hebrew, and they eclipsed the earlier, Arabic phase of Hebrew linguistics.[2] The pattern of Ibn Janaḥ's comprehensive *Tanqīḥ* was taken over by David Kimḥi. His *Mikhlol* (written close to 1200) also separates the grammar from the lexicon; it became the standard work on Hebrew language for centuries to come.

It is the aim of this article to highlight the fact that the study of the

[1] James Barr's article 'Hebrew Linguistic Literature' (*EJ* (1971) XVI, 1352–1401) conveniently summarizes both the literary history and the theoretical developments within this branch of medieval scholarship; the article includes a chronological list of bio- and bibliographical details of the individual grammarians (1379–90).

[2] A century of modern research has made these works accessible again; see Barr, 'Hebrew Linguistic Literature, 1375–9, section entitled 'The study of linguistic literature', and the various editions quoted in this article.

language of the Bible was not a matter of linguistics alone. Almost simultaneously with the linguistic description of Hebrew, the enterprise of translating the Bible into Arabic began. This was done in Karaite circles[3] and, with eventually much more influence in Judaism, by Saadya Gaon as well. It appears that these translations served as tools for interpretation. In the early manuscripts the Arabic translations are preceded by the Hebrew of the biblical text and followed by an extensive commentary, also in Arabic. This threefold layout clearly indicates that the main purpose of these translations was exegetical.[4] Although originally this also seems to have been the case for Saadya's works on the Bible, his Arabic version of the Pentateuch soon began to circulate as an independent text, apart from the commentary. Under the name *Tafsīr* ('Commentary') his translation received authoritative status.[5] Biblical exegesis then developed in close connection with linguistic literature.

Two other elements made their mark on the study of the Bible in the Middle Ages, namely early rabbinic tradition and medieval religious thought.

Classical rabbinic literature contains a wealth of interpretations of individual biblical passages. We find them mainly in the form of Midrash, but the Aramaic translations (Targumim) by their nature contain much interpretation as well. Medieval Jewish scholars neither could nor would dismiss this heritage of reading the Bible. They kept paying their respects to a tradition which was so very different from the spirit of classification and inquiry of medieval linguistics.

The other element in biblical interpretation was, however, distinctly medieval. It originated in the tension that was felt between the language of the Bible, so accessible and understandable to all, and its lofty subject, i.e. God, his attributes and his actions. Many passages in the Bible seem superficial and gross and not in keeping with God's majesty as conceived by the medieval mind. This problem was eminently and very influentially discussed by Maimonides in the first chapters of the *Mishneh Torah* and in the *Guide of the Perplexed*. He summarized the issue by the rabbinic dictum that 'the Torah speaks in human language' which he understood as a warning that the language of the Bible should not be taken at face value. It speaks to the average reader, but its real, deeper meaning can be gauged only by scholars who are aware of the true scope and portent of the biblical message. This search for a deeper meaning

[3] Meira Polliack, *The Karaite Tradition of Arabic Bible Translations of the Pentateuch from the Tenth and Eleventh Centuries CE* (Leiden, 1997).

[4] See Polliack, *Karaite Tradition*, xvi.

[5] Polliack, *Karaite Tradition*, 78–9.

of words and expressions whose literal meaning seems to collide with theological conceptions is characteristic of medieval hermeneutics to such an extent that, as we will see, even lexicographers could not escape it.

When in the following pages we try to follow the course of lexicographical description of Hebrew, we will see that Hebrew lexicography, which indeed started as a tool for reading and translating the Bible, soon came into contact with these other fields of biblical study and had to negotiate between the various strands of Jewish tradition. The morphological and semantic characteristics of the verb *nissa* , 'to try, to test', and its derivation *massa*, will provide us the pattern for this exploration. It will appear that this restriction to a single lexeme helps us to appreciate the role that this rather complicated body of texts played in medieval Jewish scholarship.

THE LEXICAL PROBLEM

There can be no doubt that the basic meaning of the biblical verb *nissa* is 'to try, to test'.[6] This fact is confirmed by repeated parallelisms with the verb *baḥan*. In a few instances this basic meaning is somewhat extended. Thus *nissa* may be used – like its English equivalent – in the sense of 'to make the attempt' (Judges 6:39), or in the sense of 'to be used to'. The latter is the case in 1 Samuel 17:39, where David has to decline the use of Saul's armour in his fight with Goliath: 'Then he tried (*wa-yo'el*) to walk, but he was not used to it (*ki lo nissa*)'.[7] The dainty woman 'who has not even tried to put a foot to the ground' (Deuteronomy 28:56 NEB; possibly a nif'al) also appears to belong in this category. Subtle as the various shades of meaning may be,[8] it is very clear that there can be no doubt on the meaning of *nissa* in biblical Hebrew in the great majority of its thirty-six occurrences.

This fact was also recognized by the classical rabbinic texts. In Bereshit Rabba 55:2, for instance, the verse 'After this God tried (*nissa*) Abraham' (Genesis 22:1) is elucidated by the quotation of Psalms 11:5, 'The Lord tests (*yivḥan*) the righteous', followed by three parables in which the idea of a test and examination is elaborated.

[6] According to most scholars the verb is exclusively used in the pi'el. However, L. Köhler and W. Baumgartner's *Hebräisches und aramäisches Lexikon zum Alten Testament*, 3rd edition (Leiden, 1967–; English trans. M. E. J. Richardson, Leiden, 1995) records four nif'al forms with the meaning 'to venture'.

[7] So the JPS translation; the RSV and NEB have slightly different translations.

[8] A slightly more difficult case is Job 4:2, usually translated as: 'If one ventures (*ha-nissa*) a word with you. . .'.

The situation with the noun *massa*, the single derivation of *nissa* in biblical Hebrew, is however slightly more complicated. In Job 9:23 *massa* probably has the plain meaning of 'trial, test'. Likewise the name Massah as a designation of a locality in the desert may be understood in this sense (cf. Deuteronomy 6:16). But in the three remaining instances (Deuteronomy 4:34, 7:19, 29:2) the word unmistakably conveys the idea of something spectacular and miraculous. In all three cases the plural *massot* is used as parallel to, and in close connection with *otot u -moftim*, 'signs and portents', so that it can hardly be taken as a simple synonym of, for example, *beḥinot*.

But it was not so much the semantic pattern of the verb *nissa* in the Bible that troubled its interpreters as its use. For the monotheistic views developed by rabbinic and medieval Judaism many instances of *nissa* in the Bible[9] offer serious difficulties.

What is the problem? When the Bible tells us that the Queen of Sheba came to test Solomon with riddles (1 Kings 10:1), the meaning is obvious. But when we are repeatedly told that the Israelites tested God by saying: 'Is the Lord in our midst or not?' (Exodus 17:7) or words of similar nature, it is difficult to imagine how an almighty God could be the object of a test by mere mortals. The solution is that this cannot be seen as a real trial, but should be considered a sinful expression of human arrogance.[10]

But the Bible is also very outspoken on the possibility that God puts man to the test. There is, for example, Exodus 16:4, where God says to Moses: 'I will rain down bread for you . . . that I may thus test them to see whether they will follow my instructions or not.' And there is, of course, the case of Abraham's trial, which opens with the well-known and ominous words: 'After this God tried Abraham' (Genesis 22:1). A trial from heaven cannot be considered a vain trial. Coming from God it must have sense and purpose. But the problem is obvious. The monotheistic conception of an almighty and omniscient God makes it very difficult to see any sense in such a test, although the Bible itself repeatedly represents God as the author of a test 'in order to know' what he did not know before.[11]

[9] For the whole spectrum see Jacob Licht, *Testing in Hebrew Scriptures and in Post-Biblical Judaism* (Hebrew) (Jerusalem, 1973).

[10] See e.g. the outspoken lines of Ps. 95:8–11, where *nissa* and *baḥan* are used synonymously. Note that rabbinic Judaism included the prohibition 'Do not try the Lord your God, as you did at Massah' (Deuteronomy 6:16) into the list of the 613 Commandments explicitly written in the Torah. See Maimonides, *Mishneh Torah*, negative commandment no. 64: 'Not to test the word of the Lord; Dt. 6:16'; H. Yesode ha-Torah, heading and X:5 (modified into testing the words of a reliable prophet); *Sefer ha-Mitsvot*, negative commandment 64.

[11] Deuteronomy 8:2: '[to] *test* you by hardships *to know* what is in your hearts'; 13:4: 'your God is *testing* you *to know* whether you really love [Him]'; and cf. Gen. 22:12: '*Now I know* that you fear God.'

The rabbis were as keenly aware of this difficulty as they were aware of the basic meaning of *nissa*, but they found ways to deal with the dilemma. Their solutions will not be discussed here in detail, but in general they are based on associating *nissa* with the word *nes*, 'banner' or 'miracle'.[12] The implication is that when God tries someone, he gives the one that is tried an occasion to distinguish himself from his fellow men: he stands out like a banner. The best-known instance of this is the beginning of Bereshit Rabba, chapter 55, where God's test of Abraham is associated with Psalms 60:6: '*Nes le-hitnoses*: "You gave those that fear you a banner to fly because of the truth forever." Trial after trial, elevation after elevation, in order to try them in the world, in order to elevate them as a sail on a ship.' The expression 'as a sail [or flag] on a ship'[13] became almost proverbial in this context.

In the eyes of the rabbis the connection between *nissa* and *nes* in the sense of 'miracle' is strengthened by the fact that, as we saw above, the noun *massot* is used for God's miraculous acts, e.g. in Deuteronomy 4:34, where Targum Onkelos resolutely renders both key words of this verse (*nissa* and *massot*) with the Aramaic equivalent of *nes*, again confirming the connection that was felt between *nissa* and *nes*.

Apart from this, we also come across an association with the verb *naśa*, 'to elevate, lift up'. Being tried by God means being elevated and being shown to others as an example.[14]

Thus, as regards the meaning of the verb *nissa*, the Rabbis left their medieval successors two different and contrasting messages: *Nissa* is synonymous with *baḥan*, but it has to be understood as derived from *nes*.

MEDIEVAL LEXICOGRAPHY

In the Middle Ages new ways to determine the meaning of biblical words and phrases developed. The works of Saadya Gaon and David

12 In the Bible, as well as in rabbinic literature, *nes* can be applied to several kinds of prominent and conspicuous objects: a banner, a flag, a mast (of a ship), a sail; cf. Bava Batra 5:1: 'If a man sold a ship, he has also sold the mast (*toren*), the sail (*nes*), the anchor, and all means for steering it.' Its metophorical meaning 'miracle' is rabbinic.

13 *Ke-nes shel sefina*; also e.g. in Bereshit Rabba 55:6. Cf. e.g. Licht, *Testing in Hebrew Scriptures*, para. 81/pp. 83–4.

14 The equation *nassot* = *gaddel* appears without any comment in Mekhilta de R. Yishmael, Yitro 9 (on Exodus 20:17/20; H. S. Horovitz and I. A. Rabin (eds.), *Mechilta d'Rabbi Ismael* (Jerusalem, 1960), 237); see also below, note 50. But Mekhilta de R. Shim'on bar Yohai (J. N. Epstein and E. Z. Melamed (eds.), *Mekhilta d'Rabbi: Sim'on b. Jochai* (Jerusalem, 1955), 155) is explicit and also adds an association with *naśa* as it is used in Kings 25:27. Note also that an identification of *nissa* with *naśa* is facilitated by the unusual spelling of *nesa* in Ps. 4:7 with samekh and he.

ben Abraham al-Fasi, a member of the Jerusalem circle of Karaite scholars, are the first representatives in this field. Their respective dictionaries, the so-called *Egron* and the *Kitāb jāmi' al-alfāẓ*,[15] are related to attempts to translate the Bible into Arabic, and both were written in that language. They are arranged alphabetically according to the first two of what their authors considered to be the base letters of the word in question. For the verb *nissa*, therefore, we have to look for an entry nun-samekh.

Surprisingly, Saadya's entry *ns* in his very concise *Egron* does not include any reference to our verb, he merely records the word *nes*, 'banner'. Neither does he list the noun *massa*. But without any doubt Saadya had a clear idea of their meaning. In his *Tafsīr nissa* is consistently rendered by forms of the Arabic verb *maḥana* (VIII) which also means 'to try, to test'.[16] Accordingly, *massa* is translated by *miḥna*, 'trial, tribulation' in Exodus 17:7 and Deuteronomy 33:8. Other cases of *massa*, however, Saadya translates by *'alam*, 'token, sign' (Deuteronomy 4:34, 7:19, 29:2), a translation which the *Egron* also offers for the word *nes*.[17] So in his eyes *massa* has two different meanings: 'trial' and 'token/banner'.

Another trace of ambivalence is apparent in Saadya's translation of *ha-nissa* in Deuteronomy 4:34 ('Or has any god tried to go . . .'), where 'tried' is rendered by 'elevated a banner' (*'aw rafa'a Allah 'alamā*). This translation is, of course, reminiscent of Hebrew *naśa*, and the use of *a'lām* for *massot* further on in the verse is completely in line with this rendering.

These data are sufficient to show that something of the ambivalence of the rabbinic ideas on *nissa* has been retained by Saadya: *nissa* means 'to try, to test', but incidentally an association with *naśa*, 'to elevate', is allowed. *Massa* means 'test', but it is simultaneously treated as a synonym of *nes*, 'banner'.

Did a philosopher like Saadya have no difficulty with the idea that 'God tries man'? Apparently he did. Abraham ibn Ezra reports in his commentary on Genesis 22:1 that 'the Gaon said that the word *nissa* means to show his [Abraham's] righteousness to mankind', adding that 'Now I know' (v. 12) is accordingly modified by Saadya into 'Now I have

[15] N. Allony (ed.), *Ha-'Egron. Kitāb 'uṣūl al-Shi'r al-'Ibrānī by Rav Se'adya Ga'on* (Jerusalem, 1969); S. L. Skoss (ed.), *The Hebrew–Arabic Dictionary of the Bible known as Kitāb Jāmi' al-Alfāẓ (Agrōn) of David ben Abraham al-Fāsī the Karaite (Tenth Cent.)*. 2 vols, (New Haven, 1936–45).

[16] E.g. in Gen. 22:1, Exod. 16:4, 17:7, 20:17/20, Deut. 8:2, 13:4, 33:8, all cases of God trying man.

[17] Allony (ed.), *Ha-'Egron*, 336. The *Tafsīr* also translates *'alam* for *nes* in Ex. 17:15 and Num. 21:8, 9, 26:10, as well as in most other places; cf. Allony (ed.), *Ha-'Egron, ad loc.*

made known'.[18] Something similar is also the case in Deuteronomy 8:2 and 13:4, where *nissa* is followed by *la-da'at* in the biblical text: to test in order to know. Saadya translates: '[to] try you in order to show to mankind'.[19]

So the conceptual difficulty involved with *nissa* when used with God as its subject has been neutralized in Saadya's translations. As the rabbis had done in their way (by association with *nes*), he also turned the trial into a proof, a demonstration. It is not God who wants to know the result of the trial, but rather men who should know it. In his commentary on Genesis 22:1 Saadya ranks this as the first and most important aspect of the trial.[20] We will see that these arguments left their trace in the history of interpretation.

Unlike Saadya, David al-Fasi provides his lexical information in a more direct way.[21] His dictionary has a composite entry nun-samekh,[22] which is mainly devoted to the noun *nes*, but also discusses the verbs *nissa* and *nus*, 'to flee'. After discussing the literal and metaphorical meanings of *nes* in the Bible ('banner' and 'token', Arabic: *band wa-'alam*), al-Fasi introduces the word *massa, massot*, which according to him has the same meaning as *nes* in its metaphorical sense, 'miracle', the *mem* merely having taken the place of the *nun*. He then proceeds to the sub-entry *ns* with the meaning 'test, trial' (*tajriba*) and lists a number of passages in which the verb *nissa* occurs,[23] all meaning test and examination (*tajriba wa-imtiḥān*).

The interesting thing for us to observe here is that al-Fasi seems to regard *massa* as a derivation or cognate of *nes*, and that he, etymologically as well as semantically, distinguishes it from *nissa*. The meaning of *nissa* is correctly identified, but no attention is given to any conceptual considerations.

A completely different picture is given in Menaḥem ben Saruq's ground-breaking *Maḥberet*, which was written around 950 CE.[24] This dictionary, written in Hebrew, is arranged alphabetically according to the roots as identified by the author. Like his predecessors, Menaḥem recognized the existence of single-letter roots, which in his alphabetical

[18] *Fa-'innī lā*[?] *'arraftu an-nās*: 'Verily, I have made known to mankind', changing a qal without object into a IInd stem with object. Note also that a causative rendering of *yada'ti* in this verse is already attested in the Midrash (e.g. Bereshit Rabba 56:6) and the Peshitta.

[19] *Maḥana* VIII followed by *ẓahara* IV. There is some slight variation and a variant reading involved; cf. J. Derenbourg (ed.), *Oeuvres complètes de Saadia ben Iosef al-Fayyoûmî*, vol. I: *Version du Pentateuque* (Paris, 1893), *ad loc.*

[20] M. Zucker (ed.), *Saadya's Commentary on Genesis* (New York, 1984), 140 (Arabic) and 399 (Hebrew trans.).

[21] On his dictionary see the introduction in Skoss (ed.), *Hebrew–Arabic Dictionary*; also Polliack, *Karaite Traditions*, 58–64.

[22] Skoss (ed.), *Hebrew–Arabic Dictionary*, vol. II, 277–80.

[23] Deuteronomy 6:16, Exod. 17:7: Israel tries God; Deut. 13:4: God tries Israel; Eccles. 7:23, Judg. 6:39; 1 Sam. 17:39, the shortened imperative *nas* in Dan. 1:12: man tries something or somebody.

[24] A. Sáenz-Badillos (ed.), *Menaḥem ben Saruq, Maḥberet. Edición crítica y introducción* (Granada, 1986).

listing directly precede the geminates.[25] It is a single-letter root samekh to which Menaḥem ascribed the verb *nissa* as well as the noun *massa*.[26] His very short entry merely contains three biblical quotations, namely Exodus 17:7: *massa u-meriva . . . 'al nassotam et-yhwh*; Psalms 95:8: *ke-yom massa ba-midbar*; Psalms 95:9: *asher nissuni avotekhem* – all instances of Israel trying God. Menaḥem refrains from giving any additional semantic information. Apparently he excluded the nun from the root because, unlike al-Fasi, he wanted to maintain the relationship between *nissa* and *massa*, which, at first sight, only have the samekh in common. His three quotations moreover strongly suggest this connection.

At this stage of Hebrew lexicography, root identification was an important issue and many of Menaḥem's decisions in this respect were disputed. These discussions offer interesting instances of the groping for a root theory in those days. In our case the relation between *nissa* and *massa* became a matter of great dispute.

It was the poet and grammarian Dunash ben Labrat who in his *Teshuvot* reacted to Menaḥem's identification of the samekh as the single common element of *massa* and *nissa*.[27] The noun *massa*, he says, cannot be adduced as proof for the fact that the nun is accidental. He sees no reason to remove the nun from the root, since the juxtaposition of *massa* and *nassotam* in Exodus 17:7 carries no linguistic weight. This is merely one of the many biblical etymologies of names that are based not on grammar but on similarity of sound. It is like the link made between *Noaḥ* and *yenaḥamenu* in Genesis 5:29, or between *Shemu'el* and *she'altiw* in 1 Samuel 1:20. According to Dunash the root of *nissa/nassotam* is nun–samekh, and *massa* is linguistically not related. His position is in fact the same as the one held by the Karaite al-Fasi.

But Menaḥem's pupils here intervened.[28] They admitted that indeed the derivations of the names of Noah and Samuel quoted by Dunash are not meant to give linguistic information and that they merely contribute to the message of the biblical story. But the relationship between *massa* and *nissa* is of a different kind and too compelling to dismiss. In Job 9:23 and Deuteronomy 7:19 *massa* is clearly not used as a name, so the parallel with Noah and Samuel is not conclusive. And since *massa* and *nissa* thus do belong together, the nun has no place in their common root.

[25] Al-Fasi, in his introduction, identifies fourteen uniliteral roots but does not include them in his dictionary. Menahem has nineteen. Cf. Skoss (ed.), *Hebrew–Arabic Dictionary*; lxviii ff.

[26] Sáenz-Badillos (ed.), *Maḥberet*, 267.

[27] A. Sáenz-Badillos (ed.), *Tešubot de Dunaš Ben Labrat. Edición crítica y traducción española* (Granada, 1980), 34* (Hebrew) and 41 (trans.).

[28] S. Benavente Robles, *Tešuḇot de los discípulos de Mĕnaḥem contra Dunaš Ben Labraṭ. Edición del texto y traducción castellana* (Granada, 1986), 44*/71.

Yehudi ben Sheshet, a pupil of Dunash, in his turn defended his master's assumption of a biliteral stem for *nissa*.[29] He considered *Massa* – which, after all, does mainly occur as a toponym – as a derivation from *nassotam* by elision of the nun, since names, he says, are subject to a special set of rules.[30] In spite of the occasional absence of a nun, *Massa* and *nissa* are related by means of the biliteral stem *ns*.

The application of the principle of the triliteral root to Hebrew by Judah Ḥayyuj exposed the essential futility of these debates. Ḥayyuj's list of weak verbs[31] includes the root nun–samekh–he.[32] He quotes four instances of its use (Genesis 221, I Samuel 17:39, Psalms 95:9, Deuteronomy 6:16) and adds the word *massa*, an indication of his conviction that the words are related. And indeed, in his introductory remarks on weak verbs beginning with a nun, he had already explicitly stated the root identity of *nissa* and *massa* which he attributed to the absorbtion of the nun into the samekh:[33] 'In *massa* (Exodus 17:7) *nun* is absorbed in *samekh* with dagesh: it is from *nissa* (Genesis 22:1), *tenassu* (Deuteronomy 6:16); *he* marks the feminine, the third radical is lost.'

The meaning of the verb is not discussed, but the grammatical argument is familiar to any modern Hebraist.

The reaction to this from Jonah (Abu 'l-Walid) ibn Janaḥ, his younger contemporary and an eager student of his works, is interesting in a number of respects.[34] In his dictionary *Kitāb al-Uṣūl*, Ibn Janaḥ has the following to say on the root nun–samekh–he:[35]

29 E. Varela Moreno (ed.), *Tešuḇot de Yehudi ben Šešet. Edición, traducción y comentario* (Granada, 1981), 19*/40.

30 Apart from elision (*migra'a*), he gives examples of addition (*tosafa*), change or mutation (? *ḥilluf*, the case of Noah), and metathesis (*tahafukha*).

31 *Kitāb (al-Af'âl Ḏawāt) Ḥuruf al-Līn* (M. Jastrow (ed.), *The Weak and Geminative Verbs in Hebrew by Abū Zakariyyā Yaḥyā ibn Dāwud of Fez, known as Ḥayyūǧ* (Leiden, 1897)); trans. into Hebrew by Moses ibn Gikatilla as *Sefer* or *Maḥberet Otiyyot ha-Noaḥ (we-ha-Meshekh)*; J. W. Nutt (ed.), *Two Treatises on Verbs Containing Feeble and Double Letters by R. Jehuda Ḥayuǧ of Fez, Translated . . . by R. Moses Ǧiḳatilia of Cordova* (London and Berlin, 1870).

32 Jastrow (ed.), *Weak and Geminative Verbs*, 191; Nutt (ed.), *Two Treatises*, 87/101.

33 Jastrow (ed.), *Weak and Geminative Verbs*, 145–6; Nutt (ed.), *Two Treatises*, 66/77.

34 There is no complete certainty about the relation between Ḥayyuj and Ibn Janaḥ. In spite of the overall dependence of the latter's books on the work of Ḥayyuj they seem never to have met. See e.g. W. Bacher, *Leben und Werke des Abulwalīd Merwān ibn Ǧanāh (Rabbi Jona) und die Quellen seiner Schrifterklärung* (Budapest, 1885; repr. in *Vier Abhandlungen über Abulwalīd ibn Ǧanāh ca. 990–1050* (Amsterdam, 1970)), 10 (and 4, 105); J. Derenbourg (ed.), *Le livre des parterres fleuris* (see below), iv). Ibn Janaḥ wrote a 'Supplement' to Ḥayyuj's books on the weak and and geminate roots (*Kitāb al-Mustalḥiq*; J. and H. Derenbourg (eds.), 'Kitab al-Moustalḥiḳ', in *Opuscules et traités d'Abou 'l-Walid Merwan Ibn Djanaḥ de Cordoue* (Paris, 1880), 1–246), which contains nothing on our verb. Ibn Janaḥ's *magnum opus* is his *Kitāb al-Tanqiḥ*, which is divided into two parts: (a) a grammar: *Kitāb al-Luma'* (ed. J. Derenbourg as *Le livre des parterres fleuris* (Paris, 1886)); trans. into Hebrew by Judah ibn Tibbon (H. Wilensky (ed.), *Sefer ha-riqma* (Berlin, 1928–30)), which contains nothing on our verb; and (b) a dictionary, *Kitāb al-Uṣūl*, translated into Hebrew by Judah Ibn Tibbon (*Sefer ha-Shorashim*) – see the next note.

35 A. Neubauer (ed.), *The Book of Hebrew Roots by Abu 'l-Walīd Marwān ibn Janāḥ* (Oxford, 1875), 438–9; W. Bacher (ed.), *Sepher Haschoraschim. Wurzelwörterbuch der hebräischen Sprache von Abulwalīd*

This root was already identified in the 'Book of the Letters of Weakness'[36] and its meaning is 'test' (Arabic: *iktibār wa-tajriba wa-miḥna*; Hebrew: *beḥina*). The noun *massa* is derived from it. The verb has a somewhat different meaning in the story of David (1 Samuel 17:39, and in Deuteronomy 4:34, 28:56, Ecclesiastes 2:1 as well); there it is used in the sense of 'to be used to' because meanings like test or trial give no sense there.[37] Abu Zakkariyya (Hebrew: *Rabbi Yehuda*) [which is Judah Ḥayyuj], did not make this distinction. But there is still a third meaning (*ma'anī tālāt/'inyan shelishi*) in *nissa* which is represented by its derivation *massa*, and that is the meaning 'miracle' (as in Deuteronomy 7:19 and 4:34), which makes the word synonymous with *nes, nissim*. This meaning is similar to what our rabbis said in the Prayer: 'As You performed a miracle (*nes*) for them, so perform miracles for us'.[38] But it is true that the words *massot* and *nissim* are apparently not derived from the same root: *Massot* is from a root with a weak third radical, and *nissim* is from a geminate root *nss*.[39]

But Ibn Janaḥ does not leave it at that. There is something which urges him still to pursue the option of a derivation of *massot* from the geminate root *nss* and thus to prove a relationship with *nes*. In fact, he says, there is a nun to be assumed in *massot*; but here this nun is not assimilated into the samekh, it is elided. This allows us to regard the stem *nss* as the root of both *massot* and *nissim*. But the process Ibn Janaḥ here proposes is very implausible. It goes on the assumption of an original form **menassot*, parallel to *meshammot* (seven times in the Bible) from the root *shmm*. An elision of the nun has to be assumed, and such elisions do occur in biblical Hebrew.[40]

It is not quite easy for us to justify Ibn Janaḥ's procedure within the parameters of the grammatical rules that he himself so ardently advocated, but it is very interesting to observe his almost desperate attempt to connect our verb *nissa* with the noun *nes*, a link so very prominent in rabbinic literature. So, unlike his predecessors, Ibn Janaḥ not only added a discussion on meaning, he also tried to pay regard to a fact of rabbinic

Merwān Ibn Ǧanāḥ (R Jona) (Berlin, 1896; repr. Jerusalem, 1966), 307. Our quotation is a paraphrase.

[36] I.e. Ḥayyuj's list of weak verbs just mentioned. The Arabic text quotes the short form of the correct title (*Kitāb Ḥuruf al-Līn*); Ibn Tibbon's Hebrew, however, has *Sefer Otot ha-Rippayon* instead of one of the usual Hebrew names of the book (see note 34).

[37] Arabic *id lam ya'tad*; Hebrew *lo hirgalti*. The Rouen MS of the Arabic text adds here to the explanation of *nissiti* in 1 Sam. 17:39: 'It is not right to say here: Since he did not try (*yujarrib*) and did not test (*yaktabir*) and did not examine (*yamtaḥin*), but rather: Since he was not used (*ya'tad*).'

[38] A conclusion of the *'Al ha-Nissim* prayer as found in ancient oriental versions; cf. I. Beer, *Seder 'Avodat Yisra'el* (Rödelheim, 1868), 101–02.

[39] This, of course, was also Ḥayyuj's derivation of *nes* (Jastrow (ed.), *Weak and Geminative Verbs*, 253; Nutt (ed.), *Two Treatises*, 113/131).

[40] Namely the elision of an alef in *wa-tazreni* (2 Sam. 22:40). Cf. also Bacher's account of this operation in *Die Hebräisch–Neuhebräische Sprachvergleichung des Abulwalīd Merwān ibn Ǧanāḥ (Rabbi Jona)* (Vienna, 1885; also repr. in *Vier Abhandlungen*), 21.

'linguistics'. As for the meaning of our verb, we saw that Ibn Janaḥ discerned three different aspects for *nissa*: 'to try', 'to be used to', and a third meaning, somehow related to 'miracle'.

Chronologically as well as with regard to content, our next lexicographer is Solomon Parḥon. Although his lexicon *Maḥberet he-'Arukh*, written in Salerno in 1161, is for the greater part a Hebrew rendering of Ibn Janaḥ's *Kitāb al-Uṣūl*, he introduced some significant new features.[41] The strictly lexical part of his lemma nun–samekh–he[42] is a short recapitulation of Ibn Janaḥ's position: The basic meaning of *nissa* is 'to try/test'; it has a special meaning in the story of David (and in Deuteronomy 4:34, 28:56, Ecclesiastes 2:1), which is 'to be used to' (*leshon nihug u-minhag*). In addition, the word *massot* in Deuteronomy 7:17 has the meaning 'miracles' (*otot*). This lexical information, however, is preceded by a lengthy discussion on the difficulties of understanding certain biblical expressions, such as the use of the verb *nissa* in the sense that God tries man.

The point of departure is the statement that 'God tried Abraham' (Genesis 22:1). This should be understood as 'human language' (*dibra Tora ki-lshon bene adam*). It is, like so many other biblical expressions, an instance of anthropomorphic speaking. God knows without a trial, but human understanding is limited and needs to be backed by tests and examinations. So the meaning of *nissa* is indeed 'to try', but in the case of God it is used in a figurative sense, which indicates that something different, something deeper has to be understood. Parḥon goes on to explain the purpose of the Aqeda in this sense, and then enlarges upon the nature of other biblical expressions, notably those related to God's attributes and actions, which have to be understood as adaptations to the limitations of the human mind. This digression on the anthropomorphic character of biblical language is not very well structured and is rather difficult to follow,[43] but the important thing for us to note here is that the old problems regarding the use of the verb *nissa* are solved in a new way, the way of philosophy and philosophical exegesis, a way that in the same span of time was to be so impressively paved by Moses Maimonides.

[41] S. G. Stern (ed.), *Maḥberet he-'arukh. Salomonis ben Abrahami Parchon Aragonensis lexicon hebraicum* (Pressburg, 1844; repr. Jerusalem, 1970). See also W. Bacher, 'Solomon Parchon's hebräisches Wörterbuch', *ZAW* 10 (1890): 120–56; 11 (1891): 35–99.

[42] Stern (ed.), *Maḥberet he-'arukh*, f. 41a–b.

[43] The editor, Solomon Stern, confesses in a note that he could hardly restrain himself from dropping this rambling piece of text. Bacher ('Hebräisches Wörterbuch', 141, note 2) mentions five other 'theologische Exkurse' in Parḥon's lexicon and discusses our passage succinctly on pp. 60–1. He does not indicate sources or dependence on others. Parḥon's view on the Aqeda contains various traditional notions without much coherence.

It is fitting to insert here a short recapitulation of Maimonides' view on the concept of trial, as he expressed it in the *Guide of the Perplexed*.[44]

When delineating his position on the biblical idea that God sometimes may put his chosen ones to the test, Maimonides starts from two presuppositions. The first is that when the Bible mentions trials on the part of God these trials cannot be meant to increase God's knowledge of his creatures, but they should rather be seen as a means to increase our knowledge of God. The second is that Maimonides refuses to ascribe any intrinsic value to the suffering implied in a trial. Suffering is punishment. A trial can, therefore, not be meant as a means to increase the sufferer's reward, either here nor in the world to come.

As a result of these principles, Maimonides maintains that when God tries his people he gives them a chance to stand out as an example of pure belief and true fear of God. We have seen that this notion was already prominent in rabbinic literature. The superficial meaning of the verb *nissa* should, after a careful reading and comparison of the various biblical verses, be modified to something like 'to demonstrate'. We are reminded here of the position of Saadya. And indeed Maimonides subtly changed the drift of the various verses which speak of 'to test in order to know' into 'to test in order to make known';[45] He thus shifted the emphasis of the trial from its subject (God) to its object (the people).

Solomon Parḥon's example in inserting a theological reflection into his lexicon was, to some extent, followed by the prince of medieval Hebrew lexicographers, David Kimḥi. As might be expected, his entry *nissa* is mainly lexical in character, but he added a philosophical observation as well. The lexical part is interesting. Kimḥi resolutely rejects Ibn Janaḥ's division into three different meanings for *nissa* and returns to the position of Judah Ḥayyuj, who indicated no subdivisions.[46] The meaning of *nissa* in all its manifestations, including the noun *massa*, is 'to test' (*kullam ʿinyan beḥina*). Even in the case of David and Saul's armour the meaning is: I have never *tried* to walk in these things before, therefore I do not know how to do it. Also in a case like Deuteronomy 7:19 the

[44] Vol. III, 24. A. van der Heide, 'Maimonides and Nahmanides on the concept of Trial (*Nissayon*)', in *Sobre la vida y obra de Maimonides*, ed. J. Peláez del Rosal (Córdoba [1991]), 305–14, esp. 307–9, and, with a different approach, J. A. Diamond, '"Trial" as esoteric preface in Maimonides' *Guide of the Perplexed*', *Journal of Jewish Thought and Philosophy* 7 (1997): 1–30.

[45] See above notes 11 and 18.

[46] J. H. R. Biesenthal and F. Lebrecht (eds.), *Rabbi Davidis Kimchi Radicum Liber, sive Hebraeum Bibliorum Lexicon* (Berlin, 1847; repr. Jerusalem, 1967), col. 439: '*Ḥalaq R. Yona ha-shoresh ha-ze li-shelosha ʿinyanim, we-enam ki im ʿinyan eḥad ka-asher ketavam R. Yehuda.*' It is an argument *ex silentio* for, as far as we can see, Ḥayyuj did not discuss meaning at all. Ibn Janaḥ, however, explicitly mentioned that Ḥayyuj did not distinguish between the meanings 'to test' and 'to be used to'.

meaning of *ha-massot ha-gedolot* is 'tests' and not 'miracles': great tests with which the Holy One tested the Israelites with his plagues to see whether they would persist in their wickedness or not.

The theological difficulties of this linguistic opinion are obvious, and it appears that Kimḥi recognized this fact. For the difficult verse '[Moses answered the people: Be not afraid;] for God has come in order to test/try you' (Exodus 20:17/20), Kimḥi quotes Maimonides' opinion in the *Guide of the Perplexed*[47] (III,24) where, as we saw, a whole series of cases of *nissa* is discussed. He does so in words that very much resemble Ibn Tibbon's Hebrew translation:

> The great sage and divine philosopher rabbi Moses ben Maimon explained here: Be not afraid of this great vision [of the revelation at Sinai] which you saw. For this was only in order that the truth may reach you, namely by being an eye-witness, so that, whenever God tests you by a false prophet who says the opposite of what you have just heard, you should remain firm in your belief and your steps will not stumble. For if you had not heard him in this great vision, it would be possible that you would listen to him [the false prophet] when he claimed to be a true prophet.[48]

What is the implication of this passage? The trial alluded to here consists of the fact that the people of Israel had to witness and endure the great signs and portents at Sinai. It was not God's intention to use these awesome phenomena as a test for his own benefit; they occurred for the benefit of Israel. They so firmly impressed God's true and reliable revelation on their minds that they would be able to recognize any rival claims of other prophets as false ones. It is interesting to see that Kimḥi felt obliged to insert this theological consideration into his lexical entry on *nissa* – albeit by way of a mere quotation.[49]

But in addition to this, Kimḥi also offers us a reference to the Midrash. In paraphrase he quotes a passage which connects the verb *nassot* with the noun *nes*: 'And in the Midrash (*Yalqut be-shem Mekhilta, remez 301*) *nissa* is explained as an expression of elevation, as from *nes*, meaning: God came to you in order to make you great and to elevate you.'[50] It is a

47 Vol. III, 24.

48 See Y. Ibn Shmuel (ed.), *Doctor Perplexorum (Guide of the Perplexed) by Rabbi Moses ben Maimon (Rambam)* (Jerusalem, 1946; rev. edn. 1981), 457–8. The same passage, including the reference to the Midrash (see below), is also included in Kimḥi's commentary on Exod. 20:17/20. There can be no complete certainty whether it was Kimḥi himself who composed the entry in this shape; our passage could be an interpolation.

49 In his commentaries Kimḥi is prepared to treat the subject in more detail, e.g. on Gen. 22:1.

50 A. Hyman and Y. Shiloni (ed.), *Yalqut Shim'oni 'al ha-Tora le-Rabbenu Shim'on ha-Darshan. Sefer Shemot*, 2 vols. (Jerusalem, 1977–80), 473 (on Exod. 20:17/20); this passage corresponds with the very succinct Mekhilta de-R. Yishmael, Yitro 9 (ed. Horowitz and Rabin, 237); see note 14 above. Rashi, *ad loc.*, adopted and expanded the same idea.

remarkable fact that the great grammarian and lexicographer, whose work is usually regarded as the crowning achievement of a long line of medieval linguistic scholarship, did not restrict his treatment of a difficult verb to lexical information alone, but included allusions to ancient rabbinic and contemporary philosophical solutions.[51]

As a contrast to the collective contribution of medieval lexicography, I shall briefly mention a rather bold solution of the intrinsic difficulty of the biblical use of the verb *nissa* which originated in the mind of an independent biblical exegete.

Rabbi Samuel ben Meir (Rashbam), a grandson of Rashi who was active around 1100, a vigorous advocate of the literal meaning in biblical exegesis but ignorant of lexicographical progress after Menaḥem and Dunash, chose an entirely different approach to deal with the problem of the meaning of *nissa*. His solution for the opening of the story of Abraham's trial is fresh and novel. I quote in paraphrase: '"And afterwards God tried Abraham" (Genesis 22:1): God's anger was kindled over Abraham because he had made a covenant with Abimelech . . . Therefore God rebuked and vexed Abraham (*qintero we–ṣi'aro*) . . . saying: You have become proud of the son whom I gave you and made a covenant between you and his sons.' Samuel ben Meir then makes a connection with the exile of the ark among the descendants of the Philistine Abimelech in the days of Samuel, and concludes with the observation that *nissa* in French means '*contraria*' – 'to thwart, to cross someone'.[52] Abraham made a grave mistake by seeking contact with the arch-enemy of his descendants, the Philistines, and now has to answer for his deeds. Later in his commentary Samuel ben Meir retains this meaning for *nissa*. In the cases of Exodus 20:17/20 and 15:25 the verb is paraphrased by *le-hokhiaḥ* – 'to rebuke', and in Exodus 16:4 the reference to Deuteronomy 8:3 shows that for Samuel ben Meir the par-

[51] I know of no other medieval lexical works which could with profit be included in our survey. Nathan ben Yeḥiel's *Sefer he-'Arukh* (Rome, early twelfth century; see A. Kohut (ed.), *Aruch Completum* (Vienna and New York, 1878–92)) is a dictionary of rabbinic literature. It does not show any awareness of the conceptual difficulties inherent in the biblical use of our verb, and *nissa* (and its later derivation *nissayon*) are not linked with *nes*. A dictionary of biblical synomyms like Abraham Bedershi's *Ḥotam Tokhnit* (thirteenth century; see G. I. Polak (ed.), *Chotam Tochnit (Hebraeische Synonymik) von Abraham Bedarschi* (Amsterdam, 1865)) merely treats *nissa* as a synomym of *bahan*. Interestingly, the entry *nissa* in the late fourteenth-century Hebrew–Italian–Arabic dictionary *Maqre Dardeqe* (printed 1488, possibly in Naples; see A. Schippers, 'A Comment on the Arabic Words in the *Maqre Dardeqe*', in *'Ever and 'Arav. Contacts between Arabic Literature and Jewish Literature in the Middle Ages and Modern Times*, ed. Y. Tobi (Tel Aviv, 1998; English section xxvii–xlvi)), still presents the traditional combination of the meanings 'to test' and 'to elevate' (Italian *atentao* and *inalzare*; Arabic *jaraba* and *rafa'a*).

[52] D. Rosin (ed.), *Der Pentateuch-Commentar des R. Samuel ben Meïr.* (Breslau, 1881), *ad loc.*: 'war entgegen'. See also D. Rosin, *R Samuel b. Meïr als Schrifterklärer* (Breslau, 1880), 92.

allelism between *nassot*, *'annot* ('to oppress') and *hir'iv* ('to make hungry') is very significant.[53]

It is clear that Samuel ben Meir was aware of the theological difficulty inherent in the verb *nissa*. He solved it by proposing a new, additional shade of meaning which is theologically acceptable. For him the meaning of *nissa* when it describes an act of God, is simply: 'to punish'. Very few exegetes, however, were prepared to accept this novelty.[54]

[53] Cf. also the preceding v. 2; Rosin (*Schrifterklärer*, 109) classified this case as the first of a series of the Rashbam's 'ansprechenden, aber unhaltbaren Erklärungen'.

[54] Few traces of it are found in the exegetical literature of the school of Rashi. Joseph Bechor Shor, for instance, took over the link with Abimelech's covenant, but remained silent on the meaning of *nissa* (Y. Nevo (ed.), *Perushe Rabbi Yosef Bekhor Shor 'al ha-Tora* (Jerusalem, 1994), 38). Later exegetical collections occasionally make mention of Rashbam's idea; cf. J. Gellis, *Tosafot ha-Shalem*, vol. II (Jerusalem, 1983), 203.

CHAPTER SEVEN

The knowledge and practice of Hebrew grammar among Christian scholars in pre-expulsion England: The evidence of 'bilingual' Hebrew–Latin manuscripts

Judith Olszowy-Schlanger

In a pioneering study on bilingual Hebrew–Latin Bible codices from medieval England, Raphael Loewe highlighted a marked discrepancy between, on the one hand, the interest displayed by Christian scholars in the Hebrew Bible and its Jewish exegesis and, on the other hand, their lack of concern with methodical or structured descriptions of the Hebrew language itself.[1] Indeed, it seems that no comprehensive treatise or textbook of Hebrew grammar was produced during the twelfth and the thirteenth centuries, a period of intensive Christian study of Hebrew sources. While they encountered a wide range of Hebrew texts, Christian scholars of the period do not seem to have displayed much interest in their purely linguistic or grammatical dimensions. The fact that a complex theory of Hebrew grammar was not developed by Christian scholars is understandable, given that Latin grammar itself was struggling at that time to acquire its status as a *scientia*.[2] What is far more surprising, however, is that there existed virtually no pedagogical aids or manuals to assist to access the original texts.

So far as the twelfth century is concerned, this indifference to the study of the Hebrew language could be related to the well-known fact that Christian scholars of the time approached the Hebrew sources through competent Jewish teachers, with whom they interacted in the vernacular French. With notable exceptions, such as Herbert of Bosham (d. after 1190) who could study Rashi commentaries by himself,[3] Christian scholars throughout the twelfth century had to call upon Jewish scholars or converts in their study of the Hebrew Bible and rabbinic literature.[4] Thus, many twelfth-century scholars whom we

[1] R. Loewe, 'The Mediaeval Christian Hebraists of England. The *Superscriptio Lincolniensis*', *HUCA* 28 (1957): 209.
[2] Cf. I. Rosier, *La grammaire spéculative des Modistes* (Lille, 1983), 9–10 and 38–40.
[3] Cf. R. Loewe, in *EJ* 8, col. 13, and his 'Herbert of Bosham's Commentary on Jerome's Hebrew Psalter', *Biblica* 34 (1953): 45.
[4] Cf. G. Dahan, *Les intellectuels chrétiens et les juifs au moyen âge* (Paris, 1990), 249.

nowadays call 'Hebraists' did not in fact master the Hebrew language well enough to gain direct access to Jewish books and scholarship.[5]

By the thirteenth century, however, knowledge of Hebrew among Christians appears to have become more widespread. Although Roger Bacon (*c.* 1214–1292) complained that fewer than four of his contemporaries actually knew Hebrew grammar well enough to be able to teach it,[6] a number of thirteenth-century sources such as *correctoria*, commentaries and translations all indicate that their authors had a very good knowledge of the language. While this knowledge could still have been acquired through Jewish tutors, it would seem that Christian scholars were by that time already able to learn Hebrew by their own means, as it were. Given the high level of linguistic proficiency displayed in some thirteenth-century sources, the virtual absence of grammatical textbooks with which to acquire basic Hebrew skills becomes all the more intriguing. In the light of this discrepancy, my purpose in this chapter is to try and find out how medieval Christian scholars actually gained their knowledge of Hebrew.

As just stated, no proper manuals of Hebrew grammar from the thirteenth century are known to us. The teaching aids that do exist consist for the most part of booklets and notes derived from the patristic tradi-

5 For example, Stephen Harding (c. 1060–1134), while stressing that knowledge of Hebrew and Aramaic is essential to establish the correct text of the Vulgate, derived his own references to the Hebrew text from the explanations he received from his Jewish tutors. Cf. C. Singer, 'Hebrew Scholarship in the Middle Ages among Latin Christians', in *The Legacy of Israel*, ed. E. R. Bevan and C. Singer, 292–3 (Oxford, 1927); S. Berger, *Quam notitiam linguae hebraicae habuerint Christiani medii aevi temporibus in Gallia* (Nancy, 1893), 9–10; R. Loewe, 'The Mediaeval Christian Hebraists of England. Herbert of Bosham and Earlier Scholars', *TJHSE* 17 (1953): 233; G. Dahan, 'Juifs et Chrétiens en Occident médiéval. La rencontre autour de la Bible', *Revue de Synthèse* 110 (1989): 9.

Andrew of St Victor (1110–75), for his part, was probably the first scholar to make extensive use of rabbinic works in his commentaries (to the point of being accused of 'judaizing'). It is probable that he knew only the rudiments of the Hebrew alphabet and grammar. Despite Roger Bacon's praise of Andrew's learning and encouragements to consult the Hebrew text whenever the translation of the Bible seems problematic, his commentaries do not contain Hebrew characters or direct quotations. On Andrew of St Victor, see R. Bacon, *Compendium Studii Philosophiae*, ed. J. S. Brewer, *Fr. Rogeri Bacon Opera quaedam hactenus inedita* (London, 1859), vol. VIII, 480–3; B. Smalley, 'Andrew of St Victor, Abbot of Wigmore: A Twelfth Century Hebraist', *Recherches de Théologie Ancienne et Médiévale* 10 (1938): 358–73; B. Smalley, *The Study of the Bible in the Middle Ages*, 2nd edn (Notre Dame, IN, 1970), 154–72.

Robert Grosseteste (*c.* 1175–1253), bishop of Lincoln, may have possessed at least one Hebrew Psalter and initiated a new literal Latin translation, but according to his admirer Roger Bacon, his knowledge of Hebrew was not sufficient to translate without the aid of proficient linguists: *Compendium Studii*, 472; cf. also D. Wasserstein, 'Grosseteste, the Jews and Mediaeval Christian Hebraists', in *Robert Grosseteste: New Perspectives on his Thought and Scholarship*, ed. J. McEvoy (Turnhout, 1995; Instrumenta Patristica 27), 361.

6 *Opus Tertium*, in *Compendium Studii*, p. 33–4.

tion, such as *Interpretationes nominum hebraicorum* (a genre of etymological lexica of transcribed Hebrew names based on St Jerome), lists of divine names, or numerous Hebrew alphabets followed by the names of the letters and their exposition.[7] These prolific literary genres amply testify to the fascination exercised by Hebrew. However, the linguistic skills they attest to are if anything very basic, comprising little more than understanding the Hebrew references in the works of the Church Fathers – in other words, the very first stage of Hebrew proficiency as defined by Roger Bacon.

In addition to these genres there existed some more specific works on Hebrew. Such was perhaps the case with a text which is unfortunately known to us only by its ambitious title, *Ars loquendi et intelligendi in lingua hebraica*, mentioned in the thirteenth-century catalogue of the Benedictine library at Ramsey.[8] A few short treatises on Hebrew pronunciation and transliteration, chief among them the preface to *De Interpretationibus nominum sacrae scripturae* in MS Paris BN lat. 36, also show genuine interest in the Hebrew language and its grammar.[9]

The most important attempt to create a Hebrew teaching aid is undoubtedly the Hebrew grammar in Cambridge MS UL Ff. 6. 13. Although the authorship of this grammar is not stated, it has been attributed to Roger Bacon on the basis of his references to a project of writing a Hebrew grammar, and because various grammatical remarks in his other works were couched in almost identical terms.[10] It consists of several folios of unstructured grammatical notes, most of which deal with the Hebrew alphabet, vowels and pronunciation. Bacon begins by providing a list of transcribed Hebrew consonants together with their names and their phonetical value. He singles out the consonants that have a double pronunciation (tav, kaf and pe), and those that have different initial and final shapes (kaf, mem, nun, pe and tzade). He then proceeds to list the vowel points, and provides them with a lengthy and rather idiosyncratic explanation (see below). After this relatively detailed account of pronunciation and transcription, Bacon moves on to a few succinct grammatical comments. Morphology is discussed in short

[7] See M. Thiel, *Grundlagen und Gestalt der Hebräischkenntnisse des Frühen Mittelalters* (Spoleto, 1973); J. Bonnard reviewed by A. Darmesteter, 'Un alphabet hébreu-anglais au XIVe siècle', *REJ* 3–4 (1881–2): 255–68.

[8] R. Loewe, 'Hebrew Books and "Judaica" in Mediaeval Oxford and Cambridge', in *Remember the Days, Essays on Anglo-Jewish History Presented to Cecil Roth*, ed. J. M. Shaftesley (London, 1966), 30.

[9] Berger, *Quam notitiam*, 21–5.

[10] Ed. S. A. Hirsch, in E. Nolan, *The Greek Grammar of Roger Bacon and a Fragment of his Hebrew Grammar* (Cambridge, 1902).

paragraphs dealing with the definite article and the 'Hebrew declension' modelled on the Latin case system (see below), with the formation of masculine and feminine plural, and with the mention of possessive and object suffixes as a 'single letter or two letters added at the end of the word'.[11] Syntax for its part is covered in a few sentences bearing on the relative pronoun, which can be expressed either by the definite article or by אשר (transcribed as *esser*).[12]

As can be seen then, Bacon's treatment of Hebrew grammar is overall extremely brief. This is generally attributed to the fragmentary preservation of the work. However, the way in which the grammar is arranged seems to indicate that there was not much more to follow. Even in this short fragment, grammatical rules receive far less attention than the discussion of the alphabet and its transcription, which even includes such details as the dagesh (referred to as *punctum infra*) and rafe (as *tractus gracilis super deleth*).[13] Moreover, the paragraphs containing grammatical remarks are inserted between two longer expositions of the alphabet and pronunciation. This makes it difficult to argue that a more developed grammatical discussion actually existed in the original manuscript and was not preserved. Even more importantly, there is evidence to suggest that Roger Bacon intended his Hebrew grammar to be easy and uncomplicated. He went so far as to state at the end of his concise grammatical remarks that 'the Hebrews have only a basic grammar and few rules'. Whether this oversimplification is due to a lack of more thorough knowledge of Hebrew by Roger Bacon, or whether it is a deliberate effort to 'teach basic Hebrew in three days' as he proposed to do in his *Opus Tertium*,[14] the use of such a tool cannot explain the much deeper knowledge of the Hebrew language attested in commentaries, *correctoria* and translations of the period.

This raises the possibility that Christian scholars in twelfth- and thirteenth-century England had access to Jewish books on Hebrew grammar. Roger Bacon, for example, complained bitterly that the lack of Hebrew books, including the Hebrew Bible and dictionary, hindered

[11] Hirsch in Nolan, *The Greek Grammar*, 204–5.
[12] Hirsch in Nolan, *The Greek Grammar*, 207–8.
[13] Hirsch in Nolan, *The Greek Grammar*, 207.
[14] *Sed certum est mihi quod infra tres dies ego quemcumque diligentem et confidentem docerem Hebraeum, ut sciret legere et intelligere quicquid sancti dicunt, et sapientes antiquii . . .*, *Opus Tertium*, in *Compendium Studii*, vol. XX, 65. According to Roger Bacon, there are three degrees of Hebrew knowledge: to use it as a mother tongue (*sicut maternam in qua natus est*), to be able to translate from Hebrew (*ut quilibet fiat interpres et transferre possit in linguam maternam Latinam scientiam de linguis illis*) and finally, to be able to understand references to Hebrew in what he calls 'Latinitas', that is the works and commentaries of the Church Fathers. It is this third and least degree of knowledge that can be learned in three days. Cf. *Compendium Studii*, vol. VI, 433.

his efforts and those of an unnamed colleague to correct the Vulgate, but he recognized that such works abounded among the Jews, and were even found among Christians in England and France.[15] However, references to such books in medieval Christian sources are very scarce indeed. Herbert of Bosham referred in his commentary on Jerome's *iuxta hebraeos* to two Spanish Jewish grammarians of the tenth century, Menahem ben Saruq (whose work *Mahberet* he called *mahberez*) and his opponent Dunash ben Labrat (called *Dones filius Leward*).[16] These grammarians were widely used by Jewish scholars at the time, and it is well known that both *Mahberet* of Menahem ben Saruq and *Teshuvot* of Dunash ben Labrat were Rashi's main source of grammatical information.[17] In addition, medieval England was the home of a well-developed tradition of Hebrew grammar (see below). Moreover, the contents of some grammatical notes (to be studied below) point to contact with the native Hebrew grammatical tradition, either through books or Jewish teachers. No Hebrew grammatical manuscripts which might have been used by medieval Christian scholars in pre-expulsion England have been identified so far.[18] All the more interest attaches to some twenty-five 'bilingual' Hebrew–Latin manuscripts of the Hebrew Bible written or used in pre-expulsion England and preserved in various English and European collections, and which were obviously the primary tool for the study of its language.

THE 'BILINGUAL' MANUSCRIPTS

These 'bilingual' manuscripts constitute together a unique body of evidence for assessing both the knowledge of Hebrew in medieval England

[15] Quoted by Nolan, *The Greek Grammar*, lviii: *Nam iamdiu est fecisset certam probationem si Bibliam Graecam et Hebraeam habuisset, et librum ethimologicarum in illis linguis quae abundant apud eos, sicut Isidorus et Papias apud nos, et sunt etiam in Anglia et in Francia, et in multis locis inter Christianos.*

[16] Cf. Loewe, 'Mediaeval Christian Hebraists', 243.

[17] Cf. W. J. van Bekkum, 'The Hebrew Grammatical Tradition in the Exegesis of Rashi', in G. Sed-Rajna (ed.), *Rashi 1040–1990: Hommage à Ephraïm E. Urbach* (Paris, 1993), 427–35.

[18] The case could however be argued for MS Bodl. Or. 135, a thirteenth-century codex containing, among other works, a Hebrew grammar by Ibn Parhon. This codex belonged to bishop of Exeter R. Grandison (1327–69). Cf. N. R. Ker, *Medieval Libraries of Great Britain. A List of Surviving Books* (London, 1941), 46. As for the codex of David Kimhi's *Sepher ha-Shorashim* annotated in Latin in St John's College, Cambridge (MS I 10, Cat. 218), tentatively included by C. Roth among Jewish books in pre-expulsion England, it is in fact a Sefardi manuscript, with annotations by a sixteenth-century hand. This manuscript belonged to the celebrated founder of Hebrew studies in Renaissance England, Robert Wakefield. Cf. C. Roth, *The Intellectual Activities of Medieval English Jewry* (London, 1949), 11; M. Beit-Arié, *The Makings of the Medieval Hebrew Book. Studies in Palaeography and Codicology* (Jerusalem, 1993), 129.

and the ways by which it was acquired. The whole topic of these manuscripts has been discussed by B. Smalley, R. Loewe, M. Beit-Arié and C. Sirat, whose studies will be referred to below. It should be noted outright that the notion of 'bilingual' is used here as a term of convenience to designate a range of different books, which can be divided in three groups according to the nature of their Latin component.

1. Bible manuscripts in which the Hebrew text and its corresponding Latin translations (one or two of the official translations: Vulgate, Gallicana, Psalter *iuxta hebraeos*) are written in parallel columns. The large majority of these manuscripts also contain an interlinear Latin translation (known as *superscriptio*, see below).
2. Bible manuscripts and one codex of Rashi's commentary on the Prophets and on the Hagiographa (MS Corpus Christi College, Oxford (MS CCC) 6) in which the main Hebrew text is provided with *superscriptio* and occasional glosses.
3. Hebrew Bible manuscripts which do not contain any specific Latin translation, but whose role in Hebrew learning by Christians is attested through various marginal annotations, glosses, Latin titles, exercises in Hebrew alphabet and vocabulary, etc.

Scribes and codicology

The actual date and place where these 'bilingual' manuscripts were written is difficult to ascertain. The manuscripts themselves do not contain any explicit indication concerning their origin. However, it has been convincingly argued on the basis of their Latin palaeography that some of these books were written in England during the twelfth and thirteenth centuries, and that others were at least read and annotated at that time.[19] A subject of particular interest raised by these 'bilingual' manuscripts is that of their scribes, and in particular the identity and religious affiliation of those responsible for the Hebrew parts of the manuscripts.[20] It would appear that some of the manuscripts, especially in groups 2 and

[19] B. Smalley, *Hebrew Scholarship among Christians in 13th century England. Paper Read to the Society for Old Testament Study* (London, 1939).

[20] Smalley, *Hebrew Scholarship*, 8–10, suggested that at least some of these manuscripts, and notably MS CCC 10, MS CCC 11 and MS Trin. R. 8. 6, were written by Christians. She based her opinion on the fact that these manuscripts were carelessly produced, and contained many errors and omissions, while books produced by Jewish scribes would necessarily be in her view of superior quality. Loewe, '*Superscriptio Lincolniensis*', 215 and 220, agrees with Smalley in the case of MS CCC 10. As for MS CCC 11 and MS Trin. R. 8. 6 (possibly both written by the same scribe), he suggests that the scribe was a convert to Christianity, since the calligraphy of the manuscripts is that of a Jewish hand, but numerous errors, omissions, and in one case an erasure of the name of God

3, were written as Jewish books which subsequently changed hands and were then used and annotated by Christian scholars (e.g. MS Bodl. Or. 3; MS CCC 6). Most of these books, however, and obviously all of group 1, were devised from the outset to be bilingual. This can be ascertained from many of their codicological and palaeographical features, and notably from the fact that the line ruling, made in advance to guide the script, took both Hebrew and Latin columns into account. What is more, some of these manuscripts were actually written from left to right, like a Latin codex (e.g. MS CCC 5; MS CCC 8; MS CCC 9, ff. 1–56).

So far as the scribes of the manuscripts are concerned, it is of course conceivable that Christians could be trained and proficient in Hebrew calligraphy.[21] However, several aspects of these manuscripts seem to indicate that the scribes in general were thoroughly trained in the Jewish scribal tradition. This is notably attested by the existence of professional ductus and the use of characteristic 'good omen' scribal formulae, often in Ashkenazi cursive script (e.g. MS Bodl. Or. 62; MS CCC 11; MS Trin. R. 8. 6). It is true that the handwriting is often careless, with many textual errors, omissions and erasures. Despite its carelessness, however, the handwriting is still very confident and fluent: this may indicate that the scribe was indeed a Jewish scribe, who simply made poor-quality copies of books that were never intended for Jewish liturgical usage. The Jewish identity of certain scribes can be further confirmed by the treatment of the name of God. Thus, in MS CCC 8 – a codex written in two Hebrew and two Latin parallel columns, from left to right, part of the text was erased in f. 145v, but great care was taken to keep the name of God intact. In fact, there is only one manuscript, Leiden Or. 4725 (Scaliger 8), and perhaps a few passages in CCC 10 (both twelfth-century Psalters), whose palaeographical features may possibly indicate a Christian hand.[22] Be it as it may, most of the 'bilingual' Hebrew–Latin manu-

seem to rule out a professional scribe. More recent studies by Hebrew palaeographers, notably M. Beit-Arié, *Hebrew Manuscripts of East and West. Towards a Comparative Codicology* (London, 1992), 16–18 and C. Sirat, 'Notes sur la circulation des livres entre juifs et chrétiens au moyen âge', tend to consider that the Hebrew text in the manuscripts in question was written by a scribe well trained in the Jewish tradition. They reach this conclusion on the basis of the handwriting and scribal practices, chief among them the presence of characteristic formulae written by pious scribes when a copied page contained an account of a disaster or calamity; see M. Beit-Arié, 'Copyists' Formulae at the End of the Pages' (Hebrew), *KS* 44 (1969): 549–53.

21 For example, a certain Maurice, prior of Augustinians at Kirkham in Yorkshire (twelfth century), apparently mastered Hebrew calligraphy to the acclaim of the local Jews. Cf. M. R. James, 'The Salomites', *JTS* 35 (1934): 289; Loewe, 'Medieval Christian Hebraists', 234; '*Superscriptio Lincolniensis*', 219.

22 MS Leiden Or. 4725; cf. G. I. Lieftinck, 'The Psalterium Hebraycum from St Augustine's Canterbury Rediscovered in the Scaliger Bequest at Leyden', *Transactions of the Cambridge*

scripts can be convincingly considered as the fruit of close collaboration between Jews and Christians, thus shedding a unique light on the professional and intellectual exchanges between the two communities in medieval England.

In the present context, however, what concerns us is the potential of these manuscripts for addressing our central questions regarding the knowledge and acquisition of the Hebrew language and grammar among Christian scholars. The very existence of these 'bilingual' manuscripts, especially those that contain Hebrew and Latin in parallel columns, attests to the importance attached to the Hebrew text in the medieval text-critical approach to the Vulgate. The practice of comparison between existing Latin versions and the original Hebrew, also recorded in medieval *correctoria*,[23] became in the bilingual manuscripts a new and highly efficient scientific tool. The production of these unusual books made the Hebrew text readily accessible, especially at a time when Hebrew books were scarce. As importantly, the potent visual device of the multi-column page layout made it possible to undertake immediate and systematic comparisons between the Latin translations and the Hebrew original.

Several codicological features of these manuscripts are of particular relevance to our concerns, since they clearly indicate that their Christian scribes – responsible for the Latin parts of the manuscripts – had at least some working knowledge of Hebrew. Indeed, in most of these manuscripts the Hebrew text was written first, and the Latin translation was then adjusted to fit the Hebrew. For example, blank spaces were left in the Latin columns of MS CCC 9 (e.g. f. 50r) in the cases when the Latin version was shorter than the Hebrew. In MS Trinity R. 8. 6, when the Hebrew text contained verses absent from the Vulgate a blank space was left in the Latin column. Such adjustments were not carried out during the writing of MS CCC 11, but when corresponding Hebrew and Latin verses did not occur exactly one in front of the other, the beginnings of these verses were linked by lines drawn in the same brown ink used for the corrections to the text (e.g. f. 72v). The implied understanding of Hebrew is even more evident in the layout of the *superscriptio*, where

footnote 22 (*cont.*)
Bibliographical Society 2 (1955): 97–104 and K. Doekes, 'Manuscript Cod. Or. 4725 (Scaliger 8). Scriptie voor Westerse Handschriftenkunde en Hebreeuws', MA thesis (Rijksuniversiteit Leiden, 1988). As for MS CCC 10, most of the Hebrew text was written by professional Jewish scribes. A few spaces left blank by them were subsequently filled by an untrained undoubtedly Christian hand, cf. Sirat, 'Notes sur la circulation'.

23 Cf. Dahan, 'La connaissance de l'hébreu', in Sed-Rajna (ed.), *Rashi*, pp. 567–78.

Latin equivalents are written directly above the original Hebrew terms. Significantly, in places where the Hebrew was corrected in the margins, the *superscriptio* follows the corrected text. As B. Smalley observed, this indicates that the scribe of the *superscriptio* must have understood something of the Hebrew text, unless he was copying from an exemplar virtually identical to his own (including the mistakes) – a very unlikely contingency given that each of the manuscripts with *superscriptio* preserved (at least fifteen) shows a different layout.[24]

Superscriptio*: vocabulary and grammar*

The knowledge of Hebrew that transpires from these codicological and palaeographical features receives further confirmation in the *superscriptio* translation itself. This new medieval Latin translation seems to have emerged from the assiduous study of the original Hebrew text of the Bible, with a view to correct the Vulgate. A systematic comparison of these translations in various manuscripts has yet to be undertaken, but it appears already now that they are not identical from one manuscript to another.[25] The *superscriptio* found in some Psalters (e.g. MS CCC 10; MS Trin. R. 8. 6) has been identified by B. Smalley as derived from a translation initiated by Robert Grosseteste.[26] As already noted, it is likely that the *superscriptio* was partly elaborated with the aid of Jewish tutors, as suggested by terms *iudeus* or *iudeus dicit* which designate the *superscriptio* in glosses in MS CCC 11,[27] or *rabi dicit* in MS Lambeth Palace 435.[28] This assistance is also suggested by the inclusion of occasional terms in French, which was then the principal vernacular means of communication between Jews and Christians.[29]

Consequently, although to a large extent based on the Vulgate, the *superscriptio* tends to follow the Hebrew text in a more literal manner. To give an example, Ezra 1:8 עַל יַד מִתְרְדָת הַגִּזְבָּר is translated in the Vulgate as *per manum Mithridatis filii Gazbar*. The *superscriptio* in MS Bodl. Or. 46 (f. 2) translates this phrase as *supra manum mithridatis ar. prefecti*, where the preposition עַל preserves its original etymological flavour 'on, above', and הגזבר is translated as an office while the Vulgate understands it as a

[24] Smalley, *Hebrew Scholarship*, 9.

[25] Cf. the collation of various *superscriptio* manuscripts for Psalm 4 by Loewe, '*Superscriptio Lincolniensis*', 231–50.

[26] Smalley, *Hebrew Scholarship*, 5–7.

[27] Smalley, *Hebrew Scholarship*, 10.

[28] Loewe, '*Superscriptio Lincolniensis*', 223.

[29] For example, in MS Bodl. Or. 46, להדרים in f. 22 is translated by *extollere* and by *hauseir*, and הנשיא in f. 1 is translated in the *superscriptio* as *maiori ar*, and in the margin as *huius principis gal maire*. Cf. Smalley, *Hebrew Scholarship*, 15; Smalley, *The Study of the Bible*, 347 ff.

proper name introduced in Latin by the word *filii*, 'son', absent from the Hebrew. In some other cases in the same manuscript, the translation of the Vulgate is deemed acceptable and is written as an alternative. For example, הֵעִיר in Ezra 1:5 is translated as *evigilavit*, but the Vulgate translation, *suscitavit*, is written in the margin.

Another characteristic feature of the *superscriptio* is the practice of what may be called 'grammaticizing translation'. Here the Latin terms are chosen in such a way as to render not only the lexical meaning of the corresponding Hebrew terms, but also to reflect their specific grammatical structure. Thus for instance, still in MS Bodl. Or. 46, the phrase וַיַּעֲבֶר קוֹל in Ezra 1:8 is translated as *transire fecit vocem*. The translation by infinitive followed by *fecit*, 'made', was chosen to reflect the factitive aspect of the Hebrew *hif'il*, while the Vulgate translation *traduxit vocem* is less specific on this point. An interesting example of a real grammatical analysis in the translation is provided by the use of *ar* (in all probability an abbreviation for *articulus*) to render the Hebrew definite article (which does not exist in Latin) in almost all manuscripts with the *superscriptio* (e.g. MS Bodl. Or. 46; MS Bodl. Or. 62; MS CCC 5; MS CCC 7).[30] For example הָאָרוֹן in Joshua 3:15 in MS St John's 143 is translated as *arcam ar*, with each element written directly above its Hebrew equivalent. It is interesting to note that the same term, *ar*, is regularly used to translate the Hebrew direct object marker אֶת, e.g. אֶת הַיַּרְדֵּן in Joshua 3:17, in the same manuscript, is translated as *iordanem ar ar*. In some contexts *ar* can also be a translation of the particle לְ, e.g., in the infinitive construct לֵאמֹר in Joshua 4:2, in the same manuscript. In other places, however, the translation of the particle לְ varies according to the context. It can be translated as *ad*, 'to, towards, for', e.g. in לַמִּלְחָמָה, *pugnandum ad*, in Joshua 4:13, as a genitive, e.g. לַחֹדֶשׁ, *mensis*, in Joshua 4:19. It appears therefore that the term *ar* was not used in a formal way to translate a specific particle, but rather that its uses depended on semantic subtleties of the text.

The translation of the definite article, as well as other parts of speech, such as the direct object marker and the particle לְ, as *ar*(*ticulus*), is surprising at first, but it is important to stress that it actually conforms with contemporary theoretical approaches to Hebrew grammar. Roger Bacon notes in his grammar: 'They [the Hebrews . . .] have also articles; הַ is the article of the nominative and genitive, לַ of the dative, אֶת of the accusative, often אֶת הַ; Whenever אֶת הַ is found in the Hebrew text, the accusative case always follows.'[31] Thus the term *articulus* covers not only

[30] Cf. Loewe, '*Superscriptio Lincolniensis*', 226.

[31] Hirsch in Nolan, *The Greek Grammar*, 204.

the definite article, but also the particles that are generally untranslatable into Latin (את), or which lose their primary meaning to be translated as Latin case endings in some contexts (ל). From Bacon's description it appears that his notion of the *articulus* is closely related to that of case declension – a concept which is foreign to the native Hebrew grammatical tradition. Seen from the perspective of the medieval Latin grammarian, the article and the untranslatable accusative particle את are regularly added to modify a name (noun or adjective), and can be translated by the Latin case endings. To express the equivalent of other Latin cases, Hebrew has prepositions, or adverbs which are clearly defined by Bacon as used 'instead of the article' (*loco articulorum*). Latin ablative is expressed by the preposition מן. Words such as מן are described as prepositions since such a part of speech exists in the Latin grammatical tradition, whereas את is called *articulus* because it does not correspond to any known Latin category. Thus both *articulus* in its broad sense and prepositions are presented by Bacon as markers of the Hebrew declension. This somewhat constrained identification is well in line with the thirteenth-century idea that there is in reality only one universal grammar which underlies different linguistic realities (i.e. different languages): *Grammatica una et eadem est secundum substantiam in omnibus linguis licet accidentaliter varietur*.[32] This universalistic approach is responsible for attempts to describe the Hebrew language in terms of Latin grammatical categories, attempts which continued down to the development of Hebrew grammatical tradition in Renaissance Europe.[33]

In addition to the somewhat indirect indications contained in the codicological features and *superscriptio* translation, the 'bilingual' manuscripts also contain more explicit evidence regarding the practical knowledge of the Hebrew language and grammar among Christian scholars. It would seem that, besides their use as reference books or source material for scholarly studies, these manuscripts also served more prosaically as convenient notebooks for recording lessons, jotting down comments and ideas about the text, and so forth. Many of the glosses and annotations found in these manuscripts concern the exegesis of relevant passages, often with reference to Jewish biblical interpretation. Several manuscripts contain the Hebrew alphabet with the names of the letters and their translation (e.g. MS Bodl. Or. 621; MS Bodl. Or. 3; MS CCC 7), the list of the names of God according to the tradition of St

[32] Roger Bacon, quoted in R. H. Robins, *A Short History of Linguistics* (London, 1967), 76.
[33] Cf. S. Kessler-Mesguich, 'Les grammaires occidentales de l'hébreu', in *Histoire des idées linguistiques*, ed. S. Auroux (Liège, 1992), vol. II, 251–70.

Jerome (e.g. MS Bodl. Or. 621: *hel ds (deus)*; *heloyim ds*; *heloi ds sabaoth virtutum*; *helion excelsius*; *adonai ds*; *egege*[34] *qui est*, based on Jerome's epistle 25), or a Hebrew translation of obviously Christian texts, such as the *Pater Noster* (e.g. MS Heb. Bodl. Or. 62, f. 3). Alongside these relatively brief and unsophisticated annotations, however, a small number of 'bilingual' manuscripts contain explicit grammatical or linguistic information which indicates an undeniable Hebrew proficiency. Particularly relevant in this respect are the linguistic and grammatical remarks found in three Latin–Hebrew manuscripts to be extensively discussed in the following pages: MS Bodl. Or. 621, MS Bodl. Or. 62 and MS Lambeth Palace 435.

MS Bodl. Or. 621 – the study of vocabulary

MS Bodl. Or. 621[35] (49 f., dimensions: 145 x 100 mm) is a Hebrew Psalter written in one column, from right to left. It contains Latin and French glosses in English hands which can be dated to the thirteenth century, as well as a Hebrew alphabet with the names of the characters according to St Jerome, epistle 30, and a list of divine names, based on St Jerome, epistle 25. The Hebrew script is an Ashkenazi gothic semi-cursive,[36] except for the first word of each psalm written in square gothic, in blue or red ink. Although it does not contain Latin translation in parallel columns or a *superscriptio*, the manuscript was probably produced for Christian use. This seems to be confirmed by the decoration of the initial in Psalm 1 with an image of King David with a lyre, just like in MS Leiden Or. 4725 (Scaliger 8), and in a number of Latin Psalters.[37] This Psalter was carefully studied by at least three Christian scholars, who furthermore used it as a kind of exercise-book. Faded notes written with a lead pencil were rewritten in brown ink by a fine thirteenth-century hand. These two earlier scholars occasionally provided selected Hebrew terms with their translation in Latin and sometimes in French, as well as some annotations. The more ancient faded hand had also left some notes in unskilful Hebrew script (e.g. hardly visible list of words on f. 7v: לב, נפש, נשמה, or the cardinal points on f. 30, following Psalm 89: דרום מזרח מערב צפון).

[34] Loewe, '*Superscriptio Lincolniensis*', 218 quotes *Ysagoge in theologiam* where Latin g is said to correspond to the Hebrew yod before e and i.

[35] No. 112 in A. Neubauer, *Catalogue of the Hebrew Manuscripts in the Bodleian Library and in the College Libraries of Oxford* (Oxford, 1886–1906), vol. I; Cf. Smalley, *The Study of the Bible*, 347; Loewe, '*Superscriptio Lincolniensis*', 224; Roth, *Intellectual Activities*, 11, note 5.

[36] Cf. Beit-Arié, *Medieval Hebrew Book*, 134, note 39.

[37] Cf. Doekes, 'Scriptie voor Westerse Handschriftenkunde'.

The marginal notes on Hebrew vocabulary made by the third hand on ff. 1–3 and 43–48 are of particular importance for reconstructing Hebrew learning methods. This third hand belongs to a scholar whose knowledge of Hebrew went well beyond the basic alphabet, and who actually used the Psalter as an aid in his methodical study of Hebrew vocabulary. This scholar proceeded by copying the relevant Hebrew words in the margins, and by providing them with vowel points which would roughly reflect their pronunciation, irrespective of the original vocalization. He then provided them with a Latin translation, often different from the Vulgate. From the choice of words dealt with in this manner we can gather that he was well acquainted with the more common vocabulary, since he translated only infrequent or difficult expressions. To grasp the subtleties of a Hebrew word better and to enrich his vocabulary, our scholar would list several of its meanings. For instance, on f. 2v he translates יהגה in Psalm 1:2 as *dolor, predicatio, loquela.* Interestingly, these translations were not intended to reflect or to shed light on the text itself. The above Latin terms do not translate the verb יהגה as it appears in the original Hebrew, as would have been the case in a *superscriptio*. Instead, the author wrote the word הֶגֶה, which, making allowances for his unconventional vocalization system, must correspond to the noun הֶגֶה. He then provided this word with several translations, which do not reflect its actual meaning, but rather various meanings of words derived from what we today would call the same root. Therefore, our scholar did not merely study words as they appeared in the text, but also sought to grasp more abstract lexical items. In so doing, he tried to attach words to their etymological basis. To give a further example, he derived the word תקות in Psalm 9:19 from a verb קַוָה noted in the margin. This verb probably corresponds to a qal form (with a patah sign instead of kamatz) which must have been taken as a basis, notwithstanding the fact that the verb 'to hope' is attested only in pi'el. In a few cases, the etymology is based on an altogether fictitious verb; the noun מורה translated as *doctor*, in f. 3v, is derived from an imaginary verb מַרַה, translated as *docuit*.

In a few, notes show that words with similar graphic shapes are studied together in order not to be confused. Thus, in Psalm 2:10, next to the verb יסר (translated here as *docuit*) our scholar writes יסד, translated as *fundamentum*. In the same vein, he studied families of words derived from the same 'root', or at least containing the same sequence of consonants. For example, on f. 2v we find חִמֵם, חַמַה *sol*, חֵימַה *ira ut furor*, חֹמַה *murus* and חֵמַת. Finally, our scholar also tried to deduce the singular of a noun written in the plural. Thus, עניים on f. 3v is not only translated in the margin, but provided with its singular עני.

MS Bodl. Or. 62 – phonetics

MS Bodl. Or. 62[38] (132 ff., dimensions 200 x 140 mm) contains the book of Ezekiel written in parallel Hebrew and Latin columns, from left to right, like a Latin codex. It also contains a complete *superscriptio* and some Latin glosses. The Latin hand seems to be datable to the beginning of the thirteenth century.[39] The Hebrew script is Ashkenazi square gothic, probably copied by two different scribes. The fly-leaves at the beginning of the manuscript contain a biblical chronology from Adam to the Babylonian exile in Hebrew and Latin, the beginning of *Pater Noster* in Hebrew and, more importantly for our purposes, a few notes on Hebrew phonetics. These brief notes present a considerable interest from the point of view of the transmission of linguistic ideas. A brief comment in f. 132r deals with Hebrew phonetics, listing the Hebrew characters in separate columns according to their place of articulation:

Ipse lettere formunt in gutture	א ח ה ע
labiis	ב ו מ ף
palato	ג י כ ק
dentales	ד ל ט נ ת
in lingua	ז ש ס ר צ

This systematic division of the consonants according to their place of articulation or organ of speech (gutturals, labials, palatals, dentals and linguals) is without precedent in the medieval Latin grammatical tradition. Roger Bacon in his grammar mentions only that alef and he are pronounced in the mouth while ayin and het are pronounced in the throat.[40] Moreover, this mention of the two places of articulation does not refer to any theoretical division, but rather attempts to describe the actual pronunciation as a practical guide to students. As for more theoretical phonetical distinctions, Roger Bacon uses terms such as aspiration, semivowels, liquid and silent letters – all common terms in the classical (Greek and Latin) tradition. On the other hand, the division of consonants according to the organs of speech was not used in Western grammatical traditions until the sixteenth century, when it was borrowed from the Hebrew grammatical tradition and applied to the description

[38] Neubauer, *Catalogue*, no. 88; Cf. Beit-Arié, *Medieval Hebrew Book*, 134, note 35.
[39] Cf. Neubauer, *Catalogue*, no. 88.
[40] Hirsch in Nolan, *The Greek Grammar*, 204.

of vernacular European languages. The first description of consonants according to their place of articulation in the Western grammatical tradition is generally attributed to the Italian Hebraist Alde Manuce, in 1501.[41] MS Bodl. Or. 62 furnishes an important piece of evidence: that already in the Middle Ages some Christian scholars were aware of the division of the consonants according to their place of articulation. Like many other achievements of thirteenth-century Christian students of Hebrew, however, this insight was rapidly forgotten, only to be rediscovered anew some two and a half centuries later.

Since this phonetic division of the consonants was not known in Latin grammatical thought, its presence in MS Bodl. Or. 62 can only be explained through some form of contact between the Christian scholars in question and the native Hebrew grammatical tradition, be it in the form of Hebrew books, or direct teaching from a Jewish tutor well versed in the Hebrew grammatical literature.[42] The division of consonants according to the organs of speech is attested from the earliest stages of Hebrew linguistic thought. First expounded in the *Sefer Yezira*,[43] it was integrated into the purely grammatical works of such authors as Sa'adya Gaon, Jonah ibn Janah, Abraham ibn Ezra, Menahem ben Saruq, Dunash ben Labrat and David Kimhi. Even more importantly for our present study, it is also attested in the Hebrew grammatical tradition developed in medieval England, and notably in the *Sefer ha-Shoham* by Moshe ben Isaac ha-Nessiya of London.[44]

The order in which the five groups of consonants are listed in MS Bodl. Or. 62 follows the alphabetical order attested in most versions of *Sefer Yezira*. It differs slightly from Menahem ben Saruq's division which contains only four groups,[45] from Dunash ben Labrat who mentions five groups but does not specify the organ of speech,[46] and from Moshe ben Isaac and David Kimhi who mention the labials at the end.[47] Probably by mistake, the MS Bodl Or. 62 lists the consonants ד ל ט נ ת under the heading 'dentals' and ז ש ס ר צ as 'linguals', while in Moshe ben Isaac's and Kimhi's grammar ד ל ט נ ת are called 'lingua.-dentals' and ש ס ר צ

41 S. Kessler-Mesguich, 'Les études hébraïques en France, de François Tissard à Richard Simon (1508–1680)', PhD thesis (University of Paris VIII, 1994), 101.

42 Roger Bacon had a very low opinion of the grammatical skills of contemporary Jews. Although many knew Hebrew, only a few could actually teach it. Cf. his *Opus Tertium*, in *Compendium Studii*, vol. X, 33, 34, and Nolan, *The Greek Grammar*, p. xxxvii.

43 *Sefer Yezira* 4: 3, ed. I. Gruenwald, 'A Preliminary Critical Edition of *Sefer Yezira*', *IOS* 1 (1971): 147.

44 B. Klar, *The Sepher haShoham (The Onyx Book) by Moses ben Isaac HaNessiah* (London, 1947), 6.

45 Menahem ben Saruq, *Mahberet*, ed. A. Sáenz-Badillos (Granada, 1986), 8*–9*.

46 *Teshuvot*, 5b, quoted in David Kimhi, *Mikhlol*, trans. W. Chomsky (New York, 1952), 11.

47 Kimhi, *Mikhlol*, 11.

ז 'dentals'. On the other hand, the order of the consonants within the first group, and notably the place of the het before the he, is consistent with the *Sefer Yezira* and most medieval Jewish grammarians, such as Moshe ben Isaac and Abraham ibn Ezra.[48] The exact Jewish source from which our Christian scholar took his division of the consonants is therefore quite difficult to ascertain. Although the list of the groups in MS Bodl. Or. 62 follows closely the alphabetical order in the *Sefer Yezira*, it seems unlikely that this work could have been used. To begin with, although the *Sefer Yezira* was studied in Jewish circles in thirteenth-century England, as attested by its two commentaries written by Elhanan ben Yaqar in the city of London,[49] there are no indications that it was known to Christian scholars. Moreover, the pronunciation of each group of consonants as described in the *Sefer Yezira* uses a different and more pragmatic wording than that of our manuscript. The consonants are said to be 'attached to the tip of the tongue, like a flame to the embers' (קשורות בראש הלשון כשלהבת בגחלת). א ח ה ע are said to be produced at the end of the tongue and in the throat (בסוף הלשון ובבית בליעה), ב ו מ ף between the lips and at the tip of the tongue (בין שפתים ובראש הלשון), ג י כ ק at the third of the tongue (על שליש הלשון), ד ט ל נ ת at the tip of the tongue (בראש הלשון), and finally, ז ס ע ר ש are said to be produced between the teeth and 'the sleeping (immobile?) tongue' (בין שיניים ובלשון). The description in *Sefer Yezira* does not mention the palate at all. In sum, despite some differences which may be due to discrepancies in manuscripts, the description in MS Bodl. Or. 62 seems to be a straightforward translation of the simple division of the consonants found in a grammatical work, such as David Kimhi or Menahem ben Saruq, or, for that matter, the local English grammarian Moshe ben Isaac.

MS Lambeth Palace 435 – vowel points

MS Lambeth Palace 435[50] (131 ff., dimensions 210 x 140 mm) is a Hebrew Psalter in one column, written from right to left and provided with a *superscriptio* and glosses. The Hebrew script is Ashkenazi, gothic square, the Latin hand can be dated to the thirteenth century, and there are

48 Cf. W. Bacher, *Abraham ibn Esra als Grammatiker* (Strassburg, 1882), 54, note 4.

49 Cf. Roth, *Intellectual Activities*, 62.

50 M. R. James and C. Jenkins, *A Descriptive Catalogue of the Manuscripts in the Library of Lambeth Palace* (Cambridge, 1930), vol. I, 607. This manuscript was written by the same scribe as MS CCC 9 and MS St. John's 143. To judge by the similar dimensions and layout of these three manuscripts it belonged together with them to the same collection of biblical books. Cf. Beit-Arié, *Medieval Hebrew Book*, 130.

some Anglo-Norman glosses which indicate English origin.[51] Of relevance to our topic are the six fly-leaves at the beginning of the manuscript. They were written by two different medieval English hands, and they contain various notes on Hebrew pronunciation and grammar.

Some of the grammatical notes found in this manuscript also point to contacts with the native Hebrew grammatical tradition. First of all, the description of the pronunciation of the Hebrew letters pays an unprecedented amount of attention to the vowel. On f. IIIr, a Hebrew alphabet is followed by a list of the vowels, written in the form of a column, which contains first the Latin sound, then the vowel point, and finally its transcribed name (*patah*, *kamez*, *segzol*, *cere*, *herek*, *holim*, *surek*). The list of the vowels also contains hataf signs, with a special note that *hataf kamez* is pronounced [o]. Particular vowels are followed by some examples of their use, and sometimes by a description of their graphic form. Thus, for instance, the hatafs are described as composed of the vowel with two superposed dots (*hataf kamez* / ֳ / *supra kamez duplex puncta*).[52] The use of *hatafs* is also associated with the gutturals. The vowels are treated as independent sounds. It is also noted that alef sounds like the vowel it bears in a given word, with examples: לא and אֶל.

While Hebrew alphabets and notes on the pronunciation of the consonants are often found in medieval manuscripts, such a detailed description of the vowels and a recognition of their independent pronunciation is very infrequent. Since the Masoretic vowel points are obviously not a part of St Jerome's legacy, their description must necessarily indicate a Hebrew knowledge ultimately acquired from Jewish rather than patristic sources. A description of the vowel points as independent sounds is also found in the preface to the *De interpretationibus* . . . (MS Paris BN lat. 36). In this work, all characters of the Hebrew alphabet except vav and yod are described as consonants, which in themselves do not have a sound and cannot be pronounced. They become speech only by addition of 'points and strokes which, by an ancient institution, have the value of the vowels'.[53] Such a definition of Hebrew vowel points and their origins was highly unusual during the Middle Ages. The more common attitude was to try to understand the Hebrew vowels in the framework of Jerome's works, or else to disregard them altogether.

An attempt to reconcile Jerome's tradition with Masoretic reality was

[51] Cf. Loewe, '*Superscriptio Lincolniensis*', 222.

[52] This description of the hatafs as having the sheva on the top of the basic vowel rather than at its right side corresponds to the way they are written in this particular manuscript, as in some other medieval manuscripts.

[53] See Berger in *Quam notitiam*, 22.

made by Roger Bacon. Himself instructed in the classical grammatical tradition, Bacon found it inconceivable that vowels should not form part of the word itself, or put otherwise, that they should be written as points. Following Jerome's tradition, he therefore considered that the gutturals א ה ח ע, just like ו and י, are vowels. The gutturals may sound like any of the Latin vowels, depending on the vowel point underneath. Consequently, a guttural with a vowel point should be always placed after a consonant proper. Thus, for instance, the possessive pronoun in 'your (fem.) son' (בנך) is described and transcribed as *caph secundo cum aleph ut benach*, which would read as בְּנאָך.[54] However, Bacon was aware that his view on the vowels was not confirmed by the Hebrew texts, where vowel points are evidently written under the consonants without any use of gutturals. Faced with the difficulty of explaining this discrepancy, he resorted to blaming the Jews for not writing the 'vowels' (i.e. א ה ח ע) and replacing them with vowel points, in order to confuse the gentiles and to make the reading of Hebrew books impossible for them.[55]

A similar status of vowels given to the gutturals is also attested in MS Paris BN lat. 36. Dealing with the name Gomora, the author of this lexicon states that the letter (i.e. consonant) g is not present in the Hebrew, and the word Gomora is written with the 'vowel ayin' (*per uocalem aym.*)[56] Since the reliability of Hebrew vocalization was put in such doubt, it is understandable that the system of vowel points was often disregarded by medieval Christian scholars in their studies of Hebrew. However, since reading a text completely devoid of vowels would present serious difficulties for the less proficient majority of scholars, the Hebrew vowel system was maintained, albeit in a drastically simplified form.

An early example of such a modified vowels system is found in *Ysagoge in theologiam*, a text written around 1150 containing arguments to be used by Christian scholars in their attempts at converting Jews.[57] To make these arguments more effective, the author proclaimed the necessity of a knowledge of Hebrew, since 'a common language leads people to a common life', and 'a Hebrew can more easily be convinced by an authority expressed in Hebrew rather than otherwise'.[58] In this vein, the second part of *Ysagoge* argued for the truth of the Christian faith, quoting in support no fewer than seventy-eight verses from the Old Testament in Hebrew. Five of these verses were provided with vowels, Latin tran-

[54] Hirsch in Nolan, *The Greek Grammar*, 205. [55] *Ibid.* [56] See Berger in *Quam notitiam*, 21.
[57] MS Trinity College Cambridge, B XIV. 33, ed. A. Landgraf, *Ecrits théologiques de l'école d'Abélard* (Louvain, 1934). [58] In the prologue, 127.

scription and translation. This vocalization has distinctive features which are later found in thirteenth-century works: all [a] sounds are expressed by a patah and all [e] sounds, except for the vocal sheva, are expressed by a cere.[59] A similar simplification is found in a number of marginal notes in our 'bilingual' manuscripts, like for instance the aforementioned קַוֵה in MS Bodl. Or. 621. Simplified vowels were also added in words provided with *superscriptio* in an originally unvocalized MS CCC 6, a Rashi commentary most probably written for Jewish use (e.g. נַתַן, רֵכֵב on f. 28v).

Most of the 'bilingual' manuscripts were, however, carefully vocalized in conformity with the Masoretic system. What is more, it appears in several instances that the vowel points were not written by the original scribe of the consonantal text, but added in an ink identical to that of the Latin gloss. This similarity of ink does not automatically indicate that the vowels in the main text were added by a Christian scribe. However, it is noteworthy that those Hebrew words that had been forgotten by the original scribe and were added in the margins by an evidently Christian hand were also given correct Masoretic vowels. At the very least, these corrections indicate that a study of the Masoretic vocalization was by no means alien to medieval Christian scholars. Clear evidence of the influence of Jewish grammatical tradition can be found in the explanation of the בגדכפת letters. Although the double pronunciation of some of them was regularly mentioned in medieval works on Hebrew pronunciation (including Roger Bacon's grammar), in MS Lambeth Palace 435 they are mentioned together as a group and refered to by the mnemotechnic term transcribed as *begazkefaz* (f. IIIr), just as in the grammars of Menahem ben Saruq or David Kimhi.

The *superscriptio* and marginal notes in MS Lambeth Palace 435 can also attest to various Hebrew learning methods. The *superscriptio* was quite sporadic, and included not only the Latin translation but also a transliteration. However, it is not the actual form as it appears in the text that is transliterated, but rather, like in MS Bodl. Or. 621, its presumed derivational basis. Thus, for instance אֹהֲבֵי שְׁמֶךָ in Psalm 5: 12 (f. 3r) is translated as *amantes*, but this translation is followed by the noun *aheba* (for אהבה) which is in turn translated *amor*. The vocabulary was studied by listing synonyms. For instance in f. 4r אֱנוֹשׁ (Psalm 8: 5) is transliterated (*enos*) and translated as *ho(mo)*, and in the margin are listed various possible equivalents of *ho(mo)*: *enos*, *is*, *adam*, *geber*, and surprisingly *gever*.

[59] J. Fischer enthusiastically defined it as a pre-Masoretic system: J. Fischer, 'Die Hebräischen Bibelzitate des Scholastikers Odo'. *Biblica* 15 (1934): 93.

Marginal notes contain also some miscellaneous grammatical information. For example, in f. 5v, transliterating and translating בַּת צִיּוֹן (*baz fillia*) in Psalm 9: 15, a remark on the plural form with possessive suffix is made: *benothecha tue fillie*. In f. 14v, there is an almost complete list of the forms of the preposition מִן 'from' with suffixes (*mimech dete*; *mimeni de me*; *mimenu de illo*; *mimenu de nobis*; *mikim de vobis*; *mihem de illis*). On the same folio can also be found a conjugation of the verb קום (*cam*; *camtim*; *cama*; *camenu*).

CONCLUSIONS

Having examined in detail the grammatical remarks included in the 'bilingual' Latin–Hebrew manuscripts that have formed the body of this study, we are now in a position to reach some conclusions regarding the knowledge and practice of the Hebrew language among Christian scholars in pre-expulsion England. Our study has confirmed the existence of a discrepancy between the enthusiastic and often very competent study of various Hebrew texts at that time and the lack of systematic descriptions of the Hebrew language which might have served as teaching aids. While they indicate a high level of linguistic proficiency in Hebrew, the annotations found in the 'bilingual' Hebrew–Latin manuscripts suggest by their *ad hoc* nature the absence of grammatical textbooks or reference works. Occurring as they do in the context of particular biblical verses whose words they transcribe and translate, or as unstructured casual remarks in the margins or the fly-leaves, these notes appear to have been jotted down in the course of a lesson, when the most appropriate or indeed the only writing support available was the book of the Bible itself. If so, these notes would indicate that the Christian scholars in question received their relevant grammatical information by oral means, through direct teaching.

The oral nature of this teaching is amply illustrated in MS CCC 6, a Rashi commentary in which only those occasional folios provided with *superscriptio* actually contain the vowel points. Unlike most 'bilingual' manuscripts, the vowels in this manuscript do not correspond to the standard Tiberian vocalization, but rather record the pronunciation of the text using a simplified vowel code. This confirms that the vowels were not copied from an existing vocalized exemplar of Rashi's commentary (which were in any case very rarely vocalized), but were put down following oral instructions. As for the identity of the teachers, there can be little doubt that some of them were Jewish 'native informants': this is explicitly stated in some of the manuscripts, and otherwise suggested by the use of French, the usual medium of communication between Christians and Jews. However, it is equally possible that some teachers of Hebrew were Christians. In the case of MS CCC 6, for instance, the Christian identity of the teacher can be argued on the basis of the idiosyncratic pronunciation as reflected in the vowels, and even more so from the fact that the vocalized words were also provided with their Latin translation. Equally significant in this respect is the use of Latin terms in various descriptions of Hebrew pronunciation, including the division of the consonants according to their place of articulation.

Together with other typical Hebrew grammatical concepts and features such as the mnemotechnic reference to *begadkefat* letters, this division seems to indicate that the Christians had at least some access to the native Hebrew grammatical tradition. These grammatical references may well have been provided by local Jewish teachers, but it is also possible that this knowledge was drawn directly from such grammatical works as the *Mahberet* of Menahem ben Saruq, or the *Sefer ha-Shoham* of Moshe ben Isaac ben ha-Nessiya. It is significant that medieval England was the most important European centre of the native Hebrew grammatical tradition outside Spain. The existence of this well-developed tradition, represented notably by Moshe ben Isaac and his teacher Moshe ben Yomtov ha-Naqdan of London, suggests that Hebrew grammatical books and teaching were readily available in thirteenth-century England.

Considered in the light of the history of Hebrew grammatical thought as a whole, the casual remarks on the topic found in our 'bilingual' Latin–Hebrew manuscripts or in Roger Bacon's grammar are not in themselves particularly outstanding. The discussion of Hebrew phonetics by some thirteenth-century Christian scholars was however both innovative and important. Besides the division of the consonants according to the organs of speech, the description of the Hebrew sounds as found in the 'bilingual' manuscripts and in Roger Bacon's grammar was also unprecedented in the Latin grammatical tradition. In contrast to the hasty treatment reserved for morphology and syntax, the consonants and vowels are described in considerable detail. Rooted in the Christian fascination with the Hebrew alphabet, such descriptions constituted above all an attempt to master the sounds of a foreign language, and particularly those (the gutturals) that have no equivalent in Latin. In attempting to describe these unusual foreign sounds and to indicate their proper pronounciation our Christian scholars had no models or precedents in the Latin grammatical literature of their times to turn to. At the same time, the issue of phonetical description initiated by this medieval tradition remained one of the chief concerns of the Christian Hebrew grammarians of the Renaissance: used as a model for the phonetic description of vernacular languages, this Hebrew-inspired approach lies at the basis of modern phonetics. While we may reasonably doubt the actual mastery of Hebrew by most twelfth-century scholars who dabbled in the subject, those anonymous scholars who commissioned, consulted and annotated the 'bilingual' Hebrew–Latin manuscripts discussed in this study displayed such linguistic proficiency as to secure them by right the title of Hebraist.

III

Prayer and poetry

CHAPTER EIGHT

The origin of the Qaddish

Michael Weitzman

As is well known, there are a number of varieties of the *Qaddish* prayer. This study is devoted to the three opening paragraphs which are always present (though they are conventionally said to make up no more than a 'half *Qaddish*'). They will be abbreviated here to Q1, Q2 and Q3.

Of these three paragraphs, the second in effect already appears in the Bible, at Daniel 2:20, להוא שמה די-אלהא מברך מן עלמא ועד עלמא. Neither the first nor the third, however, is mentioned until after the Babylonian Talmud. The usual view is that they belong to the Talmudic period.

The text of the whole *Qaddish* is first attested rather later, in the Siddur of Rav Amram (d. 875). However, Q1 at least can be carried back somewhat earlier because in the minor tractate *Soferim* we have two prayers which seem to be corrections of the phrase בעלמא די ברא in Q1. *Soferim* 19:12 states that the cantor on the Sabbath should recite the *Qaddish*, but that he should not use the formula בעלמא די עתיד לחדתא. At *Soferim* 14:12 the prayer על הכל is cited at length, and includes the phrase בעולמות שברא העולם הזה והעולם הבא. The phrases in both passages from *Soferim* are probably to be considered, as we shall see, corrections of בעלמא די ברא in the usual text of Q1. Hence the dominant view that Q1, and by implication the whole *Qaddish*, is a work of the Talmudic period.

Thanks to an unexpected source, the date of at least Q1 can be brought some centuries earlier. In the Syriac version of 1 Chronicles 29:19 we find the prayer דנתקדש שמך רבא ונשתבח בעלמא דברית קדם דחליך, 'that Thy great name may be hallowed, and praised in the world that Thou didst create before those who fear Thee'. The combination 'may Thy great name be hallowed . . . in the world that Thou didst create' is a clear citation of Q1. Significantly, the citation is in a dialect of Aramaic, the language of the *Qaddish*. The Syriac version of Chronicles has to be earlier than 344 CE, when Afrahat makes two citations from that biblical book.

This prayer in the Syriac version has nothing to do with the Hebrew text of the Chronicles passage. In fact, there are plentiful indications that the Syriac translator of Chronicles often found his *Vorlage* illegible. In the Hebrew, this verse brings to an end the last prayer of David, where he declares that Solomon will build the Temple. The translator realized that a concluding prayer was needed, and being unable to read the Hebrew substituted a phrase from the *Qaddish*, which we know to have been used at the conclusion of a sermon.[1] So we can now date Q1 to the third century.

At first sight, Q1 is a messianic prayer. The opening words, יתגדל ויתקדש, recall Ezekiel 38:23, in the apocalypse about Gog of Magog, and there is an explicit messianic reference in וימליך מלכותיה. On closer scrutiny, however, it is not so obvious that the prayer really does grow out of the messianic vision of Ezekiel, and its promise והתגדלתי והתקדשתי. First, the phrase בעלמא די ברא, which receives such prominence, has nothing to do with messianism. Second, of all the biblical representations of the coming of the Messianic Age, Ezekiel's vision of Gog of Magog is probably the most lurid, and would be an odd choice as the basis of a messianic prayer. Third, if the words יתגדל ויתקדש really are basic, why is the element יתגדל absent from the citation in the Syriac version and from the obviously related Lord's Prayer?

That the phrase יתגדל ויתקדש need not be messianic is evidenced by the prayer of thanksgiving for rain in TJ *Berakhoth* 9:2, *Ta'anith* 1:3: יתגדל ויתקדש ויתברך ויתרומם שמך מלכנו על כל טיפה וטיפה שאתה מוריד לנו. This shows that the phrase יתגדל ויתקדש need not be messianic, even though it recalls a messianic biblical phrase. There is always a potential distinction between the function of a phrase in the Bible and the function of the same phrase when it is quoted in a newly composed prayer.

If Q1 is not a messianic prayer that grows out of Ezekiel 38, where does it come from? To answer this, we must look more closely at Q2. As Pool showed,[2] there is a fundamental form, ברוך י לעולם, to which Q2 belongs. While the basic form appears in Psalms 89:53, we find variations in all three of its elements: the name, the expression for eternity, and the expression for blessing (which seemed paradoxical). This formula is ubiquitous in rabbinic prayer, where one can hardly exaggerate the inventiveness of the authors who rang the changes on these three simple elements, e.g. ישתבח שמך לעד וכל החיים יודוך סלה. It continues also in the Christian Gloria, and is even attested among the heathen of Palmyra.

[1] TB, *Sotah* 49a. [2] D. de Sola Pool, *The Kaddish* (Leipzig, 1909).

I would like to suggest that the basic formula ברוך י׳ לעולם underwent a mutation whereby it became 'Blessed be God in the world'. This was linguistically justified: עולם can mean 'world' as well as 'eternity' in rabbinic Hebrew, and the preposition ל can sometimes mean 'in' (e.g. at Genesis 4:7, לפתח חתאת רבץ, and frequently in mishnaic Hebrew). Q1 belongs basically to that mutated pattern, though obviously it has received additions. A simpler example of that same mutated form occurs in the Ashkenazi opening of the *Qedushah*, נקדש את שמך בעולם. The questions that now arise are: who brought about the mutation, what further elements are contained in Q1 and what reasons lie behind these developments?

Who, first of all, was responsible for the mutation whereby לעולם, 'for ever', became understood as 'in the world'? The evidence from the Mishnah is that this mutation did not have rabbinic approval but was due to sectarians (*minim*), usually identified with the Sadducees, who denied the resurrection:[3]

> כל חותם הברכות שהיו במקדש היו עד עולם. משקלקלו המינים ואמרו אין עולם אלא אחד התקינו שהיו אומרים מן העולם ועד העולם.

According to the above, blessings in the Temple had originally contained a single occurrence of עולם, meaning 'eternity'. The Sadducees nevertheless insisted on interpreting this word as 'world', of which they inferred that there was only one. Consequently, the rabbis were forced to lengthen the formula in blessings to מן העולם ועד העולם (which is in fact already found at Psalms 106:48), and to teach the doctrine of a second world in that way.

Yet it is unlikely that the mutation really was a Sadducean idea in origin, for, if it had been, it is surprising that a number of prayers that speak of this world and say nothing of any other should have become adopted by Jewish tradition. To begin with, we find the phrase בעלמא די ברא in the *Qaddish*, which seems to play into the hands of those who believe in this world alone. Closely similar, as already noted, is the opening of the Ashkenazic *Qedushah*: נקדש את שמך בעולם. The same is true of the common formula מלך העולם.

I would instead suggest that the new interpretation of לעולם as '(blessed be the Lord) in the world' was first invented by the rabbis, or rather by their predecessors the Pharisees. At this early stage, the main threat came, I suggest, not from the Sadducees who denied the next world but from some form of dualism, which denied this world. We can

[3] Mishnah, *Berakhoth* 9:5.

identify a number of possible movements which had in common a rejection of this world:

a. Qumran sectarians said that the world was under the rule of wickedness.
b. Jesus said that the world was under the rule of 'the prince of this world' (John 12:31 etc.).
c. The clearest evidence of this attitude, however, comes from Josephus. He said that the Essenes (who should not automatically be identified with the Qumran sect) believed that the body is a prison, and when they are freed from the bonds of the flesh they joyously ascend (*BJ* 2, 154–5). Their doctrines may have been influential elsewhere; note the cry by Aristobulus I (105–104 BCE), who was tormented by his conscience after murdering his mother and brother: 'And now, O most shameless body of mine, how long wilt thou retain a soul that ought to die?' (Josephus *AJ* 13, 317 *BJ* 1, 84).

It may be against such a background that the Pharisees reinterpreted the ancient formula ברוך י לעולם in a spatial sense.[4] As noted above, this was defensible in linguistic terms. There was also some sort of precedent in the second half of Psalms 72:19: וברוך שם כבודו לעולם וימלא כבודו את כל הארץ.

Ironically, however, this spatial interpretation of the ancient formula backfired on the Pharisees when it was utilized by heretics of the opposite extreme, who emphasized this world alone and denied any other. All these developments, I would suggest, took place in the time of the Second Temple, which is indeed mentioned in Mishnah, *Berakhoth* 9:5. In broad terms, then, the spatial interpretation of ברוך י לעולם was invented to combat Essene doctrine, but was hijacked by the Sadducees.

I am not suggesting that the final text of the *Qaddish*, as opposed to the idea that ברוך י לעולם could be interpreted spatially, goes right back to Temple times. For the dating of the *Qaddish*, the stress on creation in די ברא בעלמא is a vital clue. It suggests that the author of the prayer was protesting not merely against dualists, but against dualists who denied specifically that God created the world. That later belief is not found either at Qumran or in Christian tradition. Rather it points to gnosticism. Protest against gnosticism is attested in rabbinic literature from the second century CE onwards. When gnosticism became a major threat,

[4] By using the word 'spatial' I mean that the world to come is conceived of as another place, rather than another age. The rabbinic doctrine is that, until the coming of the Messiah, the departed live in the world to come while others live in this world. Thus in the Shabbat morning service we find the sequence: . . . לימות המשיח . . . לחיי העולם הבא . . . לתחיית המתים בעולם הזה.

the rabbis brought back their old weapon against dualism of any sort. They proclaimed that God was to be blessed in this world. Furthermore, with an explicit blow against the gnostic idea of the demiurge, he was to be blessed in the world that he created. Tentatively this would imply a date of about 200 CE for QI.

Anti-gnostic protest may likewise be the reason for the formula מלך העולם, for which our extant evidence begins early in the third century, in R. Yohanan's declaration that כל ברכה שאין בה מלכות אינה ברכה, and in the text of Grace after Meals from Dura-Europos. This motive for מלך העולם was first suggested in 1958 by J. G. Weiss, who did not however bring the *Qaddish* into the discussion. The two formulae בעלמא די ברא and מלך העולם may well have been introduced at the same time, since creation of the world and kingship over the world are closely related themes: the first implies the second, and both are embraced in the ancient title קונה שמים וארץ.

On this view, יתגדל ויתקדש שמיה רבא בעלמא די ברא is built on the formula 'Blessed be the Lord in the world', a mutation of ברוך י לעולם. Note that 'sanctify' is simply a substitute for 'bless', as at Isaiah 29:23, כי בראותו ילדיו מעשה ידי בקרבו יקדישו שמי, though it could develop new meanings: for example, the wish to 'sanctify God's name in the world' came to mean spreading his name and making converts.[5]

Before leaving QI, we have to account for its other elements. In QI we have כרעותיה; in the Syriac we have 'before those who fear thee'; the Lord's Prayer has: 'Thy will be done'. These elements of will and fearers of God are united in the על הכל prayer, as כרצון יראיו. Together they suggest reflection on Psalms 145:19, רצון יראיו יעשה, and in particular the wish to deny that this meant that God performs the will of men, R Eliezer composed a prayer which is in fact a commentary hereon: עשה רצונך בשמים ממעל ותן נחת רוח ליראיך מתחת והטוב בעיניך עשה. That tradition of interpretation of Psalms 145:19, then, has left its mark on the *Qaddish* and related prayers.

The further element that makes QI into a messianic prayer is the phrase וימליך מלכותיה. This may have been adopted in the third century, when מלך העולם was being introduced into prayers. This does not, however, lessen the fact that basically QI is founded on the model 'Blessed be the Lord in the world', which is not in itself messianic. Of course, the messianic element shed a new light on the rest of the prayer. In particular, the meaning of יתגדל ויתקדש was changed fundamentally.

[5] *Sifre Deut.* 306.

Instead of denoting the praise offered by man, it denoted the saving acts of God, as set out in Ezekiel 38.

In rabbinic tradition Q1 is not used alone: we always have Q2, so that the unmutated and mutated forms appear together. Perhaps the rabbis were aware of their common origin. Moreover, we also always have Q3, which also mentions the world (incorporating a spatial interpretation of עולם). However, Q3 says that this world is inadequate to contain the praise of God.

The basic structure of the *Qaddish* is thus:

Q1 Blessed is the Lord in the world.
Q2 Blessed is the Lord forever.
Q3 Blessed is the Lord beyond the capacity of the world.

The statement made by Q3 is in fact yet another possible interpretation of the ancient formula ברוך י׳ לעולם. One sense of the preposition ל is 'in relation to the capacity of'. In biblical Hebrew, one could say רב לך, 'it is too much for your capacity' (e.g. Numbers 16:3, Deuteronomy 3:26, 1 Kings 12:28), or יכלתי לו, 'I was too able for him, prevailed over him'. By analogy, one could describe God as ברוך לעולם, 'too blessed for the capacity of the world' (cf. Nehemiah 9:5).

The addition of this third interpretation needs to be explained. I would suggest that the motive for Q3 was that the rabbis in the third century CE faced a double threat. On the one hand they needed Q1 in order to combat gnostics who denied this world. On the other hand the emphasis on this world could provide ammunition for those who denied the world to come, and such scepticism survived the disappearance of the Sadducees. Against those sceptics, Q3 declared that this world, although God must be praised for its creation, was not everything after all. Indeed, the reason that Q1 is not cited in the Talmud may be that it was not thought to convey the whole truth; it might seem to favour those who denied the world to come.

It remains to note certain later corrections made to Q1. In *Soferim* (eighth century) the reference to the singular בעלמא די ברא was now seen to be objectionable, in that it played down the world to come. Hence we find two alternative corrections. First, בעולמות שברא העולם הזה והעולם הבא in a Hebrew prayer modelled on the *Qaddish*; second, בעלמא די עתיד לחדתא in the Aramaic of the *Qaddish* itself. The ancient text of the *Qaddish* was not, however, displaced.

There is an obvious need to see where the *Paternoster* fits into this scheme. The problem is that we have only the Greek and cannot be sure about the original Aramaic. One possibility is that it is based on the unmutated form ברוך י׳ לעולם. The element לעולם seems present at the end ('. . . for thine is the kingdom forever'). However, these words are lacking in some manuscripts of Matthew 6 and in Luke. The other possibility is that it is based on the mutated form 'Blessed be the Lord in the world'; after all, our texts all include the phrase 'on earth as it is in heaven'. However, it is not at all certain that עלמא really is the underlying Aramaic word. At all events, even if we cannot identify the basic pattern, we can still note the preoccupation with Psalms 145, which also crops up in contemporary Jewish prayers.

Obviously, there is much here that is speculative. I hope, however, to have established a number of points:

a. An early date for Q1, in the third century.
b. A structure which is superior to the conventional view of the *Qaddish* as simply a lengthy expression of praise with a brief messianic introduction.
c. The rabbinic fight on two fronts against those who rejected this world and those who affirmed this world alone.
d. The influence of those developments on Jews far from the rabbinic position, and indeed on Christianity.

CHAPTER NINE

The Journey Inward: Judah Halevi between Christians and Muslims in Spain, Egypt, and Palestine

Joseph Yahalom

Yehuda Halevi was a younger contemporary of the great chronicler of the Golden Age, Moshe ibn Ezra, and the paths of the two great poets inevitably crossed, with Ibn Ezra moving to the Christian north of Spain at the end of the eleventh century, and Halevi leaving the Christian north and heading for the Muslim south at the beginning of the twelfth century. In a poem written while he was still in the north, '*Dod bahalom nata*',[1] Halevi declares that, in the face of the cruel fate that pursued him there, he is putting his faith in the south. There, he says, he will meet Yitzhak ibn Ezra, Moshe's older brother, though he and the other residents of the south realize that he stands no chance of encountering Moshe himself, as the latter has already departed for the north. Halevi's poem concludes with an Arabic *kharja*, which is explained by the lines that precede it:

אֶל פַּאֲתֵי מִזְרָח	עֵינֵי בְנוֹת מַעְרָב
וּכְרוּב תְּמוֹל בָּרַח	לִרְאוֹת גְּבִיר וָרָב
אֶל עוֹבְרֵי אוֹרַח	קוֹרְאוֹת בְּשִׁיר יֶעֱרַב
מן חבס אלבדרא	חביבי קד אכטא
ואשגל אלסרא	עני לקד אבטא

Eyes of the west's daughter—	turned to the corners of the east
To see a lord and master	a cherub who'd fled in haste—
Call out in a song of pleasure	to those who wander past
My lover has gone	who hides the full moon (of his face?)
He's late in coming	and makes night-travel grim[2]

[1] H. Brody (ed.), *Diwan Yehudah Halevi,* vol. I (Berlin, 1894), 178.

[2] For this poem's *kharja* (ḥabībī qad aḫṭā/ man ḥabbasa l-badrā// 'an-ni la-qad abṭā/ wa-ašġala s-surā), see *Jeich ettaouchîh par Ibn al-Habib,* ed. Hilâl Nâgi and Nuhammad Mâdûr (Tunis, 1967), 50. See also J. T. Monroe and D. Swiatlo, 'Ninety-Three Arabic Harğas in Hebrew Muwaššahs: Their Hispano-Romance Prosody and Thematic Features', *JAOS* 97 (1977): 150. The poem was obviously written between about 1095, when Moshe ibn Ezra left Granada, and 1122, when Yitzhak ibn Ezra died in al-Andalus.

Moshe ibn Ezra, for his part, continued to take in interest in the young poetic prodigy, and he kept in contact with him even from his cold and alienating northern place of exile after Halevi went south and settled in Andalusia. When at the end of his life Ibn Ezra turned to write about Halevi in his book of poetics, he was able to say only that he was a 'son [resident] of Toledo' and afterward a 'son of Cordoba'.[3]

What do we know about these two centres of activity in Halevi's life? Toledo was a Christian enclave, a peninsula of sorts, jutting into the Muslim south beginning from 1086, when it was conquered by Alfonso VI, King of Castile. We have considerable testimony regarding Halevi's stay in the city. The most explicit piece of evidence comes from Halevi himself, in a poem he wrote to a poet-acquaintance of his by the name of Yitzhak ibn Alshaami. In this poem (*Hagam likhbosh ari*)[4] he describes himself as someone whose 'tent is known in the frontier of Spain, the ends of the land of Se'ir and their limit', meaning, clearly, the border areas of Christian Spain, Toledo.

In an epistolary composition in rhymed prose that Halevi wrote during his youth, the poet modestly explains to Moshe ibn Ezra that he, Halevi, is inarticulate and not a good speaker (*kevad peh ukhevad lashon*), as he has been raised in Christian territory. He confesses in this letter that he is drawn with all his heart to the centres of culture in Muslim Spain, which is known as al-Andalus, 'the west', as in *Dod baḥalom naṭa*. This was during the turbulent period of the Christian reconquest. Border-crossing was difficult and the young poet who craved knowledge and learning was repeatedly rebuffed and sent back to the north. In his letter he depicts his situation in the most unambiguous of terms. From the start, he presents himself as 'despised and young . . . from the north (Se'ir) having come / to be enlightened by the light of people of great deeds indeed / these are the great lights / the wise of Western Spain / my heart toward them trembles and turns / and ever since I've harnessed the chariots of friendship / time has worn on me heavily/ I went in search of them slowly / . . . until I arrive at the edge of their country / and was not allowed to approach their land . . .'[5] The talented young

[3] See Moshe ibn Ezra, *Sepher Ha'Iyyunim veHaDiyyunim ('al HaShira Ha'Ivrit)*, ed. A. S. Halkin (Jerusalem, 1975), 78–9, and J. Schirmann, *Toldot HaShira HaIvrit biSepharad HaMuslemit*, ed. E. Fleischer (Jerusalem, 1995), 430, and cf. Fleischer's n. 51, p. 432. See also J. Yahalom, 'Diwan and Odyssey: Judah Halevi and Secular Poetry of Medieval Spain in the Light of New Discoveries from Petersburg', *MEAH, Sección de Hebreo*, 44 (1995): 30–3.

[4] Brody (ed.), *Diwan Yehudah Halevi*, vol. II (Berlin, 1910), 287.

[5] See E. Fleischer, 'Toward a Biography of R. Yehudah Halevi in his Youth and the Beginning of his Link with R Moshe Ibn Ezra' (Hebrew), *KS* 61 (1986–7): 898–9.

man tries in vain to reach the centres of culture in the south, Cordoba and Granada, and Seville, the city of poetry, and with his hopes crushed he tells one of the great figures of Andalusian culture of his disappointment and of having to make do with inconsequential, provincial border regions of the centres that were so dear to both their hearts.

The fact of the matter is, however, that it was not entirely clear that Halevi wanted to cut himself off from Toledo, since the Christian north was a place of opportunity where one might secure a position in the service of the court. Jews often served as tax collectors and bankers, diplomats and political advisers, cultural arbitrators and translators, in addition to other occupations that brought them close to the centres of power. One such occupation was that of Halevi – physician. At the beginning of a poem that Halevi dedicates to Yehuda Ibn Giyyat, his friend from Granada (*Lemi bakhu dema'ayikh nehalim*),[6] an unnamed antagonist questions the poet: 'Your tent is pitched in the east / where creeks surround you with pleasant song // Tell me: why would you set foot in the west / which has already banished you like unwanted idols?' You are dwelling in the comfort of Christian Spain, and Andalusia, after all, promises no such satisfaction, so why are you drawn to it? Clearly the entire question would not have been raised except to set the stage for Halevi's surprising response at the beginning of the core of the poem, at its point of transition: I am drawn to Yehuda ibn Giyyat, the distinguished son of Granada. The poet then follows out the dictates of the panegyric's conventions and sings Ibn Giyyat's praises. It goes without saying that the fictional opening of the poem is rooted in a historical situation that was well known to all. The flow of Andalusian Jews from the south to the land of economic opportunity in the developing north is also well documented.[7] But in addition to being a place of promise the north was also dangerous, and the intervention of Jewish courtiers was essential and anticipated.

Echoes of the changing circumstances of Castilian Jewry can be detected in Halevi's poems. A case in point is Halevi's poem to mark the arrival in Guadalajara of Cidellus, the Jewish physician and adviser to Alfonso VI. The poem closes with surprising lines written in Romance, the spoken language of the region. Cidellus's coming to *Wadi al-Hijaara,* the river valley of stones, Halevi likens to a flood of streams of oil over streams of stones, and to a ray of light being poured across streams of

[6] Brody (ed.), *Diwan Yehudah Halevi*, vol. I, 53.

[7] See Y. Baer, *Toldot HaYehudim biSepharad haNotzrit* (Tel Aviv, 1959), 48.

stones: *desdo meu cidielu venid / tan bona al-bišāra / / com rayo de sol ešid en wād-el-ḥiğāra*).[8]

These golden days apparently did not last long. In an elegy that Halevi wrote after a pogrom in Toledo he explains that in the past Jews lived in tranquility and security in the Land of Se'ir, and even served as advisers to court ministers and to the king, Alfonso VI. Outwardly the Christian masses seemed to support the Jews of Castile, and only harboured wicked thoughts about them in secret. These thoughts found expression on a clear June day in the year 1109, when the king was killed in a pogrom. Our poet was incensed at the frequency of these bloody events. A year earlier, in May 1108, he had written a long elegy in the wake of the murder of Solomon Feruziel, the nephew of the famous Jewish statesman Cidellus. Feruziel had set out on a diplomatic mission to the kingdom of Aragon and been murdered along the way. The poet was worried about the deteriorating situation of the Jews of Castile, who were left without an honest spokesman and defender. In his poem, Halevi violently curses the heads of the Christian kingdom and its masses: 'Let the Lord pour forth torrents of wrath upon the daughters of Edom / may He destroy her from the root and crush her branches // and may He repay her with mourning and widowhood and bring / low her masses as well as all her wooden images of the Asherah' (*Zot hat-la'ah*).[9]

The anonymous elegy '*Libi aha ain li mi yahziqekha*' was apparently written at the same time. The poem laments the murder of the minister from the famous Mestre family in the city of Guadalajara. The poet, who turns to address the deceased, employs the name of the city as an image: 'Your blood was poured as a river in the river of stones / in the hands of all your enemies and tormentors // the river of stones will be wasteland and will turn to stone // and all your lightning will turn into blood / no longer will dew and rainfall grace your land / forever, and wheat shall not cover all your valleys.'[10] For Castile's Jews, rivers of oil were turned into rivers of blood. The sensitive poet wasted no time drawing conclusions. Yehuda Halevi decided to forgo the economic advantages of life in the north, as he was no longer willing to take refuge in the shadow of the dreadful Melekh–Molokh. This, it seems, is when Halevi left the seductive north behind, for good, and settled in the culturally rich south of Spain. There he eventually became a cultural

[8] Brody (ed.), *Diwan Yehudah Halevi*, vol. I, 158. Cf. S. M. Stern, *Hispano-Arabic Strophic Poetry* (Oxford, 1974), 133–4.

[9] Brody (ed.), *Diwan Yehudah Halevi*, vol. II, 98.

[10] See J. Schirmann, *Shirim Hadashim min HaGenizah* (Jerusalem, 1967), 449.

interpreter of sorts, acting as a mediator for the learned elite of the south, and for those in the north who yearned for the wisdom and knowledge that was still hidden in Arabic. This was also the turning point in his life, the beginning of his social awakening and public activity on behalf of captives who awaited redemption. We learn of these efforts from Arabic letters of his, in his own handwriting, which have been discovered in the Cairo Genizah.[11]

Of Halevi's five Hebrew epistles in rhymed prose addressed to recipients in Spain, three pertain to the matter of his correspondence with the sages of Narbonne.[12] These epistles are of great importance in understanding the tensions the poet was torn by. In a letter to David Narbonni, Halevi praises his skill in Hebrew composition and, as it were, expresses astonishment at his interest in the sciences. He also asks him, somewhat ironically: 'Would you borrow letters from other languages; do you not believe that unlike the Egyptian are the Hebrew women?' (cf. Exodus 1:19).[13] During this time, Halevi was also close to one of the prestigious scholars of Cordoba, Barukh ibn Albalia (d. 1126). In a letter in rhymed prose, dispatched in a hurry from Cordoba, he apologies to the letter's recipient, David Narbonni, for not being able to carry out the mission that the latter had charged him with. Barukh, the letter explains, has been in Lucena for some twenty days at the time of the letter's composition, and only when he returns will Halevi be able to raise David Narbonni's matter with him.[14] We might conclude from this exchange that Halevi was not willing or able to delay his response more than three weeks, something that would testify to the urgency and intensity of the correspondence with Narbonne. The urgency notwithstanding, Halevi's letter is cast in an elegant rhymed Hebrew prose that would have been acceptable to his addressees in the north.

We are able to gather some information about Barukh from Halevi's panegyric in his honour. Despite its conventional nature, the poem offers some information about Barukh's relations with the questioner, and perhaps about the nature of the questions themselves. Halevi describes him as someone who 'has erected the building of wisdom . . . and answers all those who pose questions to him / for he has found for

[11] See. S. D. Goitein, 'Documents in the Handwriting of Yehudah Halevi' (Hebrew), *Tarbiz* 25 (1956): 393–412.

[12] Two to R David Narbonni and one to the sages of Narbonne, one to R Moshe ibn Ezra and one to R Shelomo ibn Giyyat.

[13] See Brody (ed.), *Diwan Yehudah Halevi*, vol. I, 220.

[14] See J. Schirmann, 'New Fragments from the Letters of Yehudah Halevi' (Hebrew), *Yedi'ot HaMakhon LeḤeqer HaShira Ha'Ivrit* 6 (1946): 118, with new additions based on a manuscript from the Second Firkovitch Collection, Heb. 209/1, and also 208/1 and 105/12.

wisdom a spring' (*Shir ḥadash befi kulanu*).[15] Likewise from the *Book of Tradition* by Avraham Ibn Daud, who was Barukh's nephew, we learn that 'in addition to his knowledge of Torah and his learning[16] this Barukh was learned in Greek wisdom. He raised up numerous students, 'of whom I am the least'.[17] In the few other instances where it appears this sort of praise seems to have been connected with the ability to compose poems and hymns, as in the description of Moshe ibn Ezra and his teacher Yitsḥak ibn Ghiyyat.[18]

During the first quarter of the twelfth century, Halevi enjoyed the patronage of another scholar, the head of the Cordoba yeshivah, Yosef ibn Sahal, who was himself a poet of considerable repute. According to Moshe ibn Ezra, Ibn Sahal's poems of wit and satire were particularly fine. 'There was no barrier to the sharp arrows of his satirical poems, and he sent them out freely as he pleased. Most of his satirical poems were aimed at a group of men who had attacked poetry and condemned the works of the poets.'[19]

When Yosef died (Nisan 1124), the poets lost an enthusiastic supporter, one who had derived his authority from the world of religious law (*halakhah*) as well. It was more than mere rhetoric when Moshe ibn Ezra said that he was 'the last of the great dignitaries . . . after whose death the world was orphaned and evil came to men in their passing'.[20] This was certainly Yehuda Halevi's sense of the situation, as he felt that the ground had been taken out from under him with Yosef's death. He faced another blow with the untimely death of his learned benefactor Barukh Ibn Albalia. This was on the eve of Rosh Hashana 1126. At the same time the political situation was steadily deteriorating.

Towards the end of the 1120s the religious zealotry of the Almohad sect from North Africa grew increasingly intense. Halevi felt the echoes of this zealotry in Andalusia as well. In one small but highly meaningful poem – '*Aṣel halo tevosh vetikalem? Tishkav 'adei boqer vete'alem*?[21] – he berates himself for lying apathetic in his bed while the muezzins in the minarets

15 Brody (ed.), *Diwan Yehudah Halevi*, vol. I, 190.
16 G. Cohen translates 'secular learning'.
17 *The Book of Tradition*, ed. and trans. G. D. Cohen (London, 1967), 87.
18 Cohen (ed.), *Book of Tradition*, 102, 81. Apparently R Yitzḥak ibn Albalia, R Barukh's father, was the Torah scholar who wrote against R Y. Alfasi, condemning his errors in the use of Hebrew (this is the opinion put forth by the late S. Abramson in a lecture). See D. T. Banet, 'Errors in the Use of Arabic – a Subject of Debate among Spanish Halakhic Masters' (Hebrew), *Otsar Yehudei Sepharad* 4 (1961): 14–15. See also D. Sklare, 'R David Ben Se'adya Alger and his *al-Hāwi*' (Hebrew), *Te'udah* 14 (1998): 116–23, and esp. note 48.
19 *Shirat Yisrael*, ed. B. Z. Halper (Leipzig, 1924), 74, Ibn Ezra, *Sepher Ha'Iyyunim*, 76–9.
20 *Shirat Yisrael*, 74, Ibn Ezra, *Sepher Ha'Iyyunim*, 76–9.
21 Brody (ed.), *Diwan Yehudah Halevi*, vol. II, 272.

of the mosques all around thunder their prayers and supplications. He spurs himself on at the close of his brief poem in the manner of the captain who berates the prophet Jonah: 'Rise up, how can you lie there asleep; you see strangers standing at the gate, and you sleep?' During this period it seems that the emotional pressure began to take its toll on the poet's free spirit. In 1130, Almohad brigades set out on a daring campaign of conquest in North Africa, during which many of Morocco's Jews perished. In his dreams, Halevi saw the devastation of Islam approaching. In a poem employing numerous puns and homonyms he prophesies, addressing the son of Hagar in a strikingly aggressive tone: 'In the year 1130, your pride will be shattered / and you will be ashamed and disgraced for all you have wrought (*Namta venirdamta veḥared qamta*).[22] The spirit of zealotry was on the rise among Jews as well, and those who condemned poetry and the new poets began to speak out increasingly. Halevi was forced, it seems, to seek out a new centre of operations, and he managed to obtain the patronage of well-known head of the Lucena yeshivah, Yosef ibn Migash, who was a modest man of upstanding character, but far from the world of poetry and secular learning.

In an epistolary response to Ḥabib, of the city of Mahadiyyah in North Africa, in which Halevi complains of the grey that has come to his head, he bears witness to the goings on in the yeshivah and the lively give and take between Yosef ibn Migash and his students. Ḥabib was concerned at not having received an answer to his questions from the rabbi, and Halevi calms him down: 'With my own eyes I have seen your finely formulated questions in his [ibn Migash's] hands and in the hands of his disciples / and upon them were his responses / written before him, / with choice words he dictates to them / and they record.'[23]

We shall probably never know just what it was that Ḥabib had asked the head of the Lucena yeshivah and that required such an urgent response. There is, though, in Yosef ibn Migash's responsa (186) mention of a certain man who wants to make a pilgrimage to the Land of Israel, and who vows not to eat meat or drink wine until he realizes this dream of his. In his response, Yosef ibn Migash explains that the man's course of action is absolutely forbidden. Halevi perhaps found a loophole that enabled him to get around the prohibition against the vow concerning pleasure. In one of his most famous poems he says, in rhetorical fashion: 'My heart is in the east, and I at the ends of the west – / how can I taste what I eat or find it pleasing, // how could I fulfill my solemn promises

[22] Brody (ed.), *Diwan Yehudah Halevi*, vol. II, 302.

[23] See Y. Ratshabi, 'A Letter from R Yehudah Halevi to R Habib' (Hebrew), *Gilyonot* 28 (1953): 271.

and vows / while Zion is fettered by Edom and I am in Arabia's chains?'.[24] In the letter that Halevi sends to Mahadiyya, he takes a hard look at his life and attempts to come to terms with the depths to which he has fallen. His intellect, he feels, is leading him to a dead end: 'They made me the keeper of the vineyards / but my own vineyard I have failed to keep; / I have rushed into matters of medicine and therapy / but neglected matters of prophecy; / Greece and its wisdom have mired me in slime / and Qedar's darkness with its language has dimmed me / and Edom in former days doomed and muted me.' Halevi's complaints in this letter relate explicitly to matters of the spirit. The poet, it would appear, is disappointed not only with Greek philosophy and sciences, but with the primacy of Arabic literature, and with the political culture of Edom (Christianity), which made its true nature known in the past. Nor is there any demand for his own poems (of prophecy), and among the northern precincts of Christian Spain there are clearly, as he sees it, very few worthy of his poetry's sweet discourse.

It was most likely during this period that Halevi announced to the young Shelomo Farḥon, a resident of Aragon, that he, Halevi, would no longer write poetry in the quantitative meters in the manner of the Arabs. Some twenty years later (1161) the student testified to this effect in the grammatical section of his book *Maḥberet Ha'arukh*,[25] in a passage that resembles Halevi's denunciation of the Arab-style poetry in the *Kuzari*.[26] As Halevi must have said these things a short time before leaving for the Land of Israel, and as Shelomo Farḥon knew that Halevi had passed away in the east, he saw fit to state the matter plainly and powerfully: 'He repented before his death, declaring that he would never again compose poems. And in truth, this is an Arab [literally, 'Ishmaelite'] practice and it suits their language.' Halevi, when all is told, was merely seeking to avoid invitations to prophesy in poetry, especially when these invitations came from scholars in Christian Spain, who were not equipped with the refinements of Andalusian court education. They did not understand the poet's ambivalence towards Arabic culture, nor of course were they aware of the daringly hedonistic poems he was to write on the banks of the Nile in the autumn of 1140.

To counter the overbearing zealotry around him, Halevi raised the idea of the independence of the cell or the superiority of the heart among the

[24] Brody (ed.), *Diwan Yehudah Halevi*, vol. II, 155.

[25] *Maḥberet Ha'Arukh leR Shelomo Farhon*, ed. Z. Stern (Pressburg, 1844), 5a. See also the comprehensive discussion in R. Brann, *The Compunctious Poet. Cultural Ambiguity and Hebrew Poetry in Muslim Spain* (Baltimore and London, 1991), 84–118.

[26] *Kuzari* 2; 70–3.

organs and limbs of the body. His *Book of the Kuzari,* where his world-view is worked out, was written in response to a question posed to him by a Karaite from the Christian north.[27] It made perfect sense that Halevi saw things in terms of 'centre and margin'. In a letter to Cairo on the eve of his departure for the Land of Israel he adopts a similar line of thought in explaining his reasons for making the pilgrimage. 'Not every living soul is human / and not all men are of Israel / and not all of Israel's men are priests / and not all priests Moses and Aaron.'[28] And what holds good for the man who has been chosen, the prophet who comes from the chosen tribe of the Levites certainly holds good as well for the chosen place: 'And not every land is Canaan / and not all of Canaan the Gates of Heaven / and not all of the Gates of Heaven Jerusalem.'

An anonymous interlocutor raises an objection to Halevi's plans for pilgrimage and his scheme of centre and concentric circles. The objection is found in a newly discovered Judaeo-Arabic introduction to the poem *Devareikha bemor 'over requḥim.*[29] As the antagonist puts it, Jerusalem holds its advantage over other places only by virtue of being encircled and settled, but since the Jews have been murdered or expelled from the city and its environs (by the crusaders in 1099) pilgrimage no longer makes sense.[30] He is therefore of the opinion that without the outer circles there is no centre, and without 'my brethren and companions' there is no place to seek the 'house of the Lord our God' (Psalms 122:8–9). Halevi's ironic answer highlights the difference between the multiplicity of the outer circles and the oneness of the point at the centre, between Jerusalem's Jews who are buried and the buried ark inside which the eternal tablets of the commandments are kept. He asks rhetorically: 'Is it good that the dead be recalled / while the ark and the tablets are forgotten? // Would we seek out the place of the underworld and worms / and abandon the source of eternal existence? / Is our only portion the sanctuaries of the Lord, / that we abandon the mountain of his holiness?' He sets the eternal holy mountain in Jerusalem against the 'sanctuaries of the Lord', the synagogues of the Diaspora. Already at the beginning of his response he questions his antagonist's assumptions: is it for the sake of the house of our God that we pray for her (Jerusalem's) well-being, or for the sake of companions and brethren?

27 See Goitein, 'Documents in the Handwriting of Yehudah Halevi'.

28 See S. Abramson, 'R Yehudah Halevi's Letter about his Pilgrimage to Eretz Yisrael' (Hebrew), *KS* 29 (1953–4): 140–1 (with new additions from the Second Firkovitch Collection, Heb. 206, f. 41).

29 Brody (ed.), *Diwan Yehudah Halevi*, vol. II, 164; see First Firkovitch Collection, Heb. 164, f. 27.

30 See J. Prawer, *The History of the Jews in the Latin Kingdom of Jerusalem* (Oxford, 1988), 22–45.

The *Book of the Kuzari* preserves an echo of a similar argument, this time between two fictitious figures, the King of the Khazars and the wise *Ḥaver*. The *Kuzari* argues along lines similar to the argument put forward by traditionalists from northern Spain, like Avraham bar Ḥiyya from Barcelona and his friends:[31] 'What can be sought in Palestine nowadays, since the Shekhinah is absent from it, whilst, with a pure mind and desire, one can approach God in any place. Why would you run into danger on land and water and among various peoples?'[32] At this stage in the encounter the *Ḥaver* takes his leave of the king. The concluding passage reflects its author's severing of his association with his homeland and the cutting off of his former connections. One must take what he says there seriously: 'The visible Shekhinah has indeed disappeared, because it does not reveal itself except to a prophet or a favoured community, and in a distinguished place.' It sounds as though Halevi is speaking messianically, but in fact what he says relates directly and profoundly to his plans.

From what Halevi says in the most recent fragment of a letter to have been discovered in the St Petersburg library collection of manuscripts, it would appear that he sought to realize in his pilgrimage to Jerusalem the precise conditions that he had already stated would bring about the revelation of the Shekhinah in the Land. As he puts it in this letter, his intentions are to gather about him a group of priests (*kohanim*) who, under his charge, would perform the cultic rites on the Mount of Olives: 'And my soul longed / for the mountain of holiness / to bow down in the presence of the sons of Aaron / and the holy ark which has been hidden / and to say before the Lord, Rise and have compassion for Zion.' These words echo powerfully and were later passed on in the more apocalyptic formulation of Ashkenazic Hasidism: 'If three hundred priests were to stand on the Mount of Olives and recite the priestly benediction the Messiah would come.'[33] It would seem that the Ashkenazi imagination was kindled by these lines of Halevi. The poem *Tsion Halo Tish'ali*, in which Halevi gave expression to his longing for the Land of Israel, was quickly absorbed into the book of Ashkenazic dirges for the Ninth of Av, where it made a powerful impression and gave rise to a long line of Ashkenazi imitations.'[34]

[31] See M. Idel, 'On Eretz Yisrael in Mystical Jewish Thought of the Middle Ages' (Hebrew), in *Eretz Yisrael HaYehudit biYemei HaBenayyim*, ed. M. Halamish and A. Ravitzky (Jerusalem, 1991), 200–40. [32] *Kuzari* 5: 22–3.

[33] See *Perush HaRoqe'ah 'al HaTorah*, ed. S. H. Kanyevsky (Bnei Berak, 1980), vol. II, 156 (Exodus 29:29).

[34] See *Seder HaQinot leTish'ah BeAv: KeMinhag Polin uQehilot HaAshkenazim beEretz Yisrael*, ed. D. Goldschmidt (Jerusalem, 1968), 124 ff.

Among these circles of Ashkenazi Jews were people who would one day follow Halevi and take advantage of the new paths that were opened by the crusader kingdom of Jerusalem. The journey to the Land of Israel undertaken by the rabbis of France would follow the new sea-route direct to the port of Acre. In so doing these devotees would try, perhaps, to fulfil the symbolic step of the Spanish dreamer-theologian, whose pilgrimage combined ideology and reality in an indivisible bond.

CHAPTER TEN

Abraham ibn Ezra as a harbinger of changes in secular Hebrew poetry

Masha Itzhaki

I

Abraham ibn Ezra, one of the foremost Jewish scholars in twelfth-century Spain, the author of many books on philosophy, biblical commentary, astronomy, Hebrew grammar and mathematics, was also one of the famous Hebrew poets of the Middle Ages. He wrote hundreds of liturgical poems, *piyyutim*, which are still included even today in synagogue rituals, and about 250 secular poems.[1] On the one hand, his poetical work is a beautiful representation of the traditional Andalusian school, prosodically as well as thematically. On the other hand, one may easily identify in his work new poetical tendencies which should be considered as the precursors of a new period in the history of Hebrew poetry.[2]

Unlike his liturgical poetry, his biblical commentaries or his linguistic researches, Ibn Ezra's secular poetry has been relatively neglected by contemporary scholars. His secular poems have been published in three editions, all three dating from the nineteenth century: Eiger's edition,[3] based mainly on Berlin manuscript 186, a unique copy of a Yemenite *diwan* from the fourteenth century; Rosin's edition, *Reime und Gedichte des Abraham ibn Ezra*,[4] and Kahana's edition,[5] which is problematical, especially on questions of attribution and identification. All three naturally appeared too early to make use of the Genizah materials; all three are partial and very old fashioned in their modes of presentation. Nevertheless, those are the only complete editions available to the modern reader.

[1] I. Levine, *Shirey ha-Qodesh shel Avraham ibn Ezra*, 2 vols. (Jerusalem, 1975–1980), and *Yalkut Avraham ibn Ezra* (New York and Tel Aviv, 1985). No critical edition of Ibn Ezra's secular poetry has been published since the end of the nineteenth century. Having been deeply involved in this project for several years now, I hope to accomplish this work soon.

[2] M. Itzhaki, 'Megamot Didaqtiyot be-Shirat ha-Ḥol shel Avraham ibn Ezra'. In *Meḥqarim bi-Yezirato shel Avraham Ibn Ezra* = *Te'uda* 8 (1992): 2–27.

[3] Berlin, 1886.

[4] Breslau, 1885–94.

[5] Warsaw, 1894.

Selections of Ibn Ezra's secular poems have been presented in H. Schirmann's famous anthology, *Ha-Shira ha-Ivrit bi-Sefarad u-vi-Provans*[6] and later in Israel Levin's *Yalkut Avraham ibn Ezra*.[7] Nevertheless, even in those anthologies the editors follow the work of previous scholars, without studying either new sources or problems of attribution.

Most of the scholars dealing with Ibn Ezra's poetics share the same opinion: although he was very familiar with the Andalusian school, one cannot ignore the new genres he created, the strophic structures he developed, the realistic tendency and the satiric style so typical of his poetry and so very new in the history of secular Hebrew poetics in Spain.[8]

II

Studying the genres of Ibn Ezra's secular poetry, one may easily note some real changes, relating either to a different choice of genres or to new tendencies in the conventional ones, indicating a new poetical conception in relation to the traditional Andalusian school.

Ibn Ezra avoids almost totally the main subject matter of any courtly literary expression – love and passion as well as wine festivals – so typical of the previous poetical generations in Islamic Spain, beginning with Samuel ha-Nagid in the eleventh century and including his older contemporaries Moses Ibn Ezra and Judah Hallevi. Eroticism is present in Ibn Ezra's secular poetry, but in a context quite different from the previous one: not in an independent, short monorhymed poem expressing eternal love for a cruel and inaccessible beauty, so conventional in classical Hebrew poetry in Spain, and functioning as an entertainment during banquets, but either in introductions to laudatory poems, mostly strophic,[9] or in epithalamia – in most cases secular in nature – or even more so, in a humorous context, as in his famous correspondence with Joseph ibn Zaddik, a contemporary poet, on the subject of a bride whose period began on her wedding night.[10] Generally speaking, it is obvious that Ibn Ezra is very familiar with what one might consider as the erotic

6 Jerusalem and Tel Aviv, 1956. 7 New York and Tel Aviv, 1985.

8 See, for instance, I. Levin, *Abraham ibn Ezra, Ḥayav ve-Shirato* (Tel Aviv, 1970), chapter 5; H. Schirmann, *Toldot ha-Shira ha-'Ivrit bi-Sefarad ha-Noẓrit*, ed. E Fleischer (Jerusalem, 1997), 40–6; Itzhaki, 'Megamot Didaqtiyot' .

9 A typical example is the poem *Ẓura Heḥeyatni* ('The image that revived me'), dedicated to one of his patrons, Joseph ben Amram, a *muwashshah* which employs figures and images from Arabic poetry in a Hebrew version.

10 In Hebrew : *Kalla she-parsha niddatah be-leil huppatah*. See Kahana's edn, pp. 76–8.

glossary of the Andalusian school, only he is using it in a different way: not as an autonomous unity, with its own *raison d'être*, but as a vehicle for an outer message, as an instrument or a mode of transmission.

These considerations become much more self-evident when we turn to Ibn Ezra's wine poems. As a matter of fact, it is not even legitimate to speak of his 'wine poems', as this particular genre does not really exist in his corpus, not even as a metaphorical introduction serving to present another issue, as mentioned above in relation to love poems. Nevertheless, wine or wine parties figure as thematic elements in a few of his satiric poems, in his riddles and most obviously in his dispute poems.

We should be cautious in dealing with the satiric poems: as mentioned before, every scholar of Ibn Ezra's secular poetry pays a good deal of attention to his satiric style and to his humorous approach towards his contemporaries as well as towards his own destiny. In this regard, the poem *Ha-Kankan reikan* ('The empty flask'), treating the parsimony of a certain community in Provence, as well as the famous poem about the flies (*Le-mi anus*, 'Where can I find refuge?'), are very tempting examples of a real instrumental parody based on the conventional pattern of a wine party serving the cause of social critics.[11] In both cases the texts transform the traditional components of an Andalusian banquet – wine, good food and beautiful women – into a real catastrophe either by their surprising absence or by the presence of unwelcome intruders.

However, before jumping to literary conclusions and stylistic analyses, one must confront the main problem concerning Ibn Ezra's secular poetry: the identification of the author. As surprisingly as it may be, there is so far no reliable manuscript source for those two popular poems, and the same goes for another text, *Ashkim le-veit ha-sar* ('Early I set out'), as well as for *Me'il yesh li* ('I have a coat'), both considered as the best Hebrew satiric poems ever written in Spain. As a matter of fact, quite a few poems that have been considered for a long time by many scholars to be by Ibn Ezra should be viewed sceptically, and question marks should be liberally used. It seems that for at least three or four centuries copyists and scholars have been in the habit of attributing to Abraham ibn Ezra almost every sophisticated piece of poetry written in more or less Sephardic style. None of the four poems just mentioned figures in

[11] On Hebrew parody see Z. Ben Porat, 'Ha-Parodia ke-Bikoret ba-Bikoret ha-'Ivrit', in *Peles*, ed. N. Gouvrin (Tel Aviv, 1980), 232–40. For parody in Ibn Ezra's poetry see Levin, *Abraham ibn Ezra*, 202–3 and 208–10; M. Itzhaki, 'Mishte ha-Yayin be-Shirat Abraham ibn Ezra', *Tenth World Congress of Jewish Studies* (Jerusalem, 1990), 291–7; L. J. Weinberger, *Twilight of a Golden Age* (Alabama, 1997), 11–14, 65–73.

Eiger's edition, the only one based on a manuscript from the fourteenth century. *Ashkim le-veit ha-sar*, for example, figures – to the best of my knowledge – only in an eighteenth-century manuscript[12] and subsequently in anthologies and reviews from the nineteenth centuriy, such as vol. IV of *Literaturblatt des Orients*, edited by Julius Fürst (1840–51), or *Tzitzim u-Ferahim* published by A. Geiger in Leipzig in 1856, and later on in M. Friedlander's book on Ibn Ezra's commentary on Isaiah, published in London in 1873, and in *Shivhei Elohim*, published in Oran in 1884. We may trace the same poem as Ibn Ezra's at the beginning of the twentieth century in a book entitled *Et Laledet*, by Eliyahoo Alush, published in Tunis in 1911, as well as in many other publications.[13] I believe that this phenomenon – 'sure' attribution without any textual proof – is the result of a loss of information over the years. Declarations such as 'I have found in a beautiful manuscript a poem of . . .' are typical of copyists and collectors from previous generations, who forget, in their enthusiasm, to mention some useful details.

Dealing with such a problem, one must certainly continue to search for reliable sources, taking advantage of modern resources and updated studies of the Genizah manuscripts, but there is also a possibility of identifying the poet by linguistic and poetical arguments. In some cases a careful analysis of vocabulary, syntax, prosodic qualities and metaphorical language may be as useful as an authentic signature.

III

One of Ibn Ezra's most important innovations in relation to secular poetry in Spain is the introduction of the dispute poem. Admittedly, literary debate is an ancient genre in Hebrew literature. It occurs for the first time in the Bible, in the competition of the trees (Judges 9:8–15), and later on in the oriental *piyyut* or in Italian liturgical poetry where we find controversial dialogues between body and soul, good and evil, between mountains and even among the four seasons of the year.[14] This literary genre (*al-Mufakhara* or *al-Munazara)* was very popular in medieval Arabic

12 New York, *JTS* 3302, 16.

13 There is no need to give here the same information concerning the other three poems. The general pattern in each case is very similar. Are they really by Ibn Ezra? I hope to be able to give a clear answer when my work is completed.

14 See M. Steinschneider, *Rangstreit Literatur* (Berlin, 1908); A. M. Habermann, 'Reshima shel Shirei Viquaḥ le-Ma'alot be-'Ivrit'. In *A Book in Honour of Prof. Marx*, ed. David Fraenkel (New York, 1943), 59–62; H. Tourniansky, 'Shir ha-Viquaḥ ha-Yehudi', *ha-Sifrut* 32 (June 1982); W. J. van Bekkum, 'Observation on the Hebrew Debate', in *Dispute Poems and Dialogues in the Ancient and Mediaeval Near East*, ed. G. J. Reinink and H. L. J. Vanstiphout (Leuven, 1991), 77–90; E. Fleischer, 'Le-Qadmoniut Piyyuṭei ha-Ṭal va-ha-Geshem'. *Qovetz 'Al-Yad* 8 (18) (1976): 113 ff.

poetry as well, where debates between a pen and a sword, milk and wine or water and wine, sea and land, etc. occur regularly.[15]

It is rather astonishing that in spite of a continuous presence of Hebrew liturgical debates on one hand and a long Arabic tradition of poetic disputes on the other, the Andalusian Jewish secular school had not adopted this dramatic pattern. Hebrew secular poetry in Spain is based on the assimilation of Arabic literary genres, yet there is no trace of a polemic poem until Abraham ibn Ezra, the first poet who composed true literary debates.[16]

Having clear textual proofs in different manuscripts, we may mention five poems of this genre written by Ibn Ezra:

1. *Hadashim ma'asei El* ('New are the actions of the Lord'), a monorhymed introduction to a *qasida*, including a debate between the eye, the ear and the tongue, leading to the main part of the poem which is of a laudatory nature.
2. *Bein shabbat u-mo'ed* ('Between Sabbath and Holidays'), a dispute between the Sabbath and Jewish holidays, formally a classical *muwashshah*.
3. *El echad ma rabbu 'edekha* ('O one God, you have so many witnesses'), a debate between summer and winter, having a special *muwashshah*-like structure.
4. *El bor'i reshit ha-qol milay* ('God, my creator'), a quarrel between man and animals, having the same structure as no. 3.
5. *Efros kaf* ('I'll spread my hand'), a dramatic dialogue between the speaker and the sea while the former is sailing on a boat, having the same structure mentioned above.

A study of the sources of these five poems shows that their attribution to Ibn Ezra seems quite solid. Poems no. 2, 3 and 5 figure in MS Berlin 186, and hence also in Eiger's edition. Poem no. 4 is mentioned by Eiger in a list of poems known as being by Ibn Ezra, it occurs in a Genizah manuscript (T-S NS 96.55), where it is attributed to *avram* just before poem no. 3, and one can easily make out the acrostic 'Abraham be-Rabbi Meir' at the beginning of the poem. Poem no. 1, although not figuring in the *diwan*, is certainly by Ibn Ezra, as it is placed in many manuscripts at the end of the Torah commentary, with a clear title mentioning the name of the poet.[17]

15 See E. Wagner, *Die arabische Rangstreitdichtung* (Mainz, 1963); Y. Sadan, 'Ḥalav ve-Yayin', *Ha-Sifrut* 21 (1975), 21 ff.

16 There is no need to mention that this genre became quite popular after Ibn Ezra's period, especially in the Hebrew *maqama*.

17 See for example: Oxford, Bodley 222, f. 273b; Oxford, Bodley 218, f. 296b; Paris BN héb 180/2, f. 213.

Traditionally, however, there is an additional debate poem, *Bein re'im shama'ti tokhehot*, a dispute between bread and wine, officially attributed to Ibn Ezra only from the sixteenth century.[18] An attempt to justify this attribution may serve also as a systematic presentation of the poet's stylistic innovations.

IV

The nature of Ibn Ezra's dispute poems has been discussed elsewhere.[19] A short résumé would emphasize the following qualities: although dealing with different subject matters, all the poems are well constructed dramatically, and the personificated objects (whether concrete or abstract) are full of life. Four of the poems are built either in the pattern of a real *muwashshah* or on a *muwashshah*-like model. Furthermore, the texts lead, especially in the concluding strophes, towards a philosophical, if not religious, apprehension of the harmony in the universe under divine rule, as if these poems, in spite of their outstandingly secular function, have an obvious metaphysical message to convey. Two poems (nos. 3 and 5) have the acrostic 'Abraham' and one (no. 4) has an alphabetical acrostic. Taking into consideration the fact that acrostics are typical of the *piyyut*, should one regard these qualities as indicating a tendency to cross the lines between what was considered to be liturgical and secular? Could this be perceived as one of Ibn Ezra's innovations?

Our poem, *Bein re'im shama'ti tokhehot*, appears in three manuscripts: in a Genizah fragment, T-S H 10.48, the first twenty-three verses as well as any possible title are missing; the same goes for a Vatican manuscript, Ebr. 303, while the only manuscript where we find the poem as a whole is Cambridge UL Add. 377.3.10 (fol. 94b), of the sixteenth century.[20] In this source the poem – although no title is mentioned – is cited just after *El bor'i reshit ha-kol*, no. 4 in our list.

Should this lead us to attribute the poem to Ibn Ezra? Methodically, a poetical study as well as a stylistic analysis could be of great interest at this point.

In my opinion the prosodic structure of this particular poem speaks for itself: as mentioned before three of Ibn Ezra's debate poems are *muwashshah*-like and have a very particular rhyme system: a/a/a/a/a//b/b/c/c. d/d/d/d/d//e/e/f/f. etc. It seems to have the regular two

[18] See *Shirim u-Zemirot* (Constantinople, 1545), and MS Cambridge, UL Add 377 3.10.

[19] See Itzhaki, 'Megamot'.

[20] As well as in *Shirim u-Zemirot* of 1545.

parts of a traditional *muwashshah* stanza, only the *aqfal* does not really exist any more as its double rhyme changes from one strophe to another. This rhyme scheme is totally new in Hebrew poetry and does not occur in contemporary Arabic poetry either. As a matter of fact its origin is to be found in Provence in the twelfth century. Knowing that Ibn Ezra was familiar with this region, where he spent several years, it is logical to presume that he was influenced by the nature of the local poetry. In any case, *Bein re'im shama'ti tokhehot* is built according to the very same model, so new and so characteristic of Ibn Ezra.

Moreover, when we turn to the metric system things are quite similar: all four poems use the syllabic meter, usually more frequent in liturgical poetry, in an identical manner: nine syllables in the first part of the strophe and only six in the second part.[21] One should pay attention to another style marker: poem no. 3 (debate between summer and winter) uses anadiplosis (*shirshur*) as a linking device between the two parts of the strophe. This technique, so typical of the oriental *piyyutim* and so rarely used in Andalusian secular poetry, reappears in the first three strophes of the poem under discussion.

Taking all those factors into consideration, in addition to the dramatic nature of the poem as a whole and to the philosophical apprehension of the harmony in the universe, so clearly expressed in the concluding strophe, one may very readily attribute the debate between the bread and the wine to Abraham ibn Ezra.

Furthermore, this analytical experience, which leads to certain conclusions regarding attribution, enables us to identify a few of Ibn Ezra's style markers and innovations on several poetic levels: new prosodic models, new thematics and genres and, above all, a totally new tendency concerning the distinction between secular and liturgical poetry. A didactic message, treating the harmonious universe under divine providence, is an essential subject matter in his so-called secular poetry, which – poetically speaking – ignores the traditional thematic and structural distinctions between sacred and non-sacred poems.

[21] The same pattern is found in another strophic poem by Ibn Ezra: *Shim'u na el divrei ha-rofeh.*

CHAPTER ELEVEN

O Seville! Ah Castile!

Spanish–Hebrew dirges from the fifteenth century

Wout van Bekkum

I am the remnant of the exile of Spain,
and the exile of France in decline.[1]

For more than a century before their final dissolution in 1492 the Jewish communities of Spain and southern France had suffered severely from increasing animosity and repression. Already in 1378 changes of far-reaching importance were taking place: the archdeacon of Ecija, Ferrán Martínez, came to Seville and in fanatical sermons demanded the destruction of the twenty-three synagogues of the city. He asked the population of Andalusia to expel the Jews from their midst and to attack them whenever they could. In 1390 the archbishop of Seville died and Martínez succeeded him. In the same year also king Juan I died, leaving a minor as heir. Nobody could guarantee the political protection of the Jews any longer and the conditions in which a pogrom could be launched were easily created by a combination of clerical fanaticism, popular prejudice and economic considerations. The languishing state of the economy caused famine and high prices for which the Jews were blamed.[2]

I owe a great debt of gratitude to Professor Joseph Yahalom of the Hebrew University of Jerusalem for granting me permission to study MS Firkovitch (First Collection) no. 165, and for his invaluable guidance in the reconstruction of the *qinoth*. Cf. also J. Yahalom, 'The Exclusiveness of Poetry as an Expression of Spiritual Life in Late Spanish Piyyut' (Hebrew), in *Exile and Diaspora* (Festschrift for H. Beinart), ed. Aharon Mirski (Jerusalem, 1988), 337–48. The poems cited in this chapter are the first examples taken from this particular collection of Spanish–Hebrew *qinoth* to be published. A critical edition by Yahalom and myself of all the poems in MS Firkovitch 165 is in preparation.

1 MS Firkovitch no. 165 no. 201, bearing the superscription *reshut le-shabbat Shim'u*.

2 José Hinojosa Montalvo, *The Jews of the Kingdom of Valencia: From Persecution to Expulsion, 1391–1492* (Jerusalem: Magnes Press, 1993; Hispania Judaica 9); Emilio Mitre Fernández, *Los Judíos de Castilla en tiempo de Enrique III: el pogrom de 1391* (Valladolid: Secretariado de Publicaciones, Universidad de Valladolid, 1994; Estudios de historia medieval 3); Philippe Wolff, 'The 1391 Pogrom in Spain: Social Crisis or Not?', *Past and Present* 50 (1971): 4–18; Angus MacKay, 'Popular Movements and Pogroms in Fifteenth-century Castile'. *Past and Present* 55 (1972): 33–67; Franz Kobler (ed.), 'Rabbi Hasdai Crescas Gives an Account of the Spanish Massacres of 1391', in *A Treasury of Jewish Letters* (New York, 1951), vol. I, 272–5; Jaume Riera, 'On the Fate of R. Isaac Bar Sheshet (Ribash) during the Persecutions of 1391', *Sefunoth* 2, n.s. 17 (Jerusalem, 1983), 11–20.

In 1391 popular riots commenced in Seville, and spread through the entire Iberian peninsula in little over two months. The progress of the disturbances can be followed from day to day and from city to city. On 6 June 1391 a crowd entered the *judería*, directly encouraged by Ferrán Martínez. There was a series of murders and robberies and two synagogues were converted into churches. Many Jews were forced to accept baptism. From Seville the violent movement spread rapidly to Cordoba and, on 18 June, to Toledo, Madrid and Cuenca. Even in Segovia, the seat of the government, and in Burgos Jews could not be protected. From Castile the riots encroached on other kingdoms. By way of Orihuela and Alicante the kingdom of Valencia witnessed frightful scenes on 9 July and tension increased in other parts of Catalonia. From 2 August there were attacks on Jews at Barcelona, Gerona and Mallorca and soon throughout the whole region. In the meantime, tension was increasing in Aragon. The king, Don Juan I, residing in Saragossa, tried to prevent disorders in the communities under his protection and with the aid of one of his highest officials, Rabbi Hasdai Crescas, and the papal court in Avignon most communities were saved from disaster. The same is true for the kingdom of Navarre, where there were no anti-Jewish riots in spite of religious agitation.[3]

This relatively short period of ruination and decrease of the Jewish community, either by death or by conversion, had a tremendous psychological impact on Spanish Jews. Restoration was painful and mixed with demoralization. Messianic hopes arose in the midst of a deep sense of historical catastrophe which was interpreted as a manifestation of divine trial and punishment, even of God's total abandonment of his people. The dramatic echoes of 1391 can be heard throughout the fifteenth century in Spanish-Hebrew *piyyut.* A considerable number of dirges provide historical evidence regarding the incidents that took place in the summer of 1391. The composition, structure and liturgical recitation of these dirges follow a much older tradition dating back to the biblical period. The book of Lamentations played a decisive part in the development of poetic compositions on the destruction of Jerusalem and the Temple known as *qinoth.* Poetic and structural devices recur in one well-known example from perhaps as early as the third or fourth century, a *qinah* for the Ninth of Av describing how the entire universe

[3] Yizhak Baer, *A History of the Jews in Christian Spain* (Philadelphia: Jewish Publication Society of America, 1961), vol. II, 95–120; against Baer's rather 'lachrymose' way of treating Jewish history during the fifteenth century in Spain, cf. Eleazar Gutwirth, 'Towards Expulsions: 1391–1492', in *Spain and the Jews: The Sephardi Experience 1492 and After*, ed. Elie Kedourie, 51–73 (London: Thames & Hudson, 1992).

identifies with Israel's sadness about the destruction of Jerusalem and the Temple. These tragic events were mourned by the tribes of Jacob in conjunction with the sun, the moon and the stars. Specifically the *mazzaloth*, the constellations of the zodiac, are mentioned one by one in a personified and direct reaction to the misfortunes of Israel.[4] This *qinah* in many respects sets a model for the themes of numerous compositions to come up to the period of fifteenth-century Spain, an age of recurring religious oppression and persecution. A large number of conventional motifs in later *qinoth* and *seliḥoth* (penitential hymns) can be summarized as follows:[5]

First, the mourning for the historical event of the destruction of Jerusalem and the Temple after their capture by the Babylonians in 586 BCE. The main theme of Lamentations could easily be actualized in later elegiac poetry after the second destruction of Jerusalem and the Temple by the Roman legions in the years 69–70.

Second, the role of God in the history of the people of Israel, viewed from an emotional perspective. Bewilderment and despair are expressed in questions of dissent: Why are the people of Israel afflicted with calamity? Why have they lost their political and religious independence? How long will Diaspora continue? Occasionally the poet protests against God's way of ruling the people of Israel, adding a note of criticism in accordance with Lamentations 2:5: 'The Lord is like an enemy; he has swallowed up Israel, he has swallowed up all her palaces and destroyed his strongholds, and has multiplied mourning and lamentation for the daughter of Judah.'

Third, the poet expresses his concern about the success of Israel's enemies who seem to carry out God's purpose. Yet, they are held responsible for their iniquities and will eventually not escape punishment.

Fourth, the literal meaning of the word *seliḥah* is 'forgiveness'. Repentance is a necessity for the rehabilitation of Israel, strongly linked with the concept that Jerusalem and the Temple were destroyed and Israel went into exile because of the sins and crimes

4 Joseph Yahalom, '*Piyyut* as Poetry', in *The Synagogue in Late Antiquity*, ed. Lee I. Levine, 119–120 (Philadelphia: American School of Oriental Research, 1986); cf. T. Carmi, *The Penguin Book of Hebrew Verse* (Harmondsworth: Penguin, 1981), 204–6.

5 Ross Brann, 'Images of Exile in Hebrew and Arabic Qinoth in Spain' (Hebrew), in *Israel Levin Jubilee Volume*, ed. Reuven Tsur and Tova Rosen, with Hanna Dawid (Tel-Aviv: The Katz Research Institute, 1994), 45–61; Wout J. van Bekkum, 'Structures of Spanish Qinoth from the Fifteenth Century' (Hebrew), *Eleventh World Congress of Jewish Studies* C, vol. III, 21–8 (Jerusalem, 1994).

of previous generations. This implies that at the same time God has to be asked for forgiveness.

Fifth, the *qinoth* and *seliḥoth* stress God's vengeance upon Israel, but the plea for redemption is not excluded. Most post-biblical poems conclude in the same vein as Lamentations 5:21, 'Renew our days as of old', calling for restoration of Israel's glory and dignity together with the coming of the Messiah.

The thematic components of the *qinoth* and *seliḥoth* show a strong coherence and generally the poet keeps to a fixed set of themes, based upon biblical and related midrashic material. Only in an advanced stage of development within these particular poetic genres are references to contemporary events included. This is clearly the case during the fifteenth century when Spanish *payyeṭanim* turned the poetic reference to the disorders of 1391 into a historical symbol of the Jewish fate. This is a unique detail of these dirges.[6] Most compositions contain direct references to the occasions on which they were recited, and could have gradually been adopted in standard liturgy, particularly on fast days like the Seventeenth of Tammuz, a day of commemoration of the conquest of Jerusalem, and the Ninth of Av. Between these two dates there is an interval of three weeks, which was considered suitable in the Middle Ages for the recitation of *qinoth*. Many examples can be found within the Ashkenazi liturgy,[7] but with regard to the Sephardi a large collection of unknown *qinoth* for the three so-called Sabbaths of Retribution is contained in recently discovered manuscripts.[8]

One of these manuscripts is in the collection of the Russian Karaite scholar Abraham Firkovitch (1786–1874), now in the National Library (formerly Saltykov-Shchedrin State Public Library) in St Petersburg. The Firkovitch collection has enormously enriched our knowledge of Judaeo-Arabic grammar and exegesis, but Spanish-Hebrew poetry is also amply represented in it. It is obvious that the Russian Genizah will

[6] Dan Pagis, 'Dirges on the Persecutions of the year (5)151 in Spain' (Hebrew), *Tarbiz* 37 (1968): 355–73; cf. also Raymond Scheindlin, 'Secular Hebrew Poetry in Fifteenth-century Spain', in *Crisis and Creativity in the Sephardic World: 1391–1648*, ed. Benjamin R. Gampel, 25–37 (New York: Columbia University Press, 1997); Roger Boase, *The Troubadour Revival, A Study of Social Change and Traditionalism in Late Medieval Spain* (London: Routledge & Kegan Paul, 1978).

[7] Leopold Zunz, *Die synagogale Poesie des Mittelalters* (Frankfurt a.M.: Kauffmann, 1920, repr. Hildesheim: Olms, 1967), 152–333; cf. also Daniel Goldschmidt and Avraham Fraenkel, *Preces Poenitentiales quae Selichoth vocantur a poetis Germanicis et Francogallicis conscriptae* (Hebrew) (Jerusalem: Mekize Nirdamim, 1993).

[8] The incomplete MS Add. 20.747, Oriental Library, London, is another collection of approximately sixty dirges for the three Sabbaths of Retribution. MS Parma, de Rossi 1192, contains laments on the persecutions of 1391: see *Sefardi Collections of Piyyutim for Fast Days and Special Sabbaths from the Year 1481*, intro. D. S. Löwinger and J. Yahalom (Jerusalem: Makor Publishing, 1973).

contribute a great deal to the study of medieval Jewish culture in the years to come. MS Firkovitch no. 165, containing sixty leaves, has been described by Joseph Yahalom, who enumerates 118 incipits of which only 23 are known from other sources. The manuscript is incomplete, however, and may originally have included another 130 poems. The colophon states that the copyist is Jacob ben Moshe, about whose life nothing is known at present. In some of the compositions there appears the acrostic signature of Hayyim ibn Musah, who has been identified as a poet and author who died in 1460. For a number of reasons it is likely that the manuscript was copied in fifteenth-century Spain, and it becomes clear how Spanish-Jewish poets gave expression to the vicissitudes of their own time by reference to the outbreak of anti-Jewish violence in the year 1391 and the policy of the Church and the Catholic monarchs in later years. In spite of the generally conventional nature of language and style of the compositions, occasionally a glimpse of the actual situation of the Jews in Spain is given.[9]

The events of 1391 took place in the summer, just around or within the period of three weeks of mourning between the Seventeenth of Tammuz and the Ninth of Av. The Jewish communities of Spain remembered the persecutions as a traumatic experience and an obvious turn for the worse. It may not have been too difficult for the elegists of the fifteenth century to offer their historical innovative compositions to a synagogue audience in addition to older and more classical *qinoth* and *seliḥoth*. The new dirges were inserted in sometimes unexpected positions of prayers or prayer complexes, as can be learnt from the *qinah* for *Nishmat kol ḥay* ('The soul of all the living'):[10]

> How have my words of praise grown dim,
> as this sabbath on which I give my cries;
> bitterly I hit my face and my hands,
> in the month of Av, the month of my sighing.
>
> How has the blood of many pious men been shed
> in every generation by my foes and murderers;
> our God did not avenge the Jews,
> for the sake of his Law my foster children were killed.

9 The relation of poetry to history is controversial: in theory, the two are quite separate. In the case of the historical *qinoth* the events of 1391 were recorded as they actually took place, but the poets make the historical facts conform to an ornate literary style characteristic of the *qinah* genre. On *poesía* and *istórica* in contemporary Castilian poetics cf. Jeremy N. H. Lawrance, 'Juan Alfonso de Baena's Versified Reading List: A Note on the Aspirations and the Reality of Fifteenth-century Castilian Culture', *Journal of Hispanic Philology* 5 (1980–1): 101–22.

10 No. 226 in the MS, prefaced by the superscription *qinah rabba le-Nishmat kol ḥay*.

Judah is downtrodden in every place,
despite the fact that they expect my Messiah;
in murder, in conversions and in injustice,
my pains are numerous as are my troubles.

The crown of the holy Law has fallen,
and there is nobody who erects my houses, my doors;
a law of strangers is given pride of place,
it tramples upon the communities of God and my brothers.

How silent are their blood and their souls,
they do not seek for revenge on their oppressors;
it is Judah and Israel that cry,
to God they approach who has in his power
the soul of all the living.

In view of the reference to the month of Av in the fourth line of the first strophe it is likely that this elegy was inserted before the prayer *Nishmat kol ḥay*, probably on the third Sabbath of Retribution or *Shabbath Eykhah.* Many words and expressions are derived from Lamentations, and a few passages refer to a rabbinic source, but the contents of the poem allude to the actual situation: the reason for mourning is the assassination of many innocents, while the Torah seems to be put aside by the laws of the Church. Yet God does not retaliate against the enemies of Israel, and the souls of the dead remain silent, but the survivors who recite the morning prayer of *Nishmat kol ḥay* protest and mourn the fate of their people. The next *qinah* offers much more distinctive information:[11]

Hear, all ye nations how great is my grief as well as my lament,
therefore I let my eyes flow in tears and my sleep is gone.

Hear, O rivers and seas, hills and high mountains!
I weep in dust and ashes, I mourn day and night.

Hear, O earth and heavens! I cry drops of tears
about great devastation from the day I left Jerusalem.

In particular there was much wailing in the disastrous year 5151,
when the community of Seville was ruined as well as many others in Castile.

And the communities of all Andalusia; in Provence evil intruded,
in Catalonia there was looting; Aragon was caught together with them.

Judah and the people of Israel, turn away from the defiling evil inclination,
maybe God will show mercy and send to you the Redeemer.

[11] No. 206 in the MS, prefaced by the superscription *'ala Barukh she-amar*; cf. also Simeon Bernstein, *'Al neharot Sefarad* (Tel Aviv, 1956), 202.

The son of David will come and assemble them, he builds the sanctuary
and forecourt of God; every one will praise Him there,
blessed be He who spoke and the world came into being.

The opening word of the first three strophes ('Hear', Hebrew *shim'u*) hints at the second Sabbath of Retribution called *Shabbath Shim'u*, when the reading of the prophets is Jeremiah 2:4: 'Hear the word of the Lord, O house of Jacob.' A historical excursus is added to the traditional phraseology in the fourth and fifth strophes, introduced by the phrase 'in particular'. The information is accurate and reflects the development of the 1391 pogrom which started in Seville. The sixth strophe calls upon the Jewish people, perhaps specifically upon the *conversos*, to turn away from the evil of apostasy: only then will God perhaps show compassion and send the true Messiah. The two concluding strophes open with the name Judah son of David. This name occurs in many other *qinoth* as well, sometimes expanded by the name Yahya and the expressions *ha-rav* or *ben ha-rav*. Judah ben David ibn Yahya must have been a productive hymnographer, because in MS no. 165 alone some thirty poems are composed by him. Unfortunately, very little is known about his life; apparently he was a prominent communal leader and Jewish noble who associated with Christian courtiers in Castile and Aragon. We learn from one of his *qinoth* that he and his family escaped to Portugal, probably in the aftermath of the Tortosa Disputation in 1413–14 and the subsequent wave of conversions, accompanied by the fanatical sermons of the notorious preacher Vicente Ferrer. Following the standards of Spanish *piyyut*, Ibn Yahya composed short hymns for the *yozer* complex, such as *ofannim*, *me'oroth*, *ahavoth*, *zulatoth* and *ge'ulloth*, intended for the embellishment of the benedictions of the *Shema'*. These hymns open with a refrain or a biblical verse to be repeated after every strophe as a congregational response. The structure of the poem closely follows the Arabic *muwashshah*, or rather its Hebrew counterpart, but does not meet all its classical standards of metre and rhyme.[12] An example of such a *muwashshah*-type form or pseudo-*muwashshah* is the next *ge'ullah*:[13]

Joy is forgotten in our communities,
we scream loudly because of those who punish us,
for our soul is bowed down to the dust [Psalm 44:23].

12 Ezra Fleischer, *The Yozer, Its Emergence and Development* (Hebrew) (Jerusalem: Magnes Press, 1984), 486–604; Leon J. Weinberger, *Jewish Hymnography, a Literary History* (London: Littman Library of Jewish Civilization, 1998), 91–8, 117–19.

13 Bernstein, *'Al neharot Sefarad*, 274; no. 245 in the MS is prefaced by the superscription *ge'ullah laḥn yaḥpor 'alay bi-zediyyah.*

So how is a people that God calls 'first-born'
handed over to a cruel nation to whom He did not give a name?

From their Law it distracted them and caused them to sin,
saying that their Rock has hated them,
also declaring that He has uprooted them,
for our soul is bowed down to the dust.

How can God tolerate this and remain silent,
when his people is called an evil-smelling dog;
with every one's permission He punishes them:
one robs, another beats with a hammer,
another denies that our Messiah will come,
for our soul is bowed down to the dust.

Judah with Benjamin and priests,
Menasseh and loyal Levites,
are vexed by Edom and the Ishmaelites,
without being violent are fathers and sons afflicted,
in dirges we show bitterness all our years,
for our soul is bowed down to the dust.

The son of David, the Messiah, we expect,
although we do not see our signs,
in this period every year we weep
about the destruction of your sanctuary, our Father,
we longed for a sanctuary, our holy house,
for our soul is bowed down to the dust.

Pleading our cause, and our people from then,
from Egypt we went out until today,
bring near unto us the Redeemer as a ransom,
for your sake we are slain all day long,
O God, renew us for the good also today,
for our soul is bowed down to the dust.

The poetic text alludes to the historical reality of constant threat and considerable suffering as a result of religious and political oppression against the Jews, which extended to coercion to convert to Christianity.[14] The poet mentions the rejected status of the Jewish people in the hands of Edom and Ishmael, the conventional appellations for Christian and Muslim rule. The opening word *eykhah* in the first two strophes and the explicit mention of the destruction of the

[14] Stanley Evan Rose, *Poesía antijudía y anticonversa en la poesía artística del siglo XV en España* (Ann Arbor: Thesis Catholic University of America, 1975; University Microfilms International, vol. 122, microfilm series 56); Eleazar Gutwirth, 'Maestre Juan el Viejo and his Tratado (Madrid MS)', in *Proceedings of the Ninth World Congress of Jewish Studies* B, 129–34 (Jerusalem, 1986).

Temple give sufficient reason to assume that this poem was read on the third Sabbath of Retribution. The mixture of motifs in the last two strophes reflects the distressed situation of the Jews who themselves hardly believe in future salvation. Because of the trying times, the hymn writers sometimes let feelings of disappointment prevail over their firm belief in the coming Messiah. Ibn Yahya uses the expression 'pleading our cause' (Hebrew: *ha-rav rivenu*) more often in the last strophe of his dirges, both a biblical reference to Jeremiah 50:34 and an addition to his father's name within the name signature which consists of the introductory words of the last three strophes: Yehudah ben David ha-Rav. Similarly, in a composition for the first benediction of the *Shema*ʿ Ibn Yahya presents the classical themes of exile and redemption in combination with some historical statistics:[15]

> *Bitterly do the people of exiles cry*
> *to Him who made great lights* [Psalm 136:7].
>
> Judah with all my people,
> weep my day and my night,
> because God supports my foe,
> and my community is in the hands of conspirators,
> *bitterly do the people of exiles cry*
> *to Him who made great lights.*
>
> O, this exile has taken so long,
> the summer is over, the harvest is gone,
> already for 1360 years
> we are in exile and there are no redeemers,
> *bitterly do the people of exiles cry*
> *to Him who made great lights.*
>
> My sanctuary has been destroyed twice,
> two times, yes, two!
> Yet, the numerous houses of my enemy
> have been rescued in 1390 years,
> *bitterly do the people of exiles cry*
> *to Him who made great lights.*
>
> High heavens and signs of the zodiac,
> stars, constellations and hosts,
> plead with loud voices,
> that He may rescue His circumcised people,
> *bitterly do the people of exiles cry*
> *to Him who made great lights.*

[15] No. 197 in the MS, prefaced by the superscription *me'orah*.

My people Judah and its tribes
suffer from the yoke and punishments of the enemy,
return it to His places of refuge,
O Lord, living God, who heals the sick,
bitterly do the people of exiles cry
to Him who made great lights.

The son of David will revive the people who hope for him,
he will teach them to return from their guilts,
he will redeem them from amidst their enemies,
he will build the sanctuary in greatness,
bitterly do the people of exiles cry
to Him who made great lights.

How can God stand this and how
is the crown of His people trodden!
Amidst the people it is said that
the Torah of Sinai has turned into mockery,
bitterly do the people of exiles cry
to Him who made great lights.

How can people who believe in God
be called a defiling and unclean people?
How can they say that a redeemer has come,
and that he left the sanctuary in waste,
bitterly do the people of exiles cry
to Him who made great lights.

Both acrostic and name signature are inserted into this *me'orah*: Y-H-W-D-H and Judah ben David Yahya. The characteristic description of actuality in this composition is preceded by a previously mentioned classical motif: the bewailing and lamenting of the fate of Israel by the signs of the zodiac and the stars. Most famous in contemporary poetry is the moving elegy of Moses Remos, who was born in Mallorca around the year 1406 and as a youth studied and practised medicine in Palermo. At the age of twenty-four he was accused of having poisoned a Christian patient. Only conversion to Christianity could save him from the death penalty, but he refused. The signs of the zodiac play a prominent role in the elegy he composed on the eve of his execution illustrating that the use of the *mazzaloth* motif has its own long tradition in Hebrew verse.[16] The last strophe contains a cautious disapproval of the idea of Christ as the Messiah. In the second and third strophes two exact numbers are

[16] D. Kahana, *Qinah le-Mosheh Remos* (Odessa: A. M. Duchno, 1892); Carmi, *The Penguin Book of Hebrew Verse*, 438.

mentioned. Counted from the year of the destruction of the Temple in 70 CE these numbers refer to the years 1430 and 1460. The poet may be indicating that from the thirties to the sixties of the fifteenth century he himself experienced maltreatment and persecution. It is known that during this time in the aftermath of the Tortosa disputations enormous problems existed for Jews and *conversos* alike.[17] However, the use of round numbers in these *qinoth* points to stylistic elaboration rather than to an accurate historical date. Numbers and names of cities became the fixed components of the poetical version of the historical account. In other instances the mentioning of a number could implicitly be taken as a reference to the year of composition. This seems to be true in a *mi kamokha* composition by Ibn Yahya intended for insertion in the *ge'ullah* benediction after the recitation of the words taken from Exodus 15:11. The *mi kamokha* hymns in classical Spanish–Hebrew poetry are often exceedingly long, but Ibn Yahya limits himself to ten strophes according to an alphabetical acrostic and an eleventh strophe with the name signature:[18]

Lord, your love has become merciless and you have forgotten to be gracious,
from the day, 1370 years ago, that Ariel [Isaiah 29:1] was destroyed
you have sold your people to Edom and Ishmael,
The Lord was an enemy, He has swallowed up Israel [Lamentations 2:5].

Among the nations it has been heard, heaven and earth are witnesses,
that You are the King, You have appointed functionaries,
and commanded them to be the heirs and be ready,
to destroy, to slay, and to annihilate all Jews [Esther 3:13].

Our sins have become greater than the transgression of Sodom and Gomorrah,
for You have brought upon us captivity, killing and conversion,
also every sickness and every bitter affliction,
which is not recorded in the book of the Torah [Deuteronomy 28:61].

The words of Your Torah and Your commandments are despised,
from the day we went into exile and captivity,
scattered all over lands and isles,
we have become a taunt to the nations [Psalm 79:4].

Behold, since we went into exile,
and incurred burdens and insults,
we were weary and gave up but we hoped for Your salvation,
we have not seen our signs [Psalm 74:9].

17 Baer, *A History of the Jews in Christian Spain*, 244–92.

18 No. 238 in the MS, prefaced by the superscription *mi kamokha le-shabbat Eykhah*; cf. Ezra Fleischer, *Hebrew Liturgical Poetry in the Middle Ages* (Hebrew) (Jerusalem: Keter, 1975), 388–94; *The Yozer*, 575–91.

And in exile my godly and faithful men have vanished,
the blood of innocents has been poured out among my multitudes,
and there is none to search, to take revenge, to uphold my cause.
Rouse yourself! Why do You sleep, O Lord [Psalm 44:23]?

Godless men utterly derided me, and we almost abandoned hope for goodness,
and we are forced to scorn and curse Your name,
why should You leave us to rot by the punishments of exile,
remember Abraham, Isaac, and Jacob [Deuteronomy 9:27].

Cruelties, insults and curses we have suffered,
all kinds of punishments we have accepted to sanctify Your name,
therefore, if we were foolish enough to commit sins,
do not punish us because we have done foolishly [Numbers 12:11].

Before the end of this exile for which our heart is trembling,
if it still will continue and our people will not taste redemption,
Your Torah will be forgotten, and we will despair and slip away,
the name of Israel will be remembered no more [Psalm 83:5].

Judah and Israel, O God, send to release them from prison
the son of David, your Messiah, through him we will be exalted,
then they will say: the Lord has done great things for them:
Who is like You, majestic in holiness, terrible in glorious deeds, doing wonders?

The number 1370 could lead us to the date of composition in the year 1440 which seems to be consistent with the biography of the poet and his dramatic description of Israel's position in exile in which grief and despair clearly prevail over messianic hopes. Ibn Yahya, like his earlier colleagues, embellishes each strophe within this *mi kamokha* dirge by closing scriptural verses, and hardly allows himself to draw from sources other than the Bible. Some form of censorship or self-censorship could be a reason for the poet's avoidance of explicit statements. Another anonymous *mi kamokha* hymn combines the style of classical models of the genre with strong allusions to the actual situation:[19]

Hear and give ear, my multitudes,
who among you fears the Lord,
they said: the people and the priests, the ministers of the Lord, weep,
it is time to seek the Lord [Hosea 10:12].

Let me weep and cry with a bitter voice,
a cry as of a woman in travail,
who has purposed this against the bestower of crowns,
The Lord, the Lord, the Lord.

[19] No. 220 in the MS, prefaced by the superscription *mi kamokha le-shabbat Shim'u*.

Let me weep and let my tears run down,
I am utterly spent and crushed; I went about mourning,
I roar like a lion and like a bear robbed of her cubs about the killing of my community,
but as for me, my prayer is to You, O Lord [Psalm 69:14].

Let me bitterly scream about the devastation of the crown of communities on earth,
thoroughly pious men stand in the breach,
for an enemy and foe has come to kill them vigorously,
a God of vengeance is the Lord [Psalm 94:1].

Let me shout about the depositing of statues and images in our dwellings,
and about the fact that prayer has ceased from the house of the Lord,
and my princes and musicians have turned away,
the temple of the Lord, the temple of the Lord, the temple of the Lord [Jeremiah 7:4].

For whom shall I recite my dirge first,
for those who were killed sanctifying the Terrible One in deeds,
or those who against their own will left the community in exile,
and rend your hearts and return to the Lord [Joel 2:13].

Woe to the Torah which the wrongdoers have burnt,
and ceased the sabbath, the new moon and circumcision,
woe to the blood that has been shed from elder and virgin daughter,
a jealous God and avenging is the Lord [Nahum 1:2].

Woe to the elders who sit cast off in every street,
for the birds of the air to devour and the dogs to tear,
and they did not know when they committed themselves to this debt,
My people know not the ordinance of the Lord [Jeremiah 8:7].

Let me weep about the young men of Israel, the third part,
and about the killing of children who scream alas!
Because infants and babes faint in the streets of the city,
blessed be the Lord.

Let me weep about the killing of mothers with their sons,
about the daughters slaughtered before the eyes of their fathers,
their eyes look on and fail,
and they cried to the Lord [Joshua 24:7].

Woe to the women who cried but there was none to save,
and their sucking children are slaughtered by the hand of a wicked sinner,
and every one was crying and shouting aloud,
and the Lord slaughtered them.

Woe to the sale of little children who are bought
and sold, and those who are weaned from the milk are given to strange people,
and to the blood of infants and babes which is spilled in the land,
for the hand of the Lord has touched me [Job 19:21].

Woe to the children of Israel, all slain by the sword to the earth,
a proverb, a byword, fully destroyed,
they gathered them together in heaps, and the land stank,
behold, the hand of the Lord.

Let me cry drops of tears,
about the numerous times the Torah has been burnt,
O God of hosts, turn around, look down from heaven,
how long, O Lord [Isaiah 6:11]?

O Almighty, send us the chief Shepherd,
by virtue of those who were killed in unifying Your name, remember and give guidance,
that [we] may not be like sheep which have no shepherd,
I wait for your salvation, O Lord [Genesis 49:18].

Behold, we are considered as dead in the whole world,
in material loss more distressed than anyone else,
we are all guilty; do it for the sake of Your name and redeem us,
for you do I wait; and You will answer, O Lord [Psalm 38:16].

In your great mercy do not hold back Your Messiah,
from the people which You have chosen,
and He will surely come, and will not delay,
be mindful of Your mercy, O Lord [Psalm 25:6].
Concluded is *mi kamocha.*

This hymn is designed as a strong protest against everything that befell the Jews of Spain: many people lost their lives, synagogues were converted into churches by placing crosses and statues in them, Torah scrolls were burnt, and the *conversos* were equally to be lamented as those who were murdered; many people lost their incomes and jobs, humiliation by poverty and starvation had become common. It was as if God had really forsaken and forgotten his people, and the only expectation was the coming of the Messiah as the evidence of God's compassion for Israel. The poet's treatment of the genre *mi kamokha* is in full accordance with earlier examples of great poets like Shelomoh ibn Gabirol and Judah ha-Levi who also built their poems in rhyming quatrains with closing scriptural verses. Each last colon is a scriptural closing unit either cited verbatim or reformulated in order to establish a consistent rhymeme in all the strophes with the word *Adonay*. The use of scriptural references is overwhelming, and almost every colon contains one or two biblical passages.

This preliminary introduction to MS no. 165 in the first Firkovitch collection demonstrates that the *qinah* persisted as a conservative genre up to the last stage of Hebrew poetic creativity on Spanish soil. Hitherto unknown elegists who have survived almost exclusively in this manuscript envisaged the past and future of their own people in a search for and praise of their religious tradition coupled with the use of an actual historical frame of reference. These compositions represent a unique source for the spiritual anxiety of the Jews in Spain in a century of growing exclusion which was ultimately to lead to their final expulsion in 1492.[20]

20 Cf. also Yom Tov Asis and Joseph Kaplan, *Jews and Conversos at the time of the Expulsion* (Jerusalem: Zalman Shazar Centre for Jewish History, 1999).

CHAPTER TWELVE

On translating medieval Hebrew poetry

Adena Tanenbaum

The challenges of transposing medieval Hebrew poetry into English are formidable. The poems are artefacts of a culturally remote world, governed by aesthetic ideals whose formalism and classicism are alien to contemporary readers. This virtuosic verse fuses traditional Jewish piety and learning with aristocratic worldliness. Even in their synagogue poetry the Andalusians adapted and naturalized the formal and thematic innovations of their urbane, arabicizing non-liturgical verse. Whether devotional or convivial, ascetic or erotic, their poetry is written in pure biblical Hebrew, and is saturated with biblical allusions whose significance is often lost on modern audiences, while its prosody is borrowed from Arabic poetry, yielding quantitative meters, fixed rhyme schemes and enormously clever word-plays that are impossible to replicate in English. Fortunately, however, the aesthetic appeal and historical importance of this corpus have compelled some gifted translators to surmount these obstacles.

Until roughly two decades ago, the only available facing-page anthologies of Andalusian Hebrew poetry were the three volumes in the Schiff Library of Jewish Classics. Two of the volumes were translated by Anglo-Jewish literary figures active at the turn of the century, Israel Zangwill and Nina Salaman (née Davis).[1] The third[2] was translated by Solomon Solis-Cohen, a Philadelphia-born physician and Hebrew scholar of Sephardic descent, who was among the founders of the Jewish Publication Society.

In honour of my esteemed friend Professor Raphael Loewe, whose translations and contributions to the study of medieval Hebrew poetry are so elegant, profoundly learned, and thought-provoking.

[1] Israel Zangwill, trans., and Israel Davidson, ed., *Selected Religious Poems of Solomon ibn Gabirol* (Philadelphia: Jewish Publication Society of America, 1924; repr. 1974); Nina Salaman, trans., and Heinrich Brody, ed., *Selected Poems of Jehudah Halevi* (Philadelphia: Jewish Publication Society of America, 1924; repr. 1974).

[2] Solomon Solis-Cohen, trans., and Heinrich Brody, ed., *Selected Poems of Moses Ibn Ezra* (Philadelphia: Jewish Publication Society of America, 1934).

An eminent author and irrepressible wit, Zangwill took a true Victorian approach to Solomon ibn Gabirol's poetry. He saw something 'almost Swinburnian in his technical mastery, in his power of dancing in fetters', and opted for verse translations with 'English measures appropriate to [the poet's] theme' to achieve an effect analogous to Ibn Gabirol's Hebrew rhymes and meters.[3] Zangwill could not imagine omitting the 'singing element' of the poetry. Yet he was alive to the pitfalls of rhymed translation, noting that an untrammelled quest for euphony could badly bloat the structure of the original. His polished quatrains often grow out of only two Hebrew hemistichs, but even where he swells the original form he remains true to its content.[4]

Nina Salaman preferred free verse, 'with a tendency towards rhythm, and following the original, line by line'. These quite literal translations are not always as compact as they might be, yet they are carefully executed. Salaman also provided alternative rhymed and metered versions for about a dozen of the eighty poems in the anthology.[5] Her preface and translations, which now have a certain antiquarian charm, reveal great erudition and a wide-ranging familiarity with Judah Halevi's oeuvre.[6] Love songs, epithalamia and friendship poems are all included, but she judges Halevi's 'religious and national meditations and songs' to be his noblest. Salaman shows tremendous sympathy for her subject, whose stylistic mastery and lyric grace she admiringly acknowledges. If today her translations seem less than immediately appealing or accessible, they have not been entirely supplanted, for there has been no more recent attempt to produce a similarly broad anthology of Halevi's poems in English. A pioneer in her own right, Nina Salaman is to this day one of the few women to have undertaken the translation of Andalusian Hebrew poetry.

A partisan of neither rhyme nor prose, Solis-Cohen determined his forms according to the 'special content' of each poem. 'Some are in rhyme; some in more or less rhythmic prose; some in one or another form of blank verse; some in free verse. Some are consistent in meter, in arrangement of stanzas, and in rhyme schemes; others change from stanza to stanza.'[7] He regretted that rhyme and other poetic

[3] Zangwill, *Selected Religious Poems*, p. l. For the metaphor of dancing in fetters see Dryden's remarks quoted in Rainer Schulte and John Biguenet, eds., *Theories of Translation: An Anthology of Essays from Dryden to Derrida* (Chicago and London: University of Chicago Press, 1992), 18. I am grateful to my colleague Dick Davis for calling this anthology to my attention.

[4] Zangwill mentions one exception where he took the liberty of expanding upon the poet's theme; see his introduction, li.

[5] *Jehudah Halevi*, 151–74.

[6] Quite a few of Halevi's poems are included in her earlier anthology, *Songs of Exile* (Philadelphia: Jewish Publication Society of America, 1901).

[7] *Moses ibn Ezra*, foreword, xiii.

embellishments could not be preserved throughout, for Moses ibn Ezra was a master stylist whose works on Hebrew poetics reveal unparalleled familiarity with the repertoire of rhetorical figures and tropes. *Selected Poems* includes not only courtly genres, elegies, and the penitential verses for which Ibn Ezra was renowned, but even selections from the poet's book of homonymic rhymes, *Sefer ha-tarshish.* Though learned and considered, the English versions are often wordy, even allowing for their now dated diction and style. Like the Halevi volume, however, this anthology has not yet been superseded.

More recent translators may be broadly divided into those who place a premium on the lexical precision of prose and those whose preferred medium is verse. But even within these two camps distinct emphases may be discerned. As a member of the 'prose school' that includes David Goldstein and Leon Weinberger, T. Carmi stands out for his poet's sensitivity to words.[8] Not slavishly literal, the clear, unadorned language of his translations attempts 'to render the poems idiomatically and to capture something of their tone and movement, without "betraying" their literal level'.[9] Straightforward and accessible, these renderings require a minimum of explanatory notes. Yet Carmi is keenly aware of the limitations of such an approach, and concedes that he has omitted from his anthology poems whose rich sonorities and dense intertextual references could not be conveyed in translation.[10] Nor is he able to preserve the original stichometry: although he has discrete stanzas, his continuous blocks of prose give no hint of the autonomous lines, symmetry and love of balance that are the hallmarks of this poetry.

Among those who favour verse translations there is also a broad spectrum of approaches. At one end Raphael Loewe justly observes that Hebrew was not a spoken language for the Andalusian poets, who conducted their day-to-day lives in Arabic, so that even to their ears the classical diction of their poetry sounded elevated and somewhat archaic. The English of the translations should thus be formal, stately and mannered, to produce a similar effect on the contemporary reader. The translator must find fitting analogues to the rigorous rhyme schemes, regular meters, complex word-plays and allusive layerings of the

[8] See David Goldstein, *The Jewish Poets of Spain* (Harmondsworth: Penguin Books, 1971); Leon J. Weinberger, *Jewish Prince in Moslem Spain: Selected Poems of Samuel Ibn Nagrela* (University, Alabama: University of Alabama Press, 1973); Leon J. Weinberger, *Twilight of a Golden Age: Selected Poems of Abraham Ibn Ezra* (Tuscaloosa: University of Alabama Press, 1997); T. Carmi, *The Penguin Book of Hebrew Verse* (Harmondsworth: Penguin Books, 1981). See also the review of Carmi by James Kugel, 'On All of Hebrew Poetry', in *Prooftexts* 2 (1982): 209–21.

[9] Carmi, *Penguin Book of Hebrew Verse*, 11.

[10] Carmi, *Penguin Book of Hebrew Verse*, 10.

Hebrew, for the form was what defined the matter for the medieval poets. Since these authors also treated metaphysical themes, Loewe finds the closest counterpart to their school in the English poets of the sixteenth and seventeenth centuries, and models his masterful translations on their formal verse.[11]

At the other extreme is the poet Peter Cole, whose verse renderings transpose Samuel Hanagid (993–1056) into a strikingly late twentieth-century key. Cole tells us that he makes 'no attempt to duplicate the quantitative meters of the poetry', but rather uses rhythm, syntax and sound to parallel their effect. Nor does he try to reproduce the end-rhyme of the Hebrew, which in the Nagid's monorhymed poems can recur as many as 149 times. Instead, he crafts a contemporary counterpart, using 'internal and off-rhyme, assonance and consonance'.[12] These devices are, for the most part, quite effective. Cole's clean, modern diction is, in contrast with the more expansive classicizing translations, taut and compact like the Hebrew original. Occasionally the English is a little obscure, and it is sometimes difficult to recognize the Nagid's quintessentially medieval mindset in its modern guise. But it has been argued that Cole's translations are successful precisely because they are lively contemporary versions that match the emotional tone and intellectual concerns of the originals.[13]

Between the consistently classicizing and the decidedly contemporary are the fine renditions of Nicholas de Lange and Raymond Scheindlin. An accomplished translator, de Lange aims for fidelity to the substance and tone of the text as a whole, but also for an English poem that will have the same impact as the original.[14] Since the Hebrew of these poems is a 'special, artificial language, drawing heavily on biblical and liturgical Hebrew', the language of the translations must also be somewhat contrived or unnatural, although not completely arcane.[15] The remarkable allusiveness of this Hebrew defies the most skilful translation, but de Lange ably suggests its effect by exploiting the intertextual echoes of select English phrases. His translations resemble Loewe's in several

11 See Raphael Loewe, 'Abraham Ibn Ezra, Peter Abelard, and John Donne', *TAR* 1 (1988): 190–211; and his *Ibn Gabirol* (London: Peter Halban, 1989).

12 Peter Cole, *Selected Poems of Shmuel HaNagid* (Princeton: Princeton University Press, 1996), xxi.

13 See the exceptionally fine review of Cole by Andras Hamori in *Prooftexts* 17 (1997): 299–332.

14 See Nicholas de Lange, 'Reflections of a Translator' (The Sixteenth Annual Rabbi Louis Feinberg Memorial Lecture in Judaic Studies, Judaic Studies Program, University of Cincinnati, 18 March 1993), 6. My thanks to Dr de Lange for graciously providing me with several of his essays on translation, as well as some of his and Raphael Loewe's unpublished translations.

15 Ibid. For an example of such language see his translation entitled 'The Pursuit of Wisdom' in 'Four More Poems by Solomon Ibn Gabirol', *Jerusalem Review* 1 (1997) [52–64]: 59.

respects: regularly rhymed and metered, they are expertly cast in English verse forms. And, like Loewe's, they tend to be expansive, teasing two lines of English out of a single line of Hebrew, or supplying a couplet in the spirit of the original to round out the stanza. De Lange eschews colloquialisms, yet his style and diction admit some variation depending on his chosen form: lovers' plaints often become melancholy ballads, rather than stately sonnets.[16]

Scheindlin's verse translations – which are followed by brief, incisive analyses – reflect a scholarly intimacy with the cultural, intellectual and spiritual worlds the poets inhabited.[17] By giving priority to the stylistic elements of rhythm and rhetoric, they also capture the continuous play of form and sound that were so central to the poets' refined aesthetic sensibilities. To parallel the 'rise and fall' effect of the quantitative meters with their fixed patterns of long and short syllables Scheindlin uses blank verse, although some of his poems are in rhymed iambic meter. Like Cole, he avoids English monorhyme and prefers not to adopt traditional English forms, such as the sonnet. His rhyme schemes are meant to convey a sense of the original pattern of sound, particularly in the strophic poems with their *aaax bbbx* sequences. In other poems he makes effective use of alliteration, assonance, and near rhymes in place of end-rhyme. To ensure that the formal aspects of the poetry come across, Scheindlin does not restrict himself to a single register of English. In general, his translations are lean, supple and fluent, and sound quite natural to an American ear.

It is instructive to compare different treatments of the same poem. In doing so, we shall restrict ourselves to Solomon Ibn Gabirol, whose magisterial verse has attracted multiple translations. Here are de Lange's and Scheindlin's respective versions of his dark love poem *Amnon ani ḥoleh*. The poem builds on the disturbing biblical story of Amnon's lust for his half-sister, Tamar (2 Samuel 13:1–22).

de Lange:

Amnon am I lovesick – go call Tamar:
Tell her her lover struggles in a snare.
Fetch her, my friends, this is my one desire:
Adorn her with a crown and jewels fair,
Place in her hand a cup, and bring her here

[16] See, e.g., 'The Forsaken Lover' in 'Solomon ibn Gabirol: Four Poems', *TAR* 1 (1988) [59–66]: 64. On similarities to and distinctions from Loewe's translations see 'Four More Poems', 55–7.

[17] Raymond P. Scheindlin, *Wine, Women, and Death: Medieval Hebrew Poems on the Good Life* (Philadelphia: Jewish Publication Society, 1986); and his *The Gazelle: Medieval Hebrew Poems on God, Israel, and the Soul* (Philadelphia: Jewish Publication Society, 1991).

That with her kiss she may put out the fire
That sears my heart, and smooth my bristling hair.[18]

Scheindlin:

Like Amnon sick am I, so call Tamar
And tell her one who loves her is snared by death.
Quick, friends, companions, bring her here to me.
The only thing I ask of you is this:
Adorn her head with jewels, bedeck her well,
And send along with her a cup of wine.
If she would pour for me she might put out
The burning pain wasting my throbbing flesh.[19]

Meter and rhyme are central to the original Hebrew, and both translations are attentive to the flow of sound. To replicate the effect of the monorhyme, de Lange uses a series of full and near-rhymes, all similar in their final *r*, but varying slightly in the vowel that precedes it. A virtuosic feat, his rhyme scheme is perhaps even more rigorous than that of the original. Since both the Hebrew and the English build their rhymes on the name Tamar, this is a rare instance of sound similarity between the original rhyming syllable and its English counterpart. Of course, it is impossible to reproduce the subliminal effect of the Hebrew rhyming syllable *-mar*, meaning 'bitter', which colours the whole poem, reinforcing our associations with the underlying story of violent passion that turns to hatred.[20]

Scheindlin's translation is in blank verse, with alliteration and assonance in place of more formal rhyme. The opening *like* is suggested rather than explicit in the Hebrew, but it is well placed to consonate with *sick*, while anticipating the long vowel of *I*. The harshness of the final *k* sound contrasts nicely with the gentle vocalic quality of the *a* (Amnon . . . am . . . call Tamar) whose subtle variations lend the line a certain musicality, despite the bluntness of its wording. Similarly, the second hemistich of the Hebrew does not actually say *death*, but by supplying it Scheindlin sets up a crucial near-rhyme with the closing word *flesh*, forming an inclusio with the verses that speak of the lover wasting away. The altered rhythm of the final line (iamb / iamb / trochee / iamb / iamb), together with the plaintive assonance of *pain wasting*, calls attention to the lover's plight, which – as Scheindlin notes – in this poem has no neat resolution.[21]

[18] De Lange, 'The Gazelle: Hebrew Love Poetry from Muslim Spain', *In Other Words* 7 (1996) [19–23]: 22. [19] Scheindlin, *Wine, Women, and Death*, 111.

[20] On the significance of the rhyming syllable see Aharon Mirsky, 'The Significance of Rhyme in Andalusian Poetry' (Hebrew), in *Ha-piyuṭ: hitpatḥuto be-ereṣ yiśrael uva-golah* (Jerusalem: Magnes Press, 1990), 315–87. [21] See *Wine, Women, and Death*, 112–13.

Delightful, subtle differences between the two versions of the final stich highlight the interpretative challenges facing the translator from Hebrew. Unpointed, the consonantal spelling of the word meaning *if she would pour for me* could also be read as *let her kiss me*; the feminine form of the phrase which opens the Song of Songs. The pointing in most printed versions supports Scheindlin's translation, although the published texts are based on medieval manuscripts which are not usually vocalized. Moreover, the play on *le-hashqot* and *linshoq* has solid biblical precedents, going all the way back to Jacob's first meeting with Rachel by the well near her ancestral home (Genesis 29:10–11). Thematically, both readings are defensible and equally ironic, for a kiss, like wine, would not extinguish but only further inflame the speaker's desire. De Lange's penetrating near-rhymes, *fire / That sears my heart*, capture beautifully the emotional intensity and tortured passion of *esh libbi*, while Scheindlin's *put out / The burning pain* . . . preserves the original hemistich enjambment that moves us from images of an actual fire to the metaphorical plane. De Lange's carefully crafted *smooth my bristling hair* is a bit of poetic licence, perhaps suggested by Job 4:15, where the phrase 'making the hair of my flesh bristle' is one of only two biblical attestations of the verb *smr*.[22] But Ibn Gabirol's line seems to echo the other instance of *samar . . . beśari* which occurs in Psalm 119:120, 'My flesh creeps from fear of You', as well as Lamentations 3:4, 'He has worn away (*billah*) my flesh and skin.' The irony of these allusions is striking, for the speaker's flesh throbs and withers not out of fear of God, but out of unconsummated carnal desire. Such fusion of motifs borrowed from Arabic love poetry with familiar biblical themes is at once a highlight of the literature and a translator's conundrum.

Solomon ibn Gabirol was not only an exceptional poet, he was also the first Jewish philosopher in Spain. Much of his synagogue poetry blends philosophical motifs with traditional liturgical themes in a quest for heightened spirituality. He also wrote contemplative poems which were not intended for devotional purposes. These pieces do not easily fit into fixed generic categories: they are often quite lyrical, and express a strong sense of Ibn Gabirol's personality. Sometimes, however, they are concerned with universal truths, drawing on the Arabic and Hebrew traditions of aphoristic poetry and wisdom literature. *Ve-lev navuv ve-tushiyyah setumah* is a sombre meditation on life in this world. Here is Raphael Loewe's translation, followed by that of Raymond Scheindlin:

22 Scriptural verses are cited from *Tanakh: A New Translation of the Holy Scriptures* (Philadelphia: Jewish Publication Society, 1985).

Loewe:

Blank mind – like brawn's bulk blocks all else from sight,
And counsel – secret as the soul within:
The world's well-wishers snared in evil's gin,
And joylessness on earth our human plight:
The slave's fist raised to strike his lord in spite,
Whilst maid her very queen would discipline,
Son threatening parents twain in froward sin,
Daughter disdaining dam, her own sire's right.

Mine eye hath scanned the world: the world's sons hold
That best which whirls as nonsense, raving mad;
Man must bear toil while life shall onward roll,
Until he bears the weight of worms and mould
As earth at last returns to earth, and glad
The soul soars upward, homing on the Soul.[23]

Scheindlin:

The mind is flawed, the way to wisdom blocked;
The body alone is seen, the soul is hid,
And those who seek the world find only ill;
A man can get no pleasure here on earth.
The servant rises up and kills his lord,
And serving girls attack their mistresses.
Sons are raising hands against their parents,
Daughters too oppose their parents' will.
My friend, from what I've seen of life I'd say
The best that one can hope is to go mad.
However long you live you suffer toil,
And in the end you suffer rot and worms.
Then finally the clay goes back to clay;
At last the soul ascends to join the Soul.[24]

Strikingly bleak, the poem's outlook on earthly life grows out of the Neoplatonic belief that the cosmos is divided into an upper, eternally true world and a lower, ephemeral one. To Ibn Gabirol, the descent of man's pure, immortal soul into a perishable, passion-ridden body is tantamount to imprisonment. Here, that cosmic disorder is mirrored in the inversion of the accepted social and family hierarchies.[25] From the poet's vantage point, the soul's true home is in the divine world, to which it longs to return throughout its confinement here below. Life in this passing world is nothing but suffering and misery. Death, therefore,

[23] Loewe, *Ibn Gabirol*, 77–8. [24] Scheindlin, *Wine, Women, and Death*, 173.
[25] Scheindlin, *Wine, Women, and Death*, 174–5 and Reuven Tsur, *Studies in Medieval Hebrew Poetry* (Hebrew) (Tel Aviv: Daga Books, n.d), 45–8.

brings a welcome release: the body disintegrates but the soul is liberated, free to return to its celestial source in the universal Soul. Ibn Gabirol superimposes this dualistic reading on Ecclesiastes 12:7, to which he alludes in the poem's closing verse, and clinches his repudiation of mundane life with the relentless questioning of the rhyming syllable, *-mah* ('What?').

Loewe's translation is a sonnet, with two lines of English for every one of the Hebrew. Even though the monorhymed Hebrew has no stanzaic divisions, the form is well suited, for the break between octave and sestet corresponds precisely to the turn of thought following the first four verses of the original. Loewe judiciously amplifies and rearranges certain component phrases, but never loses sight of the verse's meaning as a whole. The thudding alliteration of *blank / bulk / blocks* and sighing assonance of *mind / like / sight* furnish fine counterparts to the biblical paronomasia of the opening phrase, *ve-lev navuv* (cf. Job 11:12), and the vowel harmony of *nav**u**v / **t**u**shiyyah / set**u**mah / g**u**f*. Loewe's felicitous *blank / blocks* renders Ibn Gabirol's clever *navuv / satum* which in isolation are antonyms ('hollow' / 'blocked'), but when applied to the mind and to wisdom mean much the same thing.

The intentionally archaic English diction, while it is Loewe's preferred register for all Andalusian poetry, seems particularly apt for evoking a servant rebellion and the disintegration of social hierarchies. If *parents twain in froward sin* sends some readers to the dictionary, this learned translator will not be displeased.[26] And though the concluding aphoristic verses may seem relatively straightforward, the elevated tone of Loewe's translation reminds us that the original is closer to biblical wisdom literature than folksy proverb.[27] The doubling in the sestet (world–world; bear–bears; earth–earth; soul–Soul) reflects the Hebrew faithfully, and lends unity to the poem's second part. Loewe's closing line is exquisitely wrought; its sonorous assonance in *o* and avian imagery impart a flowing motion, and its meticulously chosen verb *homing* encapsulates in one word Ibn Gabirol's doctrine of the soul's true Abode.

Scheindlin's fluid lines and clear, unaffected diction lend the poem a disarming simplicity in keeping with the gnomic quality of the original. His terse endstopped verses successfully convey the stylistic and substantive symmetries, parallelisms and antitheses of Ibn Gabirol's paired, self-contained hemistichs. The near-rhymes *ill* (2a), *will* (4b), *toil* (6a) and

[26] See Loewe, 'Keṣad metargemim?', *Biqoret u-farshanut* 32 (1998) [65–80]: 67.
[27] On the vocabulary derived from wisdom literature see Tsur, *Studies*, 45–8.

soul (7b) tie together the different strands of the poet's thought, as does the consonance of *hid* (1a), *lord* (3a) and *mad* (5b). Direct and uncomplicated, the wording avoids syntactic tangles, making this version accessible to a contemporary audience. With its pithy diction and proverbial tone, Scheindlin's translation is a fitting complement to Loewe's: the latter highlights the subtle ambiguities and occasional syntactic roughnesses that heighten the Hebrew reader's sense of disorder, while the former reflects the poem's aphoristic cadences. Taken together, they provide a rich, full impression of a distinctive and intricate literary artefact.

One of the remarkable innovations of the Andalusian school was the liturgical poem addressed to the soul. Earlier synagogue poetry petitioned God on behalf of the community, but the philosophically informed poets now looked inward, contemplating the soul and its relationship with God. They explored the act of prayer as an expression of the soul's affinity with God, focusing on the individual's spiritual quest in an unprecedented fashion. In pious tones reminiscent of a sermon, they admonished the soul to praise and fear God, and to renounce the pleasures of this world. Drawing their language and imagery from classical Jewish texts and familiar liturgical passages, they exploited the powerful religious symbolism of the Neoplatonic myth of the soul.

Ibn Gabirol pioneered the genre of *reshut*, a short, metrical and monorhymed poem, recited before certain preliminary prayers in the morning service for Sabbaths and festivals. The first of these prayers was *Nishmat*, a hymn opening with the words *nishmat kol ḥay tevarekh et shimkha*; 'The breath of every living being shall bless Your name, O Lord'. Because *nishmat kol ḥay* also meant ' the *soul* of every living being', one type of Andalusian *reshut* became a focal point for meditation on the soul and its role in praising God. By prefacing such introspective, philosophically coloured pieces to portions of the fixed liturgy, the medieval poets furnished a new way of understanding traditional prayers.[28]

Ibn Gabirol's *Sheḥi la-el, yeḥidah ha-ḥakhamah* is a fine exemplar of the genre. Its central theme draws on a series of rabbinic analogies between the human soul and God. God fills the whole world, just as the soul fills the body; they both see, but are not seen; God sustains the world, just as the soul sustains the body; they are both immortal; they are both pure; each is unique in its own domain.[29] On the basis of these similarities,

[28] See Scheindlin, *The Gazelle*, 144–8.

[29] See bBer. 10a; Pirqei de Rabbi Eliezer, ch. 34, end; Deut. R. 2:37, 'Va'etḥannan'; Midrash Tehillim 103:4; and Lev. R. 4:8, which is the fullest elaboration.

the rabbis conclude that it behooves the soul to praise God. It is this idea, refracted through a Neoplatonic lens, that motivates Ibn Gabirol's exhortation to the soul. At once intimate and urgent, this compelling poem has inspired at least five English translations from Zangwill onwards. Following are Carmi's prose version and the verse renderings of Scheindlin and Loewe.[30]

Carmi:

Bow down before God, my precious thinking soul, and make haste to worship Him with reverence. Night and day think only of your everlasting world. Why should you chase after vanity and emptiness? As long as you live, you are akin to the living God: just as He is invisible, so are you. Since your Creator is pure and flawless, know that you too are pure and perfect. The Mighty One upholds the heavens on His arm, as you uphold the mute body. My soul, let your songs come before your Rock, who does not lay your form in the dust. My innermost heart, bless your Rock always, whose name is praised by everything that has breath.[31]

Scheindlin:

Submit to God, my cerebrating soul,
  And run to worship Him in holy dread.
To your true world devote your nights and days –
  Why, why so bent on chasing empty breath?

For you, like God, have everlasting life,
  And He is hidden just as you are hid;
And is your God immaculate and pure?
  You too are pure, you too are innocent.
The Mighty One bears the heavens in His arm,
  Just as you bear the mortal, speechless clay.

My soul, greet God, your Rock, with gifts of praise,
  For nothing has He put on earth like you.
My body, bless your Rock for evermore,
  To whom the soul of All sings ever praise.[32]

Loewe:

My one true self, to God in worship bend,
Thou soul endowed with reason, haste thy flight
In reverence to serve Him, every night,
Each day, think on that world that waits thy end:
Nor chase vain bubbles, thou that canst pretend

[30] See also Zangwill, *Selected Religious Poems*, 69 and Jonathan Wittenberg, 'A Reshut to *Nishmat* by Solomon Ibn Gabirol', *Prooftexts* 8 (1988): 340–6.

[31] Carmi, *Penguin Book of Hebrew Verse*, 315.

[32] Scheindlin, *The Gazelle*, 203. See also the accompanying analysis, 204–7.

To liveliness like God's own life; from sight,
Like him, concealed; be He that formed thee hight
Purest, canst thou thy pure perfection tend:

His arm sustains the welkin, even so
Dost thou thy frame, that but for thee were dumb.
To thy Rock, then, my soul, thy singing raise,
Who made nought like to thee on earth below,
That Rock to whom shall all within me come
Blessing the One whom all that breathe do praise.[33]

One of the difficulties posed by this type of poem is its regular use of epithets. The speaker in *Sheḥi la-el* never actually says *my soul* until the penultimate stich of the Hebrew. Instead, he addresses her with the grammatically feminine phrase *yeḥidah ha-ḥakhamah*. In context, these two words carry such ramified associations that it is virtually impossible to capture all of their resonances in one concise English phrase, especially if it must also scan properly. The appellation *yeḥidah* ('only one') was derived from biblical verses in which the terms *yeḥidah* and *nefesh* (soul) worked as synonyms.[34] It was also associated with the soul in rabbinic texts. One midrashic passage identifies *yeḥidah* as one of five names for the soul because the soul is the body's only 'limb' that is not paired.[35] The sources underlying Ibn Gabirol's poem describe the soul as unique (*yeḥidah*) in the body, just as God is unique (*yaḥid*) in His world.[36] This sense of the term is reflected in the poem's penultimate verse, where the speaker reminds his soul that she has no peer on earth. Since the root *yḥd* could also mean 'individual', philosophically inclined poets like Ibn Gabirol saw in the term the Neoplatonic idea of a soul that separated from its supernal source to lodge within an individual body.[37] They used the adjective *ḥakhamah* (wise) in a similar way, to evoke poetically the philosophical notion of the soul's rational faculty. This was the seat of the intellect that distinguished man from beast, and the vehicle by means of which human beings might cling to God.[38]

How do Carmi, Scheindlin and Loewe render *yeḥidah ha-ḥakhamah*? Carmi has 'my precious thinking soul'. Technically, 'precious' translates *yeqarah*, another regular, grammatically feminine epithet for the soul. Both *yeqarah* and *yeḥidah* suggest the cherished nature of man's God-given soul, which is often personified as God's own beloved. But as

33 Loewe, *Ibn Gabirol*, 87–8. 34 See Psalms 22:21 and 35:17. 35 Gen. R. 14:9.
36 See above, n. 29.
37 See Abraham ibn Ezra's comments on Psalm 22:21, cited in Scheindlin, *The Gazelle*, 243, note 20. 38 See Loewe, *Ibn Gabirol*, 184, note 143.

Raphael Loewe has noted, the English word 'precious' carries the additional sense of overrefined or pampered, and thus may unintentionally inject a comical note into an otherwise sober poem.[39] And while thought is the distinctive domain of the rational soul, there is something awkward about the phrase 'my precious thinking soul'. Scheindlin allows that he has taken a liberty with his lushly alliterative 'cerebrating soul', and takes pains to explain the literal meaning of the Hebrew. Presumably, it is for metrical reasons that he chooses not to translate *yeḥidah*, a term whose significance he also discusses in his valuable commentary. Loewe's 'my one true self' and 'thou soul endowed with reason' build on two of the primary meanings of *nefesh*, 'self' and 'soul'. His expansion of each line of the original into two permits him to layer several of the soul's attributes, and thus capture more of the resonances of these two allusive terms.

Another set of challenges is posed by the second stich of the Hebrew. Read literally, the phrase *le-'olamekh peni* means 'to your world turn'. In Andalusian poetry, *'olam* often refers to the material world, but a medieval reader would have gathered from the possessive suffix (*-ekh*) that the soul is being exhorted to contemplate her *own*, spiritual world.[40] To ensure that the contemporary reader also understands Ibn Gabirol's shorthand, all three translators judiciously supply modifiers: 'your everlasting world' (Carmi); 'your true world' (Scheindlin); 'that world that waits thy end' (Loewe). The second hemistich clarifies this reading, urging abandonment of fleeting mundane pleasures. But it also contains an impossible pun. The hemistich opens and closes with the word *lammah*, which most commonly means 'why'. Yet, the second time it occurs, *lammah* is paired with *hevel*, as though it were a synonym for this term meaning 'empty breath' or 'vanity'. The question can thus be read as 'Why pursue vanity, why?' or 'Why seek things of which one may ask "why?"', which is to say, passing things of which one may ask 'why do they exist?'.[41] Perhaps the rhyming syllable *-mah* might then be construed not simply as 'What?' but as the more pointedly ontological, 'What for?', or 'For what purpose?'

But these questions are all rhetorical: there is nothing to be gained – and much to be lost – by chasing 'vain bubbles'. For a soul uniquely endowed with divine gifts, the only wise course of action is wholehearted devotion to God. Like most poems of the *reshut* genre, *Sheḥi la-el* hints at

[39] Loewe, 'Keṣad metargemim?', 73–4.
[40] Scheindlin, *The Gazelle*, 205; Wittenberg, 'A Reshut', 341.
[41] Scheindlin, *The Gazelle*, 204–5; Wittenberg, 'A Reshut', 341.

its liturgical station, the *Nishmat* prayer, in its closing verse. Twin allusions to Psalms 103:1 ('Bless the Lord, O my soul, and all that is within me, bless His holy name') and 150:6 ('Let all that breathes praise the Lord') lend the poem closure and guide the worshipper back into the fixed liturgy. Yet even here there is room for a philosophical reading based on medieval exegesis of these verses, so that where Loewe has 'all that breathe' for *kol neshamah*, Scheindlin has 'the soul of All'.[42] Read in the light of this profound meditation, *Nishmat kol ḥay* would have acquired additional dimensions of meaning, and the experience of prayer would have been greatly enhanced.

Ibn Gabirol's synthesis of poetry, philosophy and prayer is most impressive in his monumental *Keter malkhut*, or 'Royal Crown'. Deeply religious in sentiment, *Keter malkhut* is an unprecedented attempt at presenting a comprehensive picture of man's place vis-à-vis God and the universe within a hymnic framework. Consisting of forty cantos, it is tripartite in structure. The first part praises and reveres God while meditating on his attributes. Each canto of the second part celebrates God's creation of one of the components of the cosmos as conceived by contemporary science. The poet ascends step by step from the sublunar world through the celestial spheres that surround it, glorifying God at each successive stage. After reaching the outer limits of the universe, he explores the formation and functions of the soul. The third part then turns inward, closing with a personal prayer which is both a confession of sins and a petition for divine compassion. A source of inspiration and instruction, *Keter malkhut* was deemed worthy of inclusion in the Sephardic rite for the Day of Atonement.

The work's elevated rhymed prose has elicited translations into numerous tongues.[43] Of the four complete English versions, only Raphael Loewe's is in verse. It is a superb translation, whose extended Spenserian stanzas strike just the right tone. Where the Hebrew is at times concise to the point of being laconic, Loewe expands just enough to give the English reader his bearings. Here is the opening of the third canto, which marvels at the divine attribute of existence:

> Thou dost exist, we say, though never ear
> Gathered report of Thee, nor mortal eye

42 Cf. Abraham ibn Ezra's comment on Psalm 150:6, citing Solomon ibn Gabirol.

43 For translations into English, Spanish, Ladino, French, Portuguese, Dutch, Yiddish and German see Paula O. Benardete and David N. Barocas, eds., *Keter Malhuth* (New York: Foundation for the Advancement of Sephardic Studies and Culture, Inc., 1972). See also Christoph Correll, *Salomo ibn Gabirol: Krone des Königtums* (Berlin: Akademie-Verlag, 1994).

Hath glimpsed Thee; what existence, then, is here,
Whereof we cannot ask whence, how, and why?[44]

Fluent and graceful, this mildly paraphrastic version is far more intelligible than the literal renderings of either Zangwill or Bernard Lewis.[45] Where the latter's '. . . and how and why and where have no rule over Thee' leaves the reader puzzling, it is clear from Loewe's eloquent verses that the philosophical questions Whence? How? Why? are not applicable to God.

Keter malkhut is replete with biblical allusions, and every canto closes with a biblical verse fragment that acquires new meaning through its new context. Yet Loewe is not fazed: for the benefit of the modern reader who no longer recognizes the source of these references, he deftly works in an identifying hint. When Ibn Gabirol extols God for exalting his throne of glory above all else in the cosmic hierarchy (canto 26), he describes his seat as a realm of divine mystery, beyond which lies the impenetrable divine essence. To signal that this is the limit of human apprehension, the poet alludes to Exodus 34:3, where God commands Moses to ascend in preparation to receive the second set of tablets. In its original context the admonition *ve-ish lo ya'aleh 'immakh* ('no man may ascend with you') is addressed to Moses, who alone is granted a first-hand experience of revelation. In its new poetic setting, however, the phrase is addressed to God and suggests that the human intellect cannot reach up beyond the realm of the throne, to know God in his essence. Remarkably, Loewe's rendering captures both the original and the new senses of the verse:

Upon thy throne of might Thou dost retreat,
Nor may man climb that Sinai's peak to share thy seat.[46]

It is impossible to do justice to this extraordinarily felicitous translation by quoting snippets; for the full effect one must read it in its entirety. It is a labour of love; a surpassing homage to the poet whose 'honeyed words and reasoned argument'[47] Professor Loewe so admires.

44 Loewe, *Ibn Gabirol*, 121.
45 See Zangwill, *Selected Religious Poems*, 82–123; Bernard Lewis, *The Kingly Crown* (London: Vallentine, Mitchell, 1961). The most recent translation is David Slavitt, *A Crown for the King* (New York: Oxford University Press, 1998), see my review in *Prooftexts* 20 (Autumn, 2000).
46 Loewe, *Ibn Gabirol*, 139. See also 'Keṣad metargemim?', 78.
47 From the English version of a poem Professor Loewe composed in honour of the 950th anniversary of Ibn Gabirol's birth; see his *Ibn Gabirol*, 163–4.

IV

The world outside

CHAPTER THIRTEEN

Hebrew apologetic and polemical literature

William Horbury

Like a row of thorns by a Cambridgeshire chalk-pit, this title masks a series of pitfalls with a steep drop. To begin with, the term 'Hebrew' does not always fully suit the medieval apologetic writings preserved in Hebrew.[1] They arise in large part from literary composition and oral converse in languages shared by Jews and non-Jews, from Greek and Arabic to Italian. Thus a gem of this literature is the twelfth-century *Kuzari* of Judah ha-Levi, but its Hebrew form is a translation from Arabic. Moreover, 'Hebrew' does not quite invariably imply 'Jewish'. In almost all cases these writings defend Judaism, against Christianity or Islam, or both; but they include one or two works issued in Hebrew in the Christian interest, following a practice which seems already to be attested in thirteenth-century England, but is perhaps best known from Alphonsus of Valladolid, formerly Abner of Burgos, whose fourteenth-century polemic circulated in both Hebrew and Castilian.[2] Attention is focused below on Hebrew works in rebuttal of Christianity.

These glosses on the term 'Hebrew' have already verged on a question posed by the next three words of the title of this chapter: in what sense can this literature be called 'apologetic' or 'polemical'? These works were no doubt written in most cases with more than one end in view, and then as they circulated will have fulfilled a number of functions. Nevertheless, the two uses that have been to the fore in discussion of these texts are in fact well represented by 'apologetic' and 'polemical' respectively; for interpreters have often put the main emphasis either on defence and internal use, on the one hand, or on attack and external reference, on the other.

Thus a long-standing scholarly recognition of the function of this

1 These works are listed with comment in the bibliographies by J. M. Rosenthal (1960–1) and Krauss and Horbury (1996: 201–61).

2 See Horbury (1999: 17–18); on Alphonsus, see Krauss and Horbury (1996: 94 and note 13); del Valle (1992b).

literature as defence is further developed by H. Trautner-Kromann, reviewing works from France and Spain between 1100 and 1500. Stressing the inaccessibility of these Hebrew writings to non-Jews, rather than the relationship noted above between Hebrew texts and literary and oral argument in other languages, she interprets the literature as intended primarily for internal use, to strengthen adherence to Judaism despite Christian pressure.[3] This defensive and inner-communal purpose and function is clearly important, and it includes a response to the need for what can be called communal self-identification in a broad sense; but perhaps there is more to be said, as the possibility of assessing the use of Hebrew in different ways may already suggest.

An interpretation in which, by contrast, polemic comes to the fore is put forward by Bernhard Blumenkranz, reviewing western Europe between 430 and 1096 (Blumenkranz 1960; 164–71, 216; 1954). He mentions a short but important series of surviving Jewish polemical writings from this period, including in Hebrew the Toledoth Jeshu, and in Latin the fragmentarily preserved arguments of the ninth-century proselyte Bodo from the court of Louis le Débonnaire, who took the name Eleazar and settled in Cordoba. Blumenkranz gives full weight to Christian complaints and quotations of Jewish invective and controversy, and to our knowledge of a number of other proselytes as well as Bodo. He urges accordingly that Jews skilfully imitated the Christian literary polemic against Judaism;[4] in the service of what can be called a Jewish mission, they brought to this genre their own characteristically mordant irony and scorn.

The difference between his summary and that of Trautner-Kromann can be partly but not wholly explained by the difference between the periods in question, respectively before and after the First Crusade. Certainly Christian pressure was heavy in the years reviewed by Trautner-Kromann, especially from the thirteenth century onwards, debate was often undertaken only under compulsion, and the need for restraint in argument on the Jewish side came to be emphasized; but remarkably frank exchanges are still reflected in the Hebrew apologies of the high Middle Ages.[5] It seems probable that, throughout the

3 Trautner-Kromann (1993: 13–18); defence was the keynote of the influential survey of Hebrew polemic by Geiger (1865–71, vol. III: 96–111), and is stressed by E. I. J. Rosenthal ([1960] 1971; 1968–71).

4 Christian writings directed against Judaism are enumerated and discussed by Williams (1935); Schreckenberg ([1982] 1990; 1991; 1994) (the fullest study); and Krauss and Horbury (1996: 26–149).

5 Compare Urbach ([1935] 1999: 59–64) (opposing Graetz's view that freedom in discussion with Christians could hardly be envisaged in France after the twelfth century).

centuries during which this literature flourished, allowance should be made for a desire to commend Judaism and to controvert Christianity or Islam, as well as for the ever-present needs of defence and communal reassurance.[6] The link between communal self-identification and the desire to refute error and win proselytes was brought out especially clearly from halakhic and pietist Hebrew literature of the later medieval west by Jacob Katz.[7]

These works then are first of all apologetic, for they were written, normally for Jewish minority populations under Muslim or Christian government, to provide an 'answer', *teshubhah,* Greek *apologia*. Herein they follow the rabbinic maxim which they often echo, 'Be alert to learn Torah, (and know) wherewith to make answer to an unbeliever (*Epicurus*)' (Aboth 2:14 [18, 19], and Sanh. 38b, in the name of Eleazar ben Arakh); compare the roughly contemporary Greek Christian counsel to be 'ready always for *apologia*' (1 Peter 3:15). 'Answer' often occurs in the relevant Hebrew book titles (for examples see the next paragraph), and E. I. J. Rosenthal correspondingly called his introduction to this literature 'Jüdische Antwort'.

It is true that these writings commonly functioned as apologies only indirectly, for their Hebrew form was rarely accessible to non-Jews, and in other languages too they were probably kept for the most part within the community. In the sixteenth century and later it became possible to print Latin or modern-language apologies addressed directly to non-Jews, like Isaac Cardoso's *Las excelencias de los Hebreos* (Amsterdam, 1679); but these works usually avoid the outspoken argument against Christian biblical interpretation and ecclesiastical teaching and custom that characterizes the Hebrew literature considered here (Yerushalmi [1971] 1981: 352–7, 408–12). Nevertheless, it seems clear that the Hebrew apologies helped to shape the oral argument that they often reflect, and that at least sometimes literary texts were made known directly to the opponent. Thus *Nestor ha-komer* (ninth century, in the east, perhaps Syria or Iraq) purports to be a letter from a proselyte to a Christian following up earlier discussion (compare the contemporary Latin remarks of Eleazar, formerly Bodo), and Jacob ben Reuben (twelfth century, in Gascony or Aragon) says that his book arises from talks with a learned clerk who had tried to bring him over to

[6] Comparable debate over the purposes of early *adversus Iudaeos* texts is reviewed by Carleton Paget (1997).

[7] Katz (1961: 81, 90–2, 96–7, 105), drawing especially on Rashi, the Tosaphists, the *Sefer Ḥasidhim* and Hebrew martyrology.

Christianity; these settings may be fictitious, but they are clearly regarded by the authors as lifelike. In sixteenth-century Constantinople the Spanish exile Isaac Akrish describes himself as holding daily discussions (sometimes at considerable risk) with Christians and Muslims, and as using a series of Hebrew apologies – a *Nizzahon*, and work by Profiat Duran, Ibn Shaprut, and Moses Tordesillas; Akrish sponsored both the copying and the printing of Hebrew polemic (Krauss and Horbury 1996: 168 n., 205, 211). Now and then, no doubt exceptionally, such apologies were directly known to Christians. Nicholas de Lyra (early fourteenth century) notes in his treatise *De Christi adventu* that he read 'a little book written in Hebrew' in which trinitarian doctrine was questioned, and in a second treatise, on Jewish objections to St Matthew's gospel, he rebuts a (possibly identical) Jewish work which is close to Jacob ben Reuben's treatment of the gospel.[8] A work *L'Official*, which seems likely to be Joseph Official's *Joseph the Zealot*, discussed below, was listed in 1429 among Jewish books confiscated at Trévoux in Savoy.[9] Don David Nasi says that by request he expounded (in Crete, *c.* 1430) three Hebrew apologies to his patron and Hebrew pupil archbishop Francisco Bentivoglio; Don David himself wrote a fourth, especially for the archbishop (Krauss and Horbury 1996; 235). Partly through Nicholas de Lyra's commentaries, often printed with the Vulgate, medieval Hebrew 'answers' became familiar in early modern Christian theology; '[Rashi] laid down that [Psalm 2] should rather be interpreted of David [than of the messiah]: לתשובת המינים, *that he might answer the heretics*' (Denis Pétau (Petavius), *De theologicis dogmatibus*, part 2, *De Trinitate* (1644), 2.7.15; Venice, 1721, 93).

Despite qualifications, therefore, 'apologetic' is a justified description; these arguments were indeed important in Jewish self-identification, and in Hebrew they had an almost entirely Jewish circulation, but the arguments themselves were not restricted to the Jewish community. Moreover, the adjective 'polemical' which is often applied to the Hebrew apologies is also appropriate, for their defence includes attack, expressing the desire to confute and even to win over the adversary which has been noted above. Confutation is aimed above all at Christian understanding of the Hebrew Bible, in line with the link between Torah and apology which Eleazar ben Arakh's saying can suggest.

The titles of the Hebrew apologies range accordingly from the imagery of debate to that of conflict, just as happens in Christian con-

[8] See Blumenkranz ([1964] 1977: 135 note 16) (envisaging two distinct Jewish works); Dahan (1991: 113–15).

[9] Loeb (1885: 52), suggesting that this was a book of prayers ('offices').

troversial literature. So Christian book-titles, from the often-used *Against the Jews*, *Dialogue* or *Disputation* to *Dagger of Faith* (Raymund Martini, *c.* 1278) and *Victory against the Jews* (Piero Bruti, bishop of Vicenza, 1488), find correspondence in a range of Jewish titles. Defensive response is suggested by the widespread *Answer(s) to the* Minim ('heretics', often used for 'Christians', as by Rashi quoted above; e.g. Johanan Loria, early sixteenth century) or *to the Christians* (e.g. Benjamin of Rome, fifteenth century) and *Disputation* (*wikkuahī*, sometimes reflecting compulsory oral debate, as with the Disputations of Jehiel of Paris and Nachmanides). More militant are *War of Obligation* (Meir ben Simeon of Narbonne, thirteenth century, neatly implying (cf. M. Sotah 8:7) that this 'war' is an inescapable duty), *Shield and Sword* (Leone Modena, seventeenth century), or *Nizzahon* ('confutation' or 'victory'), a title often used from the fourteenth century onwards (for several anonymous works, and for the widely current apology by Lipmann Mühlhausen, who was a spokesman for Judaism under attack in Prague (1399–1400), among other places). Defence is of course implied by the provision of 'shield' as well as 'sword', and it forms the keynote of titles like *Help of Faith* (Moses Tordesillas, fourteenth century; one of the works used by both David Nasi and Isaac Akrish), *Shield of the Fathers* (Simeon Duran, fifteenth century, against Islam as well as Christianity) or *Bulwark of Faith* (Isaac Troki, sixteenth century).[10] Both polemic and apologetic titles current among Jews are echoed in anti-Judaic Latin writing by Jews who had received baptism, as with William of Bourges, *War of the Lord* (early thirteenth century) or Victor of Carben, *Bulwark of Christian Faith* (Cologne, *c.* 1510).

Finally, 'literature' itself might seem an appropriate term only if understood in its broadest sense. The apologies overlap with other literary genres in which apologetic plays a part, most obviously biblical commentary and theology, but also mystical, halakhic and pietist writing.[11] Moreover, the apologies themselves can appear to lack literary quality. Like the corresponding Christian *adversus Iudaeos* tracts, these works are often compilations, they can give an impression of sameness, and they seem to allow pat answers to great questions; their combination of stylistic nonchalance and doctrinal confidence can repel. Yet here too the apologies have an answer. They simply follow the manner of controversy in their times. As their arguments made their way into the opposite camp, they will indeed have done something to challenge certainty and deepen

[10] The mingling of defence and attack is brought out by Schiller-Szinessy (1876: 224).
[11] See for example Bacher (1891) and J. Katz, as cited in note 7, above.

knowledge.[12] Their sameness should not be overestimated, for they reflect the individuality of a series of authors and situations. Apologists of high literary gifts include not only Judah ha-Levi, mentioned already, but such authors as David Kimchi, Nachmanides, Profiat Duran and Leone Modena; and compilations such as *Joseph the Zealot* or *Nizzahon* 'vetus', which are formed on a skeleton of Old and New Testament texts, can excel in vivid and pointed reports of oral exchange. Moreover, the content of the Hebrew apologies is not without broader historical and theological significance. They shed light on Jewish–gentile converse and relations, Jewish participation in non-Jewish culture, and a still wider range of historical topics, as Raphael Loewe has pointed out (Loewe 1969; 25–7). In their measure they also illuminate the image of Judaism and Christianity in the medieval Jewish community, and contribute to an understanding of what customs and tenets have been held dear by Jews and Christians.[13]

Now a sketch of this genre of medieval Hebrew literature, as it may with all reservations be called, will be followed by brief comment on its origins. The writings in question are mainly but not solely medieval. Their first traces emerge in the Geonic period. *Nestor ha-komer* or *The Book of Nestor the Priest*, mentioned above, is the earliest book of this kind which fully survives in Hebrew, and is once again a translation from Arabic. It can perhaps be assumed that controversial writing of this kind was current at least from the eighth century, although an earlier date is not impossible.[14] A closing date for the genre can be roughly set a thousand years later, at the time of the French Revolution. The last great new efflorescence of this literature was in eighteenth-century Italy, represented by authors such as Jonah Rappa and Joshua Segre, although the copying and translation of Hebrew apologetic continued in the nineteenth and twentieth centuries. Judah Rosenthal in his bibliography counted about a hundred and ten named writers in Hebrew down to the eighteenth century, and thirty-six anonymous works. This rough total of 146 books (liable to increase as further texts become known)[15] gives an average of nearly one and a half in every decade of the millennium from the eighth to the eighteenth centuries; absurd though it is to envisage so even a distribution, this mechanical apportionment gives some idea of the extent of the Hebrew apologetic literature in question.

12 Jewish–Christian debate reflected in Meir ben Simeon is assessed on these lines by Stein (1969: 22).
13 Compare Rankin (1956: viii), on polemic as gradually exposing issues of long-term importance.
14 Thus fragmentarily preserved Genizah material of this kind was tentatively ascribed to the period from the eighth to the tenth century by Mann (1937–8: 413).
15 For an example of a newly recognized polemical text see de Lange (1990).

The non-Jewish awareness of these writings noted above was enhanced from the sixteenth to the eighteenth centuries through discussion and printing of polemical works, notably by Sebastian Munster, Theodor Hackspan (editing Lipmann's *Nizzahon*), J. C. Wagenseil (editing *Nizzahon* vetus, Toledoth Jeshu, and other works), and J. C. Wolf in his Hebrew bibliography.[16] At the same time some Jewish printing of this literature also took place in havens such as Constantinople, Leghorn and Amsterdam. At the end of the eighteenth century the great Hebraist G. B. de Rossi summed up the whole area of study, issuing his own learned apology *Della vana aspettazione degli ebrei del loro ré messia* (Parma, 1773), and amassing the manuscripts and printed books that form the basis of his fundamental bibliography, *Bibliotheca Judaica Antichristiana* (Parma, 1800). This literature was not of primary interest to the scholars of the *Wissenschaft des Judentums* (with notable exceptions such as A. Geiger), but much further knowledge of it was gained through the bibliographical work of M. Steinschneider, A. Neubauer and others. At the beginning of the twentieth century Adolf Posnanski prepared a corpus of Hebrew polemical writings, but could print it only in part; his handwritten editions and commentaries passed to the Jewish National and University Library (Simonsen 1935). Two books from this period present a section through the whole range of the Hebrew apologies, printing much unpublished material: Neubauer, S. R. Driver and E. B. Pusey on Jewish interpretation of the fifty-third chapter of Isaiah (1876), and Posnanski's *Schiloh*, on both Jewish and Christian interpretation of the messianic prophecy of Jacob in Genesis 49:10 (1904). Samuel Krauss re-edited the Toledoth Jeshu in his *Das Leben Jesu nach jüdischen Quellen* (1902), and revised and supplemented de Rossi's bibliography.[17] Later in the twentieth century E. E. Urbach studied the Hebrew polemic of northern France and the Rhineland (1935), J. M. Rosenthal's bibliography (1960–1) and editions once again did much to sum up the whole polemical literature, and its interest and variety were brought out by O. S. Rankin (1956). Countries which have been to the fore in subsequent study of the Hebrew apologies include Canada, the USA, Spain and Israel. Perhaps especially noteworthy are editions with translation and comment, for example by F. E. Talmage (Joseph and David Kimchi, among much other relevant publication), D. Berger (*Nizzahon* vetus) or D. Lasker and S. Stroumsa (*Nestor*), and editions of unpublished works, for example the *Answers to the Men of Iniquity* now shown probably to be by Profiat Duran (J. V. Niclós and C.

[16] On these authors see Loewe (1971).

[17] See note 1, above.

del Valle), or the *Asham Talui* of Joshua Segre (D. Malkiel). Although many of the sources have been utilized by historians, much basic work of edition and interpretation remains to be done.

Where and when did this literature most flourish? As is already obvious, it was composed both in the East and the West. Authors include a notable series of Karaites: Qirqisani (ninth-century Mesopotamia); Judah Hadassi (twelfth-century Constantinople; his polemical passages were edited by W. Bacher); and Isaac Troki (sixteenth-century Lithuania). Other authors and works mentioned so far represent Syria or Iraq (*Nestor*), Gascony or Aragon (Jacob ben Reuben),[18] Majorca and Algiers (Simeon Duran), Spain (Judah ha-Levi, Moses Tordesillas), Alsace (Johanan Loria), the Rhineland more broadly and northern France (Joseph Official, and the *Nizzahon* 'vetus', the oldest work bearing this title), Rome (Benjamin) and northern Italy (Modena, Rappa and Segre). Although Christian Europe and Byzantium can claim the largest number of texts, Simeon Duran is not an isolated instance of an anti-Christian polemist under Muslim rule; other authors range from David Muqammiṣ in Mesopotamia (Arabic; ninth century) to Isaac Lopez in Aleppo (1695) (see Steinschneider 1877; Lasker 1990–1). The free discussions of Christianity by Maimonides (Cairo, twelfth century), notably in his *Code* and *Epistle to the Yemen*, can also be reckoned under this heading.

Clusters of writings can sometimes be identified in times and places of intensive biblical, halakhic and philosophical work within the Jewish community, or of intensive Christian disputation and writing against Judaism, often in connection with royal and ecclesiastical measures to implement the conversion or segregation of the Jews. Thus the authors of Hebrew apologies include the grammarians and exegetes Joseph and David Kimchi in twelfth-century Provence, and the philosophical theologians Hasdai Crescas and Profiat Duran in fourteenth-century Spain. Yet, partly because works were translated into Hebrew if not written in Hebrew, this was an international literature; *Nestor* from the East was quoted and copied in Spain, and the voluminous Spanish apologetic of the fourteenth and fifteenth centuries was subsequently copied in Italy and the East. Sometimes particular Christian pressure evoked a composition, but 'answers to the *minim*' were a long-term and everyday requirement, and work elicited by crises drew accordingly on a long continuous tradition of apologetic and polemic.

18 See R. Schmitz, 'Jacob ben Rubén y so obra Milḥamot ha-šem' and C. del Valle, 'Jacob ben Rubén de Huesca. Polemista. Su patria y su época', in del Valle (1992a: 45–58, 59–65).

Links can therefore be traced between apologetic and other Jewish literary activity, between apologies from different regions, and between answers in time of crisis and the long apologetic tradition.[19] The complexity these links display in particular cases can be illustrated from thirteenth-century northern France. Here the public disputations held in Paris by royal command in 1240 during the examination of the Talmud, and again from 1269 onwards, gave rise to the Hebrew compositions (1) *Disputation of R Jehiel of Paris*, (2) answers given when 'in the year 29 of the sixth millennium [1269] an apostate [probably Paul Christiani] came from Montpellier', and (3) *Answers to the* Min *who rose up against us in the year 32* [1272]; these, however, are connected in turn with the mid-century apologetic work *Joseph the Zealot*, called by this name after its author Joseph Official of Sens, who also drew up the Hebrew account of the 1240 disputation of Jehiel.[20] A Paris manuscript containing both the texts for which Joseph was responsible is itself dated around 1270–80, in or near the second period of disputation.[21]

These three works also attest the interconnection of apologetic with other literary genres, and the contacts between apologetic works composed in different places. Joseph's book collects 'answers to the *minim*' attributed to northern French scholars of the twelfth and thirteenth centuries. Those named include Jehiel of Paris himself, the Tosaphists Rabbenu Tam and Isaac ben Judah ha-Levi, and the biblical commentators Samuel ben Meir (Rashbam) and Joseph Bekhor Shor. Many of these names recur in *Nizzahon vetus* and in other related controversial collections. They attest the link between Jewish apologetic and the biblical and Talmudic comment of Rashi and his successors, especially in the prolific northern French school of biblical exegesis (compare Rashi's comment on Psalm 2, quoted above). At the same time they suggest that apologetic in this tradition probably became known in the East, for Jehiel's son Joseph and other Parisian Jewish scholars settled in Acre in the Latin kingdom of Jerusalem (Prawer 1988: 274–6). Lastly, the later period of disputation, as reflected in Hebrew narrative, included arguments for Christianity from the Talmud like those answered by Nachmanides at the 1263 Barcelona disputation; and Latin sources show that the Dominican Paul Christiani who put these arguments at

[19] On debate and apologetic see Ben-Shalom.
[20] Krauss and Horbury (1996: 150–61, 218) (Joseph Official, Jehiel); Shatzmiller (1994).
[21] MS. BnF héb. 712, described with photograph of the beginning of the *Disputation of R Jehiel* by Garel (1991: 87, no. 58); Shatzmiller (1994: 21–2).

Barcelona was in Paris in 1269.[22] In this context it seems natural that the Hebrew polemical text (2), ascribed to northern France at this period and showing contact with material used by Joseph Official, includes a summary of the answers of Nachmanides in Barcelona.[23]

What kind of books are the Hebrew apologies? They range from doctrinal or biblical treatises with an apologetic dimension (exemplified in works by Saadia and David Kimchi, respectively) to writings in epistolary form, as already noted (Profiat Duran's satirical epistle *Be Not Like thy Fathers* is particularly famous), and to the humbler summary aide-mémoire (a striking instance is the short *Remembrance of the Book Nizzahon*, in Hebrew rhyme to be sung to the tune 'Herzog Ernst').[24] For the most part, however, they look like a counterpart to the Greek, Latin and Syriac Jewish–Christian dialogues issued by ecclesiastical authors from the second century onwards. A very substantial Christian production in this genre continued throughout the millennium of Hebrew apologetic literature just identified. Like the Christian works, the Hebrew apologies often take the form of dialogues, imaginary or with some basis in events. The speakers sometimes bear emblematic and assonant names, like Heretic (*min*) and Faithful (*ma'amin*), in Joseph Kimchi's *Book of the Covenant*, Saint (*qadosh*) and Sodomite (*qadesh*), in Meir of Narbonne, or Affirmer (*ma'amir*) and Apostate (*memir*), in Moses Tordesillas; but sometimes personal names appear, as in the Hebrew narratives of disputation in Paris and Barcelona noted above, and sometimes, as in the anecdotes of *Joseph the Zealot*, there is a half-way position, with at least a place-name; so (again on a theme of the 1240 disputation) 'A clerk from Paris said to his pupils, Come and see the heresy of those Jews, who say that Leviathan is a great fish, and in the time to come they are going to eat him' (*Joseph*, no. 132).

The mainstay of the Hebrew apologetic throughout is, just as in the Christian works, argument concerning biblical texts. It is urged that the Old Testament passages brought forward in the New Testament and the Church Fathers, in the Christian argument from prophecy, should be given another interpretation. Further, it is argued that the New Testament itself suggests a non-Christian Jewish interpretation of Jesus the Nazarene and his followers. A widespread form of apology treats a

[22] His presence in Paris in 1269 is therefore attested independently of the question whether, as Shatzmiller (1994: 15–20) argues, he is the 'Paul' mentioned in the Hebrew account in connection with 1272 and 1273, and on the face of it as a Franciscan, not a Dominican.

[23] See Urbach ([1935] 1999: 56–72); Shatzmiller (1994: 20–1, 36–43); on the context of the summary, see Horbury (1998: 245–6).

[24] On the works mentioned see Krauss and Horbury (1996: 211, 221, 229, 240).

series of texts from the Hebrew Bible, often followed by a series from the New Testament, as in Jacob ben Reuben, Joseph Official, Lipmann Mühlhausen (Hebrew Bible only) and Isaac Troki. This biblical content of the apologies remained primary from the beginnings to the eighteenth century, but it was supplemented by other approaches; a list of six was drawn up by Joseph ben Shem Tob (fifteenth century) in comment on Profiat Duran's epistle.[25] These reflect in various ways the philosophical influence on medieval Judaism and Christianity, the tendency of Christian argument to include post-biblical Jewish literature, especially the Talmud and Jewish prayers (criticized systematically in the Paris proceedings) and the reference of Jewish argument to ecclesiastical rites, customs and authors as well as the New Testament (the Christian cult of the saints and use of pictures and images is consistently criticized, from *Nestor* to Jonah Rappa).[26]

The combination of approaches can be exemplified by the varied content of the *Touchstone* of Shem Tob ibn Shaprut, from Castile at the end of the fourteenth century.[27] The longer of the two main forms in which this comprehensive work was current comprises sixteen books, divided as follows: I, principles of Judaism; II–X, proof-texts from the Hebrew Bible brought forward by Christians (based on Jacob ben Reuben's work, now judged to be too outspoken, and in this form of the *Touchstone* including answers to the refutation of Jacob ben Reuben by Alphonsus of Valladolid, known before his baptism as Abner of Burgos); XI, narratives from the Talmud (*haggadoth*) attacked by Christians or interpreted in favour of Christianity; XII, articles of Christian belief, including topics such as the trinity, the incarnation and the eucharist (this book probably draws on the extended critique of Christian principles by Ibn Shaprut's contemporary, Profiat Duran); XIII, on the gospels, again developing Jacob ben Reuben and now including an entire Hebrew translation of Matthew and part of Mark, interspersed with refutation; XIV, answering the parts of Alphonsus's refutation of Jacob ben Reuben which deal with the gospels, the resurrection of the dead and the coming of the messiah; and finally XV and XVI, on the resurrection and the messiah respectively, written originally without knowledge of this work of Alphonsus. This table of contents shows how the ancient biblical discussion was itself expanded and developed, and also how it was

[25] See Neubauer (1888: 90–1); Lasker (1977: 13–15); on the wide diffusion of philosophical argument, see Lasker (1996). [26] On Rappa see Krauss (1904).

[27] On the arrangement of the books, Horbury (1998: 263–5); the text is edited by José V. Niclós (Madrid, 1997).

supplemented by defence of the Talmud and by a topical treatment of Jewish and Christian belief, corresponding to the philosophical and doctrinal systematizations popular among Jews and Christians alike in this great age of Jewish creeds, articles and principles.[28]

Supplementation also embraced in due course other sources drawn into the argument, such as Jewish mystical writings. Such developments are perhaps less striking overall, however, than the continuity of a few central themes, treated in varying ways, throughout the whole period under review. One such, already noted, is the attack on images and the cult of the saints, consistently maintained through times of inner-Christian division on images (from the eighth to the tenth century, and then again from the sixteenth century) and of Jewish approximation, especially but not only in pilgrimage, to a cult of the fathers and their sepulchres.

Another such abiding theme is the presentation of a non-Christian view of the rise of Christianity, owing something to the Talmud and the Toledoth Jeshu as well as the New Testament. Thus in *Nestor* the argument that New Testament and apocryphal accounts of the conception, birth, family, baptism, temptation, arrest, suffering and execution of Christ are incompatible with divinity converges with a portrait derived from the Toledoth Jeshu of Christ as a helpless fugitive from Jewish justice. Through his commandments the institutions of Moses are changed. Alternatively, argument can follow the line taken in the Toledoth Jeshu, that Paul (also Peter), secretly acting on behalf of the Jews, deliberately divided Christians from Jews by a series of new commandments. This view is reflected in the elucidation of a phrase in the Mishnah on gentile festivals (A Z 1:3 'the day of the *genesia* of their kings') in Rashi's commentary on the Babylonian Talmud (AZ 10a); 'the Romans' writing and speech came to them from another people; others established all their books for them' – and these were 'John, Paul, and Peter, who were Jews'.[29] Talmudic or Toledoth Jeshu traditions can have a striking prominence, as when the Hebrew narrative of the 1240 disputation states that Mary's husband's name was John, 'and so it is written in the gospel' (whereas in the gospels the name is Joseph, but it is John in a widespread version of the Toledoth Jeshu). On the other hand, the

28 On these see Kellner (1986); Loewe (1999: 76–84) brings out the strength of a less confidently assertive strand in medieval Jewish theology.

29 Zunz (1865: 5); see R. Rabbinowicz, *Variae Lectiones in Mischnam et in Talmud Babylonicum*, vol. X (Munich, 1879), 23, note 9, reprinting a full text of the commentary from Jacob ibn Habib, *'Eyn Ya'aqobh* (Saloniki, 1516); Greenstone (1950: 100).

main polemical point can be made by giving primacy to Christian sources. An outstanding later medieval example is Profiat Duran, who constantly cites the epistles as well as the gospels of the New Testament to show that Jesus and his followers, even including Paul, went astray rather than leading others astray, as the later ecclesiastical teachers did – for the New Testament throughout shows that Jesus himself kept the Mosaic law, and that the first Christians exalted him, but did not deify him.[30] In the seventeenth century, by a further step, Leone Modena in his Hebrew apologetic dismisses the Toledoth Jeshu as a hostile fable, and gives his own sketch of Christian origins from consideration of Jewish and Christian writings; Jesus is assessed as a divergent Pharisee.[31]

Lastly, the very ancient theme of messianic prophecy has a like tenacity in the Hebrew apologies. Christian interpretation of prophecy is of course rebutted, but rebuttal is often strikingly accompanied by the assertion of a specifically Jewish messianic hope. True interpretation of prophecy (it is argued) shows that the error of Christianity was itself foretold, and that the Messiah will surely come to confound error, redeem Israel and bring in God's kingdom.[32] In *Nestor* (180a, 185) these assertions are linked with proof-texts including Ezekiel 28:8–9, on the slaying of the man who claims to be God, Jeremiah 23:5–8, on the Davidic righteous branch in whose days the exiles shall return, and Jeremiah 16:19, 'the gentiles shall come unto thee from the ends of the earth, and shall say, Surely our fathers have inherited lies'. The same pattern of rebuttal and assertion shapes the chapter on redemption in Saadia's *Beliefs and Opinions*, and the famous declaration of a non-miraculous messianic hope in the Code of Maimonides (14:11–12); here Christ and Muhammad are prophesied and providentially intended to prepare for the King Messiah, at whose coming their followers will know their traditions for lies (cf. Jeremiah 16:19). In the thirteenth century, by contrast, the disputation of Nachmanides includes an influential denial that messianic hope is of the essence of Judaism, and apologies of this and other periods can give greater prominence to the simple exclusion of Christian messianic

30 The argument is summarized by E. I. J. Rosenthal (1970: 349–54); its probable antecedents include earlier Jewish polemic, contemporary Christian use of the criterion of apostolicity, and (as suggested by Cohen 1993) Christian attacks on Judaism as a departure from primitive tradition.

31 *Magen wa-Herebh*, 3:9, ed. S. Simonsohn (Jerusalem, 1960), 43–4. On Modena see Le Brun and Stroumsa (1998: xiii–xxxii).

32 A comparably continuous recollection in medieval *piyyut*, especially for Purim and Passover, of the promise that latter-day foes would fare in the future redemption like those of old was noted by Zunz (1855–9: 126).

exegesis than to assertion of Jewish expectation; a well-known example is the movement away from messianic interpretation of Isaiah 52:13–53:12 – mainly, however, towards an application to Israel's exile which once more permits expression of the hope of redemption.[33] The assertion of Jewish messianic expectation is accordingly still prominent in apologetic, for instance in *Joseph the Zealot* (beginning with a collection of 'consolations' to the Jewish people from prophecy) and in a work of unknown authorship, perhaps from the fourteenth century, related to *Nizzahon* 'vetus' (here Ezekiel 28:8–9 and Jeremiah 16:19 are again important) (Horbury 1998: 254–60). Jewish messianic assertion receives classic later expression in Isaac Abravanel and in perhaps the most influential of all the apologies, the sixteenth-century work of Isaac Troki.[34]

The three themes just singled out can be traced through the whole period surveyed above, and they probably antedate the earliest surviving Hebrew apology, for they are attested in the arguments ascribed to Jews in Latin Christian works from the seventh century onwards (Blumenkranz [1948] 1977: 139–46). This attestation forms one of the considerations bearing on the question of the origins of Hebrew apologetic literature. To what extent was the emergence of this literature from the eighth and ninth centuries onwards, in Arabic and then in Hebrew, anticipated in earlier Jewish writing?

Medieval polemists naturally held that they were taking up rabbinic apologetic. Eleazar ben Arakh's maxim is frequently in view; it is twice quoted, for instance, in the introduction to *Joseph the Zealot*, and 'What shall I answer to Epicurus?' begins the mnemonic *Remembrance of the Book of Nizzahon*;[35] Isaac Pulgar called his reply to his former teacher Abner of Burgos, now baptized Alphonsus, 'Answer to Epicurus' (del Valle 1999). Somewhat comparably, the Hebrew account of the disputation of Nachmanides begins with a quotation of the legendary but lively passage in the Babylonian Talmud (Sanh. 43a) describing a battle of proof-texts fought against the five disciples of Jesus. 'It was necessary to answer all the vain and empty arguments which they brought. And so I also am writing down the remarks which I made in answer to the errors of Fra Paulo.'[36]

33 The passage was applied to Israel by authors including Rashi, Joseph and David Kimchi, Jacob ben Reuben, Shem Tob ibn Shaprut, Lipmann Mühlhausen, Isaac Troki, Isaac Lopez and Joshua Segre; see E. B. Pusey in Neubauer, Driver and Pusey ([1876] 1969, vol. II: lx–lxiii).

34 See Deutsch (1873: I, 1, 6, 34, 44; II, 49).

35 Rosenthal (1970: 15–16); 'Carmen memoriale libri Nizzachon', in Wagenseil ([1681] 1970: 105; Rankin (1956: 60).

36 M. Steinschneider (ed.), *Nachmanidis Disputatio* (Berlin, 1860), 5, translated by Rankin (1956: 178–9); the association of contemporary with rabbinic polemic is still attested if, as H. Maccoby

Admittedly the Talmudic accounts of controversy are scattered and anecdotal, but they already, as in Sanhedrin 43a, attest the centrality of the discussion of biblical texts in apologetic. So in the Babylonian Talmud Eleazar ben Arakh's saying, which can itself be taken, as noted above, to link Torah with apology, is brought together with another almost equally famous saying on biblical proofs: Whatever text the *minim* distort, their answer is beside it (Sanh. 38b, in the name of R Johanan). This probably third-century maxim is quoted in the Palestinian Talmud (Ber. 9:1, 12d–13a, here in the name of R Simlai) in connection with a series of texts which might suggest a plurality of heavenly powers, but can be rescued for the affirmation of one God by attention to nearby words or phrases.[37] Further passages from Talmud, Midrash and Targum confirm that there was a tradition of biblically based apologetic and polemic which left its deposit in rabbinic literature (Urbach [1971] 1999; Loewe 1966; Visotzky 1990; Horbury 1998: 203–5; Hadas-Lebel 1999). It was perhaps also embodied in written texts which no longer survive, like the anti-Roman propaganda conjectured by R. Loewe (in connection with Simeon ben Yohai's anecdote on Trajan in the Palestinian Talmud, Sukkah 5:1, 55b) as a Jewish counterpart to the pagan Greek Acts of the Alexandrians; the story of the five disciples and their proof-texts, noted above, has comparable points of contact with Greek propaganda literature (Loewe 1961). Rabbinic polemic forms, in any case, an important antecedent of the later apologies, and one often recognized by the apologists themselves.

Secondly, at least one of the Hebrew apologetic and polemical works mentioned above, the Toledoth Jeshu, goes back in substance to the ancient period. It was known in early ninth-century Gaul as a written text read by Jews, and its earliest manuscript attestation is of about the same time; but its agreements with the speeches of the Jew of Celsus in Origen and with Jewish argument as envisaged by Tertullian and Commodian show that much of its content was current in connected form in the second and third centuries. Once again, lost written texts from this period (perhaps in Aramaic or Greek) can reasonably be envisaged.

Thirdly, the indications of Jewish argument on Christ, the saints and messianism noted above in Latin Christian texts from the seventh century and onwards can be connected with a canon of the Twelfth Council of Toledo (681) forbidding Jews to read 'books which the Christan faith rejects'; it is not certain that these were apologies, but the

suggests (see Krauss and Horbury 1996: 161, note 54), this introductory passage is an editorial addition. [37] Visotzky (1988), noting further parallels.

issue of an anti-Jewish treatise on the sixth age of the world by Julian, bishop of Toledo 680–90, suggests the possibility that the forbidden books included an apologetic statement of Jewish hope.[38] Jewish works in Latin can be envisaged in this setting.[39]

Lastly, to return to literature preserved within the Jewish community, a link between late antiquity and the medieval apologists is formed by the polemical elements of the *piyyut*, for example in connection with the hanging of Haman or the expectation of Edom's overthrow.[40] These elements have long been recognized, both by students of Hebrew poetry and by ecclesiastical censors;[41] but Egyptian papyri and Cairo Genizah texts have shown that *piyyut* flourished much earlier than was thought in the nineteenth century. Discovery or reconsideration of texts has accordingly made it plain that developed anti-Christian polemic (in which representations of Christ and the claims made for him form a prominent target) was current in the Aramaic and Hebrew poetry of Byzantine Palestine, from the fifth century onwards.[42] This material, viewed together with the similarly trenchant argument ascribed to south Arabian Jews in the sixth-century Greek disputation of Herbanus and Gregentius,[43] in turn strengthens the likelihood that some now lost polemical compilations, perhaps in Aramaic or Greek, circulated in this period side by side with early forms of the Toledoth Jeshu.

It seems, therefore, that the debate among Jews, Muslims and Christians which forms the setting of the earliest surviving Hebrew apologies was itself continuous with earlier Jewish apologetic and polemic directed against Christianity, both in Byzantium and in the kingdoms of the west. The four separate lines of argument just considered converge to suggest a fair probability that apologetic was embodied in written texts now lost, in Aramaic, Greek or Latin. The apologetic elements in Talmud and Midrash, Targum and *piyyut* would then form echoes or remnants of a Jewish apologetic literature which preceded the

38 Blumenkranz (1960: 164–6); for varying opinion on the books intended see also Krauss and Horbury (1996: 59, note 23).

39 Compare the trilingual fifth or sixth century Tortosa epitaph (*CIJ* 661) discussed by Noy (1993: 247–53, no. 183).

40 Cf. note 32, above.

41 Zunz (1855–9: 125–6, 437–55). A censored Passover *piyyut* of Yannai on Edom, from the thirteenth-century MS. BnF héb. 650, is illustrated in Garel (1991: 160, no. 116).

42 For examples see Rabinowitz (1965: xxx–xxxi); van Bekkum (1993); Sokoloff and Yahalom (1999: 216–17, no. 33, lines 85–90); Sivan (2000).

43 Christ was a duly executed Sabbath-breaker, Christianity is the idolatry of those 'adversaries of Judah' (Isaiah 11:13) whose doom is foretold (*PG* 86.1, cols. 625, 629, 692, 754–6).

later Hebrew literature considered here. Yet, even apart from this suggestion, and apart from the widespread agreements between Jewish and non-Jewish evidence for Jewish argument, it can be seen simply from the surviving literature of the Jewish community that the main arguments used in the Hebrew apologies were current among Jews before the time of the apologies themselves.

Apologetic literature is almost by definition a disputed topic. It may therefore at least indicate areas of continuing discussion if, in conclusion, some opinions advanced above are recapitulated in a short list.

(1) Medieval Hebrew apologies played a great part internally in the Jewish community among the gentiles, contributing to self-identification and the defence and confirmation of Judaism, very often under severe pressure; but this literature is also polemical, reflecting a desire to confute error and, if it may be, to win opponents over to Judaism.

(2) Hebrew works often reflect oral and written debate in other languages and their arguments were known outside the Jewish community.

(3) These works are criticized for monotony, shapelessness and a doctrinaire manner; but they give access, often vividly, to varied situations and gifted authors, and they contribute to an historical understanding of Judaism and Christianity.

(4) This literature was international, and its manifestations in times of crisis drew on a long-standing tradition of apologetic for everyday use.

(5) Despite rich variety and innovation in the millennium during which Hebrew apologetic literature flourished, there is a striking continuity in the use of arguments on representational art and the cult of the saints, on the rise of Christianity, and on the assertion of specifically Jewish messianic hope.

(6) These arguments antedate the earliest apologies; they were probably incorporated into older polemical writings which no longer survive, but in any case Talmud and Midrash, Targum and *piyyut* show that the main apologetic and polemical themes were continuously current between the times of the rabbinic and the early medieval literature.

To offer these comments to Raphael Loewe is to bring prose to a poet, and owls to an Athens of learning; but it gives me a valued chance of expressing admiration for his work, and gratitude for his kindness and instruction over many years.

LITERATURE

Bacher, W. 1891. 'Judaeo-Christian Polemics in the Zohar'. *JQR* 3: 781–4

1896. 'Jehudah Hadassi's "Eshkol Hakkofer"'. *JQR* 8: 431–44

van Bekkum, J. W. 1993. 'Anti-Christian Polemics in Hebrew Liturgical Poetry (*Piyyut*) of the Sixth and Seventh Centuries'. In *Early Christian Poetry: A Collection of Essays*, ed. J. den Boeft and A. Hilhorst, 297–308. Leiden, New York and Cologne: Supplement to Vigilae Christianae 22

Ben-Shalom, R. 2000. 'Between Official Debate and Private Polemic: The Case of Christian Spain and Provence in the Late Middle Ages'. *AJS Review* 25

Berger, D. 1979. *The Jewish–Christian Debate in the High Middle Ages: A Critical Edition of the Nizzahon Vetus, with an introduction, translation and commentary*. Philadelphia

1986. 'Mission to the Jews and Jewish–Christian Contacts in the Polemical Literature of the High Middle Ages'. *American Historical Review* 91: 576–91

Blumenkranz, B. 1960. *Juifs et chrétiens dans le monde occidental 430-1096*. Paris

[1948] 1977. 'Die jüdischen Beweisgründe im Religionsgespräch mit den Christen in den christlichen lateinischen Sonderschriften des 5. bis 11. Jahrhunderts'. *TZ* 4: 119–47; repr. in Blumenkranz 1977

[1954] 1977. 'Un pamphlet juif médio-latin de polémique antichrétienne'. *RHPR* 34: 401–13; repr. in Blumenkranz 1977

[1964] 1977. 'Anti-Jewish Polemics and Legislation in the Middle Ages: Literary Fiction or Reality?'. *JJS* 15: 125–40; repr. in Blumenkranz 1977

1977. *Juifs et chrétiens: patristique et moyen age*. London

Carleton Paget, J. N. B. 1997. 'Anti-Judaism and Early Christian Identity'. *ZAC* 1: 195–225

Cohen, J. 1993. 'Profiat Duran's *The Reproach of the Gentiles* and the Development of Jewish Anti-Christian Polemic'. In *Shlomo Simonsohn Jubilee Volume: Studies on the History of the Jews in the Middle Ages and Renaissance Period*, ed. D. Carpi et al., 71–84. Tel Aviv

Dahan, G. 1991. *La polémique chrétienne contre le judaïsme au Moyen Age*. Paris

Deutsch, D. 1873. *Befestigung im Glauben von Rabbi Jizchak, Sohn Abrahams neu herausgegeben*, 2 vols. in 1, 2nd edn. Sohrau and Breslau

Garel, M. 1991. *D'une main forte: manuscrits hébreux des collections françaises*. Paris

Geiger, A. (1865–71). *Das Judenthum und seine Geschichte*, 2nd edn, 3 vols. Breslau (1865, 1865, 1871)

Greenstone, J. H. 1950. 'Jewish Legends about Simon-Peter'. *Historia Judaica* 12: 89–104

Hadas-Lebel, M. 1999. 'Hezekiah as King Messiah: Traces of an Early Jewish–Christian Polemic in the Tannaitic Tradition'. In Targarona Borrás and Sáenz-Badillos (eds.), vol. I, 275–81

Horbury, W. 1998. *Jews and Christians in Contact and Controversy*. Edinburgh

1999. *Christianity in Ancient Jewish Tradition*. Cambridge

Katz, J. 1961. *Exclusiveness and Tolerance*. Oxford

Kellner, M. M. 1986. *Dogma in Medieval Jewish Thought*. Oxford

Krauss, S. 1902. *Das Leben Jesu nach jüdischen Quellen*. Berlin
1904. 'Un atlas juif des statues de la Vierge Marie'. *REJ* 48: 82–93
Krauss, S. and W. Horbury 1996. *The Jewish–Christian Controversy from the Earliest times to 1789*, vol. I: *History*. Tübingen
de Lange, N. 1990. 'A Fragment of Byzantine Anti-Christian Polemic'. *JJS* 41: 92–100
Lasker, D. J. 1977. *Jewish Philosophical Polemics against Christianity in the Middle Ages*. New York
1990–1. 'The Jewish Critique of Christianity under Islam in the Middle Ages'. *PAAJR* 57: 121–53
1996. 'Jewish Philosophical Polemics in Ashkenaz'. In Limor and Stroumsa (eds.), 195–213
Lasker, D. J. (ed.) 1990. *R Hasdai Crescas, Sefer Bittul Iqqarei ha-Nozrim, translation of Joseph ben Shem Tov*. Ramat Gan and Beer Sheva
Lasker, D. J. (transl.) 1992. *The Refutation of Christian Principles by Hasdai Crescas*. Albany
Lasker, D. J. and S. Stroumsa 1996. *The Polemic of Nestor the Priest*, 2 vols. Jerusalem
Le Brun, J. and G. G. Stroumsa 1998. *Les juifs présentés aux chrétiens: textes de Léon de Modène et de Richard Simon*. Paris
Limor, O. and G. G. Stroumsa (eds.) 1996. *Contra Iudaeos: Ancient and Medieval Polemics between Christians and Jews*. Tübingen
Loeb, I. 1885. 'Un épisode de l'histoire des juifs de Savoie'. *REJ* 10: 32–59
Loewe, R. 1961. 'A Jewish Counterpart to the Acts of the Alexandrians'. *JJS* 21: 105–22
1966. 'Apologetic Motifs in the Targum to the Song of Songs'. In *Biblical Motifs* , ed. A. Altmann, 159–96. Cambridge, MA
1969. 'Prolegomenon'. In Neubauer, Driver and Pusey (eds.), vol. II, 1–38
1971. 'Hebraists, Christian (1100–1890)'. In *EJ* vol. VIII (1971), cols. 9–71
1999. 'Credat Judaeus Apella?'. *JJS* 50: 74–86
Mann, J. 1937–8. 'An Early Theologico-polemical Work'. *HUCA* 12–13: 411–59
Neubauer, A. 1888. 'Jewish Controversy and the *Pugio Fidei*'. *The Expositor*, third series, 7: 81–105, 179–97
Neubauer, A., S. R. Driver and E. B. Pusey (eds.) [1876] 1969. *The Fifty-third Chapter of Isaiah according to the Jewish Interpreters*, 2 vols. Oxford, 1876; repr. with a prolegomenon by R. Loewe, New York, 1969
Niclós Albarracín, J. V. 1999. *Profiat Durán, Cinco cuestiones debatidas de polémica. Edición crítica bilingue con anotaciones de C. del Valle*. Madrid
Noy, D. 1993. *Jewish Inscriptions of Western Europe*, vol. I. Cambridge
Posnanski, A. 1904. *Schiloh, ein Beitrag zur Geschichte der Messiaslehre, Erster Teil, Die Auslegung von Genesis 49, 10 im Altertume bis zu Ende des Mittelalters*. Leipzig
Prawer, J. 1988. *The History of the Jews in the Latin Kingdom of Jerusalem*. Oxford
Rabinowitz, Z. M. 1965. *Halakha and Aggada in the Liturgical Poetry of Yannai*. Tel-Aviv
Rankin, O. S. 1956. *Jewish Religious Polemic of Early and Later Centuries, a Study of Documents here Rendered in English*. Edinburgh

Rosenthal, E. I. J. [1960] 1971. 'Anti-Christian Polemic in Medieval Bible Commentaries'. *JJS* 11 (1960): 115–35; repr. in E. I. J. Rosenthal, *Studia Semitica*, 2 vols. Cambridge, 1971, vol. I, 165–85

[1968–70] 1971. 'Jüdische Antwort'. In *Kirche und Synagoge*, ed. K.-H. Rengstorf and S. von Kortzfleisch, vol. II, 307–62, 2 vols. Stuttgart, 1968, 1970; repr. in E. I. J. Rosenthal, *Studia Semitica*, Cambridge, 1971, vol. I, 187–242

Rosenthal, J. M. 1960–1. 'Anti-Christian Polemics from its Beginnings to the End of the Eighteenth Century' (Hebrew). *Aresheth* 2 (1960): 132–79; 3 (1961): 433–9

Rosenthal, J. M. (ed.) 1970. *Sepher Joseph Hamekane, Auctore R Joseph ben R Nathan Official*. Jerusalem

Schiller-Szinessy, S. M. 1876. *Catalogue of the Hebrew Manuscripts Preserved in the University Library, Cambridge*, vol. I. Cambridge

Schreckenberg, H. [1982] 1990. *Die christlichen Adversus-Judaeos-Texte und ihr literarisches und historisches Umfeld (1.-11. Jh.)*, Europäische Hochschulschriften, Theologie 172. Frankfurt a.M., 1982; repr. with addenda et corrigenda, 1990

1991. *Die christlichen Adversus-Judaeos-Texte (11.–13. Jh.): Mit einer Ikonographie des Judenthemas bis zum 4. Laterankonzil*, Europäische Hochschulschriften, Theologie 335. Frankfurt a.M.

1994. *Die christlichen Adversus-Judaeos-Texte und ihr literarisches und historisches Umfeld (13.-20. Jh.)*, Europäische Hochschulschriften, Theologie 497. Frankfurt a.M.

Shatzmiller, J. 1994. *La deuxième controverse de Paris*, Collection de la Revue des Etudes juives. Paris and Louvain

Simonsen, D. 1935. 'Eine Sammlung polemischer und apologetischer Literatur'. In *Festschrift für Aron Freimann*, ed. A. Marx and H. Meyer, 114–20. Berlin

Sivan, H. 2000. 'Synagogal Poetics and Polemics: Jews, Jerusalem and the Sassanids'. *SCI* 19

Sokoloff, M. and J. Yahalom 1999. *Jewish Palestinian Aramaic Poetry from Late Antiquity*. Jerusalem

Stein, S. 1969. *Jewish–Christian Disputations in Thirteenth-century Narbonne*. London

Steinschneider, M. 1877. *Polemische und apologetische Literatur in arabischer Sprache, zwischen Muslimen, Christen und Juden*. Leipzig

Targarona Borrás, J. and A. Sáenz-Badillos (eds.) 1999. *Jewish Studies at the Turn of the Twentieth Century: Proceedings of the 6th EAJS Congress, Toledo, July 1998*, 2 vols. Leiden, Boston and Cologne

Trautner-Kromann, H. 1993. *Shield and Sword: Jewish Polemics against Christianity and the Christians in France and Spain 1100-1500*. Tübingen

Urbach, E. E. [1935] 1999. 'Etudes sur la littérature polémique au moyen-âge'. *REJ* 100 (1935): 49–77; repr. in E. E. Urbach, *Collected Writings in Jewish Studies*, ed. R. Brody and M. D. Herr, 347–75. Jerusalem

[1971] 1999. 'The Homiletical Interpretations of the Sages and the Expositions of Origen on Canticles and the Jewish–Christian

Disputation'. *Scripta Hierosolymitana* 22 (1971): 247–75; repr. in E. E. Urbach, *Collected Writings in Jewish Studies*, ed. R. Brody and M. D. Herr, 318–46. Jerusalem

del Valle, C. (ed.) 1992a. *Polémica Judeo–Cristiana: Estudios.* Madrid

1992b. 'El libro de las Batallas de Dios, de Abner de Burgos'. In del Valle (ed.), 75–119

1999. 'La *Contradicción del Hereje* de Isaac ben Polgar'. In Targarona Borrás and Sáenz-Badillos (eds.), vol. I, 552–60

Visotzky, B. L. 1988. 'Trinitarian Testimonies'. *USQR* 42 (1988): 73–85

1990. 'Anti-Christian Polemic in Leviticus Rabbah'. *PAAJR* 56: 83–100

Wagenseil, J. C. [1681] 1970. *Tela Ignea Satanae.* Altdorf, 1681; repr. Farnborough

Williams, A. L. 1935. *Adversus Judaeos*: A *Bird's-Eye View of Christian* Apologiae *until the Renaissance.* Cambridge

Yerushalmi, Y. H. [1971] 1981. *From Spanish Court to Italian Ghetto. Isaac Cardoso: A Study in Seventeenth-century Marranism and Jewish Apologetics*. New York, 1971; repr. Seattle and London, 1981

Zunz, L. 1855–9. *Die synagogale Poesie des Mittelalters.* Berlin

1865. *Literaturgeschichte der synagogalen Poesie.* Berlin

CHAPTER FOURTEEN

Biblical commentaries and Christian influence: the case of Gersonides

Colette Sirat

> There is barely any philosophical system, from the ancient Greek schools down to the modern materialists, that has not found its adherents and advocates in Jewish schools or its place in the Jewish Commentaries on the Bible; the latter retain, more or less, indications of the intellectual atmosphere in which their authors lived.[1]

The aim of this brief overview is to show that these 'indications' include the structure and literary arrangements of the commentaries as well as some basic assumptions about the relations between the 'sacred page' and philosophy, be it Arab or Christian.

The debt of Jewish to Arab philosophy has been acknowledged from the start of the history of philosophy as a discipline. Not only do Jewish philosophers write in Arabic, they also quote from Arabic authors. In Christian Europe, on the other hand, if Jewish philosophers knew Latin they generally do not say so, and, except in Italy, no Jewish philosopher or exegete quotes from Christian scholars. Although the influence of Christian thought on medieval Jewish exegesis has been recognized in a few instances, it is mostly the polemical aspects that are highlighted.[2] The comparison between Jewish and Christian doctrines and ideas has yielded only meagre results, and we may wonder whether Jewish philosophers were really deaf to the culture within which they lived.

I do not presume to answer this question in the present study, but only to look at a few texts, in the hope that they may reveal some new facts.

Jewish biblical commentaries[3] can be classified into two types, accord-

[1] M. Friedlaender, *Essays on the Writings of Abraham ibn Ezra* (London, 1877; repr. Jerusalem, 1964), 108.

[2] D. L. Lasker, *Jewish Philosophical Polemics against Christianity in the Middle Ages* (New York, 1977). Jewish influence on Christian exegesis has been thoroughly studied, e.g. by R. Loewe, especially 'The Medieval Christian Hebraists of England. The *Superscriptio Lincolniensis*'. *HUCA* 28 (1957): 205–52; B. Smalley, especially *The Study of the Bible in the Middle Ages*, 3rd edn (Oxford, 1983); G. Dahan, *Les intellectuels chrétiens et les juifs au moyen âge* (Paris, 1990).

[3] A brief and consistent sketch is given by E. I. J. Rosenthal, 'The Study of the Bible in Medieval Judaism', in *The Cambridge History of the Bible*, vol. II, ed. G. W. H. Lampe (Cambridge, 1969),

ing to the presence or absence of an introduction. The commentaries that lack introductions are first the Midrashim,[4] and secondly the commentaries of Rashi (1040–1105)[5] and his successors. These commentaries begin with the first verse of the book and continue, verse by verse, until the end. The explanation may concern a single word or expression or the whole verse, but it follows faithfully the order of the text. General remarks, when they exist, are tied to the more particular ones. As befits the 'seventy-two faces' of the Torah, more than one explanation is often proposed by the compiler or the author. In the Midrashim, the divisions of the text are those of the scriptural reading in the synagogue: the three-year Palestinian cycle. In the commentaries by rabbis of Ashkenazic countries, however, the division of the text is that of the Babylonian one-year cycle of liturgical biblical readings which was universally adopted in the course of the twelfth century.

These commentaries have reached us in written form; however, there is no doubt that they were composed in the surroundings of an oral and collective study. No introduction was necessary: the Bible was God's revelation and this fact was not open to question. The whole biblical text is of utmost interest: every verse is as worthy of explanation as any other, every letter as significant as another, every detail of every letter heavy with sense. This conception of the Torah has a long history going back to the Talmud and the *Sefer Yesirah*, flourishing in the kabbalah and letter mysticism; it is as alive today as it was two thousand years ago. In this way of thinking of God and humanity the Torah is central, as is the Jewish people, in an absolute and largely unconscious world view.

This does not mean that these commentaries are devoid of reasoning and argumentation. On the contrary, they display a high level of authentic linguistic perspicacity, logical discussion, explanations by means of comparison with the material and social surroundings. But all this intellectual activity is circumscribed within limits drawn by the traditional sources of the written and oral law.

Philosophical commentaries, on the other hand, take into account another source of relation to God: reason. Although the definition of reason is diverse, and its relevance to revelation given more or less importance, it is always recognized as the heritage of all human beings.

252–79. Cf. also A. Neubauer, *The Fifty-third Chapter of Isaiah according to the Jewish Interpreters* (London, 1876; repr. New York, 1969).

4 E. Z. Melamed, *Bible Commentators* (Hebrew) (Jerusalem, 1978), vol. I, 5–128.

5 Melamed, *Bible Commentators*, vol. I, 353–449 on Rashi; pp. 453–513 on Rashi's grandson, Samuel ben Meir of Ramerupt (Rashbam). For other commentators see A. Grossman, *The Early Sages of France. Their Lives, Leadership and Works* (Jerusalem, 1995) and *The Early Sages of Ashkenaz. Their Lives, Leadership and Works (900–1096)* (Jerusalem, 1988) (both in Hebrew).

All medieval philosophical commentaries have introductions, which ultimately have their source in the philological scrutiny of classical Greek literature. The earliest of these medieval philosophical commentaries were composed by the Rabbanite Geonim Saadya Gaon[6] (882–942), Samuel ben Hofni[7] (*c.* 997–1013) and Aaron ben Sargado[8] (eleventh century) who, in the words of Abraham ibn Ezra, 'introduce in their commentaries an excess of extraneous matter', and the Karaites, 'those who entirely reject tradition and solely rely on their own reasoning': Jacob al-Kirkisani (*fl. c.* 930–940),[9] Salmon ben Jeroham (mid-tenth century, Jerusalem), Japheth ben Eli[10] (d. after 1004–5 in Jerusalem) and many others.

All of these lived in the Middle East and wrote in Arabic. To this group are to be added the Spanish halakhist, scholar and poet Isaac ben Judah ibn Ghayyat (Lucena, 1038–1089), author of a commentary on the Ecclesiastes, and Joseph ibn Aknin (twelfth century), author of a commentary on the Song of Songs.

Saadya's Commentary on Genesis[11] is an illustration of this kind of work. The general introduction to the Torah subdivides the text into parts, with different aims and different literary formulations.

1) It stipulates the place of the Torah vis-à-vis rational knowledge, axiomatic and derivative: reason precedes revelation, which is followed by oral tradition.
2) The central part of the Torah is made of laws: commandments and prohibitions. The two other parts of the Torah – promises of reward and punishment and the stories of righteous and wicked men – are meant to encourage man to obey divine laws and to deter him from disobedience: these two subjects are subdivided into eighteen parts.
3) After a lengthy refutation of the Karaites' claims against the oral law, Saadya enumerates the requirements of correct biblical exegesis, i.e. the harmonization of the biblical text with the other sources of human knowledge.

[6] Saadya's commentaries have been published mostly by Y. Kafih. The edition by M. Zucker, *Saadya's Commentary on Genesis* (New York, 1965), brings together Genizah fragments. His notes are a fountain of knowledge, as is his *Rav Saadya Gaon's Translation of the Torah* (New York, 1959).

[7] D. E. Sklare, *Samuel b. Hofni Gaon and his Cultural World* (Leiden, 1996), and A. Greenbaum, *The Biblical Commentary of Rav Samuel b. Hofni According to Geniza Manuscripts* (Jerusalem, 1979).

[8] Cf. Zucker, *Saadya's Commentary*, 12 and 27 of the introduction.

[9] Jacob al-Kirkisani's principles of biblical exegesis are translated in L. Nemoy, *Karaite Anthology* (New Haven and London, 1952; new edn 1980), 53–68.

[10] On Salmon ben Jeroham and Japheth ben Eli see G. Vajda, *Deux commentaires karaïtes sur l'Ecclésiaste* (Leiden, 1971), and P. Birnbaum, *The Arabic Commentary of Yefet ben Ali the Karaite on the Book of Hosea* (Philadelphia, 1942).

[11] Cf. Zucker, *Saadya's Commentary*.

4) One has to take into account the rules of rhetoric.
5) The cases where lexicographical and exegetical rules are to be applied.

The commentary itself is divided in three parts:

1) an Arabic translation of the text;
2) an explanation of the way the translation was made and the reason for the lexical choices;
3) a commentary, which sometimes proceeds verse by verse and sometimes discusses a group of verse.

However, the limits of the three parts are blurred and their succession is irregular.

Another example is the introduction of Jacob al-Kirkisani to his commentary on the non-legal parts of the Pentateuch:[12]

> It is our purpose to undertake a commentary upon the Book of our Lord, which he revealed to us through Moses, namely the Law, and to elucidate that part of its subject matter which is other than laws and ordinances . . .
>
> Scripture is one of the foundations of philosophy . . . We must prove the validity of rational speculation and philosophical postulates from Scripture by mentioning some passages in it which point and lead to them . . . The Sages of our nation had engaged in such investigation . . . This in fact is what the Greek and other philosophers quote in his [King Solomon's] name and is now incorporated in their books.

Thirty-seven preliminary rules are enumerated, and they are followed by five principles of correct exegesis, which are thoroughly discussed, as may be seen in the following summary of the first of them:

1. We must know that our prophet and master Moses was the one who wrote the Pentateuch, from its beginning to its end.
2. Scripture as a whole is to be interpreted literally, except where literal interpretation may involve something objectionable or imply a contradiction.
3. The Hebrew language is the primordial tongue.
4. Scripture addresses mankind in a manner accessible to their understanding.
5. Scripture does not recount a false statement in an unqualified way.
6. When Scripture quotes the words of persons . . . who are not of the children of Israel, does it do so in the same language the words were spoken . . . ? Some say . . . Those who oppose this view say . . . To this, the holders of the former opinion reply . . . Their opponents then answer

[12] Cf. Nemoy, *Karaite Anthology*, and G. Vajda, 'Du prologue de Qirqisani à son commentaire sur la Genèse', in *In Memoriam Paul Kahle*, ed. Matthew Black and Georg Fohrer (Berlin, 1968), 222–31.

. . . The opinion of these latter seems, up to this point to be more convincing . . . However . . . Therefore, not everything recounted in Scripture in the Hebrew language was originally spoken in Hebrew . . .

A third example is the commentary on Ecclesiastes by Isaac ibn Ghayyat.[13] It is divided into blocks of verses which are explained together, and the explanation may include a conclusion. Here is a very brief resumé of the introduction:

Rhetoric is a means of conveying a given intention in a clear and concise way. It was used in sacred scripture, and the author of this commentary will use it too. Thus, eight questions are to be answered:

– who is the author?
– what is his surname?
– for whom was the work produced and when?
– is this book one of the venerated ones?
– is the work a personal composition or was it inspired by God?
– were the contents known or unknown at this period?
– what are the fundamental principles the work is based on?
– is the aim of the work general or particular?

Chapter 1, verses 1–4 are the introduction to the book. It gives the name of the author and his genealogy, and expresses the aim of the book.

Chapter 1, verses 5–7 discuss the radiance of the sun which has a perpetual movements which divides the day from the night; the circular movements of the planets which directs the seasons; the winds, etc . . .

[Conclusion] By these, the Sage wanted to teach us four things:

1) that the sun and planets have an eternal existence and all the other creatures in the generated world are transient.
2) how time is related to the two heavenly movements; the function of rivers and of the four constitutive elements of this world.
3) the life of the terrestrial world depends on the two movements of the sun and planets.
4) in the same way as the celestial bodies long to return to their principle, the four elements which composed the generations have returned to their constituant element.

[13] I am grateful to Steven Harvey for reminding me of this important text, published and translated into Hebrew by Y. Kafih, *Hamesh Megillot* (Jerusalem, 1962, 161–296), as a commentary by Saadya Gaon. My lapse of memory was the more unforgivable since I was a pupil of Georges Vajda when he lectured on this text in 1971/2 at the Ecole Pratique des Hautes Etudes (see *Annuaire de l'EPHE, Section des sciences religieuses*, vol. 79, 233–7). The authorship of Isaac ibn Ghiyyat has been demonstrated by S. Pines (*Tarbiz* 33 (1963/4): 212 ff.), added to by G. Vajda (*The Seventy-fifth Anniversary Volume of the Jewish Quarterly Review* (1967): 518–27). The introduction has been translated to French by H. Zafrani and A. Caquot, *L'Ecclésiaste et son commentaire 'Le Livre de L'ascèse'* (Paris, 1989).

Joseph ben Judah ben Jacob ibn Aknin, a contemporary of Maimonides, introduces the duality of exoteric and esoteric meaning in the Bible. He wrote *The Divulgence of Mysteries and the Appearance of Lights,* on the Song of Songs.[14] After a lengthy introduction, recapitulating the order of the spheres and of the intellects and describing the relations between the lowest intellect – the Agent intellect – and the human soul, he divides his commentary into three parts: the exoteric sense, which is essentially grammatical and literal; the rabbinic sense, an explanation concerned with the fate of Israel based on the Midrash, which he calls 'the way of our masters' (*shitat rabotenu*); and a 'scientific' one, endowing each word with physiological, psychological, logical and philosophical implications, opening with the formula 'according to my conception'.

The Jewish authors of these biblical commentaries were steeped in Arabic philosophy, be it the kalam or some other trend of Arabic thought. The Torah was the only divine law, but this divinity was in harmony with rational arguments. The biblical text was thus to be investigated like any other text, using the common scientific tradition garbed in inherited literary structures. These are partly known: the parallels drawn with Qur'ānic exegesis by Moshe Zucker[15] are illuminating; the parallels with Christian Syriac exegesis look promising (the list of questions asked by Ibn Ghayyat clearly shows that the classical tradition had already been adapted to the scriptures) and this influence may have come through David al-Muqammis.[16]

The Jews of Christian Europe had no access to these Arabic philosophical Bible commentaries, which were lengthy and old fashioned when philosophical books began to be translated from Arabic into Hebrew. We know them owing to the Genizah fragments recovered since the end of the last century and from Yemenite manuscripts since their arrival in Israel fifty years ago. Only short quotations entered what was to be the mainstream of Rabbanite Judaism, the Hebrew-reading European tradition which grew up during the eleventh and twelfth centuries.

[14] It was edited and translated into Hebrew by A. S. Halkin, *Divulgatio Mysteriorum Luminumque Apparentia* (Jerusalem, 1964).

[15] *Saadya's Commentary*, introduction, 35–57.

[16] Who is cited by Kirkisani: 'Daud ibn Marwan al-R'akki, known as al-Muqammis, has written a fine book containing a commentary on Genesis, which he translated from the commentaries of the Syrians . . . Another scholar of our own time also composed a fine book on this subject in which he followed a method similar to that of Da'ud' (Nemoy, *Karaite Anthology*, 54, note 9). Cf. S. Stroumsa, *Dawud ibn Marwan al-Muqamis's Twenty Chapters* (Leiden, 1989), 20. To my knowledge, the second scholar has not been identified, but the Syriac lead has not been thoroughly followed – again, to the best of my knowledge.

The twelfth century was a turning point in the intellectual history of Jews, in Islam as well as in Christian Europe. The growth of a stricter Aristotelianism exacerbated the conflict between philosophy and revelation, a conflict that came to a head in lengthy polemics between reason and faith. The Jewish communities of Europe were divided: in northern countries, the scholars were outside the world of 'sciences'; they studied the Talmud and produced the biblical commentaries we spoke of at the beginning. In the south (Provence, Spain, Italy), the scholars aspired to learn the sciences. Both groups of communities were introduced to the new kind of biblical commentary through Abraham ibn Ezra (*c.* 1089–*c.* 1165), the first philosopher who wrote in Hebrew and, through his travels, promoted his work in all parts of Europe.

Abraham ibn Ezra[17] divides his readers into two classes: the general public, able to understand only the received explanations, and liable to be endangered if they are exposed to philosophical truth; and the privileged few, who have enjoyed education – i.e. studied the sciences – to whom he may entrust his suggestions and views, his 'secrets'.

'He who is wise will understand,' he writes when he wants his reader to discover by himself the explanation of the more difficult passages of the Bible based on his astrological Neoplatonism.

In the Muslim countries, where Maimonides and Ibn Aknin lived, and where Abraham ibn Ezra originated, calling philosophy 'a secret truth' conformed to the philosophical view – found for example in Averroes – that the revealed books are political laws, altogether different from philosophical demonstrations.

The reasons for this secrecy were the differences between philosophy and revelation concerning the doctrines of creation, resurrection and so on. However, for Abraham ibn Ezra, as for Maimonides in his *Guide of the Perplexed*, the reason for the defence of revealing the secrets was the conservation of social peace, possible only by the moral way of life of the vulgar, itself possible only with the help of the law.[18]

For Christians the secret was not a secret. On the contrary, it was well publicized, as Samuel ibn Tibbon already remarked at the beginning of the thirteenth century. Nonetheless the topos of the 'secret' and the accusation of 'revealing the secrets' were at the heart of the controversy on the teaching of philosophy that engulfed the Jewish communities of

[17] See Friedlander, *Abraham ibn Ezra*; cf. Melamed, *Bible Commentators*, vol. II, 517–714 and R. Jospe, 'Biblical Exegesis as a Philosophic Literary Genre: Abraham ibn Ezra and Moses Mendelssohn', in *Jewish Philosophy and the Academy*, ed. E. L. Fackenheim and R. Jospe, 48–92. (Madison and London, 1996).

[18] The bibliography on this subject is considerable. The clearest account is that of S. Pines in the introduction to his English translation, *Moses Maimonides, the Guide of the Perplexed* (Chicago, 1963).

France, Provence and Spain during the thirteenth century.[19] In the fourteenth century the issue of 'revealing the secrets' was as hotly debated as during the controversy; this is clear from the attacks against Joseph ibn Caspi (*c.* 1280–after 1332).[20] Nissim ben Moses of Marseille, writing between 1315 and 1330, uses the word *sod* (secret) six times in the first sentence of his commentary on the Pentateuch.[21]

Ibn Ezra's biblical commentaries also introduced the literary structures of the philosophical commentaries.

They are preceded by introductions. The introduction to the Pentateuch lists the classes of commentaries written before him and contrasts their methods with the correct one: that which uses the rules of grammar and common sense. Thus he will explain first each word of the weekly section, and then the sense and context of the whole. As noted by Friedlaender, 'it seems that most of the commentaries were originally arranged according to this plan; it is preserved only in a fragment of a second recension of the Commentary on the Pentateuch, in the commentaries of Job, on the Song of Solomon, on the book of Lamentations, and traces of it are also discernible in the printed Commentary on the Pentateuch'.

An example is given in the Hebrew text printed by Friedlaender at the end of his English study: after the introduction (pp. 1–10), we find ten weekly pericopes called *diqduq* (pp. 10–18) and the explanation of subjects called *perush* (pp. 19–46), etc. The Song of Songs (Song of Solomon) is divided into three parts: explanation of the grammatical sense of the songs, their literal meaning and their allegorical (midrashic) meaning.

In subsequent biblical commentaries written in Spain, Provence and Italy, there are always introductions of one type or another.

It is with Samuel ibn Tibbon, coming after Abraham ibn Ezra, that the proper *accessus ad auctorem* entered the Jewish tradition. As pointed out by Sarah Klein-Braslavy, 'he not only implemented the conventional preliminary topics in his works but contends explicitly that this prologue-paradigm is a literary convention and that the eight-point preface should precede any *philosophical* treatise'.[22] He introduced his commentary on Ecclesiastes in this way.

Samuel ibn Tibbon does not mention his sources. He may have found this tradition in the philosophical treatises of al-Farabi or Averroes, which

[19] See C. Sirat, *History of Jewish Philosophy in the Middle Ages* (Cambridge, 1990), 222–6, and the bibliography, 434–5.

[20] See B. Mesch, *Studies in Joseph ibn Caspi* (Leiden, 1975), 43 ff.

[21] See Sirat, *History of Jewish Philosophy*, 277–82. I quote from Paris BNF MS hébr. 720, f. 1v.

[22] S. Klein-Braslavy, 'The Neo-platonic Prologue Tradition in the Writings of Samuel ibn Tibbon and Gersonides', a lecture given during the Dibner/Israel Conference in the History of Science: 'Medieval Hebrew Science. The Contexts', Jerusalem, 5–8 July 1999. I am very grateful to S. Klein-Braslavy for giving me a copy of this lecture.

he may have read in Arabic; he could also have been influenced by the Christian milieu. In the final chapter of his *Ma'amar Yiqawu ha-mayim* he affirms that he saw it as a duty to reveal the secrets of the doctrines of the ancient sages, because 'I saw that the truths which were concealed since then, since our prophets and the sages of our Torah, are all of of them well known by the Gentiles; in conformity with these truths, they explain the secrets of the Torah of the prophets and in most cases of those who were inspired by the Holy Spirit when our people is ignorant of them.'[23] As long as the Jews are ignorant, the truths can only be alluded to. This is not the case for gentiles and Arabs: 'I have seen that the true sciences have become much more publicised (*nitparsemu*)[24] among the nations under whose rule and in whose countries I live, more and more than in the lands of Ishmael.'

Indeed, philosophical questions were openly debated in Christian countries beginning in the twelfth century. Some Jewish philosophers could not fail to be impressed by the free exposition of subjects which were considered, in Arabic and Jewish societies, as dangerous 'secrets'. Those who knew enough of Christian philosophy to be impressed by these public debates could not fail either to see the difficulty of interpreting the Bible in Aristotelian terms.

The study of the New Aristotle and of Averroes' commentaries in the arts faculties indeed exacerbated the conflict between philosophy and revelation. The Christian opponents of philosophy – and its excess – reacted by condemning some theses. In any case, for them philosophy was the servant of theology. It was to be learnt openly but its ancillary status was to be acknowledged.

It seems that only two Jewish philosophers were steeped enough in Christian thinking to realize fully the problems and propose solutions, which are, however, very different one from the other.

The first of these is Judah ben Moses ben Daniel Romano (*c.* 1292–*c.* 1325). He lived in Rome and had first-hand knowledge of the Christian scholastics: he translated into Hebrew numerous works by Christian scholars[25] and drew on them freely.[26] His commentary on Genesis begins with the following verses:

[23] Ed. M. C. Bisliches, 173–5. (Pressburg, 1837).

[24] The Hebrew word *nitparsemu* has been translated by S. Pines (*Guide*, 52) by 'much more famous'; however, this fame is tied to proclamation; *lefarsem* means 'to make public' (see E. Ben Iehuda, *Thesaurus totius hebraitatis et veteris et recentiores* (Tel Aviv, 1949), s.v. *prsm*).

[25] See J. B. Sermoneta, 'La dottrina dell' intelletto e la 'fede filosofica' di Jehudàh e Immanuel Romano', *Studi medievali*, 3rd series, 6 2 (1965): 1–76.

[26] W. M. Reedijk, 'Some Observations on the Influence of Christian Scholastic Authors on Jewish Thinkers in the Thirteenth and Fourteenth Century', *Bijdragen, Tijdschrift voor Filosofie en Theologie* 51 (1990): 382–96.

The star of innovation will shed light/
And my light shall settle on the explanation/
And I shall not be satisfied with strange offspring/
Today because I shall inherit them
Lest I drink from the waters of their springs
And I forget the law of the poor and their poverty.[27]

The introduction is constructed according to the schema of the four Aristotelian causes – which was the university fashion at this time.

Also at this time, some Christian exegetes favoured an 'infinite interpretation' which is defined by Gilbert Dahan as 'les paroles divines croissent avec celui qui les lit',[28] and by G. Sermoneta explaining Judah's way of explaining the scripture:

> If we assume that there is no need for exact correspondence between Scripture in all its details, on the one hand, and the philosophical teaching of the Aristotelian schools, on the other; if we are content with the principle that the scriptural text is merely a channel for the dissemination of the rational truth among the learned, while retaining its status of exemplary truth, then we have preserved *in toto* the truth of Scripture as well as its philosophical meaning. It can be understood that in every generation we continue to discover the truth, which is revealed to those who search for it. The principle can thus be preserved even if we admit that the scriptural text has multiple meanings and even if we grant the philosopher total freedom of interpretation . . .
>
> What matters in the philosophical interpretation of Scripture is not the uncovering of a single truth, hidden in the verse, expressed there as an *exemplum* which the commentator must be able to show corresponds to the *examplatum*, which is one of the principles of Aristotelian philosophy. This new kind of exegesis is guided by the performance of a formal exercise, the sole aim of which is to extract a certain rational truth from the verse. At the moment when the interpreter applies his intellectual faculties to the verse, there is no importance to the content itself, or to the sequence of the matters related in the passage before him. Any sort of content and any abstract idea derived from the verse will constitute the discovery of a formal and rational truth. The sequence of matters and the number of explanations which he may extract from the verse or impose on it is of absolutely no importance.[29]

Thus for a single verse Judah Romano proposes fifteen different explanations.[30]

Immanuel ben Solomon of Rome (*c.* 1270–*c.* 1330) quotes extensively from his younger contemporary. He orders his commentaries in two

[27] Vatican Library, MS Urb ebreo 38, f. 1r, translated in G. Sermoneta, 'Prophecy in the Writings of R Yehuda Romano', in *Studies in Medieval Jewish History and Literature*, ed. I. Twersky, vol. II, 354, note 30 (Cambridge and London, 1984) (some emendations made to this translation).

[28] See G. Dahan, *L'exégèse chrétienne de la Bible en Occident médiéval, XIIe–XIVe siècle* (Paris, 1999), 71.

[29] Sermoneta, 'Prophecy', 342–4.

[30] Sermoneta, 'Prophecy', 347.

parts: the literal and grammatical explanation is followed by the philosophical one; more than one explanation is sometimes given but never as many as in Judah's commentaries. He calls the literal commentary *diqduq ha-millot* and the general interpretation *'inyan ha-pasuq*.[31]

In fact both Judah Romano and Immanuel of Rome were influenced by a Christian exegetical trend which was already out of fashion. During the thirteenth century Christian exegesis had already abandoned the complexity of the 'infinite' number of explanations, so dear to Judah Romano. In order to build on the *pagina sacra* a scientific theological argumentation, some theologians, such as Thomas Aquinas, first extended the field of the *littera*. Instead of relying on the traditional 'four senses' of scripture, they affirm that the first *intentio* of the divine author is the *littera*. This *littera*, however, has three stages, each requiring different techniques and knowledge: the *littera* strictly defined is textual analysis; the *sensus*, a study of the historical context; the *sententia*, a philosophical and theological approach. Thus both figurative expressions and moral injunctions may be part of the literal sense.[32]

John Van Engen remarks: 'The shift to the literal sense as foundational arose in part from a self-conscious exegetical program, a repudiation of endless "unscientific" spiritual interpretations, and in part from the cultural shift that made of scripture, hence its words and sentences, a classroom textbook.' The second move was to interpret the *littera* not only as the first *intentio* of the text but also as the sign of universal and intelligible truths.

To make Scripture true and theology a science, the master had to overcome all the confusions and distractions thrown up by its variety and its literal meanings to discern what the author – God – intended; this counted as scientific exegesis . . . What implicitly worried these theologians, once they had acquired this overwhelming knowledge of the words and *gesta* in their Text was to make universal truths claims out of such a mass of particulars . . . Masters and students were further confounded by the impact of an Aristotelian model of *scientia,* generating in most thirteenth-century *summae* the first question, whether theologia, meaning the study of Holy Scripture, could qualify as a science . . .

How could science, Albert the Great wondered, be based upon *gesta singularia* which could not count either as *intelligibilia or universalia ?* . . . These were potentially universal in nature, each historical particular, like one eclipse, teaching a more universal truth . . . These particulars understood as universals could yield the nodal points of theology as a science.[33]

[31] Parma, Bibliotheca palatina, MS de Rossi 404. [32] Dahan, *Exégèse*, 240–1.
[33] J. Van Engen, 'Studying Scripture in the Early University', in *Neue Richtungen in der hoch- und spätmittelalterlichen Bibel exegese*, ed. R. E. Lerner, 30–3 (Munich, 1996).

In stating these transformations in Christian exegesis, we are already describing the exegesis of Gersonides.[34]

Gersonides (1288–1344) lived in Provence.[35] His biblical commentaries are preceded by introductions of the *accessus ad auctorem* type: like Samuel ibn Tibbon, he had read the commentaries of al-Farabi and Averroes (although he read them in Hebrew). Like him, he was acquainted with Christian personalities, and probably but not certainly knew (and perhaps owned) Samuel ibn Tibbon's commentary on Ecclesiastes.[36]

Gersonides' relations with the Christian milieu have been a subject of dispute among historians of Jewish philosophy for a hundred years. Although he collaborated with Christian scholars and worked for Christian patrons, unlike Judah and Immanuel Romano, he never quotes a Christian philosopher. Notwithstanding this fact, the principle laid out by Shlomo Pines seems like sound common sense: 'It is indeed unreasonable to surmise that individuals who were alive in their foreign environment, who were undoubtedly at home in its vernacular – some probably even knowing Latin – would have been sealed off from the philosophical currents, the problems and the crucial, even occasionally stormy, arguments which engaged that environment'.[37]

The comparison of the structures of his biblical commentaries with Christian ones may add new arguments. Eli Freyman[38] has pointed out three features which are characteristic of Gersonides' commentaries:

1. the division in two separate parts: a literal commentary (*be'ur ha-millot*) precedes a general interpretation (*be'ur ha-parashah*).
2. the division of the weekly pericope into smaller units.
3. the use of 'lessons' (*to'aliyot*) which specify what we learn from each of the commented units.

[34] S. Feldman, 'Gersonides and Biblical Exegesis', in *The Words of the Lord*, vol. II (Philadelphia, New York and Jerusalem, 1987), without comparing them to Christian exegesis.

[35] M. Kellner has given two lists of studies on this author, the more recent being 'Bibliographia Gersonideana: An Annotated List of Writings by and about R Levi ben Gershom', in *Studies on Gersonides: A Fourteenth-century Jewish Philosopher-Scientist*, ed. G. Freudenthal, 367–414 (Leiden, 1992).

[36] G. Weil, *La bibliothèque de Gersonide d'après son catalogue autographe* (Louvain, 1991), and Klein-Braslavy, 'Neo-Platonic Prologue Tradition', 13–16. The arguments of Ruth Ben Meir in favour of the influence on Gersonides of Ibn Ghayyat's commentary on Ecclesiastes (in her PhD thesis, Jerusalem, 1994, 117–52) do not seem convincing, as I hope to show in a future publication.

[37] *Scholasticism after Thomas Aquinas and the Teachings of Hasdai Crescas and his Predecessors* (Jerusalem, 1967; repr. in *The Collected Works of Shlomo Pines*, vol. V, 489–589 (Jerusalem, 1997).

[38] 'Le commentaire sur le Pentateuque de Gersonide: éditions et manuscrits', in *Gersonide en son temps*, ed. G. Dahan, 117–124 (Louvain and Paris, 1991).

1. In fact, the first feature is not as original as it looks: it is not only used by Abraham ibn Ezra, but we have noticed it in Immanuel Romano's commentary on the Pentateuch.
   Nonetheless, this division does parallel the well-known Christian distinction between *littera* and *sensus* or *littera* and *sententia.*
2. The division of the weekly pericope into smaller units is the well-known *divisio textus*, each division being preceded by an introduction. Gersonides' divisions do not parallel the ones found in the conventional contemporary Christian Bible commentaries. Indeed, these divisions depend on the themes discerned by the various exegetes, although the *divisio textus* is used by all university teachers, whether in the arts or theological faculty.[39]
3. The 'lessons' are the most important personal feature of Gersonides' commentary; they are not found in any other Jewish exegesis, but are paralleled by the universals and intelligibles which were the 'nodal points' of Christian theology.

At the start of his exegetical period, Gersonides wrote commentaries on Job, the Song of Songs, Ecclesiastes, Esther and Ruth, and began his commentary on the Torah. The commentary on the Song of Songs[40] is the best example of the extension of the literal sense to all the senses intended by the 'author'. Gersonides explains that

1. the intention of this book is to guide the 'few' (the philosophers) to their ultimate felicity: cognizing and knowing God as far as man is able to do it;
2. this intention is the *pshat,* the *littera* of the text;
3. this *pshat* is only *hiqquyim, figures.* There is no other literal meaning, besides this allegorical one.

As Menahem Kellner says:

> A few examples here will suffice to give the flavour of the whole: *Jerusalem* stands for man. Just as man, among all the compounded entities, is set apart for the worship of God, so is *Jerusalem* set off from other cities. Furthermore, the name *Jerusalem* is derived from the Hebrew word perfection: man is the most perfect of all the sublunar entities and thus called *Jerusalem.* The faculties of the soul are *the daughters of Jerusalem* while *Solomon* refers to the intellect. Since *Zion* is the worthiest part of Jerusalem, *the daughters of Zion* refer to those faculties of the soul

[39] For the arts faculty see the examples given by O. Weijers, *Le maniement du savoir, Pratiques intellectuelles à l'époque des premières universités* (XIIIe–XIVe siècles) (Turnhout, 1996), 44, and for the faculty of theology G. Dahan (ed.), *Gersonide et son temps*, 112, 271–5.

[40] See *Commentary on the Song of Songs, Levi ben Gershom (Gersonides)* translated from the Hebrew with an introduction and annotations by M. Kellner (New Haven and London, 1998).

closet to the activity of the intellect. Gersonides continues in this vein, interpreting in this fashion many of the expressions found in *Song of Songs*.[41]

Extending the literal sense to include the allegorical one was a way to make clear the 'first intention' of the text: the 'scientific' one. This is what Gersonides did in his Bible commentaries, dividing the text in order to isolate the themes that yield the *universals*, the *intelligibles*, the *to'alyot* intended by God to guide the human being to their felicity. These *universalia intelligibilia* may be of three kinds:[42]

1) commandments, positive or negative ones, dealing with faith or actions;
2) political science;
3) knowledge of the science of existent beings.

The third kind of knowledge is not acquired by human investigation or perhaps with great difficulty.

The three kinds of *universalia* and *intelligibilia* are found also in the Talmud and Gersonides gives the title of the chapters of all the Talmudic treatises.

Both Bible and Talmud are thus the repositories of theology, the science which is to be studied after the completion of the study of mathematics, the study of physics, the study of metaphysics.

All this is explained by Gersonides many times, very clearly, in all his commentaries. The *universalia* and *intelligibilia* are certainly not those found by the Christian exegetes. Gersonides has not copied them. What he took from them is their methods, the way a science may be deduced from the Bible.

Interestingly enough, the *to'aliyot*, the universals and intelligibles, which are, for Gersonides, the basis of the highest science have never been studied. Denying the influence of scholasticism on one of the greatest Jewish philosophers has had for consequence the neglect of what is perhaps the only true Jewish theology.

41 'Gersonides' Commentary on Song of Songs', in Dahan (ed.), *Gersonide en son temps*, 86.

42 *Rabbinic Pentateuch with Commentary on the Torah by R Levi ben Gershom*, edited from MSS and provided with introduction and notes by B. Braner and E. Freiman (Jerusalem (Maalyot), 1993). I intend to translate Gersonides' introduction into French in the collective book to be edited by S. Klein-Braslavy and myself, *Les méthodes de travail de Gersonide*.

CHAPTER FIFTEEN

Jewish scholarship and Christian tradition in late-medieval Catalonia: Profiat Duran on the art of memory

Irene E. Zwiep

Medieval Christian scholars were well aware of the tension between reading and remembering exactly what they had read. Petrarch articulated the quandary in a much-discussed passage in the *Secretum* (1347–53), a fictional dialogue between himself (alias 'Franciscus') and 'Augustinus', modelled after Augustine's *Confessiones* but in fact largely dependent on Ciceronian ethics and psychology. In Book II of the *Secretum* Franciscus and Augustinus pursue their analysis of the misery that comes with the Seven Deadly Sins. Within this context they review various intellectual habits that might lead to arrogance and thus conflict with prudence. One of these potentially harmful habits was reading, a custom which, though ultimately wholesome and beneficial to the soul, was not without its intrinsic problems. When Augustinus tells the author to go and find a remedy against his weakness in the books of Seneca and Cicero, Franciscus retorts that in fact he has read both but has forgotten most of their precepts. Books, he found, are a great help while you are reading; once you put them away, however, their impact disappears. Augustinus acknowledges that only too many nowadays pursue this kind of reading and hastens to offer practical guidelines as to how to memorize effectively the contents of one's reading. The belief that reading and memorizing were closely connected yet somehow incompatible had an ancient pedigree. In Plato's *Phaedrus* (274c–275b), Socrates formulated a critique of writing with the help of ancient Egyptian mythology. The myth related by Socrates tells us how Theuth or Thoth, the divine creator of various arts, invented script and presented it to the supreme god and ruler Thammuz-Ammon, claiming it would make the Egyptians wiser men since it was a recipe for memory and thus for wisdom. Ammon, however, exposed writing as a mere semblance of wisdom, pointing out that it would stimulate 'reminding' rather than the

The author would like to thank Shlomo Berger and Emile Schrijver for their advice.

actual memories of his subjects. In Socrates' version of the story, writing was suspect because it would create a class of literate but essentially ignorant readers who, like 'Franciscus' in Petrarch's *Secretum*, would rely on external sources of knowledge rather than exercise their own minds and use their own, internalized or innate wisdom.[1]

Throughout the ages the frailty of human memory and its cultivation, both naturally and artificially, remained an important theme within the Western tradition. It was explored by the ancient pagan orators, who depended on their memories when delivering their speeches, and re-examined by various scholars of the Middle Ages, who transformed the classical art of memory into a component of Christian ethics and an instrument to be applied within the wider context of reading and education.[2] By contrast, in spite of the lively preoccupation with practical mnemonics (*simanim*) in the rabbinic and masoretic literature of the first millennium CE, which had expressed itself in a great number of technical proverbs, catchphrases and acrostics, the Jewish scholarly tradition of the later Middle Ages seems to have been less immersed in memory training. One exception to this rule is the section on the fifteen 'ways of reading and studying' that would stimulate memory, which the Catalonian scholar Profiat Duran appended to the preface of his Hebrew grammar *Ma'aseh Efod* (The making of the Efod) of 1403.[3] Notwithstanding the fact that Duran had been forcibly converted to Christianity during the persecutions of 1391, the *Efod* turned out a very Jewish book. Methodologically, it was intended as a rehabilitation of the linguistic approach of the Hebrew grammarians of eleventh-century Andalusia.[4] Ideologically, it was an attempt to promote the study of Torah among his Jewish co-religionists,[5] and to provide them with a basic tool for its understanding. In the more theoretical chapters, however, the *Efod* betrays various Christian, scholastic, influences.[6] As

[1] For an analysis of various modern interpretations of the passage and its meaning within the dialogue, see G. R. F. Ferrari, *Listening to the Cicadas. A Study of Plato's Phaedrus* (Cambridge: Cambridge University Press, 1987), 204–32.

[2] For various trends and developments within the *ars memorativa* before the Renaissance period, see the classical study by Frances A. Yates, *The Art of Memory* (London: Routledge & Kegan Paul, 1966), esp. 1–104 and, more recently, and with a much broader scope, Mary Carruthers, *The Book of Memory. A Study of Memory in Medieval Culture* (Cambridge: Cambridge University Press, 1990).

[3] Jonathan Friedländer and Jakob Kohn (eds.), *Maase Efod. Einleitung in das Studium und Grammatik der Hebräischen Sprache von Profiat Duran* (Vienna: J. Holzwarth, 1865), 18–25.

[4] *Ma'aseh Efod*, introduction, 16. [5] See *Ma'aseh Efod*, 17f.

[6] See Irene E. Zwiep, *Mother of Reason and Revelation. A Short History of Medieval Jewish Linguistic Thought* (Amsterdam: J. C. Gieben, 1997), chap. 2, which discusses such typical features as Duran's definition of language in terms of material and formal causality, and his primarily extensional, object- rather than concept-oriented view of signification.

we shall see, the section on the art of memory too shows traces of Christian concerns and motifs.

One such motif was the doubtful harmony between reading and memory, recorded by Duran at the end of his preface, in which he critically reviewed the various ways of achieving scholarly perfection current in his days. His words are not so much reminiscent of Socrates' reservations in the *Phaedrus*, but rather remind us of Franciscus's desperation in the *Secretum*, completed exactly fifty years before Profiat Duran wrote his *Efod*. Commenting upon the best way to conduct one's studies Duran explained that, as contemporary scholarship had it, the knowledge best remembered was *ha-yedi'ah 'al peh*, the knowledge learnt by heart:

> Among the philosophers, too, he is not thought truly wise whose wisdom is not stored in his heart and who puts his trust in the skins of dead animals.[7] Of this it is said: every wisdom that does not enter the bath with its owner is no wisdom at all. This contrasts sharply with the majority of those who study Torah nowadays and believe that it is more than enough to know its contents from the book itself – once they have closed its doors and their eyes no longer see it, their hearts cease to be enlightened.[8]

The analogy between Duran's characterization of modern reading habits and Petrarch's observations in the *Secretum* is striking enough. First of all, while berating their contemporaries for putting their trust in books, both authors approached the issue from a distinctly moral angle. Duran's stipulation that 'religious reading should be conducted . . . in such a way that the knowledge derived from it is stored in the heart and in the faculty of memory . . . This is an indication of the love of God'[9] can be read as a pious restatement of Augustinus's more secular belief that Seneca's letters and *De tranquilitate animi*, combined with Cicero's *Tusculan Disputations*, would constitute 'a remedy written in the mind' (*velut in animo conscripta remedia*) against Franciscus's melancholy. Duran's Torah students, whose hearts were no longer enlightened by the divine

[7] *We-yivtach 'al 'orot ha-behemot ha-metot*, an obvious topos within this context, though not entirely unambiguous. The 'skins of animals' may be deemed unreliable because they distinguish neither truth nor falsehood. Cf. R. I. Moore, *The Rise of Popular Heresy* (London: Edward Arnold, 1975), 14, who describes a group of eleventh-century heretics denouncing the gospel as 'fabrications which men have written on the skins of animals'. According to Socrates, 'the trouble with a written composition is that it becomes detached from its author . . . falling into ignorant as well as learned hands. The educational value of writing thus depends upon the knowledge and quality of the person who reads it'; cf. Carruthers, *The Book of Memory*, 30. Parallel to Petrarch's view, however, Profiat Duran's objection concerns the fact that the contents of Torah should be written 'in the mind' rather than 'on the skins of dead animals'.

[8] *Ma'aseh Efod*, 18.

[9] *Ibid.*

word once they had closed their books, closely resemble not only Petrarch's forgetful Franciscus, pictured above, but also the *literatorum flagitiosissimos greges* immediately adduced by his tutor, the crowd of literati who were unable to put into action what they had learned in the classroom. In both accounts the obstinate reader, whether studying Torah or Seneca, failed to internalize the ethical precepts he had read and remained as unable to integrate those precepts into his everyday life and conduct as he had been before reading them. In short, in both accounts the reader, while trying to improve himself, actually ran the paradoxical risk of failing to become a better person.

But the two passages have more in common than their overall theme and wording. In their discussions of reading and memory Duran and Petrarch, each in his own way and within his own cultural context, evoked more or less the same image: that of the private reader, the man who read and studied by himself. Being the more subjective and introspective of the two, Petrarch concentrated on his own cultural and moral dilemmas and voiced the frustrations of the man of letters, the humanist reader-author on the brink of a new epoch. Duran chose to be more practical and instructive, and offered the Jewish reader an unprecedented set of techniques that would support and improve his private studies. Against the background of his own tradition, however, Duran could not help contrasting those novel techniques with the most ancient and, one might say, archetypically Jewish way of learning: the study of Talmud.

Even the basic proficiency to which the knowledge of Talmud was reduced in his days, Duran pointed out, was acquired through a single, essential technique: that of *shimmush*, i.e. visiting the yeshivah, where attending to the rabbis and cursory immersion in their teachings seemed more effective than the study of their actual writings. By contrast, the solitary reader addressed in the *Efod* was no longer part of a community and would acquire his knowledge not through contact with other living minds, but from written texts only. The argumentation in this part of the preface is in fact quite suggestive and almost emphatically Jewish. By structuring the text as he did, Duran could imply that he had noticed the disparity between the two methods and that he realized that, since he more or less rejected the (collective) study of the Talmud[10] in favour of the (solitary) study of Torah as the foundation of Jewish intellectual and spiritual life, he would have to compensate for the absence of a

[10] Cf. his discussion of the Talmudists, *Ma'aseh Efod*, 4ff.

traditional communal context. And so he decided to equip the private reader with fifteen 'ways of reading (*'iyyun*) and studying (*'eseq*) Torah, through which that which is learnt will be best remembered'.[11]

Again, it is not unlikely that this was a secondary justification. For indeed Duran's section on 'the art of memory' contains various interests and motifs that suggest it had been inspired, however circumstantially, by foreign, Christian trends. I have pointed to the analogy between Duran's digression on memory and Petrarch's *Secretum* II.16, which reveals the same ethical dimension and the same emphasis on the problems and possibilities of internalizing moral or religious values. Yet to appreciate this analogy better one should also take into consideration the remainder of Duran's excursus and examine its contents, terminology, cultural and scientific context, both against the background of the contemporary Christian tradition, with its long-standing preoccupation with memory, and against that of Duran's Jewish heritage. This examination may illustrate not only how Christian concerns could influence a Jewish scholar in Catalonia in the years after 1391, but simultaneously shed some light on the Jewish (and Christian) reading habits and memory strategies of that period.

Before coming to an evaluation of those habits and strategies one should of course establish the overall theory of memory on which Duran's 'fifteen rules' were modelled. Fortunately, quite a few of those rules contain information that helps us reconstruct its basic constituents. Hardly surprisingly, the vast majority of the instructions reveal that Duran's approach to memory was firmly rooted in the psychological tradition that had been developed out of Aristotle's – and Avicenna's – writings on the soul. Yet even when compared to Aristotle, whose *oeuvre* contains at least a few scattered observations on the practical art of memory,[12] the medieval Islamo-Judaic branch of that tradition was theory oriented rather than practical and didactic, bent on refining previous descriptions of mental processes rather than on guiding those processes. In view of this tradition, Duran seems to have trodden new ground when combining psychological theory and practical mnemonics.

His overall starting point was the theory of knowledge as formulated in Aristotle's *De anima*, according to which all knowledge, even intellectual, abstract, knowledge, has its ultimate origin in the sensory world. In an attempt at refuting Plato's view that knowledge consists only of innate

[11] *Ma'aseh Efod*, 18.

[12] The four passages where Aristotle incidentally discusses mnemonics are collected in Yates, *The Art of Memory*, 31–5.

ideas, Aristotle had postulated that all human knowledge ultimately rests on sense perceptions. These perceptions are brought in by the external senses, whereupon they are received by the so-called 'common sense' and subsequently transformed into images by the faculty of imagination, the chief intermediary between perception and thought. Thus memory represents the final stage in the sensory process of acquiring and retaining knowledge. It was defined by Aristotle as a set of mental images derived from sense impressions of things perceived in the past.[13] The images, stored in the sensitive part of the soul, become the material of intellectual thought, yet remain essentially physiological affectations. Therefore recollection, i.e. the deliberate, rational search for certain memory-images, is physiological too and always involves the body. Defective recollection should likewise be attributed to specific physiological peculiarities.[14]

It should be noted here that although his psychology ultimately depended upon Aristotle, Duran offered his readers a piece of mnemonic advice that was radically different from the elementary instructions that had been formulated by the master himself. Witness Aristotle's *De memoria et reminiscentia*, his most explicit work on memory that belonged to the *Parva naturalia*, a cluster of short treatises dealing with the interface between psychology, biology and anthropology. As the title of the treatise suggests, Aristotle had made a clear distinction between, on the one hand, the passive *memoria*, i.e. the more or less permanent collection of mental images derived from sense impressions that had become part of the soul[15] and, on the other, *reminiscentia*, the act of recovering existing knowledge or previous sensations.[16] He had postponed the discussion of actual memory techniques to the second chapter ('on reminiscence'). There he offered various suggestions as to how to stimulate and guide the process of recollection. In the previous chapter ('on memory'), he had paid due attention to the nature of the mental images that constituted memory. At no point, however, did he mention the stimulation and manipulation of the sense impressions and their ensuing images as a prerequisite of memory. He concluded his first chapter by claiming that when it came to memorizing, frequent meditation would do the trick and that 'exercizes safeguard memory by reminding one'.[17]

[13] *De memoria et reminiscentia* 449b9.
[14] *De memoria et reminiscentia* 453a4–453a31.
[15] *De memoria et reminiscentia* 450a25.
[16] *De memoria et reminiscentia* 451a18.
[17] *De memoria et reminiscentia* 451a12; English translation in Richard Sorabji, *Aristotle on Memory* (Providence, RI: Brown University Press, 1972), 52.

In the medieval philosophical usage, Aristotle's distinction between *memoria* and *reminiscentia* was generally maintained, even if the two were sometimes classified under one faculty. In the *Canon* Avicenna had referred to a controversy among the philosophers as to whether memory and recollection constituted one or two faculties; in his influential *Shifā'*, however, he had made no distinction between the two.[18] In less specialized contexts, especially in medieval Latin texts dealing with rhetoric, the term *memoria* usually represented both memory and recollection.[19] We shall see that, compared to this dual interpretation, Duran's conception of memory, in this text at least, was rather one dimensional. Throughout his excursus he concentrated not on the act of recollection but on the set of mental images, using the potentially ambiguous term *zikkaron* as synonymous with *koaḥ ha-zokher*, the retentive faculty of memory.[20] Unlike Aristotle, he did not instruct his readers as to how to improve recollection by training their powers of association, but rather described how they could enhance the retentive function of their memories by increasing the impact of the sense impressions. In accordance with Aristotle's conception of memory as an essentially physiological state, Duran proposed a series of predominantly somatic techniques, discussing various kinds of sensual and physical stimulation – through sound, vision and bodily movements – that would improve his readers' memories. To facilitate the discussion, let us summarize the most relevant material from Duran's preface:

Rule no. 5: One should always read from one book, i.e. from the same copy (*qovets*). When reading by oneself, the reader should not switch from copy to copy . . . but always read from the same copy. This improves the memory (*zikkaron*) of what one has read, because when one moves from copy to copy, the forms of the [mental] images from which the intelligibles are derived become confused and their impression disappears from the faculty of imagination (*koaḥ ha-medammeh*) and the common sense (*koaḥ ha-meshuttaf*), and this weakens the faculty of memory (*ha-koaḥ ha-zokher*).

[18] Cf. Harry Austryn Wolfson, 'The Internal Senses in Latin, Arabic, and Hebrew Philosophical Texts', *HTR* 28 (1935): 99.

[19] Cf. Carruthers, *The Book of Memory*, 46.

[20] Duran's interpretation of the faculty of imagination as a predominantly retentive faculty, whose function is a continuation of that of the common sense (the initial recipient of the sense impressions), is consistent with his emphasis on the retentive function of memory. Almost without exception he mentions the common sense and the imagination in the same breath as the stage where the impressions reside before becoming intelligibles. Aristotle had distinguished between two kinds of imagination. Besides the formal, retentive imagination he postulated a deliberative, compositive imagination, responsible for the actual composition of the images. Duran does employ two terms (*koaḥ ha-medammeh* in rule 5 next to *dimmayon* elsewhere), but I see no reason to differentiate between the two. Finally, when mentioning the composing of images he does not refer to the (compositive) faculty of imagination.

Rule no. 7: One should always study Torah aloud and through audible speech . . ., by moving all the organs of speech and all the faculties of the body . . . When one studies like this, the natural heat (*ha-ḥom ha-tiv'i*) is aroused and with it all the faculties are strengthened.

Rule no. 9: One should always read Torah or Gemara from a book in *ktav ashuri* . . ., which most people call *ketivah meruba'at* (square writing), for because of its beauty the impression of this script remains in the common sense and in the imagination (*dimmayon*) . . . I learnt this from my teachers, may they rest in Paradise, i.e. that this script has characteristics that enhance the faculty of memory . . . and I thought they were exaggerating. But then I tried it during my own reading and found it was true . . .

Rule no. 10: One should always read books whose script tends to be bold . . . because the impression of a bold script remains in the common sense and the imagination more than that of fine script . . .

Rule no. 11: One should teach someone else. When one teaches someone else, the knowledge one has grasped is repeated and comes from potentiality into actuality. Thus the *'inyanim* enter the soul, where their impression is strengthened, and the storage in the hearts is strengthened because of this . . .

Rule no. 12: One should always study in peace and quiet, with a tranquil mind and at a moderate pace . . . This is only natural, for haste is the most harmful thing when acquiring knowledge . . . To be impressed upon the soul, the forms of the [mental] images, that are first of all a likeness of the material things and not abstracted from materiality at all, need a fixed time until their impression becomes visible in the common sense and the imagination and is preserved and strengthened there . . . The philosophers too are of this opinion. Their *rosh* said that mental perception happens more effectively in rest, and that is precisely what I meant.

Rule no. 13: One should study Torah for its own sake, i.e. one should not give it another goal, like searching honour or financial gain . . . and one should clear one's mind of all other, worldly, things . . . This is a natural thing too, for confused thinking leads to confused mental perception, and the things that are impressed like images upon the soul are almost erased with the changing of one's thoughts, the later forms obliterating previous forms . . .

Rule no. 14: One should appoint a fixed time for studying Torah, during which one's mind is free from all other business . . . to ensure that whatever one grasps will remain in the heart . . . The best time of day for this is the night, because at night one is free from worldly business . . . Readers from all nations agree on this.[21]

First of all we notice that Duran's elaborate descriptions of the workings and failures of memory show a basic familiarity with Aristotle's concise

[21] *Ma'aseh Efod*, 21–4.

teachings in *De memoria et reminiscentia*, even if his classifications of memory and of the role of the common sense and the imagination seem much less complex and exhaustive than Aristotle's. There is one passage which at first glance suggests a more direct acquaintance. In rule 12 Duran spelled out the consequences of haste, the most harmful factor when it comes to acquiring knowledge. When the intellect grasps the intelligibles without taking time for abstraction, the impressions will not remain in the common sense and in the faculty of imagination long enough for the images to be impressed upon the soul properly. 'Just like [water],' Duran concluded. 'Upon fast-flowing water the likeness of a form cannot be impressed . . . In standing water, however, or in gently flowing water, the likeness will be visible.'[22] This metaphor of impressing forms upon water obviously paraphrases the imagery in *De memoria et reminiscentia* 450a32, where we read that 'memory does not occur in those who are subject to a lot of movement . . . just as if the change and the seal were falling on running water'.[23] Yet we cannot know for certain whether Duran's imagery was based directly upon a Hebrew version of the treatise[24] or whether he borrowed the metaphor from a (popular, Latin, oral?) adaptation. For apart from differences in the *Wortlaut*, there is a significant difference in meaning. Duran adduced the metaphor to illustrate the importance of reading slowly in order to allow the impressions to sink in and be abstracted from all material qualities. Aristotle, on the other hand, brought it up while relating the various qualities and conditions of the human soul and their respective dispositions for receiving a sensory imprint.

Despite his ultimate reliance on Aristotle, Duran's exclusive focus on the retentive function of memory wholly ignores Aristotle's guidelines for recollection and instead reflects an emphasis on preparing and arranging one's memory that had been prominent throughout the Christian tradition. The ancient pagan sources of that tradition, notably the pseudo-Ciceronian rhetorical textbook *Ad herennium* (first century

[22] *Ma'aseh Efod*, 22. [23] English translation in Sorabji, *Aristotle on Memory*, 50.

[24] From the thirteenth century onwards the *Parva naturalia* were accessible in Hebrew. Averroes' compendium *al-Hass wa-'l-mahsûs* (*De Sensu et Sensato* [!]), of which *adh-Dhikr wa-'t-tadhakkur* (*De memoria et reminiscentia*) was the second treatise, was translated 1254 by Moses ibn Tibbon (*Sefer ha-hush we-ha-muhash*) and 1323–39/40 by Samuel ben Judah of Marseille (the rare *Ma'amar ba-nefesh*); cf. Moritz Steinschneider, *Hebräische Übersetzungen des Mittelalters und die Juden als Dolmetscher* (Berlin: Kommissionsverlag des bibliographischen Bureaus, 1893; repr. Graz: Akademische Druck- und Verlagsaustalt, 1956), pp. 153 ff. We find echoes from *De memoria et reminiscentia* in the definitions of memory in Shem Tov ibn Falaquera's *Sefer ha-nefesh*, in Meir Aldabi's *Shevile emunah*, Simon ben Zemach Duran's *Magen avot* and in *Sefer ha-gedarim*, the Book of Definitions compiled by Profiat Duran's contemporary and fellow-townsman Menachem ben Abraham Bonafos.

BCE), promoted an *ars memorativa* that urged the orator to imprint upon his memory various highly symbolic images that would bring to mind the subject matter of his speech.[25] In later ages the medieval scholastics, especially Dominican scholars like Albert the Great and Thomas Aquinas who made extensive use of Aristotelian philosophy in their defences of Roman Catholicism, tended to justify their adaptations of these ancient techniques with the help of Aristotle's *De memoria et reminiscentia*.[26] Their efforts resulted in concatenations of practical suggestions backed up by scientific knowledge. In Duran's preface we encounter, *mutatis mutandis* of course, a similar combination of memory precepts and Aristotelian psychology.

Among the 'fifteen rules' we encounter quite a number of clichés from the medieval Christian corpus on studying and memorizing, even if Duran's ultimate interpretation of those clichés often deviates from their original sense. Since the vast majority of those shared topoi strike one as pre-eminently sensible and practical, it is not always easy to determine whether each coincidence should be ascribed to sheer 'common sense' or to a common (Christian) source of inspiration. Duran's recommendation to stick to one codex when reading by oneself (rule 5), for example, was put forward by the twelfth-century abbot Hugh of St Victor (d. 1141), a prolific writer of mnemonic lessons. In his *Didascalicon* Hugh advised his pupils 'to pay close attention to the shapes of the letters and the colors on the page in order to fix a memorial image of the text',[27] hinting that if they absorbed the formal, visible characteristics of a page, the contents of that page would necessarily become part of their memories too. As Mary Carruthers pointed out, while formulating such basic precepts Hugh was not so much trying to be original as to offer an elementary introduction to studious techniques that had prevailed for centuries[28] and would probably continue to be employed by following generations. If Duran actually adopted the rule from a Christian source, he at least took great pains to rewrite its rationale in terms of Aristotelian epistemology.

A further example of a 'Christian topos' in a novel garb is Duran's second precept, i.e. that of 'brevity'. In Christian sources the emphasis on brevity was often inspired by the awareness that the human mind is incapable of concentrating for an extended period of time. Therefore Christian scholars repeatedly discussed the precept of *brevitas* in

[25] Yates, *The Art of Memory*, 4–17.
[26] Yates, *The Art of Memory*, 57–78.
[27] Carruthers, *The Book of Memory*, 215.
[28] Carruthers, *The Book of Memory*, 95.

connection with *divisio*, the breaking up of a text into shorter passages that could be remembered more easily than longer episodes.[29] Duran's concept of brevity was somewhat different and in fact much less negative. 'Brevity *of expression*', he reasoned, '. . . improves the memory and bestows upon the mind wit and *pilpul*. For most brief sayings are quite deep and since thorough study is required [to understand them] they will be stored in the hearts more effectively.'[30] In her pre-war study of medieval mnemonic writings, Helga Hajdu already mentioned the 'Ballung und Straffung des Inhaltes', the internal structuring and economizing of a text, as a mnemonic device that may eventually have inspired the rich medieval 'Summen–literatur'. All in all, she summarized, the focus on memorization greatly influenced the form, length and contents of virtually every medieval schoolbook.[31]

Profiat Duran furthermore agreed with 'the readers from all nations' that 'the best time for studying Torah is the night' (rule 14), because at night one is free from worldly cares.[32] In the Christian tradition the advantages of studying at night-time were sometimes propounded in connection with the need for *silentium*. In these texts, silence was a major prerequisite of concentration and a necessary condition for successful *meditatio*, the actual memorizing of what one had read. Often *silentium* was associated with silent reading, a habit that was less common in antiquity and medieval times than it is today and that was considered more acceptable to the internal senses than the full voice.[33] By contrast, Duran explicitly cautioned his readers that they should always study Torah 'in a loud voice and through audible speech . . ., by moving all the organs of speech and all the faculties of the body' (rule 7), because 'when one studies this way, the natural heat is aroused and with it all the faculties are strengthened'. Duran indicated that he was describing a vital Jewish tradition, and that 'a few authors already wrote that this is the reason why those who study Torah move [their bodies] backward and forward, i.e. [that they do so] in order to arouse the natural heat[34] so that the knowledge gained from [reading] will remain in the faculty of memory'.

29 Carruthers, *The Book of Memory*, 83, 146.

30 *Ma'aseh Efod*, 18.

81 Helga Hajdu, *Das mnemonische Schrifttum des Mittelalters* (Vienna, Amsterdam and Leipzig: Franz Leo & Co., 1936), 53 ff.

32 A locus classicus is Martianus Capella's *De nuptiis Philologiae et Mercurii* book IV, where Capella offered a few practical rules that more or less went back to Quintilian, *Institutio oratoria* XI, ii, 17–26.

33 See Carruthers, *The Book of Memory*, 171 f. Capella, in the passage referred to in the previous note, recommended memorizing 'with a murmur'.

34 The Friedländer–Kohn edition (p. 20) erroneously reads *chush* for *chom*.

Perhaps Exodus 20:18 ('and all the people [present at the *mattan torah* at Sinai] *saw* the *qolot*') was a *remez* to the belief that Torah is studied more effectively this way. 'And I think that because of this the sages called the Hallowed Book *miqra*,' Duran concluded, 'as if through this name they wished to explain that it should be studied in a loud voice and through *qeri'ah*.'

A further ancient and widespread mnemonic device that makes its appearance in numerous Latin works from Quintilian to Petrarch is outlined in Duran's 'fourth way':

> Rule no. 4: The reader should always place signs (*simanim*) next to what he is reading and then repeat or learn, for this is one of the techniques that help memory very much . . . The *ba'ale ha-Talmud* followed this routine, as did the *soferim* and the masoretes.[35]

To gloss the words of Victoria Kahn, this marking of passages was a matter of preserving the memory in one's text in order to preserve the text in one's memory.[36] Hajdu stresses the importance of writing in general as an external, visual aid to memory in medieval education.[37] Carruthers traced and described the extensive use of marginal *notae* or *notulae* as a recurrent feature of memory training since antiquity.[38] As numerous sources reveal, readers would mark well-defined pericopes with associative signs or a key-words, punctuation marks or abbreviations (the so-called *notataria*) to facilitate their mental marking of the contents of each page. Many modern scholars assume that it was common practice among medieval (Christian) scholars to rehearse their knowledge by regularly 'thumbing books to pick up previously marked passages'.[39] This insoluble bond between reading and memorizing persisted throughout the Middle Ages. Consulting one's memory was not, as Walter Benjamin defined it centuries later, a tentative 'Spatenstich' into the dark realm of things past. The medieval memory was more like a well-sorted library: its scope was neither eclectic nor critical but comprehensive and reproductive. The individual books were accessible through the marginal *notae* that would serve as 'indices' to the often immense collections.

Petrarch too would read this way. In the passage from *Secretum* II quoted earlier, Augustinus encourages Franciscus, the forgetful reader, to

[35] *Ma'aseh Efod*, 19.
[36] Victoria Kahn, 'The Figure of the Reader in Petrarch's *Secretum*', in *Petrarch: Modern Critical Views*, ed. Harold Bloom (New York and Philadelphia: Chelsea, 1989), 159 f.
[37] Hajdu, *Das mnemonische Schrifttum*, 50.
[38] Carruthers, *The Book of Memory*, 107–14. In the passage mentioned in notes 32 and 33, Capella had advised 'to write down *notae* next to items we wish to remember'.
[39] Carruthers, *The Book of Memory*, 158.

employ the same technique (*tu vero, si suis locis notas certas impresseris, fructum ex lectione percipies*). In reply to Franciscus's query as to the nature of these *notae*, he tells him to write marks next to morally edifying *sententiae* and then to make each entry familiar through strenuous meditation (*multoque studio tibi familiare effice*) so that each moral precept will be as if 'written in the mind' (*habeas velut in animo conscripta*).[40] A few lines further on, when Augustinus repeats once more that his pupil should meditate on useful sentences with the help of 'clear marks', he qualifies these marks as *unci memoria*, 'hooks in the memory'[41] that will serve as a mental concordance to his pupil's reading. As we see from 'rule no. 4', Duran adopted the general practice but was again anxious to provide it with an incontestable Jewish precedent. And so he alluded to the mnemonic references and quotations used in Masoretic literature and to a passage in bEruv 54b, where the importance of studying Torah with the aid of mnemonic signs is deduced from various scriptural verses.

Let us turn to a final example that appears to be quite instructive as to the cultural environment of Duran and his intended audience. In rule 6 we read:

> One should always study from beautifully made books that have elegant script and pages and ornate adornments and bindings, so that the *meqomot ha-'iyyun*, i.e. the *bate ha-midrash*, are well built, for this enhances the love of reading. Memory derives much benefit from this, for reading while looking at pleasant forms and beautiful images[42] and drawings quickens and stimulates the soul and strengthens its faculties . . . Therefore it is permitted to paint images and drawings on buildings, utensils and clothes, for [otherwise] the soul will be exhausted and thought will be impossible . . . Therefore it is proper, even obligatory, to decorate the books of God.[43]

Quoting various proof-texts – borrowed from 'the physicians' and the *ba'ale gematria* alike – Duran efficiently countered potential objections, inspired by the Second Commandment (Exodus 20:4 and Deuteronomy 5:8), to the use of graven images in Hebrew books. It is unlikely, though, that such objections were often heard in Duran's upper-class environment. Throughout the fourteenth century the Jewish aristocrats of Catalonia, especially the wealthy dignitaries associated with the royal court in Barcelona, had supported a number of workshops that manufactured illuminated Bibles, *haggadot* and other, philosophical, medical

40 *Secretum* 16.2, 106. Dotti adds that Petrarch was indeed 'un dilligentissimo postillatore di codici'.
41 *Secretum* 16.10, 110.
42 See Joseph Gutmann, *No Graven Images. Studies in Art and the Hebrew Bible* (New York: Ktav, 1971), xvii.
43 *Ma'aseh Efod*, 19.

and scientific manuscripts.[44] Judging by the decorative style of those manuscripts, which reflects the latest innovations in contemporary Christian illumination, this aristocratic patronage must have resulted, partly at least, from the continuous exposure of the Jewish elite to the neighbouring Spanish culture. Given this strong tradition, not even a consequential event like the persecutions of 1391 could stop the Catalan workshops from producing Hebrew manuscripts that joined a traditionally Jewish iconography to a distinctly 'Latin' style.[45]

According to Joseph Gutmann, '[a] Spanish Jewish aristocrat like Profiat Duran, functioning at and in contact with the Christian courts of the peninsula' was inevitably 'familiar with the beautiful Christian codices of the milieu.'[46] Gutmann's statement may have been a trifle intuitive, however, for not only Duran's biography, but also the kind of books he may have encountered in his daily milieu and the degree of his acquaintance with those books and their contents remain to be established with greater precision. As Frank Talmage contended, much of our information about Duran seems based upon conjecture.[47] However, since Richard Emery's research in the departmental archives in Perpignan, conducted in the late 1960s, we are able to reconstruct at least a few data with some plausibility. One of the results of Emery's search suggests that, shortly after his forced baptism in 1391, Duran was referred to in an Aragonese record as the court astrologer of King Joan I,[48] who throughout his reign from 1387 until 1396 had 'kept up the same friendly relations with Jewish scholars as . . . their father had always maintained'.[49] That within such a climate the Jewish and Christian courtiers of Aragon could get together and discuss shared cultural or scholarly interests has been demonstrated by Warren Zev Harvey.[50] Through a comparison of the psychological theory in *Or Adonai* by Hasdai Crescas (d. 1410/11?) and the concept of the soul in the first

44 Bezalel Narkiss, *Hebrew Illuminated Manuscripts in the British Isles I: The Spanish and Portuguese Manuscripts* (Jerusalem and London: Israel Academy of Sciences and Humanities and the British Academy, 1982), 15; further information and examples are found in Michel Garel, *D'une main forte. Manuscrits hébreux des collections françaises* (Paris: Seuil/Bibliothèque Nationale, 1991), 25–84.

45 Narkiss, *Hebrew Illuminated Manuscripts*, 51.

46 Gutmann, *No Graven Images*, xvii.

47 Frank Talmage, 'The Polemical Writings of Profiat Duran', *Immanuel* 13 (1981): 1 and note 1.

48 Richard W. Emery, 'New light on Profayt Duran "The Efodi"', *JQR* n.s. 58 (1967/8): 331; see also Amada López de Meneses, 'Crescas de Viviers, astrólogo de Juan I el Cazador', *Sefarad* 14 (1954): 103 (Crescas de Viviers died in August 1391).

49 I. Baer, *A History of the Jews in Christian Spain* (Philadelphia: Jewish Publication Society of America, 1978), vol. II, 92.

50 Warren Zev Harvey, 'Hasdai Crescas and Bernat Metge on the Soul' (Hebrew), *Jerusalem Studies in Jewish Thought* 5 (1986): 141–54.

dialogue of *Lo somni* (The dream) by the Catalan humanist poet Bernat Metge (1340/6–1413), Harvey was able to support with plain textual documentation various general notions about the existence of such contacts.

In an article published in 1992, Harvey discussed two remarkable correspondences in the physics of Crescas' teacher, Nissim ben Reuben of Gerona (*c.* 1310–*c.* 1380), and William of Ockham's *Reportatio* and *Summulae physicorum*.[51] Harvey pointed out that he could not determine whether 'RaN studied Ockham's writings directly, or whether he was influenced by them through an unknown Hebrew or Latin intermediary', yet he was inclined to believe that Rabbenu Nissim based his views on a direct reading of Ockham's Latin original.[52] One possibility that Harvey did not consider, but which cannot be ruled out in view of what we know today about the role and nature of oral transmission within medieval scholarly circles, was that Rabbenu Nissim may have encountered Ockham's teachings through oral communication rather than via a written text. The possibility of such intermediary oral sources has been neglected in a number of other cases as well. Thus, for example, when modern scholars stress that Duran's polemical writings reveal his knowledge of such Christian classics as Peter the Lombard's *Sententiae*, Vincent of Beauvais' *Speculum historiale* and the *Postilla* of Nicholas of Lyra,[53] they describe these coincidences in general terms without attempting to establish whether it was through written versions or through hearsay accounts that Duran acquired this knowledge. In the case of Duran's 'fifteen rules', too, there are ample points of contact with Christian mnemonic motifs, yet each of these – including what I called the 'striking analogy' between Duran's characterization of modern reading habits and Petrarch's *Secretum*[54] – turns out to be so elusive that it seems futile to try to determine any written source(s) with greater precision.

The search for these sources is of course closely connected with the more general question as to what inspired Duran to include this exhaustive survey of mnemonic techniques in an otherwise rather conventional grammar of biblical Hebrew. Again it is difficult to come up with a definitive answer, but perhaps one may point to a similar trend in con-

51 Warren Zev Harvey, 'Nissim of Gerona and William of Ockham on Prime Matter', *Jewish History* 6.1/2 (1992): 87–98. 52 Harvey, 'Nissim of Gerona', 93 f.

53 E.g. Talmage, 'The Polemical Writings of Profiat Duran', 79.

54 For Petrarch's (rather limited and one-sided) impact upon late fourteenth-century 'Catalan humanism' in general, see Francisco Rico, 'Petrarca y el humanismo catalán', in *Actes del Sisè Col.loqui Internacional de llengua i literatura Catalanes, Roma, 28 setembre–2 octubre 1982*, ed. G. Tavani and J. Pinell (Abadia de Montserrat, 1983), 257–91.

temporary devotional literature. In *The Art of Memory* Frances Yates discussed a series of fourteenth-century ethical treatises written by Dominican friars for a steadily growing class of literate lay readers. She noticed that various authors included some form of *ars memorativa* to help their readers remember the virtues, vices and spiritual intentions described in their books. The most explicit legitimization of the use of such auxiliary mnemonics was supplied by the author of the Italian *Rosaio della vita* of 1373, who introduced his section on *ars memorie artificialis* by stating that 'now that we have provided the book to be read, it remains to hold it in memory'. From this and other examples Yates inferred that during the *Quattrocento* 'artificial memory begins to appear as a lay devotional discipline fostered and recommended by the friars'.[55] Profiat Duran, writing for the solitary lay reader too, may have come across this particular literary custom and then decided to adopt it, but only after casting it into a distinctly Jewish mould, as we have seen from the examples discussed above.

Even if Duran's contribution to the medieval art of memory leaves us with a number of questions, it unambiguously illustrates one specific, not altogether undisputed, point. It reminds us once more that, when applied to medieval scholarship, the opposition of 'orality' versus 'literacy', assumed by various modern scholars, is an artificial if not an ideological construct.[56] As we may learn from Carruthers' *Book of Memory*, in medieval western Europe memorizing – primarily an oral activity, even when ultimately based upon written texts – was very much part of the literate mentality. It had an intellectual complexity of its own, which expressed itself, in the medieval Latin tradition at least, in an abundance of mnemonic techniques, strategies, precepts and metaphors. Finding his ultimate inspiration in that Latin tradition, Profiat Duran formulated his 'fifteen rules of reading and studying Torah from which memory will benefit', to guide the solitary Jewish reader and compensate for the absence of the traditional scholarly community.

[55] Yates, *The Art of Memory*, 85–91.

[56] For a discussion of the most relevant modern publications on this controversy, see Mayke de Jong, 'Geletterd en ongeletterd. Zin en onzin van een tegenstelling', in *Oraliteit en schriftcultuur*, ed. R. E. V. Stuip and C. Vellekoop (Hilversum: Verloren, 1993), 9–13.

A select bibliography of the writings of Raphael Loewe

1947 ''*Akdamuth*: A Liturgical Fossil'. *The Jewish Outlook* 12 (May, 1947): 3 (article and verse translation). Translation repr., *Service of the Synagogue*, *Pentecost*, 14th edn (London: Routledge & Kegan Paul, 1954), 210–11

1949 'Jerome's Rendering of עולם'. *HUCA* 22 (1949): 265–306, 432

1950 'Orthodox and Liberal'. *JC* (20 Jan. 1950): 12 (leading article, unsigned)

1952 'Jerome's Treatment of an Anthropopathism' [נחם] *VT* 2 (1952): 265–306, 432

1953 (i) 'The Mediaeval Christian Hebraists of England: Herbert of Bosham and earlier Scholars'. *TJHSE* 17 (1953): 225–49

(ii) 'Herbert of Bosham's Commentary on Jerome's Hebrew Psalter: A Preliminary Investigation into its Sources'. *Biblica* 34 (1953): 44–77, 159–92, 275–98

1954 'An Early Instance of *Orange* in French'. *Archivum Linguisticum* 6, ii (1954('55): 122–5

1955 (i) 'The Earliest Biblical Allusion to Coined Money?'. *Palestine Exploration Fund Quarterly Statement* (May–October 1955): 141–50

(ii) 'Jewish Ceremonial and Liturgy'. In Ephraim Levine (ed.), *The Jewish Heritage* (London: Vallentine, Mitchell, 1955): 29–50

1956 (i) 'Anglo-Jewish Sacred Literature'. *JC*, special tercentenary supplement (27 Jan. 1956): 20–2

(ii) 'Handwashing and the Eyesight in the *Regimen Sanitatis*'. *BHM* 30 (1956): 100–8

1957 (i) 'The Jewish Midrashim and Scholastic Exegesis of the Bible'. *Studia Patristica* 1 (= *Texte und Untersuchungen* 63) (1957): 492–514

(ii) 'The Mediaeval Christian Hebraists of England: The *Superscriptio Lincolniensis*'. *HUCA* 28 (1957): 205–52

1958 'Alexander Neckam's Knowledge of Hebrew'. *MRS* 4 (1958): 17–34 (repr. in W. Horbury (ed.), *Hebrew Study from Ezra to Ben-Yehuda* (Edinburgh: T. & T. Clark, 1999): 207–23

1959 (ii) 'Which-hunting (Who is a Jew?)'. *JC* (5 June 1959): 28

1960 'Jewish Scholarship in England'. In V. D. Lipman (ed.), *Three Centuries of Anglo-Jewish History* (Cambridge: Heffer, for the Jewish Historical Society of England, 1960): 125–48

1961 (i) Foreword to Roy A. Stewart, *Rabbinic Theology* (Edinburgh and London: Oliver & Boyd, 1961): v–viii

(ii) 'The Moral Issues of the Eichmann Trial' (letter). *JC* (14 April 1961): 20
(iii) 'A Jewish Counterpart to the Acts of the Alexandrines'. *JJS* 12 (1961): 105–22

1962 *Judaism: Privilege and Perspective* (Southampton: Parkes Library Pamphlet, 1962)

1963 (i) Latin Alcaic version of אדון עולם, with English translation by P. Hartog. Privately printed (repr. *Common Ground* 17/ii 17–19)
(ii) 'Tribute to Leon Roth'. *Common Ground* 17/ii (1963): 25–7
(iii) 'The Polarity of "Holiness"'. *Conservative Judaism* 18/i (1963): 55–9

1964 (i) 'Towards a Definition of Judaism', *Jewish Quarterly* 14/iv (1964): 4–9
(ii) (with Chloe Loewe), 'Treatment of Calculus in a Fragmentary Hebrew Pharmacopoeia'. *JJS* 15 (1964): 57–79

1965 (i) 'Defining Judaism: Some Ground-clearing'. *Jewish Journal of Sociology*, 7 (1965): 153–75
(ii) *Order of Service for the* הקפות, London: Spanish and Portuguese Jews' Congregation
(iii) 'The Divine Garment and *Shi'ur Qomah*'. *HTR* 58 (1965): 153–60
(iv) 'The "Plain" Meaning of Scripture in Early Jewish Exegesis'. *Papers of the Institute of Jewish Studies* 1 (all published), ed. J. G. Weiss (Jerusalem: Magnes Press, 1965), 140–85 (repr. Lanham, MD: University Press of America, Brown Classics in Judaica, 1989)
(v) 'The Laws Regarding Slavery as a Source for Social History of the Period of the Second Temple, the Mishnah and Talmud' (translation of article in Hebrew by E. E. Urbach, *Zion* 25 (1960). In *Papers of the Institute of Jewish Studies* 1 (all published), ed. J. G. Weiss (Jerusalem: Magnes Press, 1965), 1–94 (repr. Lanham, MD: University Press of America, Brown Classics in Judaica, 1989)

1966 (i) 'Hebrew Books and "Judaica" in Mediaeval Oxford and Cambridge'. In John M. Shaftesley (ed.), *Remember the Days: Essays on Anglo-Jewish History Presented to Cecil Roth* (London: Jewish Historical Society, 1966), 2–48
(ii) (ed.), *Studies in Rationalism Judaism and Universalism in Memory of Leon Roth* (London: Routledge & Kegan Paul, 1966); includes the following items contributed by R. L: Preface (ix–xiii); 'Memoir' (1–11); 'Potentialities and Limitations of Universalism in the *Halakhah*' (115–50); Bibliography of the Writings of Leon (*Hebraice* Ḥayyim Yehudah) Roth (323–36) (the latter repr. in 1999, ii)
(iii) 'Apologetic Motifs in the Targum to the Song of Songs'. In Alexander Altmann (ed.), *Biblical Motifs: Origins and Transformations*, Studies and Texts 3 (Cambridge, MA: Harvard University Press, 1966), 159–96
(iv) *The Position of Women in Judaism* (London: SPCK, 1966)

1967 (i) 'Judaism in a Secular Age'. In Philip Longworth (ed.), *Confrontations with Judaism* (London: Anthony Blond, 1967), 35–60
(ii) ווידוי לערב יום הכפורים. *Tarbuth* (Tishri 5728): 59–61

1968 (i) 'Solomon Marcus Schiller-Szinessy, 1820–1890: First Reader in Talmudic and Rabbinic Literature at Cambridge'. *TJHSE* 21 (1968): 148–89

(ii) 'Divine Frustration Exegetically Frustrated – Numbers 14: 34 תנואתי'. In P. R. Ackroyd and B. Lindars (eds.), *Words and Meanings: Essays presented to David Winton Thomas* (Cambridge: Cambridge University Press, 1968), 137–58 (see correction, 1970, i)

1969 (i) 'Prolegomenon' to the re-issue of S. R. Driver and A. Neubauer, *The Fifty-third Chapter of Isaiah according to the Jewish Interpreters*, Library of Biblical Studies (New York: Ktav, 1969), vol. I, 1–38

(ii) 'The Medieval History of the Latin Vulgate'. In G. W. H. Lampe (ed.), *The Cambridge History of the Bible*, vol. II: *The West from the Fathers to the Reformation* (Cambridge: Cambridge University Press, 1969), 102–54 (paperback edn, 1975)

(iii) 'Solomon Ibn Gabirol's Lament for a lost Leader'. *Judaism* 18 (1969): 343–53

1970 (i) 'Abraham ibn Ezra on Numbers xiv: 34'. *JJS* 21 (1970): 65–8 (correction to 1968, ii)

(ii) 'Cecil Roth', obituary notice. *The Times*, 22 June 1970 (unsigned)

1971 'Dr Cecil Roth', obituary tribute spoken at the Anglo-American Jewish Historical Conference. *TJHSE* 23 (1971): 103–5

1972 Contributed articles, mainly biographical, to *EJ* (Jerusalem: Keter, 1972), in particular 'Hebraists, Christian (1100–1890)' VIII, 9–71

1973 (i) 'Dr Phyllis Abrahams', obituary notice. *The Times*, 30 March (joint obituary contribution, with J. D. P[earson] and D[avid] G[oldstein])

(ii) 'La poesía de Salomon ibn Gabirol'. In *Seis conferencias en torno a Ibn Gabirol* (Malaga: Ayuntamiento, 1973), 21–6; also Hebrew poem, 56–7

1974 (i) 'Rabbi Joshua ben Hananiah: Ll.D or D. Litt?'. *JJS* 25 (1974): 137–54

(ii) Prolegomenon' to the re-issue of C. G. Montefiore and H. Loewe, *A Rabbinic Anthology* (New York: Schocken, 1974) (unpaginated)

1975 (i) 'The Evolution of Jewish Student Feeding Arrangements in Oxford and Cambridge'. In D. Noy (ed.), *Studies in the Cultural Life of the Jews of England* (Jerusalem: Folklore Research Center Studies, 1975), v, 165–84

(ii) 'Dr David Diringer', obituary notice. *The Times*, 19 February 1975 (unsigned)

1979 (i) 'Erwin Rosenthal 75'. *A*[ssociation of] *J*[ewish] *R*[efugees] *Information* 34 (1979): 7.

(ii) '*'Omnam Ken*: Anglo-Jewry's Penitential Hymn'. *JC* (28 September 1979): 27

(iii) (ed., with S. Stein), *Studies in Jewish Religious and Intellectual History presented to Alexander Altmann* (Alabama: University of Alabama Press); includes R. L., 'Ibn Gabirol's Treatment of Sources in the *Kether Malkhuth*' (183–94)

1981 (i) '"Salvation" is not of the Jews'. *JTS* n.s. 32 (1981): 341–68

(ii) 'The Spanish Supplement to Nieto's *'Esh Dath*'. *PAAJR* 48 (1981): 267–96

1982 (i) גלגולי מרבעים: *Omar Khayyam and Edward Fitzgerald, Rubaiyyat*, translated into Hebrew (Jerusalem: Magnes Press, 1982)

(ii) 'The Bible in Medieval Hebrew Poetry'. In J. A. Emerton and S. C. Reif (eds.), *Interpreting the Hebrew Bible: Essays in Honour of E. I. J. Rosenthal* (Cambridge: Cambridge University Press, 1982), 132–55

(iii) 'The Implications of Covenant'. *L'Eylah* 2, iii (1982): 35–41

(iv) 'Window of the Seven Heavens'. *JC* Colour Magazine (24 September 1982): 36–7

1983 (i) Introduction to L. Loewe (ed.), *Diaries of Sir Moses and Lady Montefiore*, repr (London: JHSE and Jewish Museum, 1983), 6–10

(ii) 'שיר הירקלייטוס של קלימכוס ותרגומיו'. *Prozah* 60–3 (1983): 98–9

1984 'Judaism and the Jenkins Factor'. *The Times*, 28 July 1984

1985 (i) 'Dr Charlotte Klein', obituary notice. *JC* (15 March, 1985): 16

(ii) 'Jewish Evidence for the History of the Crossbow'. In G. Dahan (ed.), *Les Juifs au regard de l'histoire: mélanges en l'honneur de Bernhard Blumenkranz* (Paris: Picard, 1985), 87–107

(iii) 'Louis Loewe: Aide and Confidant'. In Sonia and V. D. Lipman (eds.), *The Century of Moses Montefiore* (Oxford; Oxford University Press, for the Littman Library of Jewish Civilization, 1985), 104–17

1986 (i) 'Yehezkel Abramsky', and 'Israel Brodie'. In *DNB Supplement 1971–80*, 34 and 90–1

(ii) 'Una diatriba trilingüe contra Pilato'. *Sefarad* 46, *Volumen en homenaje al Prof. Pérez Castro* (1986): 295–308

1987 (i) 'Dr Alexander Altmann', obituary notice. *The Times*, 8 June, 1987 (unsigned)

(ii) 'Judaism's Eternal Triangle'. *Religious Studies* 23 (1987): 309–23

(iii) 'לשון עברית ומדבריה: עבד ורבו'. *'Am wa-sepher*, n.s. 4 (1987): 11–52 (see below, 1990, i, for Italian translation, and extended English version, 1994, i)

1988 (i) *The Rylands Haggadah: A Medieval Spanish Masterpiece in Facsimile* (London: Thames & Hudson; New York: Abrams, 1988)

(ii) 'David Goldstein', obituary notice. *Bulletin of the British Association for Jewish Studies*, January 1988

(iii) 'Abraham ibn Ezra, Peter Abelard, and John Donne'. *TAR* 1 (1988): 190–211

(iv) 'In Memoriam Richard David Barnett, 1909–1986'. *TJHSE* 29 (1988): xv–xvii

(v) 'A Medieval Latin–German Magical Text in Hebrew Characters'. In A. Rapoport-Albert and S. J. Zipperstein (eds.), *Jewish History: Essays in Honour of Chimen Abramsky* (London: Peter Halban, 1988), 345–68

(vi) 'שנאנים שאננים לר׳ שלמה אבן גבירול'. In A. Mirsky *et al.* (eds.), גלות אחר גולה *Studies presented to Professor Haim Beinart*, [i] (Jerusalem: Ben-Zvi Institute, 1988), 114–33

1989 (i) *Ibn Gabirol* (London: Peter Halban; New York: Grove Weidenfeld, 1989)

(ii) Translation of Yosef Kaplan, *From Christianity to Judaism: The Story of Isaac Orobio de Castro* (Oxford: Oxford University Press, for the Littman Library of Jewish Civilization, 1989)

(iii) 'Cambridge Jewry: The First Hundred Years'. In W. Frankel and H. Miller (eds.), *Gown and Tallith: In Commemoration of the Fiftieth Anniversary of the Founding of the Cambridge University Jewish Society* (London: Harvey Miller, 1989), 13–37

(iv) 'Dedication, to the Memory of David Goldstein'. *Transactions*, Jewish Historical Society of England, 30 (1989): v

1990 (i) 'La linguistica ebraica'. In Giulio C. Lepschy (ed.), *Storia della linguistica* (Bologna: Mulino, 1990), vol. I, 119–66 (cf. Hebrew Original, 1987, iii; English, 1994, i)

(ii) 'Jewish Exegesis'. In R. J. Coggins and J. L. Houlden (eds.), *A Dictionary of Bible Interpretation* (London: SCM Press, 1990), 346–54

(iii) 'Dr Vivian Lipman', obituary notice. *The Times*, 15 March 1990 (unsigned)

(iv) 'Dedication in Memory of Vivian David Lipman'. *TJHSE* 31 (1990): v. [*Note*: The article 'A "Miniature Sanctuary" at Clapton House, 1781', part-authorship of which was courteously credited, despite protest, to R.L., is entirely the work of Malcolm Brown.]

(v) 'The Influence of Solomon ibn Gabirol on Abraham ibn Ezra'. In Fernando Díaz Esteban (ed.), *Abraham ibn Ezra y su tiempo*, Actas del Simposio Internacional (Madrid: Asociación Española de Orientalistas, 1990), 199–210

1991 (i) 'The Contribution of German-Jewish Scholars to Jewish Studies in the United Kingdom'. In W. E. Mosse (ed.), *Second Chance: Two Centuries of German-speaking Jews in the United Kingdom* (Tübingen: J. C. B. Mohr, 1991), 437–62

(ii) 'Solomon Marcus Schiller-Szinessy'. *Österreichisches biographisches Lexicon 1815–1950*, 47. Lieferung, 136–7 (abbreviation of 1968, i)

(iii) 'E. I. J. Rosenthal', obituary notice. *The Times*, 7 June 1991 (unsigned)

(iv) 'Israel's Sovereign Statehood and Theological Plumb-lines'. In D. Cohn-Sherbok (ed.), *Problems in Contemporary Jewish Theology* (Lampeter: Edwin Mellen Press, 1991), 161–88

(v) 'Professor Moshe Goshen-Gottstein', obituary notice. *The Guardian*, 15 October, 1991, 37

(vi) 'Truth, Faith and Tradition' (review article of F. Lachower and I. Tishby, *The Wisdom of the Zohar: An Anthology of Texts*). *L'Eylah* (March, 1991): 47–9

1992 (i) Translation of poems and targumim in Jeremy Schonfield (ed.), *The Barcelona Haggadah* (companion vol. to facsimile) (London: Facsimile Editions, 1992)

(ii) 'Midrashic Alchemy: Exegesis, Ethics, Aesthetics in Judaism'. In H. J. Blumberg *et al.*, *"Open Thou Mine Eyes . . .": Essays on Aggadah and Judaica Presented to Rabbi William G. Braude* (Hoboken, NJ: Ktav, 1992), 109–37

1993 (i) 'רננות רעננות גם ברכה', poem for the re-opening of the Spanish and Portuguese Synagogue, Bevis Marks, London, after repair of bomb damage, 29 August 1993. *Sephardi Bulletin* 47 (January–February 1993): 11

(ii) *Khayyamidis Quaternionum Selecti Latine.* Privately circulated

1994 (i) 'Hebrew Linguistics'. In Giulio Lepschy (ed.), *History of Linguistics* (Harlow: Longman, 1994), vol. I, 97–163 (extended version of the Hebrew (1987, iii) and Italian (1990, i) texts)

(ii) 'רחוצות בנהר שלום ורצון'. *Hadoar* (18 March 1994): 26

1995 'Dr Myer Salaman', obituary contribution. *JC* (3 March, 1995): 19

1998 (i) ‘כיצד מתרגמין?’, בקורת ופרשנות/*Criticism and Interpretation* 32 (1998): 65–80
(ii) ‘Michael Weitzman’, obituary notice. *Daily Telegraph*, 10 April, 1998, 29 (unsigned)
(iii) ‘Sir Moses Montefiore, Sheriff of London, 1837’. In *A Service of Thanksgiving following the Admission of the Right Honorable the Lord Mayor Lord Levene of Portsoken, KBE, at the Spanish and Portuguese Jews’ Synagogue, Bevis Marks, City of London*, 17–19 (repr. from *Sephardi Bulletin* 46 (November–December 1992): 9–11
1999 (i) ‘Credat Judaeus Apella?’. *JJS* 50 (1999): 74–86
(ii) Translation of Leon Roth, ‘Imitatio Dei and the Idea of Holiness’. In Leon Roth, *Is there a Jewish Philosophy? Rethinking Fundamentals* (London: Littman Library of Jewish Civilization, 1999), 15–28; also xvii–xx, ‘(biographical) Note’, and reprint of Roth’s bibliography (see 1966 ii, 323–36)
(iii) Entries in John H. Hayes (ed.), *Dictionary of Biblical Interpretation* (Nashville, TN: Abingdon Press, 1999): on Abravanel (i, 3–4), Wilna Gaon (330–1), Malbim (ii, 114), Moses de Leon (164–5), Sforno (466–7)
(iv) ‘Gentiles as Seen by Jews after CE 70’. In William Horbury *et al.* (eds.), *The Cambridge History of Judaism*, vol. III: *The Early Roman Period* (Cambridge: Cambridge University Press, 1999), 250–66
2000 (i) ‘*In Memoriam* Sir Isaiah Berlin, OM, CBE, MA, FBA (1909–1997)’, *TJHSE* 35 (2000): v, xvi–xviii
(ii) Introductory matter and translations of liturgical poems in J. Schonfield (ed.), *The Rothschild Haggadah* (Companion vol. to facsimile) (London: Facsimile Editions; Jerusalem: Israel Museum, 2000), 17–22, 49–56, 65–78

IN PRESS AND FORTHCOMING

‘Censorship in Jewish History: A. Antiquity and Early Middle Ages’. In D. Jones (ed.) *Censorship: An International Encyclopaedia* (London: Fitzroy Dearborn)

Translation of liturgical poems in *The Rothschild Haggadah* (London: Facsimile Editions)

Meshal haqadmoni: Fables from the Distant Past by Isaac ibn Sahula (Littman Library of Jewish Civilization)

‘The Structure of the Hymnic Insertions into the Jewish Liturgy’. In *JSS*

‘Ark, Archaism, and Appropriation (the versional treatment of ארון)’. In A. Rapoport Albert (ed.), *Michael Weitzman Memorial Volume* (Sheffield Academic Press)

‘Raphael Meldola’. In *The New DNB*

Poem, Hebrew and English, for the tercentenary of the Spanish and Portuguese Jews’ Synagogue, Bevis Marks, London, in 2001

Index of names